London

BARS
PUBS & CLUBS

timeout.com

Time Out Guides Limited
Universal House
251 Tottenham Court Road
London W1T 7AB
Tel + 44 (0)20 7813 3000
Fax + 44 (0)20 7813 6001
Email guides@timeout.com
www.timeout.com

Contributors

Ravneet Ahluwalia, James Aufenast, Simone Baird, Alex Brown, Paul Burston, Nuala Calv, Simon Coppock, Peterjon Cresswell, Jonathan Derbyshire, Alexi Duggins, Dominic Earle, Janice Fuscoe, Kate Fuscoe, Ottilie Godfrey, Charlie Godfrey-Faussett, Rob Friedrich, Will Fulford-Jones, Sarah Guy, Edmund Gordon, Hugh Graham, Steve Gwynn, Phil Harriss, Martin Horsfield, Emma Howarth, Ruth Jarvis, Emily Kerrigan, Rhodri Marsden, Jenny McIvor, Brendan McKeown, Norman Miller, Jenni Muir, Rachel Mulrenan, Anna Norman, Matt Norman, Sharon O'Connell, Cath Phillips, Holly Pick, Gemma Pritchard, Nick Rider, Adam Scott, Cyrus Shahrad, Andrew Shields, Lucy Smallwood, James Smart, Andrew Staffell, Carmel Turner, Patrick Welch, Rachel Williams, Elizabeth Winding. **Insider Knowledge** Nuala Calvi.

Maps john@jsgraphics.co.uk

Cover artwork by Ming Tang-Evans at Idlewild, see page 109.

The editor would like to thank Guy Dimond.

Photography by pages 3, 20, 36, 40, 41, 43, 46, 47, 52, 63, 79, 85, 114, 115, 139, 208, 210, 212, 213, 216, 220, 221, 233, 224, 225 Ming Tang-Evans; pages 7, 8, 11, 107, 158, 159, 230, 231, 237, 241, 244, 249, Jonathan Perugia; pages 25, 26, 33, 54, 55, 59, 72, 73, 97, 102, 104, 142, 152, 153, 160, 176, 198 Hayley Harrison; pages 51, 81, 101, 149, 168, 183, 189, 223 Marzena Zoldaz; pages 60, 68, 69, 165 Michael Franke; pages 89, 122, 123, 129, 132, 133, 184, 185, 192, 193, 200, 201, 205 Nerida Howard; pages 99, 170 Tricia de Courcy Ling; page 111 Alys Tomlinson.

Printer St Ives (Web) Ltd, Storeys Bar Road, Eastern Industrial Estate, Peterborough, PE1 5YS
ISBN 978-1-905042-18-0

Distribution by Seymour Ltd (020 7429 4000)
Distributed in US by Publishers Group West
Distributed in Canada by Publishers Group Canada
For further distribution details, see www.timeout.com

About the guide

Opening times
We list only the opening times of the bar or pub at the time of going to press. We do not list those of any attached shop, restaurant or brasserie (though these may be the same).

Food served
We list the times when food is served in the bar or pub or, where relevant, in any attached restaurant or brasserie. 'Food served' can mean anything from cheese rolls to a three-course meal. When the opening times and food serving times are run together (Open/food served), it means food is served until shortly before closing time.

Admission
In some cases, particularly in central London, pubs and bars charge admission after a certain hour. Where there is a regular pattern to this, we list the details. Note that more and more venues are becoming members-only after a fixed time (usually when pubs close), although the rules are often blurred. We've chosen not to include in this guide places that are strictly members-only.

Credit cards
The following abbreviations are used: **AmEx** American Express; **DC** Diners Club; **MC** MasterCard; **V** Visa.

Babies and children admitted
Under-14s are only allowed into gardens, separate family rooms and restaurant areas of pubs and wine bars, unless the premises has a special 'children's certificate'. If the establishment has such a certificate, children are allowed in as long as they're accompanied by an adult. Those aged 14-17 can go into a bar, but only for soft drinks. It's an offence for a licensee to serve alcohol in a bar to anyone under 18. Unless drinkers can prove they're at least 18, the licensee can refuse to serve them and may ask them to leave the premises.

Disabled: toilet
If a pub claims to have a toilet for the disabled, we have said so; this also implies that it's possible for a disabled person to gain access to the venue. However, we cannot guarantee this, so it's best to phone in advance to check.

Smoking
A smoking ban came into force in London in 2007 so we no longer include smoking information in our listings. The fine for smoking in an indoor public place is £50. We have listed venues that offer slightly more salubrious environs for puffers in the **Where to go for...** section (starting on p255).

Star ratings/New entries/Hot 50
Those venues that we like are marked with a ★ in this guide. Those that we consider to be quintessentially 'London' venues are marked **HOT 50**. Those added since the last edition are marked **NEW**. These aren't necessarily brand-new businesses, but they are new inclusions to the guide.

Themed index
This guide is arranged by area because that's how most people drink. But if you're after something other than just the closest or most convenient pub or bar, turn to **Where to go for...** (starting on p255), an index of establishments arranged by theme.

During the year-long lifetime of this guide, bars and pubs will inevitably change name, change hands or close. We strongly recommend giving the venue a ring before you set out – especially if your visit involves a long trip.

Reviews featured in this guide are based on the experiences and opinions of *Time Out*'s reviewers. All pubs and bars listed are visited – anonymously – and *Time Out* pays the bill. No payment or incentive of any kind has secured or influenced a review.

Contents

GATE

| Acoustic sounds upstairs | Salsa Mondays | Notting Hill's longest running Hip Hop and R&B Night | supper · wine live music · dj | The 80's Revival |

The Gate Restaurant, Bar and Club form the hub of Notting Hill's social scene. Spread over two venues dominating the junction at the very heart of Notting Hill, the Gate offers everything one could need for a great night out.

The establishment comprises a restaurant, bar, lounge, club and private rooms and offers homemade international tapas, delicious bar snacks, canapés for private functions, fine wines and great cocktails. With a different DJ every night of the week offering up everything from R&B, Funky House and 80s Soul to a live music Supper Club and Salsa night, the party never ends at the Gate.

GATE RESTAURANT, BAR & CLUB

Gate Bar and Private rooms, 90 Notting Hill Gate W11 3HP
Gate Bar and Lounge, 87 Notting Hill Gate W11 3JZ
Gate Restaurant and Club, 87 Notting Hill Gate W11 3JZ

Website: www.gaterestaurant.co.uk

Restaurant reservations & private hire

Contact Chloe Campbell on 020 7727 9007
Email: General@gaterestaurant.co.uk

Freaks, the lot of you

Simone Baird takes the temperature of London's alternative nightlife scene, and finds it healthier – if stranger – than ever.

'I'm surprised,' admits cabaret mogul Paul L Martin, whose MMP cabaret agency (www.millionthmuse.com) celebrates its tenth anniversary this year. 'I thought we'd get two good years out of the cabaret revival and then the bubble would burst. But now I don't think it will, just as long as we come up with new ideas. What I've always said is that people no longer want to sit in a club and be quiet, they want to be a star as well. They have that chance by dressing up and having fabulous attitude, and that's why the scene continues to be so successful.'

The burlesque and cabaret scene really took off in London when event organiser Warren Dent 'discovered' the **Bethnal Green Working Men's Club** (*pictured, see p242*) in 2002. Like many working men's clubs in England, this one boasted sticky carpets, rewind-to-the-1970s decor and was in dire financial straits – it was no secret that the club was a hefty £40,000 in debt. It took three years before he finally sorted out the quagmire of licensing problems, but by early 2006, disparate London scenes – 1920s-'60s music fans, vintage dressers, burlesque performers and quirky club promoters – had found a place to call home.

While wearing second-hand tea dresses and learning to dance to 1940s swing was a giggle, it was soon overshadowed by girls stripping down to frilly knickers and nipple pasties (the things the tassels hang off). Burlesque clubs such as Whoopee (www.thewhoopeeclub.com) and the Flash Monkey (www.theflashmonkey.biz) were suddenly the height of fashion; Immodesty Blaize and Dita Von Teese ▶

were absolutely everywhere and there was a run on red lipstick.

Still, waving a couple of fans around or popping balloons stuck to your underwear – two of burlesque's most famous, and overdone, routines – only amuse for so long. Increasingly savvy audiences demand greater thrills. They want dangerous circus stunts and ukulele playing, preferably at the same time. Step forward… the variety revival.

'It was really useful for cabaret artists when burlesque appeared properly about two or three years ago,' says Martin. 'It gave an inroad into something very fashionable, which cabaret never was. I think it wasn't until the beginning of 2007 that we were really working together as a united cabaret and burlesque scene.'

Jamie McLaren, publisher of *Run-Riot*, a weekly mail-shot of underground happenings, isn't surprised that those leading the way are the same people who've been doing so from day one. 'What's really exciting is how these artists are now in a great position to take audiences on really arty cabaret and performance experiences. Audiences are recognising the intelligence, wit and charm of these leading artists, and are being tested and pushed. There is more trash out there, it's true, but on the front line, things are really exciting.'

Martin responded to the ever-changing nature of London's alternative nightlife scene by launching SideShow, held at the Arts Theatre (www.artstheatrelondon. com) every other Thursday. The line-up is full of, well, freaks. Sword swallowers, naked synchronised swimmers, midget burlesque roller skaters, gimp mask-wearing DJs.

Variety shows were made for supper clubs, and there's also – you guessed it – been a phenomenal resurgence in these. Venues range from covetable purpose-built spaces such as the **Pigalle Club** (*see p248*), kitted out like a 1940s supper club and home to the weekly Kitsch Lounge Riot (www.kitschloungeriot.com), through to newer restaurants such as Brickhouse

(www.thebrickhouse.co.uk) on Brick Lane, which adds nightly burlesque, aerial and cabaret performers to its menu. Bonobo Presents… is a once-a-month supper club held in the opulent Grill Room at the Café Royal (www.bonobopresents.com). Tickets might push £65 (including a three-course dinner and some drinks), but it's hard to top for a special night out.

Bethnal Green Working Men's Club

Still, there are circus freaks and then there's the seriously freaky. Take the alternative drag performers, for starters. Forget men looking as best they can like women and lame miming to disco classics, these blokes are all about the art. Bursting out of venues such as **Bistrotheque** (*see p242*) and Bar Music Hall (www.barmusic hall.com) with an edgy take on cross-dressing – they might wear make-up, but they're never in traditional drag – comparisons are often made with the mid 1980s clubbing phenomenon headed by Boy George and Leigh Bowery. Indeed, when it comes to forward-thinking cabaret, Bistrotheque is top of the pile. Twice a year, performer Lisa Lee puts on a ten-week run (UnderConstruction) at the venue, where established performance artists such as ▶

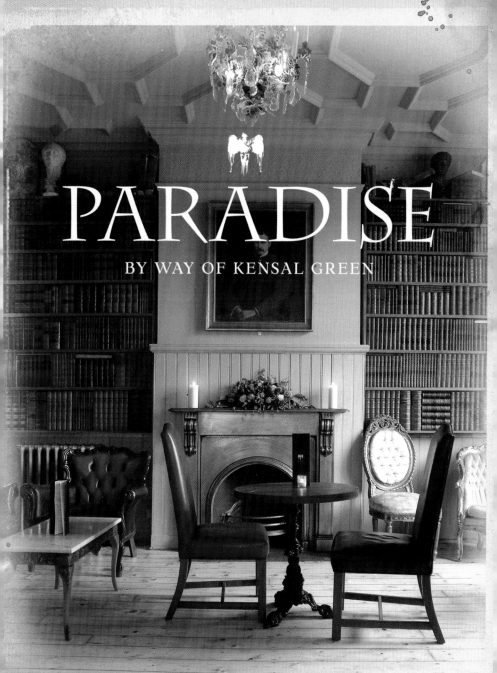

PARADISE

BY WAY OF KENSAL GREEN

AVAILABLE FOR PARTIES AND PRIVATE HIRE

020 8969 0098 · WWW.THEPARADISE.CO.UK

"This is without doubt the best place to buy or drink wine in London - you can browse the shelves like a bookshop and the staff are brilliant. It makes you realise how much fun drinking wine can be"

A satisfied and (as far as we know) sober customer

Green & Blue Clapham
20 - 26 Bedford Road
Clapham
London SW4 7HJ
T: 0207 498 9648

www.greenandbluewines.com

Green & Blue Lordship Lane
38 Lordship Lane
East Dulwich
London SE22 8HJ
T: 0208 693 9250

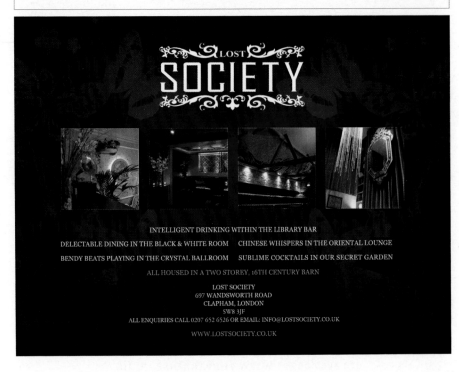

INTELLIGENT DRINKING WITHIN THE LIBRARY BAR

DELECTABLE DINING IN THE BLACK & WHITE ROOM   CHINESE WHISPERS IN THE ORIENTAL LOUNGE

BENDY BEATS PLAYING IN THE CRYSTAL BALLROOM   SUBLIME COCKTAILS IN OUR SECRET GARDEN

ALL HOUSED IN A TWO STOREY, 16TH CENTURY BARN

LOST SOCIETY
697 WANDSWORTH ROAD
CLAPHAM, LONDON
SW8 3JF
ALL ENQUIRIES CALL 0207 652 6526 OR EMAIL: INFO@LOSTSOCIETY.CO.UK

WWW.LOSTSOCIETY.CO.UK

Soho Revue Bar

Scottee, Jonny Woo and Ryan Styles get an opportunity to try out new material. It may be very, ahem, 'under construction', but it's a rare insight into the creative process.

On the other side of London, the legendary gay boozer **Royal Vauxhall Tavern** (*see p150*) is every bit as ragged around the edges, but is more importantly home to London's longest-running cabaret club, Duckie (www.duckie.co.uk). Every Saturday night, cabaret performers from all walks of life – eye-watering magicians who pull red cloths from places they shouldn't; envelope-pushing performers such as Marisa Carnesky – step on stage. 'Dark prince of cabaret' Dusty Limits hosts his neo-Weimar Kabarett here once a month, while VauxhallVille Cabaret is the weekly Thursday happening led by post-modern puppeteer Nathaniel-de-Ville and the hairy burlesque bears, Bearlesque.

It's not just about strange-looking performers, though. Cabaret singers such as Bourgeois & Maurice – all camp 1980s cast-offs and gorgeous cheekbones – might look like achingly fashionable East End types when they descend on their regular haunt **CellarDoor** (*see p242*), but listen closely. This young duo write cabaret songs with names like 'Cyber Lament' ('so sick of these friend requests/ and the leaking from my silicone breasts/ I've got Botox tears in my eyes').

There's more to it than simply cabaret and surreal drag shows though. Londoners just can't get enough of the quirky and unusual. Club goers are encouraged to be morose at Feeling Gloomy (www.feelinggloomy.com) – School Disco meets Morrissey on a comedown – while onions are chopped at Loss (www.thelasttuesdaysociety.org)

to encourage free-flowing tears among the funeral-parlour classical music and Victorian costumes. Speed daters are turned into bile-spewing haters at Down With Dating (www.downwithdating.com) – think of the best insults you can hurl rather than trying to sell yourself – while a flash mob of Viennese waltzers recently descended on Piccadilly at dusk.

As long as promoters and performers can satisfy the incessant demand for the new, it seems London's cabaret and burlesque revival isn't going anywhere. What's in vogue seems to change every six months or less. Right now it's circus freaks – although as companies such as Circus of Horrors (www.circusofhorrors.co.uk) and FireTusk PainProof Circus (www.fire tusk.com) up the ante to out-gross each other, it's a lifetime since Jim Rose's rock-fuelled shenanigans seemed shocking – and close-up magicians. For the latter, check out Magic Night, every first Friday of the month at the **Soho Revue Bar** (*see p250*). It's quickly progressed from a handful of magicians working the room throughout the night to ten magicians, and it's getting bigger. But what's next? We've already had the trend for all things 1920s a couple of years back, but there's heavy betting on the scene rewinding even further.

'I think it'll be music halls,' says Martin, and he's got good reason to think so. More and more Londoners are discovering old music halls – such as the Hackney Empire (www.hackneyempire.co.uk) and Wilton's (www.wiltons.org.uk) – and performers are taking the opportunity to come up with fresh material that satirises and well as amuses. 'After all,' quips Martin, 'variety's the word!'

Time Out's Hot 50

The editors of *Time Out Bars, Pubs & Clubs* have picked 50 places, quite subjectively, that offer some of London's most interesting drinking experiences. From glamorous hotel bars to old-fashioned boozers, each adds something life-enhancing to our city. Each venue is marked with a `HOT 50` in its relevant chapter.

Anchor & Hope
South p150
Waterloo's finest gastropub, with a superb wine list and real ales.

Anglesea Arms
Central p74
Entering this trad boozer is like taking a step back in time.

Auld Shillelagh
North East p200
Guinness lovers should head straight for this temple to the black stuff.

Balham Bowls Club
South p136
Bowls club rules no longer apply, but the quirky interior is a reminder of this bar's previous life.

Bar Estrela
South p148
A corner of south London that's forever sunny Portugal.

Boisdale
Central p80
A whisky drinker's paradise, with a heated cigar terrace.

Boot & Flogger
South East p167
Worth a visit for the wood panelling and personal service as much as for the wine.

Bread & Roses
South p144
Community spirit rules at this Workers Beer Company pub.

Bricklayer's Arms
South West p128
The oldest pub in Putney serves the full range of Timothy Taylor ales, including mild.

Brown Dog
South West p120
A superior gastropub in the backstreets of Barnes.

Café Kick
Central p24
Table football and European bottled beers galore.

Canbury Arms
Outer p237
A refugee from Gordon Ramsay's kitchen cooks up a storm here.

Candy Bar
Central p66
London's longest-established lesbian bar has an equally lengthy happy hour.

Cellar Gascon
Central p24
The wines of the French south-west are the speciality at Pascal Aussignac's cosy bolthole.

Charles Lamb
North p215
A delightful pub in a quiet Islington side street that does gastro to perfection.

Charlie Wright's
East p184
A Hoxton original that's spot on for late-night debauchery.

Cow
West p117
Irish oysters, real ales and perfectly poured Guinness.

Crazy Bear
Central p39
Cocktails are the order of the day in this glam basement.

Duke of Cambridge
North p217
Civilised Islington establishment that is Britain's first certified organic gastropub.

Eagle
Central p26
London's gastropub pioneer is still doing the business.

Ebury
Central p81
A classic wine bar with a vast selection on offer.

Establishment
South West p127
For a pub, this Parsons Green boozer does a fine line in wine.

French House
Central p70
De Gaulle had his wartime HQ at this Soho institution where beer is still served by the half-pint.

Galvin at Windows
Central p58
Superior cocktails and one of the best views in town.

Gladstone Arms
South East p168
A cosy local that's a destination for some of the hippest indie-folk acts around.

Golden Heart
City p88
Sandra Esqulant's wonderful take on the East End boozer.

Gordon's
Central p77
Purveyor of ports and sherries since the reign of Queen Vic.

Hakkasan
Central p42
This sleek and glamorous cocktail bar does amazing things with saké.

Harringay Arms
North p210
No food, no frills, just beer and banter. An unreconstructed triumph of a pub.

Hawksmoor
City p89
Go east for seriously stylish cocktails and fine steaks too.

Holly Bush
North West p229
This Hampstead boozer does a pitch-perfect impersonation of a country pub.

Lost Society
South p140
A glamorous and opulent bar, with a cocktail list to die for.

Milk & Honey
Central p71
An atmospheric Soho members' bar that lets all comers in on the act (before 11pm).

Monkey Chews
North p209
A relaxed lounge bar that's NW5's best-kept secret.

Old Red Lion
North p220
Unpretentious old-school boozer below the fringe theatre of the same name.

Pig's Ear
South West p125
A notably successful gastro conversion.

Pineapple
North p222
A north London institution with a convivial vibe.

Polo Bar
Central p58
A gem of a hotel bar – with fine cocktails.

Prince Arthur
North East p197
This top-notch Hackney gastropub is beautifully restored.

Retro Bar
Central p77
An appealingly eccentric gay bar.

Richard I
South East p165
Trad Greenwich local that's holding its own against newer venues.

Royal Oak
South East p169
A rare London outpost of Sussex brewery Harveys, whose wide range of ales tempts discerning drinkers.

St John
Central p32
Adjoins Fergus Henderson's famous restaurant and serves quality bar snacks and wine.

Seven Stars
City p84
Roxy Beaujolais's atmospherically cramped pub has a bohemian feel.

Sir Richard Steele
North West p228
This endearingly scruffy Belsize Park venue has traditional boozer appeal.

Sultan
South West p134
An much-loved ale drinker's paradise in South Wimbledon.

Vertigo 42
City p91
Worth visiting for the stupendous view from the top of Tower 42 if nothing else.

Wenlock Arms
East p191
A bit battered round the edges, this N1 boozer is all about real ales, quizzes and local banter.

Ye Olde Mitre
City p84
With its atmospheric hidden location and old-fashioned feel, this is something close to pub nirvana.

Ye Olde White Bear
North West p231
A charming NW3 pub that's all muddy dogs and real ale.

Hot 50

Central

Central

From Clerkenwell and Farringdon in the east to Mayfair and Belgravia in the west, central London offers almost unimaginable choice to the discerning drinker. Traditional boozers and raucous DJ bars, real ale and high-end cocktails – you really can have it all here. Though it's a nightclubbing Sodom and Gomorrah these days, Soho still boasts some of the capital's best pubs. The diminutive **Dog & Duck**, the **Endurance** gastropub and old-time literary haunt the **Pillars of Hercules** are our favourites. Despite being a tourist magnet, Covent Garden is blessed with some lovely little pubs too – 'little' being the operative word in the case of the **Lamb & Flag**. And worth a detour if you're a lover of Belgian beer is **Lowlander**. A little way north, the revamped, Grade II-listed **Princess Louise** flies the flag for Yorkshire's Samuel Smith's brewery. Head a mile or two west along Oxford Street and the atmosphere is rather more elevated: Mayfair has some of London's best hotel bars. **Galvin at Windows** commands stunning views from the summit of the Park Lane Hilton, while the **Polo Bar** at the Westbury Hotel is all effortless art deco chic. Oh, and fantastic cocktails.

Aldwych

Edgar Wallace
40 Essex Street, WC2R 3JE (7353 3120/ www.edgarwallacepub.com). Temple tube. **Open** 11am-11pm Mon-Fri. **Food served** noon-9.30pm Mon-Fri. **Credit** MC, V. **Pub**
His bust sitting attentively on the bar counter, the pre-war penman would have appreciated this neat, well-run pub serving handpump ales and decent wines to a mainly legal clientele from the Royal Courts of Justice. The demise of nearby Fleet Street has done little to dull the manly chatter here, fuelled by ten types of red (Louis Latour pinot noir, £17), ten whites (Chablis Chablisienne, £18) and a steadily interesting changeover of ales. Edgar's own Pale Ale is currently complemented by 1648 Hop Pocket, Woodforde's Wherry and Bishops Farewell. Wraps and a veggie brunch (£6) balance out the steak sandwiches (£8) and burgers (£8).
Babies and children admitted (restaurant only). Function room (capacity 40). Restaurant. TVs. **Map p275 M6.**

George IV
26-28 Portugal Street, WC2A 2HE (7955 7743). Holborn or Temple tube. **Open** noon-11pm Mon-Fri. **Food served** noon-10pm Mon-Fri. **Credit** MC, V. **Pub**
Set on an unassuming, traffic-free junction of three streets, the spruce George IV attracts orderly students and staff from the London School of Economics opposite. While BBC's *News 24* silently broadcasts from a corner flat-screen TV, learned, chatty types fire into their soup of the day (£2.95) or torpedo rolls (with kettle chips, £3.95) and pints of Pedigree, Thwaites Lancaster Bomber or Everards Tiger. Wines, ranging from a Casa La Joya merlot (£10.65) to a Pouilly Fuissé Chablis (£18.90), are also available in number and two of them, more unusually, are on draught. The upstairs games room is a convivial option.
Function room (capacity 100). Games (darts). TVs. **Map p275 M6.**

Lobby Bar ★
One Aldwych, WC2B 4RH (7300 1070/ www.onealdwych.com). Covent Garden or Temple tube. **Open** 8am-11.30pm Mon-Sat; 8am-10.30pm Sun. **Food served** noon-5pm, 5.30-11pm Mon-Sat; noon-5pm, 5.30-10.30pm Sun. **Credit** AmEx, DC, MC, V. **Hotel bar**
The signature bar of the upmarket urban hotel One Aldwych is known for the range and quality of its cocktails and for a sculpture of a bemused rower. From one of the elegantly high-backed chairs, select your own martini spirit from a range that includes Wyborowa (£9.40) and Kauffman Luxury Vintage 2003 (£20) – that is, if none of the 20 listed martinis (£9.95), such as a Gazpacho with lemon-infused Tanqueray, green pepper, Midori and elderflower cordial,

grabs you. A Number One from the six-strong 'One Aldwych Selection' (£9.95-£12.75) of Wyborowa, raspberry liqueur, passion fruit and De Venoge champagne also stands out. Various sandwiches (£9) and working lunch plates (beef carpaccio, £11.95) make classy accompaniments. *Babies and children admitted. Disabled: toilet. Function room (capacity 100).* **Map p275 M7.**

Belgravia

Blue Bar
The Berkeley, Wilton Place, SW1X 7RL (7235 6000/www.the-berkeley.co.uk). Hyde Park Corner tube. **Open/food served** 4pm-1am Mon-Sat; 4-11pm Sun. **Credit** AmEx, DC, MC, V. Hotel bar
The crowd at this sleb-favoured hotel haunt is very see-and-be-seen, but it's nice to see the staff don't greet them with the complacency they probably deserve. This is a handsome, cosy room, made lovelier by the low lighting, and the drinks are terrific. On the colourful cocktail list, the bar staff make good on the basics (an impressive whisky sour made with egg whites) and the inventions: our Amber Manhattan, essentially a perfect manhattan made with Macallan ten-year and titivated with maple and pecan liqueur, vanilla, Cointreau and orange bitters, was every bit as stunning as it should have been given its outlandish £16 price tag. Bite your lip and brave the throng.
Disabled: toilet (in hotel). Dress: smart casual.

Library ★
Lanesborough Hotel, 1 Lanesborough Place, Hyde Park Corner, SW1X 7TA (7259 5599/ www.lanesborough.com). Hyde Park Corner tube. **Open** 11am-1am Mon-Sat; noon-10.30pm Sun. **Food served** noon-midnight Mon-Sat; noon-10.30pm Sun. **Credit** AmEx, DC, MC, V. Hotel bar
Surprisingly, those books are real. But the whole place is otherwise a fabulous illusion: despite its olde worlde appearance, the Lanesborough was a hospital until the '80s, and only opened as a hotel less than 20 years ago. Whereas the bars at other nearby hotels – the Berkeley, say, or the Mandarin Oriental – are dressed to the eights and nines and draw a younger, more boisterous crowd, the Library remains gentle and mellow long into the night, partly thanks to a tinkling pianist and perpetually low lighting. Attentive staff and above-par cocktails help things run along very smoothly.
Disabled: toilet. Function rooms (capacity 180). Music (pianist 6.30pm daily; free). Restaurant.

Nag's Head
53 Kinnerton Street, SW1X 8ED (7235 1135). Hyde Park Corner or Knightsbridge tube. **Open** 11am-11pm Mon-Sat; noon-10.30pm Sun. **Food served** noon-9pm daily. **Credit** MC, V. Pub
It's unusual to see a landlord's name plastered on the front of a pub, but then there aren't many like Kevin Moran left in the trade. The Nag's Head reflects Moran's exuberant eccentricity, both by design (mobiles are banned; the walls are cluttered with everything from cartoons to baseball reports, garden tools to vintage penny-slots) and, most strikingly, by accident (the rooms could scarcely be wonkier, one stepped awkwardly above the other with a bar that somehow serves them both). The ale is from Adnams and only OK, but the appeal of this place isn't really to do with the beer.
Games (antique what-the-butler-saw machine). No mobile phones. Tables outdoors (1, pavement).

Star Tavern
6 Belgrave Mews West, SW1X 8HT (7235 3019). Hyde Park Corner or Knightsbridge tube/Victoria tube/rail. **Open** 11am-11pm Mon-Sat; noon-10.30pm Sun. **Food served** noon-4pm, 5-9pm Mon-Fri. **Credit** AmEx, MC, V. Pub
During the '50s and '60s, this mews pub is said to have drawn a mix of the very high and the very low: on the one hand, the moneyed Belgravians who've long dominated the area; and on the other, the underworld types who aspired to it (the Great Train Robbery was reputedly planned upstairs). These days, it's a little less vibrant, but still a pleasant place, spruced up in a recent refurbishment and enlivened in summer by its fabled hanging baskets. A Fuller's pub, it's one of only a handful of London pubs to have been included in every edition of CAMRA's *Good Beer Guide*.
Babies and children admitted. No piped music or jukebox.

Bloomsbury

AKA
18 West Central Street, WC1A 1JJ (7836 0110/ www.akalondon.com). Holborn or Tottenham Court Road tube. **Open** 6pm-5am 1st Tue of mth; times vary Wed; 8pm-3am Thur; 6pm-4am Fri; 7pm-5am Sat; 10pm-5am Sun. **Food served** 6-11.30pm Tue-Fri; 7-11.30pm Sat. **Admission** £5 after 11pm Tue; £5 after 10pm Thur; £7 after 11pm Fri; £10 after 9pm Sat; varies Sun. **Credit** AmEx, DC, MC, V. DJ bar

Central

Just off the bustle and tat of Shaftesbury Avenue, this airy cocoon – sister venture to the End – claims to have been London's original DJ bar, and it's still grooving along nicely. The two-floor interior is assured and modern, with balconies reaching into brickwork and black sofas sitting low in the artful gloom; the zinc bar has separate cognac, champagne and 'fine spirits' menus. Needless to say, this isn't your typical clubbing scuff's hangout, although presumably the punters' styled locks are let down a little at the Saturday morning post-club session. The rest of the time, it's pre-club sets; on our last visit there was noodly jazz-funk early on and more pumped-up house and techno later. *Bar available for hire. Comedy (7.30pm 2nd Thur of mth; £8). Disabled: toilet. Film night (6pm, Tue; free). Music (DJs 10pm nightly; free).* **Map p272 L6.**

All Star Lanes ★

Victoria House, Bloomsbury Place, WC1B 4DA (7025 2676/www.allstarlanes.co.uk). Holborn tube. **Open/food served** 5-11pm Mon-Wed; 5pm-midnight Thur; noon-2am Fri, Sat; noon-11pm Sun. **Bowling** £8.50 (per person, per game). **Credit** AmEx, MC, V. **Bar/bowling alley**
Of Bloomsbury's two subterranean bowling dens, this is the one with aspirations. Walk past the lanes and smart, diner-style seating, and you'll find yourself in a comfortable, subdued side bar with chilled glasses, classy red furnishings, glitterballs, an unusual mix of bottled lagers (try the delicious Anchor Steam) and an impressive cocktail selection. It's a fine place for lounging, although the rumble of bowling balls and clink of beer buckets should serve as a reminder that leisure entertainment is very much the name of the game. There's a sister branch in Bayswater (7313 8363), and another planned for Brick Lane. Booking ahead is a good idea.
Babies and children admitted (until 6pm). Disabled: toilet. Music (DJ 10pm-2am Fri, Sat). Private bowling room (capacity 75). **Map p272 L5.**

Bloomsbury Bowling Lanes

Basement, Tavistock Hotel, Bedford Way, WC1H 9EU (7691 2610/www.bloomsbury live.com). Russell Square tube. **Open** noon-2am Mon-Wed; noon-3am Thur-Sat; 1pm-midnight Sun. **Food served** noon-10pm Mon-Fri; noon-midnight Sat; 1-9pm Sun. **Bowling** from £36/hr 1 lane. **Credit** AmEx, MC, V. **Bar/bowling alley**
Although its near-neighbour All Star Lanes (*see above*) makes a good stab at sophistication, BBL

knows it's a big kids' playground. As well as the eight lanes, there's pool by the hour, table football, karaoke booths and, beside the entrance, a small cinema. Bands add to the mayhem on some weekend nights, when the floor buzzes with squiffy revellers, their eyes ablaze with sport. The rest of the place is pretty functional, with a large horseshoe bar (serving Bitburger, Bernard and Meantime), retro bowling instructions on the walls and a smokers' alley at the back. If you want a piece of the bowling action (or karaoke), be sure to book ahead.
Disabled: toilet. Games (pool tables, table football). No under-18s after 4pm. Karaoke (private rooms, capacity 25; from £40 per hour). Music (bands 9pm Mon, Wed, free; 9pm Fri, Sat, £3-£8). **Map p272 K4.**

Duke ★

7 Roger Street, WC1N 2PB (7242 7230/ www.dukepub.co.uk). Chancery Lane, Holborn or Russell Square tube. **Open** noon-11pm Mon-Sat; noon-10.30pm Sun. **Food served** noon-10pm Mon-Sat; noon-9.30pm Sun. **Credit** MC, V. **Gastropub**
For review, *see p20.*
Babies and children admitted. Restaurant. Tables outdoors (3, pavement). **Map p274 M4.**

Lamb ★

94 Lamb's Conduit Street, WC1N 3LZ (7405 0713). Holborn or Russell Square tube. **Open** 11am-midnight Mon-Sat; noon-10.30pm Sun. **Food served** noon-9pm daily. **Credit** AmEx, MC, V. **Pub**
Founded in 1729, this Young's pub is the sort of place that makes you misty-eyed for a vanishing era. The Lamb found fame as a theatrical haunt when the A-list included Sir Henry Irving and stars of music hall; they're commemorated in vintage photos, surrounded by well-worn seats, much polished wood and a few vintage knick-knacks. Food is of the soak-it-up variety – try the 1729 Celebration Pie – and in summer there's a patio at the back. Punters range from discerning students to Gray's Inn barristers, though on our last visit we chatted to a pair of fur-coated old dears three sheets to the wind and happy as Larry (Olivier, perhaps).
Function room (capacity 40). No piped music or jukebox. Tables outdoors (3, patio; 3, pavement). **Map p274 M4.**

Museum Tavern

49 Great Russell Street, WC1B 3BA (7242 8987). Holborn or Tottenham Court Road tube. **Open** 11am-11.30pm Mon-Thur; 11am-

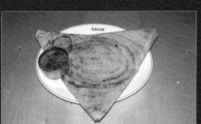

Duke ★

Its nondescript brick facade may echo the primary school opposite, but the Duke (of York, as the sign outside helpfully adds in brackets) is itself something of an education in quirky style. Seating in the tiny main bar is a mix of vintage wooden booths and brightly coloured, Formica-topped tables dotted around on scuffed parquet. A shiny red piano beckons from one side, though you'd have to know your chops, since cool jazz is the music of choice. Monochrome portraits of vintage film starlets set the 1930s to '50s mood, but the food is pure modern gastropub – fried bream, perhaps, or the 'pie of the week', served in a separate wood-lined dining room. For beer, Adnams and Greene King are on tap. *For listings, see p18.*

midnight Fri, Sat; noon-10.30pm Sun. **Food served** 11am-10.30pm Mon-Sat; noon-8pm Sun. **Credit** AmEx, MC, V. Pub

When a boozer boasts logoed T-shirts and its own history book, you might be wary; but this venerable corner pub opposite the British Museum pulls in its fair share of locals as well as tourists. Though the premises date from the 1720s (when it was known as the Dog & Duck), the current incarnation is Victorian, all engraved mirrors and windows, ornate ceiling and walls whose muted brown and red chimes with the historic air. Past customers have included JB Priestley, Sir Arthur Conan Doyle and Karl Marx, who unwound here after hours of reading in the old British Library. Today, the excellent guest ales are well worth anyone's Kapital, though the food is basic proletarian pub fare.

Children admitted (until 5pm). Tables outdoors (8, pavement). **Map p272 L5.**

mybar

11-13 Bayley Street, WC1B 3HD (7667 6050/www.myhotels.com). Goodge Street or Tottenham Court Road tube. **Open** 7am-midnight Mon-Thur, Sun; 7am-1am Fri, Sat. **Food served** 7am-10.30pm daily. **Credit** AmEx, DC, MC, V. Hotel bar

Tucked down a side street just off Tottenham Court Road, this hotel bar is coolly contemporary: white walls decorated with modern art of the not painted variety (sculpture, photo installations), big pale tables for impromptu brainstorms, and judicious amounts of metal, including a tiny zinc-topped bar. Interesting bottled beers like Lapin Kulta augment a copious cocktail list of around 50 options (from £6.50), a 'Wellbeing' selection of mocktails, and a decent wine list. Like the hotel it's attached to, the place is well thought-out and stylish, and without trying to be at the cutting edge, still pretty sharp.

Bar available for hire. Disabled: toilet. Function rooms (capacity 60). Tables outdoors (7, pavement). **Map p272 K5.**

Perseverance

63 Lamb's Conduit Street, WC1N 3ND (7405 8278/www.theperseverancepub.com). Russell Square tube. **Open** noon-11pm Mon-Thur, Sat; noon-midnight Fri; noon-10.30pm Sun. **Food served** noon-4pm, 5-10pm Mon-Sat; noon-6pm Sun. **Credit** AmEx, MC, V. Pub

Occupying a large corner site near Great Ormond Street hospital, this is a popular spot for medics seeking to soothe the stresses of their jobs. A recent refurb put mock vintage gilding and aged-looking red pillars under a browny-red

ceiling, embossed with period patterns. But why have an old 'Ale & Stout' engraved window when the only ale amid the lagers is Greene King IPA? Fine if you just want to drink, eat (various things, mostly with chips) and forget a hard day; if you want good beer and real atmosphere, the Lamb is a hundred yards away.

Babies and children admitted (until 6pm). Function room (capacity 40). Tables outdoors (3, pavement). **Map p274 M4.**

Queen's Larder NEW

1 Queen Square, WC1N 3AR (7837 5627). Russell Square tube. **Open** 11.30am-11pm Mon-Sat; noon-10.30pm Sun. **Food served** noon-3pm daily. **Credit** MC, V. Pub

Set on the west side of Queen Square, this pub is well placed to bag custom from Great Ormond Street hospital and among the learners and lecturers of neighbouring Mary Ward Centre; it also draws business types down the alley from busy Southampton Row. Not that many can get in, mind you, given the tiny ground-floor bar, although an equally petite space upstairs does cater for a small amount of overspill. Reds dominate the decor, and over the bar a strange gaggle of toy clowns watch proceedings. A trio of ales – Old Speckled Hen, Greene King IPA and a guest ale (Fireside on our visit) – are served, as is basic pub grub.

Babies and children admitted. Function room (capacity 50). Tables outdoors (7, pavement). TVs. **Map p272 L4.**

Truckles of Pied Bull Yard

Off Bury Place, WC1A 2JR (7404 5338/ www.davy.co.uk). Holborn or Tottenham Court Road tube. **Open/food served** 11am-10pm Mon-Fri; (summer only) 11am-3pm Sat. **Credit** AmEx, DC, MC, V. Pub

Its ghastly name sounds like an old-fashioned shop, though this is actually part of the Davy's wine chain. As a bar, Truckles is something of a one-trick pony – think summer, think terrace. In all other ways, it's completely unremarkable. Large windows wrap around a space as corporate as a hundred others; office types pour into this goldfish bowl to lunch on standard brasserie fare, then return in the evening for some post-work vino or a pint of Old Wallop. Come summer, the drinkers take over a large swathe of the Pied Bull Yard piazza to sip Davy's plonk and babble in the sunshine.

Babies and children admitted (restaurant). Bar available for hire. Dining room (available for hire, capacity 12). Quiz (6.30pm last Mon of mth; £15/ team). Tables outdoors (35, courtyard). **Map p272 L5.**

Central

Clerkenwell & Farringdon

Al's Café Bar

11-13 Exmouth Market, EC1R 4QD (7837 4821). Angel tube/Farringdon tube/rail. **Open** 9am-midnight Mon; 9am-2am Tue-Sat; 9am-11.30pm Sun. **Food served** 9am-6pm Mon-Wed, Sun; 9am-10pm Thur-Sat. **Credit** AmEx, MC, V. **Bar/café**

Part bar, part caff, part late-night boozing magnet: everyone round here knows Al's. It's a breakfast-to-bedtime operation, serving a hotchpotch of punters with fry-ups (house variety with cumberland sausage, £6.95), bagel towers (with poached eggs, £6.95), burgers (£7.50), tapas, ciabattas and spot-on pints of golden König Ludwig beer from 10.30am onwards. Also on offer are the likes of Leffe and Hoegaarden, plus bottled Budvar and Warsteiner, flavoured teas (somewhat at odds with the prosaic red and black setting) and cocktails (watermelon collins, passion fruit mojito). Make a beeline for the pavement seating at the first sign of sun.

Babies and children welcome. Function room (capacity 40). Music (DJ 11pm Fri, Sat; free). Tables outdoors (12, pavement). TVs. **Map p274 N4.**

Apple Tree

45 Mount Pleasant, WC1X 0AE (7837 2365). Farringdon tube/rail. **Open** noon-11.30pm Mon-Fri; 3-10.30pm 2nd & last Sun of mth. **Food served** noon-3pm, 6-9pm Mon-Fri. **Credit** AmEx, DC, MC, V. **Gastropub**

This smart gastropub and post-work glughouse has a superior feel about it, thanks to high ceilings, tall house plants and a quality drinks list. Draught beers include Greene King and Budvar, wines a Ropiteau Chablis (£18) and a decent merlot and chardonnay by the glass; malts include the likes of Auchentoshan and Bunnahabhain. Food is similarly a notch above, like house beef burger (£8) with mature cheddar, caramelised red onion and salsa; alternatively, you can wolf down a ciabatta for under a fiver. Brown couches in a far corner and wooden benches outside offer respite from telly talk and blokey guffaws.

Bar available for hire (Sat, Sun). Entertainment (poker 7pm Wed; £2). Function room (capacity 50). Music (Americana/bluegrass, 3pm, 2nd & last Sun of mth; free). Tables outdoors (3, pavement). **Map p274 N4.**

Betsey Trotwood ★ **NEW**

56 Farringdon Road, EC1R 3BL (7253 4285/ www.thebetsey.com). Farringdon tube/rail.

Open noon-11pm Mon-Wed; noon-11.30pm Thur; noon-1am Fri, Sat. **Food served** noon-3pm, 6-9pm Mon-Fri. **Credit** MC, V. **Pub**

It isn't only Clerkenwell's media types who are thankful for the Betsey's long-overdue facelift. The spruce-up extends beyond the fresh flowers, retro lighting and crazy, coppery wallpaper; the upstairs bar still hosts great soul nights, the downstairs box still shoehorns in geektastic indie outfits and, on our visit, the soundtrack appeared to be Dylan on a loop. Musos aside, all can enjoy great eating and drinking. Spitfire and Bishops Finger ales are joined by guest Whitstable Bay (from £3), a decent choice of wines by the glass (from £3), a dozen malt whiskies, 'special' bloody marys (glass or pitcher), and proper coffees and herbal teas. Appetites can be sated with regularly changing menus that always include delicious pies fresh from Borough Market.

Babies and children admitted (until 6pm). Bar available for hire. Function rooms (capacity 50). Music (folk, 8pm alternate Thur, £3; bands/comedy Fri, Sat; check website for details). Tables outdoors (2, pavement). **Map p274 N4.**

Bishops Finger

9-10 West Smithfield, EC1A 9JR (7248 2341/ www.shepherdneame.co.uk). Farringdon tube/rail. **Open** 11am-11pm Mon-Fri. **Food served** noon-3pm, 6-9pm Mon-Thur; noon-3pm Fri. **Credit** AmEx, MC, V. **Pub**

Faversham brewery Shepherd Neame runs this rather splendid, sleek and varnished boozer on a quiet crescent near Smithfield Market. It once had a Smithfield 375 telephone number, hence the sign inside mixed in with brewery publicity and paraphernalia. The titular BF, Master Brew, Spitfire and Porter are kept company on tap by the usual SN options of Holsten Export and Oranjeboom, plus Asahi. Wines (£12-£18.50) include a Domaine de la Bouronnière Chablis, although the choice of a dozen juicy sausages attracts a more blokey, beer-quaffing clientele. There's now a laptop area in one corner and an attractive upstairs room has been recently renovated.

Babies and children admitted. Bar available for hire. Disabled: toilet. Function room (capacity 40). Tables outdoors (3, pavement). TV. **Map p274 O5.**

Bleeding Heart Tavern ★

Bleeding Heart Yard, 19 Greville Street, EC1N 8SJ (7404 0333/www.bleeding heart.co.uk). Farringdon tube/rail. **Open** 7am-11pm Mon-Fri. **Food served** *Bar*

7-10.30am, 12.45-10.30pm Mon-Fri. *Bistro/ tavern* noon-2.30pm, 6-10.30pm Mon-Fri. **Credit** AmEx, DC, MC, V. **Wine bar**
For review, *see right.*
Babies and children admitted. Disabled: toilet. Function rooms (capacity 120). No piped music or jukebox. Restaurant. Tables outdoors (16, terrace). **Map p274 N5**.

Café Kick ★ HOT 50

43 Exmouth Market, EC1R 4QL (7837 8077/ www.cafekick.co.uk). Angel tube/Farringdon tube/rail. **Open** noon-11pm Mon-Thur; noon-midnight Fri, Sat; (Mar-Dec) 4-10.30pm Sun. **Food served** noon-3pm, 6-10pm Mon-Fri; noon-10pm Sat; 4-9.30pm Sun. **Credit** AmEx, MC, V. **Bar**

Clerkenwell's most likeable bar is this table-football themed gem, now ten years old. The soccer paraphernalia is authentic, retro-cool and mainly Latin (though you'll find a Zenit St Petersburg scarf amid the St Etienne and Lusitanian gear); equally, bar staff, beers and bites give the impression you could easily be in Lisbon. Vitor and his crew plonk bottled Sagres, Super Bock, Brahma, Cusqueña and Krombacher on to the zinc counter, at the end of which a modest open kitchen ('we don't microwave or deep-fry') dishes out tapas, sandwiches and charcuterie platters. Kick cocktails (£6.50), two dozen martinis and drinks long and short, involve football-related names shaken to the background rattle of table football and victorious whooping.
Babies and children admitted (until 5pm). Games (table football, 3 tables). Tables outdoors (4, pavement). TVs (widescreen). **Map p274 N4**.

Cellar Gascon ★ HOT 50

59 West Smithfield, EC1A 9DS (7600 7561/ 7796 0600/www.cellargascon.com). Barbican tube/Farringdon tube/rail. **Open** noon-midnight Mon-Fri; 6pm-midnight Sat (2 Sat/ mth). **Food served** noon-11.30pm Mon-Fri; 6pm-midnight Sat (2 Sat/mth). **Credit** AmEx, MC, V. **Wine bar**

Comprising a strand of cheek-by-jowl tables facing a low-lit bar, and a cosy gallery at the back, this pocket-sized joint is one third of chef Pascal Aussignac's trio of Smithfield temples to the food and drink of south-west France. Here the bias is towards wine (and lots of it), with a list that's an insider's guide to some of the best producers in the region, each entry supplied with compelling, haiku-like tasting notes. The small plates that make up the food offerings are similarly high quality; Aussignac's Gascon-focused loyalties

Bleeding Heart Tavern ★

Casual drinkers may be put off by reviews of this place describing it as a bijou bistro or a top-notch grill-style restaurant; and within the various rooms that comprise the Bleeding Heart 'complex' you'll certainly find both of these things. But at street level there's an unpretentious pub, serving Adnams ales, lager by tap or bottle, and a lovingly compiled wine list at between £4.50 and £7 a glass. The punters queuing in barely concealed frustration at the Eagle around the corner would be well advised to pop in here instead: the grub is hearty (shepherd's pie or steak at around a tenner), the atmosphere convivial; and although standing room is at a premium, the wait for a seat is marginally shorter. Although the Bleeding Heart has succumbed to the inescapable forces of gentrification, it's a relief that this long-standing drinking location has retained at least some of its honest boozing history. *For listings, see p23.*

make this one of the few places in London where you can enjoy foie gras just as a bar snack. An indulgent place to sink into and totally relax of an evening.
Babies and children welcome. Bar available for hire. Tables outdoors (3, pavement). **Map p274 O5**.

Charterhouse

38 Charterhouse Street, EC1M 6JH (7608 0858/www.charterhousebar.co.uk). Farringdon tube/rail. **Open** noon-11pm Mon, Tue; noon-midnight Wed, Sun (by request); noon-2am Thur; noon-4am Fri; 5pm-4am Sat. **Food served** noon-9.30pm Mon-Fri; 5-9.30pm Sat; noon-5pm Sun. **Credit** AmEx, MC, V. **Bar**

Opposite Smithfield Market, this bar shaped like a Trivial Pursuit wedge is a pleasantly understated affair. A modest counter dispenses draught Kronenbourg and San Miguel, and a decent range of £6 cocktails. Twisted Classics include a Krupnik sour with the titular honey vodka, lemon juice and Angostura bitters, and a blueberry daiquiri with Green Island spiced rum and vanilla syrup. Wines run to a £21.50 Charles Pierre Chablis, and the £5.50 pasta of the day would suit most budgets and appetites. The only decorative touches of note are three red globes glowing over the bar staff. The basement DJ space proves popular with trendy office types on Fridays and a laid-back local crowd on Saturday nights.

Central

Bar available for hire. Function rooms (capacity 100). Music (DJs 8pm Fri, Sat; free). Tables outdoors (3, pavement). TVs (big screen). **Map p274 O5**.

Coach & Horses ★

26-28 Ray Street, EC1R 3DJ (7278 8990/ www.thecoachandhorses.com). Farringdon tube/rail. **Open** 11am-11pm Mon-Fri; 6-11pm Sat; noon-4pm Sun. **Food served** noon-3pm, 6-10pm Mon-Fri; 6-10pm Sat; noon-3pm Sun. **Credit** AmEx, MC, V. **Gastropub**
This gastro gem is invariably packed with staff from the nearby *Guardian* offices, whose splashes decorate the wood-panelled interior. Inside, pub and restaurant areas are divided by an island bar serving both. Ale drinkers get Adnams, Timothy Taylor Landlord and Fuller's London Pride; winos, meanwhile, are spoilt for choice. Eight of each colour come by the glass, five by the half-bottle and 30 each by the bottle, complementing a daily-changing menu whose ingredients are meticulously and regionally sourced (fish comes from Ben's Fish on Mersea Island, for example). The day's eight starters and mains might include a pheasant and chestnut salad (£5.60) and roasted Hereford sirloin (£14); a six-strong bar menu (chorizo with egg and chips, £7.20) provides levity. *Babies and children welcome: high chairs. Restaurant (available for hire, 35). Tables outdoors (6, garden).* **Map p274 N4**.

Dollar

2 Exmouth Market, EC1R 4PX (7278 0077/ www.dollargrills.com). Farringdon tube/rail. **Open** noon-5pm, 6pm-1am daily. **Food served** noon-5pm, 6-11pm Mon-Thur; noon-5pm, 6-11.30pm Fri, Sat; noon-5pm, 6-10.30pm Sun. **Credit** AmEx, MC, V. **Cocktail bar**
'Grills & Martinis' runs the gaudy red neon sign of this incongruous slice of Americana set behind a black-fronted façade on the corner of Exmouth Market. And sure enough, Dollar steak burgers there are (£10.95), with cashew sauce, sweet-cure bacon and Dollar relish, along with Porn Star martinis (£8) of Cariel vanilla vodka and passion fruit purée – one of 20 cocktail options. A 40-strong wine list includes a Domaine de Charmoy Chablis (£29) and Viña Alicia Lujan de Cuyo Mendoza malbec (£42), and a surprisingly eclectic European bottled beer list has Salzburg Stiegl and Estonian Viru. Below ground, the evening-only Martini Lounge is red lit, seductive and packed with frocked up girls with *Sex and the City* complexes most weekends. As a touching reminder of less glamorous times (as the Penny Black – so named as it's right by the Mount Pleasant sorting office) 'Watney's Public Bar' remains etched into the main window. *Babies and children admitted. Bar available for hire. Music (DJs 8pm Fri, Sat; free). Restaurant. Tables outdoors (5, pavement). TV.* **Map p274 N4**.

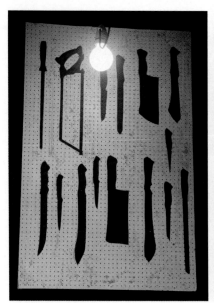

Medcalf. *See p29.*

Eagle ★

159 Farringdon Road, EC1R 3AL (7837 1353).
Farringdon tube/rail. **Open** noon-11pm Mon-
Sat; noon-5pm Sun. **Food served** 12.30-3pm,
6.30-10.30pm Mon-Fri; 12.30-3.30pm, 6.30-
10.30pm Sat; 12.30-3.30pm Sun. **Credit** MC, V.
Gastropub
Gastropub pioneer the Eagle was founded by
Michael Belben and David Eyre way back in
1991 – you'll find signed copies of the weighty
tome *Gastropub Classic* (£18) by the famous
open kitchen. The excellent Mediterranean and
Modern European cuisine still draws a barful of
discerning diners at every sitting; bagging a
spontaneous table can prove impossible at peak
times. The dozen wines by the glass include a
Reserva Nieto merlot (£4/£16) and Blanco
Cosecha Rioja (£3.75/£14.75); draught beers
Eagle IPA, Bombardier and Red Stripe. Bottled
Sagres maintains the southern European mood,
and determined bar-hoppers can eschew food
for a Dark & Stormy cocktail (£5) of Havana 7,
fresh lime and ginger beer.
Babies and children welcome; children's
portions. Tables outdoors (4, pavement).
Map p274 N4.

Easton

22 Easton Street, WC1X 0DS (7278 7608).
Farringdon tube/rail. **Open** noon-11pm
Mon-Thur; 12.30pm-1am Fri; 5.30pm-1am Sat;
12.30-10.30pm Sun. **Food served** 12.30-3pm,

6.30-10pm Mon-Fri; 6.30-10pm Sat; 1-4pm,
6.30-9.30pm Sun. **Credit** MC, V. **Gastropub**
A white indoor paint job in January 2008 has
sharpened the contrast with the red banquettes,
creating a neat decorative backdrop at this solid-
quality gastropub. Draught Hoegaarden and
Red Stripe are served from a long bar counter,
as are bottled Australian VB and Sol – though
the Easton's after-work drinkers are more of a
wine-glugging bunch. They have plenty to
choose from: Beau Chêne pinot noir, Enate
cabernet merlot or Terra Anzica sauvignon blanc,
perhaps? All fine potential accompaniments to
dishes such as harissa roast organic chicken
(£11.50) or pan-fried sea bass fillets with walnut
bagna calda (£12.95) from the regularly changing
menu. A 'No Dancing' sign offsets mildly erotic
images dotted around the expansive room.
Babies and children admitted (until 9pm).
Tables outdoors (4, pavement). **Map p274 N4.**

Fluid

40 Charterhouse Street, EC1M 6JN (7253
3444/www.fluidbar.com). Barbican tube/
Farringdon tube/rail. **Open** noon-midnight
Mon-Wed; noon-2am Thur; noon-4am Fri;
7pm-4am Sat. **Food served** noon-10pm
Mon-Fri. **Admission** £3 after 9pm, £5 after
10pm Fri, Sat. **Credit** AmEx, DC, MC, V. **Bar**
Wantonly tacky, petite two-floor Fluid brings
Japanese pop sensibilities to Clerkenwell. Manga
art and retro computer games feature above, and
downstairs a brash mural of Tokyo by night

offers something to gawp at while DJs spin a laid-back house and electro mix (most nights of the week). Ginseng beer complements the Sapporo, Kirin and draught Asahi, chased by sakés from Azeki (£5) to Yancha (£12). Sushi, sashimi and tempura comprise the 30-strong snack list, and a list of 25 cocktails (£7-£7.50) includes specialities such as a saké sling. Low, communal seating upstairs fosters a conspiratorial atmosphere.

Babies and children admitted (until 9pm). Function room (capacity 100). Games (retro video games). Music (DJs, 7pm Tue-Sat). Tables outdoors (3, pavement). TV. **Map p274 O5**.

Fox & Anchor ★ NEW

115 Charterhouse Street, EC1M 6AA (7250 1300/www.foxandanchor.com). Barbican or Farringdon tube/rail. **Open** 8am-11pm Mon-Fri; noon-11pm Sat. **Food served** 8am-11pm Mon-Fri. **Credit** AmEx, MC, V. **Pub**

The meat workers of Smithfield (and countless clubbers) were up in arms when this early-opening boozer closed in 2006. They have Malmaison to thank for its return, and especially for the fact that its beautiful interior has been restored and updated but largely left unspoiled. The long bar is still there (now with a pewter top), as are the wood fixtures, the lovely snugs and the 8am weekday opening (try the full English at £8.95). Aside from the six hotel rooms upstairs, the most eye-catching change is the addition of a TV in a spot not central enough to be of much use, but visible enough to be a distraction. However, with an array of rarely seen bottled beers supplemented by six cask ales, the Fox is a beer-drinker's paradise. The vigorous cooking is also a couple of cuts above: oysters, picture-perfect steak pie, or an awesome ham hock, sourced from the Ginger Pig. Time will tell if the traders will embrace the more upmarket feel but Clerkenwell's trendy types have already been checking it out.

Babies and children admitted (until 7pm). Disabled: toilet. TV. **Map p274 O5**.

Green

29 Clerkenwell Green, EC1R 0DU (7490 8010). Farringdon tube/rail. **Open** noon-11pm Mon-Wed, Sun; noon-midnight Thur-Sat. **Food served** noon-3pm, 6-10pm Mon-Thur, Fri; noon-4pm, 6-10pm Sat; noon-4pm, 6-9pm Sun. **Credit** AmEx, MC, V.

Bar/restaurant

Part-French and part-Spanish in its gastronomic leanings, the street corner Green attracts a discerning professional clientele

thanks to the quality of its cuisine and wines. Under a bloody great clock, suited types loosen their ties and tuck into one of five daily specials (dishes like grilled tuna steak or roast partridge, £12.50) or superior tapas (manchego and quince £3, chorizo in red-wine sauce £3.80), available after 5pm. Some 30 wines (ten by the glass) are served, including a decent house Santa Isidro Pegões for £3.50/£13.50. Draught beers include König Ludwig, Leffe and Adnams, with Duvel and Belle-Vue Kriek by the bottle. An upstairs bar offers the ideal intimacy to ignite an office romance.

Babies and children admitted. Bar available for hire. Disabled: toilet. Function room (capacity 100). Music (DJ 9pm Fri; free). Tables outdoors (5, pavement). **Map p274 N4**.

Gunmakers

13 Eyre Street Hill, EC1R 5ET (7278 1022/www.thegunmakers.co.uk). Farringdon tube/rail. **Open** noon-11pm Mon-Fri; noon-5pm Sun. **Food served** noon-3pm, 6-10pm Mon-Fri; noon-5pm Sun. **Credit** MC, V. **Gastropub**

One of many gastropubs within easy reach of the *Guardian* offices, Gunmakers is popular with lunching hacks but also operates as an excellent natter-filled bar. Draught Young's, Bombardier and Staropramen are consumed with as much relish as the wine list of 16 varieties, whose Italian influence harks back to the time when this area was known as Little Italy. Frame makers and organ builders worked here, as did Hiram Maxim, inventor of the machine gun – hence the pub's name. In any case, there's a D'Istinto sangiovese (£3.65/£15.50) or Provincia di Pavia pinot grigio (£16) to go with your fennel and mascarpone risotto or pasta of the day (both £8.50). The underused white-walled back room allows dining space but not much sociability.

Babies and children admitted (until 6pm). Bar available for hire (Sat). Tables outdoors (7, conservatory). **Map p274 N4**.

Hand & Shears

1 Middle Street, EC1A 7JA (7600 0257). Barbican tube. **Open** 11am-11pm Mon-Fri. **Food served** noon-3pm Mon-Fri. **Credit** AmEx, MC, V. **Pub**

'Established 1532', says the sign, but a pub stood here even centuries before that. Oval-shaped, with an island bar of similar outline, the Hand & Shears is named after the Tudor tailors' guild that frequented it, and continues in a traditional fashion with little pretension. Courage Best, Wadworth 6X and Adnams are served from the wooden bar as punters' soles scuff the bare

Central

floorboards. The menu is of the 'sausage and mash for a fiver' variety, although you can tuck into an 8oz rump steak too. Black-and-white images of old London complement the low-key atmosphere. *Function room (capacity 50). Games (darts). No piped music or jukebox. Restaurant.* **Map p274 O5**.

Hat & Feathers

2 Clerkenwell Road, EC1M 5PQ (7490 2244/ www.hatandfeathers.com). Barbican tube/ Farringdon tube/rail. **Open** noon-1am Mon-Sat. **Food served** noon-10.30pm Mon-Fri; 6-10.30pm Sat (noon-10.30pm in summer). **Credit** AmEx, MC, V. **Gastropub**
Traffic roared around this forgotten building for years, but only recently did anyone care enough to put this two-floor bar and restaurant in it, magnificent yellow stucco exterior, statues and all. Inside, gaslights flicker in the etched glass, and the bar menu reflects the quality of the Modern European fare above – onion and port soup (£4.50) and pork belly (£14.50) are among the options. Beers have been similarly cherry-picked: you don't see draught Elman's Pond, Paulaner and Cruzcampo everywhere. Cocktails come by the glass (£6-£8) or pitcher (£19.95), including a Hat & Feathers Breeze of Smirnoff Black, cranberry and pineapple juice. The wine list numbers 50, six each by the glass. A side terrace is heated in winter and breezy in summer: lovely if you can manage to ignore the honking Clerkenwell Road traffic. *Babies and children admitted. Bar available for hire. Disabled: toilet. Restaurant (available for hire, capacity 60). Tables outdoors (30, terrace).* **Map p274 O4**.

Jerusalem Tavern ★

55 Britton Street, EC1M 5UQ (7490 4281/ www.stpetersbrewery.co.uk). Farringdon tube/ rail. **Open** 11am-11pm Mon-Fri. **Food served** noon-3pm Mon, Fri; noon-3pm, 5-9.30pm Tue-Thur. **Credit** AmEx, MC, V. **Pub**
Tilting, creaking and uneven, the cosily tatty JT serves the sought-after ales of Suffolk's St Peter's brewery. Behind the bar, seemingly hidden amid the timber divides and occasional raised seating, is a row of barrels, above which a board lists beers and their ABVs: Suffolk Gold, Grapefruit, Cinnamon & Apple, Organic, the whole range. A rag-tag and decidedly loyal crowd muses over the *Evening Standard* crossword and, in winter, a homely fireplace smell encourages the desire for warm sustenance. Fantastic haddock and salmon fishcakes and various sausages (especially on Tuesdays) fit the bill nicely. A fine place to unwind.

Bar available for hire (weekends only). No piped music or jukebox. Tables outdoors (2, pavement). **Map p274 O4**.

Match EC1

45-47 Clerkenwell Road, EC1M 5RS (7250 4002/www.matchbar.com). Farringdon tube/rail. **Open** 11am-midnight Mon-Wed; 11am-1am Thur, Fri; 6pm-1am Sat. **Food served** noon-10.30pm Mon-Fri; 6-10.30pm Sat. **Credit** AmEx, DC, MC, V. **Bar**
The stickers on Match EC1's door boast of bar awards won a decade or so ago; and though the world has moved on, the original of three Match bars (there's another on Margaret Street in W1; for Sosho *see p191*) has hardly changed. To be fair, little has arrived to match its commitment to mixed drinks. Each year a 'Match Original' cocktail created by an incumbent bartender is added to the list; John Cowley's Anniversary Fizz (Beefeater gin, Aperol, fresh lemon juice, passion fruit syrup and soda, £7) marks a decade of discerning drinking. Celebrated New York mixologist Dale DeGroff still dominates, with his five 'Original Recipes' (£6.50-£8), including a Japon Cocktail of Gran Centenario Reposado, fresh pink grapefruit, saké and cassis) and film-themed 'Matchnificent Seven' inventions. 'Sharing blocks' (£12-£13) of meze and charcuterie provide quality nutrition. *Babies and children admitted (before 5pm). Bar available for hire. Disabled: toilet. Tables outdoors (4, pavement).* **Map p274 O4**.

Medcalf ★

38-40 Exmouth Market, EC1R 4QE (7833 3533/www.medcalfbar.co.uk). Farringdon tube/rail. **Open** noon-11pm Mon-Thur, Sat; noon-12.30am Fri; noon-4pm Sun. **Food served** noon-3pm, 6-10pm Mon-Thur, Sat; noon-3pm, 6-10.30pm Fri; noon-4pm Sun. **Credit** MC, V. **Bar**
With rustic breads on shop-window boards where butcher Albert Medcalf's meats used to be displayed, this namesake bar is an exercise in practical good taste. A main room of scuffed wooden tables (each with a small white dish of salt and dwarf pepper grinder) leads to a square bar lounge and an adjoining decked terrace (five sought-after tables and splashes of shrubbery). Back in the main room, bare bulbs hang over a high bar, beside which a side room with a Shoreditch feel stages DJs, exhibitions and casual daytime chess games. The bar's short and sweet menu attracts a stream of diners with the likes of roast pumpkin soup (£4.50), barbary duck breast (£14.50) and honey roast black figs (£5). Five wines by the glass include an unusual

Central

Marqués de Aleila pensa blanca (£4.30/£15.75) from Barcelona; a classy Guitton Michel Chablis (£35) shines among the 30 bottles. There's plenty of choice by way of draught beer too, with Paulaner, Erdinger and Brugse Zot from across the Channel, Old Speckled Hen from Greene King in Suffolk, and Meantime from Greenwich. Vedett, Blanche de Bruxelles and Negra Modelo are the pick of the bottles. Booking is advised if you want to sample the food.
Art exhibitions (daily). Babies and children welcome (until 7pm): high chair. Disabled: toilet. Function room (capacity 50). Tables outdoors (5, garden; 4, pavement). **Map p274 N4.**

Old China Hand

8 Tysoe Street, EC1R 4RQ (7278 7678/ www.oldchinahand.co.uk). Angel tube. **Open** noon-2am Mon-Sat; noon-10pm Sun. **Food served** noon-3pm, 6-10pm Mon-Fri; 6-10pm Sat. **Credit** MC, V. **Gastropub**
Once your average corner boozer, the Old China Hand is now a dainty dim sum drinkery. It's a neat, two-area venue, featuring rustic-looking furniture and decor with a global, ethnic vibe. International draught beers include Kirin, Red Stripe and Hong Kong Sun Lik. Whitstable East India pale ale and Dark Star Hophead offer rare finds for UK ale lovers. Bottled Greek Mythos, Singapore Anchor, Indonesian Bitang, Laotian Lao and New Zealand Mac's Gold, plus Columba wheat beer from Corsica, comprise one of London's most eclectic choices. Chef Ngan Tung Cheung's expert dim sum (£4-£5) come in 13 varieties, including a ngan see beng of steamed and pan-fried Chinese sausage.
Babies and children admitted (until 6pm). Bar available for hire. Function room (capacity 30). Tables outdoors (4, pavement). Takeaway service. **Map p274 N3.**

Peasant ★

240 St John Street, EC1V 4PH (7336 7726/ www.thepeasant.co.uk). Angel tube/Farringdon tube/rail. **Open/food served** noon-11pm Mon-Sat; noon-10.30pm. **Credit** AmEx, MC, V. **Gastropub**
Gin palace turned gastropub, the pleasant Peasant exudes a contemporary tone with its continental draught beers and posters of punk rock stars. Where did they get that one advertising Iggy Pop in San Sebastián? Antwerp De Koninck is another rare find on tap, accompanied by Erdinger Weissbier, Cruzcampo and Leffe; Breton cider and Belgian Trappist treats come by the bottle. Pub touches from a previous life include the provision of Bombardier and Crouch Vale Brewers Gold, and a striking mosaic of

George and the dragon in tiled-floor form. A superior bar menu (try the steak sandwich) can be had with your choice of a dozen-plus wines by the glass; the Sunday roast is a killer.
Babies and children welcome (until 9pm): high chairs. Bar available for hire. Games (board games). Restaurant (available for hire, capacity 85). Tables outdoors (4, garden terrace; 5, pavement). **Map p274 O4.**

Potëmkin

144 Clerkenwell Road, EC1R 5DP (7278 6661/www.potemkin.co.uk). Farringdon tube/rail. **Open/food served** noon-11pm Mon-Fri; 6-11pm Sat. **Credit** AmEx, DC, MC, V. **Bar/restaurant**
Potëmkin ('Potyomkin') is a smart and well-stocked Russian bar with more than 50 varieties of vodka in clear, unusual, berry, fruit, citrus and herb 'n' spice categories. Most come in at around £3.50 a 25ml shot, the standouts being Chaika grape, Polmos rowanberry, Cristall blackcurrant and Sputnik horseradish flavours. Beers to chase them include bottled Baltika 3, Zhigulevskoe and Estonian Viru, with Georgian wines (Kindzmarauli £27, Khvanchkara £35) also available. Zakuski to nibble include raznosoly pickled vegetables (£3.75) and pod shuboy herring cake (£6), with sturgeon solyannka soup and rye bread (£6) for stronger appetites. Heartier mains, pelmeni dumplings (£9.50) or marinated shashlik (£13.50) are best taken in the equally neat restaurant down a staircase lined with black-and-white photographs of Russian sailors.
Babies and children admitted (dining only). Bar available for hire. Booking advisable. Restaurant. Takeaway service. TV. **Map p274 N4.**

Slaughtered Lamb NEW

34-35 Great Sutton Street, EC1V 0DX (7253 1516/www.theslaughteredlambpub. co.uk). Barbican tube/Farringdon tube/rail. **Open** noon-11pm Mon-Thur, Sun; noon-1am Fri, Sat. **Food served** noon-10pm Mon-Sat; 1-8pm Sun. **Credit** MC, V. **Pub**
Friday nights are a scrum in this art gallery turned gastro-ish pub. Just as well it's a big, lively space, the central bar being particularly well positioned for eyeing up the rather attractive clientele (think trendy, bespectacled publishing folk and architects). The basement hosts the odd poetry reading or performance, and some popular (sometimes ferociously trendy) gigs. The tunes upstairs meanwhile can be anything from Pink Floyd to people you've never heard of. No matter, simply kick back in one of the leather sofas with a plate of fish and chips or a roast, and

Central

• cocktails • beers • wine • shooters • jugs • bar food •
• spirits • champagne • spirits by the bottle • dj's •

**40 Hoxton Square, Shoreditch
London N1 6PB**
alternative entrance at 331 Old Street EC1V 9LE

• Happy hours daily from 5.30pm • Open til 2am (sunday midnight) •
• Basement bar available for private hire • No hire fee •
• Deposit and minimum spend required • Table reservation available •
• Pole dancing lessons hosted by www.polestars.net (women only) •

pr@trafikinfo.co.uk • 020 7613 0234 • www.trafikinfo.co.uk

one of the many international beers (Kirin from Japan, Sagres from Portugal or NYC's Brooklyn). *Babies and children admitted. Disabled: toilet. Function room (capacity 120). Music (bands 8pm Mon-Thur; £5).* **Map p274 O4.**

St John ★ `HOT 50`

26 St John Street, EC1M 4AY (7251 0848/ 4998/www.stjohnrestaurant.com). Barbican tube/Farringdon tube/rail. **Open/food served** 11am-11pm Mon-Fri; 6-11pm Sat. **Credit** AmEx, DC, MC, V. **Bar/restaurant**
Like bar, like restaurant: St John is quality through and through. Stark to the point of institutional, this eaterie of considerable renown offers a selection of gastronomic delights and a vast wine selection to those happy to hang out in the bar rather than the restaurant proper. As well as sourdough, light rye or any other bread baked here, discerning visitors might tuck into kedgeree (£14) or celeriac and bacon soup (£6.40) listed on the blackboard by the artisanal pile of loaves. A commendable number of wines come by the glass, including a Domaine Boudau Patrimoine Côtes de Roussillon Villages (£8.65) or a Domaine Chataigneraie-Laborier La Roche Pouilly-Fuissé (£9.10). Black Sheep bitter appears among other draught options provided by the Meantime brewery based at the equally renowned Greenwich Union bar (*see p164*). *Babies and children welcome. Disabled: toilet. Function room (capacity 18). Restaurant.* **Map p274 O5.**

Three Kings of Clerkenwell ★

7 Clerkenwell Close, EC1R 0DY (7253 0483). Farringdon tube/rail. **Open** noon-11pm Mon-Fri; 7-11pm Sat. **Food served** noon-3pm, 6.30-10pm Mon-Fri. **No credit cards. Pub**
The Three Kings remains a wonderful place to drink in, despite the apparent disappearance of the equally wonderful black pub cat whose style and attitude fitted so perfectly. Rhino heads, Egyptian felines and Dennis Bergkamp provide the decorative backdrop against which a regular bunch of discerning bohos glug Scrumpy Jack, Beck's Vier, Old Speckled Hen or London Pride, and tap the well-worn tables to the Cramps and other gems from an outstanding jukebox. Bottles of Tyskie and Lech point to a recent invasion by jaw-droppingly gorgeous Poles of both sexes. This would sit well in Shoreditch or Camberwell; here in Clerkenwell, it's a proper oasis of alternative taste. *Babies and children admitted (until 5.30pm). Function rooms (capacity 70). Games (board games). Jukebox. Quiz (9pm Mon; £5 per team). TV.* **Map p274 N4.**

Vinoteca ★

7 St John Street, EC1M 4AA (7253 8786/ www.vinoteca.co.uk). Farringdon tube/rail. **Open** 11am-11pm Mon-Sat. **Food served** noon-2.45pm, 6.30-10pm Mon-Sat. **Credit** MC, V. **Wine bar**
Inspired in name and approach by the Italian enoteca (a blend of off-licence and wine bar, with bar snacks thrown in for good measure), Vinoteca is actually more of a gastropub in spirit. It places much greater emphasis on the robust and strictly seasonal food than its European counterparts might: hardly surprising, as its chef, Carol Craddock, earned her stripes at Simon Hopkinson's Bibendum across town. But even if you're not in the mood for anything more than a plate of bread and olive oil, this place is worth heading to for its impressive 200-bottle wine list, of which a changing range of 19 are available by the glass. All are modestly marked up, making this a fine place to swot up on grape varieties and regions. *Babies and children admitted. Bookings not accepted for dinner. Function room (capacity 30). Off-licence. Tables outdoors (4, pavement).* **Map p274 O5.**

Vivat Bacchus

47 Farringdon Street, EC4A 4LL (7353 2648/www.vivatbacchus.co.uk). Chancery Lane tube/Farringdon tube/rail. **Open/food served** noon-10.30pm Mon-Fri. **Credit** AmEx, DC, MC, V. **Wine bar**
Although the hedonists of EC1 might instinctively head for the area around Smithfield Market, Vivat Bacchus – on the 'wrong' side of Farringdon Street – knocks nearly all of those joints into a cocked hat. Many people will come here for the acclaimed Modern European grub, which is served on the ground floor; vinophiles tend to nip up the stairs into a spacious, airy wine bar, where they can sniff and swill their way through an incredibly well-stocked cellar. If you peer in from the street and are put off by the faux-industrial chic, with a ceiling full of pipes and vents that may well be totally cosmetic, be reassured: this is as down-to-earth as modern wine bars get, with staff falling over themselves to assist and advise you. All the by-the-glass selections can be tasted before you buy, not that you're likely to be disappointed (the Jordan Stellenbosch should be administered by force to anyone who sneers at chardonnay), and the quality is consistently, fantastically high. *Bar available for hire. Disabled: toilet. Off-licence. Restaurant (booking advisable). Wine club (7pm Mon; £15). TV (satellite).* **Map p275 N5.**

Vinoteca

Central

Covent Garden

Box

*32-34 Monmouth Street, WC2H 9HA
(7240 5828). Covent Garden or Leicester
Square tube.* **Open** 11am-11pm Mon-Sat;
noon-10.30pm Sun. **Food served** 11am-5pm
daily. **Credit** MC, V. Café/bar

At first glance, this gay café-bar seems a pretty
standard joint (leather banquettes, big windows,
mirrors); however, its Covent Garden location
makes a fine break from the manic Old Compton
Street scene. The Muscle Mary contingent – the
chiselled bar staff once had their own beefcake
calendar – comes as something of a surprise too.
On weekend evenings the tables are pushed
back, the music pumped up and the place fills
with queens for some pre-club drinking. There
are 13 wines and five bottled beers (including
Peroni, Cobra and Tiger), and bar snacks
include pistachios and dried fruit. By day, the
place has a laid-back vibe, with alfresco seating
in summer. In fact, shoppers might not even
realise they're in a gay bar until they clock the
'Gay men and steroids' pamphlets in the loos.
*Babies and children admitted. Music
(DJs 8pm Thur-Sat; free). Tables outdoors
(2, pavement).* **Map p273 L6**.

Brasserie Max

*Covent Garden Hotel, 10 Monmouth Street,
WC2H 9LF (7806 1000/www.coventgarden
hotel.co.uk). Covent Garden tube.* **Open/food
served** 7am-11pm Mon-Fri; 8am-11pm Sat;
8am-10.30pm Sun. **Credit** AmEx, DC, MC, V.
Hotel bar

Under the row of flags on the stern, stylish
Covent Garden Hotel, this bar-restaurant is one
to impress with. Join the crowd of well-to-do
creative types for champagne-fuelled powwows
and sophisticated banter. The seven modish
cocktails (£10.50) show daring: take the Lady
Marmalade, comprising Hennessey cognac,
Cointreau, lime, own-made marmalade and
lemonade. The similarly priced signature
martini is a Max Passion of Belvedere Orange,
Passoa liqueur, Chambord, passion fruit and
lychee juice. Wines start with a Telero Bianco
del Salento at £6.50/£22. House platters include
a ploughman's at £25, beefburgers are £15.50
and bellinis start at £11.50. Waiters squeeze
their way between the half-moon chairs from the
zinc bar creating a buzzy, brasserie atmosphere.
*Babies and children welcome. Disabled: toilet.
Function rooms (capacity 50). Restaurant.
Screening facilities (dinner & film, 8pm
Sat; £35). Tables outdoors (7, pavement).*
Map p272 L6.

Café des Amis

*11-14 Hanover Place, WC2E 9JP (7379 3444/
www.cafedesamis.co.uk). Covent Garden tube.*
Open 11.30am-1am Mon-Sat. **Food served**
11.30am-11.30pm Mon-Sat. **Credit** AmEx,
DC, MC, V. Wine bar

As French as its name and namesake restaurant
upstairs, the cosy C des A is more basement bar
than café, but stylish for all that. A buzzy bunch
of shoppers and showgoers clink glasses around
an island bar, the minimal space made bigger
by wall mirrors. The French-dominated wine list
is 70 strong, with some 20 by the glass, from a
humble Le Bosq (£3.95/£14) to a Puligny
Montrachet Remoissenet 2005 (£63) and some
seriously pricey Bordeaux. A glass of Chat
Rouge Beaujolais comes in at £5.60. There are
five cocktails (£7.50), bottled Kronenbourg, and
a tidy menu of bar food that includes lunchtime
omelettes (honey roast ham and cheese, £7.50),
tapas and steak tartare (£8.50/£16).
*Bar available for hire. Function room
(capacity 120). Tables outdoors (12, terrace).*
Map p273 L6.

Christopher's Martini Bar ★

*18 Wellington Street, WC2E 7DD (7240
4222/www.christophersgrill.com). Covent
Garden tube.* **Open** 11.30am-11.30pm daily.
Food served noon-3pm, 5-11pm Mon-Fri;
11.30am-3pm, 5-11pm Sat, Sun. **Credit**
AmEx, DC, MC, V. Cocktail bar

Christopher's rightly calls itself the American
Bar, not only because the original at the nearby
Savoy is closed for refurbishment, but because
the quality of its martinis is tremendous. Also
known as the Martini Bar, it comprises maroon-
striped booths and swivel bar chairs, globe
lights and a large black and white portrait of
Roger Moore. Classic martinis are mixed from
20 spirits of your choice in three measures, be
it an U'Luvka (£11) or a Belvedere (£10); the 20
contemporary varieties (from £7.50) include a
Marcotini of Zubrówka, pomegranate juice,
lime and amaretto muddled with red pepper.
Other cocktails are also classic or contemporary,
with a lovely 'Neo Classic' range, all kumquats
and lemongrass. Bar snacks include courgette
tempura (£3.50) and classic hamburgers (£9).
*Babies and children welcome. Function room
(capacity 40).* **Map p273 L7**.

Cross Keys

*31 Endell Street, WC2H 9EB (7836 5185).
Covent Garden tube.* **Open** 11am-11pm
Mon-Sat; noon-10.30pm Sun. **Food served**
noon-3pm Mon-Sat; noon-2.30pm Sun. **Credit**
MC, V. Pub

Quirky, atmospheric and nicely unpretentious, the Cross Keys begs one question. What the hell is it doing in tourist-mobbed Covent Garden? Catering to ordinary folk and regulars, that's what; yep, this place does exactly what a pub is supposed to do. You'll find Bombardier, Courage Best, John Smith's and Guinness on draught, alongside doorstep sandwiches and pub bites. Most first-time visitors find themselves peering through the dim light to gawp at a poster for the Beatles' Royal Command Performance of 1963, Elvis Presley's napkin and a newspaper article relating to the landlord's successful £500 bid for it. Any man who pays £500 for a soiled napkin deserves to be celebrated. *Function room (capacity 40). Games (fruit machine, quiz machine). Tables outdoors (3, pavement).* **Map p273 L6**.

Detroit

35 Earlham Street, WC2H 9LD (7240 2662/ www.detroit-bar.com). Covent Garden or Leicester Square tube. **Open** 5pm-midnight Mon-Sat. **Credit** AmEx, DC, MC, V. **Bar**
Subterranean Detroit's cave-like alcoves combine a sense of below-radar cool with the uneasy feeling you've stumbled on a *Flintstones* theme park; it's not for claustrophobes, either. Lovers and intimate circles of friends whisper and cackle in dark corners, while sassy staff serve up contemporary drinks from a long bar of equal attraction. Fifteen long drinks (£6.95) include a Rosemary's Son of vodka, rosemary, raspberry, raspberry eau de vie, elderflower cordial and ginger beer; ten martinis (£6.95) include a Detropolitan of citrus vodka, cassis, Cointreau, cranberry and lime juices. More pricey, absinthe-laced 'Overproof' cocktails (£9.80) are balanced out by a '7 Heaven Happy Hour', when two drinks are £7. Cusqueña, Viru and Asahi are among the beers; satays, skewers and focaccia are the booze-soaking edibles. *Function rooms (capacity up to 200). Music (DJs 8pm Fri, Sat; free). Tables outdoors (2, pavement).* **Map p273 L6**.

Freud

198 Shaftesbury Avenue, WC2H 8JL (7240 9933/www.freudliving.com). Tottenham Court Road tube. **Open** 11am-11pm Mon-Wed; 11am-1am Thur, Sat; 11am-2am Fri; noon-10.30pm Sun. **Food served** noon-4.30pm daily. **Credit** MC, V. **Bar**
Back in the day – the late 1980s to be precise – Freud was the hottest ticket in town. Below the shop of the same name, this hidden cellar bar (reached via a metal staircase) retains the cool industrial feel, fans and slate seating that

brought discerning drinkers flocking here 20 years ago. What's more, it still impresses today. The 30-odd cocktails (£6-£7), stencilled on a board above the busy bar counter, are strong and served with ceremony. Fifteen-odd types of bottled beer include St Helier, Kastel Cru and Estrella, and the wholesome food is wonderfully cheap for the area – £5 salads and £3.50 soups. Mick Stump's charcoal images of London and New York add a stylish decor touch. *Babies and children admitted. Music (jazz 3pm occasional Sun; free). TV.* **Map p272 L6**.

Lamb & Flag ★

33 Rose Street, WC2E 9EB (7497 9504). Covent Garden tube. **Open** 11am-11pm Mon-Sat; noon-10.30pm Sun. **Food served** noon-3pm Mon-Fri, Sun; noon-4.30pm Sat. **Credit** MC, V. **Pub**
A pub for over 300 years and a fixture on Rose Street for longer, the unabashedly traditional Lamb & Flag is always a squeeze, but no one seems to mind. Character is in short supply around Covent Garden, and this place has bags of the stuff. On tap are draught Young's, Greene King and Courage Best, bottled Budvar and Peroni, and a daily menu usually including a ploughman's with a choice of eight cheeses (£5.25), roast beef pork or lamb with all the trimmings (£8.50) and cumberland sausage with french bread (£5.25). The afternoon-only bar upstairs is 'ye olde' to a fault. Pictures of passed-on regulars – 'Barnsey', Corporal Bill West et al – testify to its neighbourhood feel. *Babies and children admitted (lunch only). Games (darts). Music (jazz 7.30pm Sun; free). No piped music or jukebox. TV.* **Map p273 L7**.

Langley

5 Langley Street, WC2H 9JA (7836 5005/ www.thelangley.co.uk). Covent Garden tube. **Open/food served** 4.30pm-1am Mon-Sat; 4.30pm-12.30am Sun. **Admission** £3 after 10pm Thur; £8 after 10pm Fri, Sat. **Credit** AmEx, MC, V. **Bar**
This cavernous, bare-brick basement bar caters to an up-for-it crowd eager for fun and eye contact. Nine-to-fivers mingle around the main Geneva Bar before breaking out to the Vault and other alcove areas of greater intimacy. On the menu are 20 wines, a dozen by the glass, including a £3.55/£12.95 Italian sauvignon chardonnay and a Babich pinot noir (£24.95). Standard cocktails come by the glass (£6), seven by the jug (£16), and most prices drop by about a third between 5pm and 7pm. Early drinking

Central

Crazy Bear. *See p39.*

encourages the consumption of burgers (£7) or fish finger sarnies (£3.50) as the night draws on. *Bar available for hire. Disabled: toilet. Music (DJs 8pm Thur-Sat). Restaurant. TVs.* **Map p273 L6.**

Lowlander ★

36 Drury Lane, WC2B 5RR (7379 7446/ www.lowlander.com). Covent Garden or Holborn tube. **Open/food served** 10am-11pm Mon-Sat; noon-10.30pm Sun. **Credit** AmEx, MC, V. **Café/bar**
Brightly logoed and Benelux-themed, the smart Lowlander fills its expansive, long-tabled space easily, thanks to an impressive range of draught and bottled beer. The efficient table service adds extra appeal to knackered workers, shoppers and the terminally lazy. Sit back and relax as you take your pick from 15 tap beers, by the half-pint glass or two-pint jug, including Palm Speciale, Poperings Hommelbier and St Louis Premium. Of the 100 bottled varieties, Charles Quint, Achel and St Feuillien Blond stand out among the 20 abbey types, and the lambic

Cantillon Rose de Gambrinus (£5.50) is a rare find. Stoemp (£3.25) stew is ubiquitous in Belgium and perfectly made here; mussels (£5.95/£11.95) come in four sauces. A pleasant mezzanine is often occupied by private parties. *Babies and children admitted (until 6pm). Tables outdoors (2, pavement). TV (big screen, satellite).* **Map p272 L6.**

Maple Leaf

41 Maiden Lane, WC2E 7LJ (7240 2843). Covent Garden tube. **Open** 11am-11pm Mon-Thur; 11am-midnight Fri, Sat; noon-10.30pm Sun. **Food served** noon-9.30pm daily. **Credit** (over £10) AmEx, MC, V. **Pub**
'This public house is dedicated to the friendship between Britons and Canadians', says the sign. Inside, a recent refurb has kept the log-cabin atmosphere which, with a Mountie's uniform and ice-hockey paraphernalia, fosters warm bonhomie. Brits and Canucks can seal the deal over draught Sleeman or Labatt, a bottle of Moosehead, or a small (£4.50) or large (£6.99) portion of ML's 'famous chicken wings'. As

well as other specialities such as Quebec poutine and lumberjack meatloaf, the menu lists a serious selection of mains (28-day-matured rump steak, £8.75) sure to keep the wolf from the door.
Babies and children admitted (before 5pm). Bar available for hire. Games (fruit machine, quiz machine). TV (satellite). **Map p273 L7**.

Porterhouse

21-22 Maiden Lane, WC2E 7NA (7836 9931/www.porterhousebrewco.com). Covent Garden tube/Charing Cross tube/rail. **Open** 11am-11pm Mon-Wed; 11am-11.30pm Thur-Sat; noon-10.30pm Sun. **Food served** noon-9pm Mon-Sat; noon-7pm Sun. **Credit** AmEx, MC, V. **Bar**
Irish by nationality but remarkably global by nature, this gleaming, multi-spaced hostelry has a gregarious, no-nonsense vibe. Underpinning it all are draught stouts and ales rarely seen outside Ireland: Wrasslers, for example, popular in West Cork in the early 1900s. Along with the titular Porterhouse are An Brain Blást and oyster stout; tap lagers Temple Bräu and Hersbrucker are of the same family. The bottled beer list is simply mad – Albanian Tirana, Indonesian Bir Bintang, Israeli Macabee, Mozambican Laurentina Clara, Palestinian Taybeh and Tahitian Hinano – and goes down a treat with the multinational crowd that packs the place to bursting for key sporting fixtures.
Disabled: toilet. Function room (capacity 100). Music (bands 9pm Wed-Sat; Irish band 4.30pm Sun; free). Tables outdoors (3, pavement). TV (big screen, satellite). **Map p273 L7**.

Euston

Positively 4th Street

119 Hampstead Road, NW1 3EE (7388 5380/www.positively4thstreet.co.uk). Euston tube/rail. **Open** 5-11pm Mon-Thur; 5pm-1am Fri; 7pm-1am Sat. **Food served** 5-9.30pm Mon-Fri. **Credit** MC, V. **Cocktail bar**
You've got a lotta nerve… to put a Japan-themed, NY-style cocktail bar on a nondescript street corner halfway to Camden; but, like the Dylan song, it works. In an atmosphere that's half speakeasy, half colonial clubhouse (note the disconcerting lines of leaf-shaped fans above), the dozen or so cocktails served are wonderfully inventive. In the Zimmerman Revisited, 'the bile and bitterness of tequila is tamed temporarily', in this case by raspberry liqueur and passion fruit. A Japanese cosmopolitan includes Finlandia Mango, Midori,

lime and cranberry. Perhaps even more incongruously, Tetley's features among the draught beer options (Red Stripe, Leffe, Grolsch); sakés, umeshu and udon noodle soups (£5.95) add a further twist.
Bar available for hire. Function room (capacity 50). Music (DJs 8pm Fri; free).

Somers Town Coffee House

60 Chalton Street, NW1 1HS (7691 9136/www.somerstowncoffeehouse.com). Euston tube/rail. **Open/food served** noon-11pm daily. **Credit** AmEx, MC, V. **Gastropub**
French sisters Vanessa and Sabine ought to be commended for creating this thoroughly professional operation. Gallic in management and sensibility, the SCH has a carefully chosen and thoughtfully priced wine list of nearly 30 types to accompany quality lunch and evening menus, fixed and à la carte. Nearly 20 come by the glass, all in the £3 to £4 range, such as a Les Jamelles viognier and a Château de Carré Beaujolais Villages. Draught beers include Bombardier, Kirin, Wells Eagle, Red Stripe and Erdinger Weissbier, and there's a decent all-day bar menu (Somers Town beef burger with emmental, £8.75). A front terrace, back garden and back room with fireplace complement the spacious front bar and restaurant areas.
Babies and children admitted (until 5pm). Bar available for hire (Mon-Wed). Tables outdoors (10, terrace; 10, garden).

Fitzrovia

Annex 3 ★

6 Little Portland Street, W1W 7JE (7631 0700/www.annex3.co.uk). Oxford Circus tube. **Open** 5pm-midnight Mon-Fri; 6pm-midnight Sat. **Food served** 6.30-11pm Mon-Sat. **Credit** AmEx, MC, V. **Bar**
This is one of a trio of innovative enterprises run by Malaysian-born Hassan Abdullah, Frenchman Michel Lasserre and Swede Stefan Karison: the others, both in Shoreditch, are French restaurant Les Trois Garçons and bar Loungelover (*see p189*). All three share a swank-camp sensibility when it comes to design – so prepare to be dazzled by starburst chandeliers, foil, brocade and fairy lights on glass-topped tables. As original as the decor are the 20-odd cocktails defined as 'Old' and 'New Flames' (£8-£9), the former including a Loungelover of Annex 3 fig liqueur, sweet vanilla, lemon oil and prosecco, the latter a Wasabi Kiss of wasabi, basil, kiwi, Skyy vodka and Drambuie. Panch cocktails (£16) are the house speciality, modern

BOSTON'S FAVOURITE BAR IN LONDON'S PICCADILLY CIRCUS

Cheers®
LONDON

SIT, RELAX AND SOAK UP THE ATMOSPHERE IN AN AUTHENTIC RE-PRODUCTION OF THE ACTUAL BAR FROM THE LEGENDARY TELEVISION SERIES.

DINE, DANCE, DRINK TIL 3AM
DJ FROM 10.30PM EVERY NIGHT

RESTAURANT OPEN EVERYDAY FROM MIDDAY

FOR RESERVATIONS CALL:
020 7494 3322
72 REGENT STREET, W1B 5RJ.

www.cheersbarlondon.com

I ♥ SO.HO.
www.ilovesoho.co.uk

takes on 17th-century recipes from Charles H Baker's *Jigger, Beaker & Glass*; try the East Meets West of fresh blueberries, saké, Whitley Neill gin, rose syrup, pressed apple and ginger ale. Wines, four each by the glass, run from a house Terra Ventoux (£4.50/£16) to vintages costing three figures; an early-evening prix fixe menu (two courses for £14.95, three for £19.95) is a snip considering the quality of the fare on offer. Booking a table is advisable most nights. *Bar available for hire. Disabled: toilet. Music (DJs Sat; free).* **Map p272 J5.**

Bourne & Hollingsworth NEW

28 Rathbone Place, W1T 1JF (7636 8228/ www.bourneandhollingsworth.com). Goodge Street or Tottenham Court Road tube. **Open** 5pm-midnight Mon-Thur; 5pm-12.30am Fri, Sat. **Credit** (over £12) MC, V. **Bar**
Not so much a bar as a reproduction of your granny's sitting room, Bourne & Hollingsworth is not easy to find (walk down some steps at the junction of Percy and Rathbone Streets), but it warrants the effort – particularly on Tuesday nights, when good bands entertain cool, young boozers. For the rest of the week, it's hip pop, which sometimes triggers impromptu dancing – surprising, as the lounge is tiny. It all adds to the cosy feel of the place, as do the standard lamps, old fireplace and granny's flowery (but so chic) wallpaper. The range of cocktails is good, and prices even better (£5-£7), which – with the friendly atmos – make this a fine venue. *Bar available for hire. Music (bands 8.30pm Tue; free).* **Map p272 K5.**

Bradley's Spanish Bar

42-44 Hanway Street, W1T 1UT (7636 0359). Tottenham Court Road tube. **Open** noon-11pm Mon-Sat; noon-10.30pm Sun. **Credit** MC, V. **Bar**
Is it the jukebox? Is it the tatty velvet furniture and wobbly stools? Is it just habit? Whatever the reason, people still love Bradley's, a cornucopia of tack at the Oxford Street end of Hanway Street. A hotchpotch of local workers, shoppers and amorous foreign exchange students fills the cramped two-floor space, enraging passing taxi drivers as they spill on to the narrow street outside. All are happy to pay slightly over the odds for draught Cruzcampo, San Miguel and Budvar and bottled Estrella, Beck's and Warsteiner as they strain to chat over 'Geno' playing for the umpteenth time on the juke. All that's changed since the early 1990s is the staff – they're mainly Hungarians these days. *Jukebox.* **Map p272 K5.**

Carpenter's Arms NEW

68-70 Whitfield Street, W1T 4EY (7307 9931). Goodge Street tube. **Open** noon-11pm Mon; noon-11.30pm Tue-Thur, Sat; noon-midnight Fri; noon-10.30pm Sun. **Food served** noon-10pm daily. **Credit** AmEx, MC, V. **Pub**
A once-sad Fitzrovia boozer was transformed by the people behind the nearby Crown & Sceptre (*see p41*) in the spring of 2007. It shares its stablemate's taste for tap beers – Peroni, Belle-Vue Kriek and Franziskaner Weissbier included – with Singha, Pacifico Claro and Chimay Red available by the bottle. All are served from a lengthy bar that divides drinkers from diners, the former sat in a Macmillan-era living room, the latter in comfortable and contemporary surroundings. The Belle Bar upstairs and airy roof terrace offer alternatives to the main bar, though the punters (plenty of media types) tends to huddle outside on the pavement during the busy post-work slot. *Babies and children admitted. Bars available for hire. Disabled: toilet. Quiz (7pm Mon; £2). Tables outdoors (4, roof terrace; 12, pavement). TVs.* **Map p272 J4.**

Crazy Bear ★ HOT 50

26-28 Whitfield Street, W1T 2RG (7631 0088/www.crazybeargroup.co.uk). Goodge Street tube. **Open/food served** noon-10.45pm Mon-Fri; 6-10.45pm Sat. **Credit** AmEx, DC, MC, V. **Bar/restaurant**
This is the London outpost of Oxfordshire's upmarket hotel and bar Crazy Bear. A charming hostess leads you to a low-lit, Lilliputian basement bar of quiet chatter, padded alcoves, swivel cowhide stools and low-slung leather armchairs. Swanky cocktails (£8.50/£9.50 for champagne variants) are the order of the day, and mixed to perfection. There are classics with a twist (lychee mojitos, strawberry and basil mules) and quirky originals like a Ginger Bear of Koko Kanu rum, chocolate liqueur, ginger and lemongrass. If mixed drinks don't appeal, there are three champagnes (Gallimard, Pol Roger Reserve and Billecart-Salmon) available by the glass, as are a dozen wines; a full wine list is also available. Beers are bottled and include Singha, Monteith's and Tiger. Whatever your choice, a level of sobriety is required for the incredibly glam but disorientating loos (the doors are hidden in the walls and ev⋯⋯ ⋯ng is mirrored). Bar snacks include dim spring rolls and satays. *Babies and children admitted (lun Bar available for hire (Mon-Wed'* **Map p272 K5.**

Bountiful Cow ★

The nondescript modern exterior gives no hint of the Cow's cosy red and brown interior. Owned by Roxy Beaujolais (of Seven Stars fame, *see p84*), it's more a bar than a pub, with diner-style bar stools, booth seating, film posters (try not to sit opposite zombie flick *Raw Meat* while eating) and mounted bull horns. Although there's beer from Adnams, Harveys and Timothy Taylor, plus Aspall Suffolk Cyder and a short but sweet wine list, food – meat, mainly – takes pride of place; the clue's in the name. Decent steaks and mighty hamburgers form the backbone of the menu; veggies have to eat welsh rarebit or go hungry. A pleasant joint, but not one for traditionalists. *For listings, see p45.*

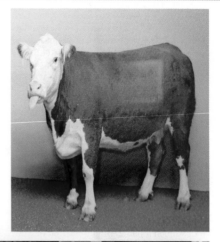

Crown & Sceptre

*26-27 Foley Street, W1W 6DS (7307 9971).
Goodge Street, Oxford Circus or Tottenham
Court Road tube.* **Open** noon-11pm Mon-Sat;
noon-10.30pm Sun. **Food served** noon-
10.30pm Mon-Sat; noon-9.30pm Sun. **Credit**
AmEx, MC, V. **Pub**

Choice is king at this busy and well-run pub, so
steer straight for the horseshoe bar and start
making your mind up. The beer options span
Timothy Taylor Landlord, Greene King IPA,
Angram, Beck's Vier, Schneider Weisse,
Hoegaarden, Budvar dark, Staropramen, Früli,
Kirin, Maredsous Blonde, Leffe and Frambozen.
Bag a table if you can, or join the inevitable
throng of after-work hedonists on the quiet
pavement in summer. Within, a loungey area to
one side lends itself more to diners, who can
plump for snacks or heartier mains (burger and
chips, £6.90). Most labels on the lengthy wine
list are available by the glass and bottle.
*Disabled: toilet. Music (DJ 7pm Sat; free).
Tables outdoors (3, pavement).*
Map p272 J5.

Eagle Bar Diner

*3-5 Rathbone Place, W1T 1HJ (7637 1418/
www.eaglebardiner.com). Tottenham Court
Road tube.* **Open/food served** noon-11pm
Mon-Wed; noon-1am Thur, Fri; 10am-1am
Sat; 10am-6pm Sun. **Credit** MC, V.
Bar/restaurant

Part diner, part bar, but as adept at mixing
cocktails as griddling burgers, the Eagle brings
American standards of service and sustenance
to Oxford Street shoppers and Fitzrovia night
owls. The drinks menu features an Eagle Fizz
of Grey Goose Le Citron, clementine, ginger and
Mercier (£8.50); a Björk Punch (£6.95) of Reyka
vodka, guava and lychee is inspired, as are the
alcohol-charged Boogie Shakes (£7.50). Bottled
beers include Anchor Steam and Brooklyn, with
Bud on draught. During the day, most people are
here for the food: of the burgers, Caledonian
Crown (£6.95) with monterey jack, red salsa or
jalapeños extras is a good bet, or you could try
crocodile, bison, kangaroo, springbok or ostrich
from the 'Something Wild' (£6.50) selection.
Breakfasts are another strong suit.
*Babies and children admitted (until 9pm if
dining). Disabled: toilet. Music (DJs 7pm
Wed-Sat). Restaurant. Takeaway service.*
Map p272 K5.

Green Man ★ NEW

*36 Riding House Street, W1W 7ES (7307
9981). Goodge Street or Oxford Circus tube.*
Open noon-11pm Mon-Sat; noon-10.30pm

Central

Sun. **Food served** noon-10pm Mon-Sat; noon-9.30pm Sun. **Credit** AmEx, MC, V. Pub

Since the tableau on the back wall was painted, the floors have been stripped, the walls have been cream-washed and the lights have been undimmed. So far, so so, but this is one pub where modernisation works. The Green Man's USP is draught ciders: five on our visit, with several in bottles, a couple of ales and ice-cold Sierra Nevada on tap. Aided by matey staff and a busy yet not noisy vibe, it's also a fine place for a drink and a chat. If the incongruous '80s-indie soundtrack isn't up your alley, the darker, sleeker upstairs bar may be mellower.
Function room (capacity 70). Games (board games, classic arcade machine). Music (DJ/bands 7pm Thur, Fri; free). Tables outdoors (3, pavement). TV. **Map p272 J5**.

Hakkasan ★ HOT 50

8 Hanway Place, W1T 1HD (7907 1888). Tottenham Court Road tube. **Open** noon-12.30am Mon-Wed; noon-1.30am Thur-Sat; noon-midnight Sun. **Food served** noon-3pm, 6-11.30pm Mon-Wed; noon-3pm, 6pm-12.30am Thur, Fri; noon-4pm, 6pm-12.30am Sat; noon-4pm, 6-11.30pm Sun. **Credit** AmEx, MC, V.
Bar/restaurant

This thin, aquamarine sliver of a cocktail bar is as renowned as the upmarket Chinese eaterie that surrounds it. Tucked down a dog-leg alley behind Hanway Street, Hakkasan is reached via a staircase and blossom-scented cloakroom – a descent into another world of beautifully lit, oriental sophistication. Drinkers must negotiate the dining room's interlocking booth dividers to get to the long, back-lit bar; then it's simply a case of sitting pretty and soaking up the glamour. Some 15 martinis and 26 long drinks (£9) are made with spirits such as 'Nikka whisky from the barrel' and 'Ciroc grape distilled vodka'. The signature Hakkatini mixes Campari, Belvedere Pomarancza, Grand Marnier, fresh apple and orange bitters; a Hakka is saké, Ketel One, lychee juice, passion fruit and coconut cream. Saké is a key ingredient: note the Purple Emperor with Matusalem 10 and jasmine tea, and the Chinese mule with ginger, coriander and Platinum vodka. Sold separately cold (£20-£96) and hot (£19.50),saké comes in Kubota Manju and Kenbishi varieties; other premium spirits (Buffalo Trace bourbon, Gran Centenario Reposado) come in £6.50 measures.
Babies and children admitted (until 7.30pm). Disabled: toilet. Function room (capacity 65). Music (DJs 9pm nightly; free). Restaurant (available for hire, capacity 150).
Map p272 K5.

Hope

15 Tottenham Street, W1T 2AJ (7637 0896). Goodge Street tube. **Open** 11am-11pm Mon-Sat; noon-10.30pm Sun. **Food served** 11am-3pm, 6-9pm Mon-Fri; noon-4pm Sat, Sun. **Credit** AmEx, MC, V. Pub

Welcomingly unpretentious, Hope serves decent ales and good sausages to a lunch-break and post-work, mainly white-collar crowd. Ales include Wadworth 6X, Adnams, Fuller's London Pride, John Smith's and Timothy Taylor Landlord; the sausage selection changes daily, but you can probably count on it including something tasty with venison. Canteen-style mains (beef goulash, fish and chips, £5.95) are produced to an equally high standard. You'll find a Ropiteau sauvignon blanc and a Cape Province pinotage among the wines, and may prefer a table in the upstairs dining room to the scuffed-floorboard bar at street level.
Babies and children admitted (weekends, until 7pm). Comedy (8pm Tue; £4). Function room (capacity 30). Games (fruit machine). Tables outdoors (3, pavement). TV.
Map p272 J5.

King & Queen NEW

1 Foley Street, W1P 7LE (7636 5619). Goodge Street tube. **Open** 11am-11pm Mon-Fri; noon-11pm Sat; 7-10.30pm Sun. **Food served** noon-2.30pm Mon-Fri. **Credit** AmEx, MC, V. Pub

The King & Queen has barely been touched since the day Bob Dylan played his first London show here, and it still has a monthly folk night. Most come to this dark, expansive saloon for the beers, which include St Austell Tribute, John Smith's, Adnams, Deuchars and San Miguel. Sport plays on a TV on the back wall – it's not a bad place in which to watch the Saturday results unfold – and mounted cricket souvenirs from the 1970s point to a personal involvement. Sandwiches include corned beef and pickle, and sales are rung up on an old cash register.
Babies and children admitted (until 7pm). Function room (capacity 60). Music (folk club 7.30pm mthly Fri; £3-£4). TVs (satellite).
Map p272 J5.

Long Bar

The Sanderson, 50 Berners Street, W1T 3NG (7300 1400/www.sandersonlondon.com). Oxford Circus or Tottenham Court Road tube. **Open/food served** 11.30am-2am Mon-Wed; 11.30am-3am Fri, Sat; noon-10.30pm Sun. **Credit** AmEx, DC, MC, V. Hotel bar

The Long Bar's early noughties glory days (the clientele is more civilian than celebrity in 2008)

Harrison. *See p47.*

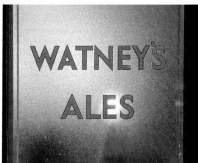

may be a faded memory, but there's still easy glamour for the taking. The long bar in question is a thin onyx affair, though nabbing one of the eyeball-backed stools is an unlikely prospect. A better bet is the lovely courtyard, where table service, candlelight and watery features make a much nicer setting for cocktails. And, really, it would be wrong to order anything else, with a list of enticing flutes (£14), long drinks (£11) and martinis (£12) to choose from: try a Santa Rosa (Stoli raspberry, crème de framboise and pêche, fresh raspberries and Laurent Perrier) or a Vesuvio martini (Ketel One Citron, lychee liqueur, lemongrass cordial and a dab of fresh chilli). High-end spirits include Chivas Regal and Sauza Hacienda (£8), and the wine selection is kept short. Bar snacks are priced high (BLT for £14, burger for £16), though this is unlikely to be a problem for most of the punters.
Babies and children admitted (terrace).
Disabled: toilet (in hotel). Function room (capacity 80). Music (DJ 10.30pm Fri; free). Tables outdoors (20, terrace).
Map p272 J5.

Market Place

11-13 Market Place, W1W 8AH (7079 2020/www.marketplace-london.com).
Oxford Circus tube. **Open** 11am-midnight Mon-Wed; 11am-1am Thur, Fri; noon-1am Sat; 1-11pm Sun. **Food served** 11am-3.30pm, 6.30pm-midnight Mon-Wed; 11am-3.30pm, 6.30pm-1am Thur, Fri; noon-1am Sat; 1-11pm Sun. **Admission** £7 after 11pm Fri, Sat. **Credit** AmEx, MC, V. **Bar**
Market Place attracts a gregarious global crowd to its ground-floor bar and basement DJ den. Come Friday evening, there's no standing on ceremony; if you don't have a mate to share a litre bottle of Cruzcampo with at the start of the night, you will have by the end. Those familiar with Cargo (*see p242*) or the Big Chill bars (*see p47 and p175*) will recognise the Cantaloupe Group's USP: eclectic music policy, Med/Latin street food and an array of unusual bottled beers. The place comes into its own for summer boozing, with a large terrace out front and cocktails by the jug or glass – try a Rosella (Belvedere vodka, fresh grapefruit, kiwi, peach and passion syrup). The 15-strong, largely Mediterranean wine list includes rarer finds such as a Corsican pinot noir and a rosé from Chapel Down in Kent. The pick of draught beers is a König Ludwig Hefe-Weizen; Innis & Gunn and Moretti are the top finds by the bottle.
Disabled: toilet. Music (DJs 8pm nightly).
bles outdoors (8, terrace).
ᵥ p272 J6.

Newman Arms

23 Rathbone Street, W1T 1NG (7636 1127/ www.newmanarms.co.uk). Goodge Street or Tottenham Court Road tube. **Open** noon-midnight Mon-Fri. **Food served** noon-3pm, 6-9pm Mon-Fri. **Credit** MC, V. **Pub**
The cabin-like Newman Arms has had the decorators in, but is still in touch with its history. A poster for the Italian version of Michael Powell's *Peeping Tom*, filmed right here in 1960, faces a black and white portrait of former regular George Orwell above the bar. Upon the bar are taps of London Pride, Adnams and Guinness (when will they get a decent lager?), but here beer is only half the story. Pies are the staple, best enjoyed in the Famous Pie Room upstairs (you may have to book); numerous fillings include chicken and broccoli in leek and pepper sauce, lamb and rosemary, or beef and Guinness, all at £8.95.
Children admitted (restaurant only).
Restaurant (available for hire, capacity 30).
Map p272 J5.

Nordic

25 Newman Street, W1T 1PN (7631 3174/ www.nordicbar.com). Tottenham Court Road tube. **Open** noon-11pm Mon-Wed; noon-11.30pm Thur; noon-midnight Fri; 6pm-midnight Sat. **Food served** noon-3pm, 5.30-10pm Mon-Fri; 6-10pm Sat. **Credit** AmEx, MC, V. **Bar**
The inventive management at this Scandinavia-themed bar may have had to ring a few changes of late (bringing in £4.95 lunch deals, for example), but Nordic remains the same kooky cellar of yore; the day they remove the triptych of Max von Sydow sinking an akvavit is the day you have to worry. In the meantime, expect the usual 29 cocktails (£7) – try the Northern Light (muddled fresh mint, mango and white peach purée, Absolut mandarin and blue curaçao). The shots (£3) are as cheeky as their names (Flaming Volvo, Sven Goran Erection), and the beers include Zeunert Original and Lapin Kulta. Scando smörgåsbords complete the picture.
TVs. **Map p272 J5.**

Nueva Costa Dorada

47-55 Hanway Street, W1T 1UX (7631 5117/www.costadorarestaurant.co.uk). Tottenham Court Road tube. **Open** noon-3am Tue-Fri; 5pm-3am Sat. **Food served** 5pm-3am Tue-Sat. **Credit** AmEx, DC, MC, V. **Bar**
Tapas and flamenco, vino tinto and cortado coffees: you could never complain that Nueva Costa Dorada isn't authentic. You could,

however, note that this cavernous basement, formerly a pretty cheesy affair, has become a rather sleek operation. A lengthy cocktail menu offers Flamenkitos made with Absolut Kurrant, Licor 43 and cranberry juice, and El Matadors with Havana 3, mint and lime, complementing a wine list drawn from all over Spain. A Joan Sarda chardonnay is a nice find at £21.50; a standard Rioja of either colour will set you back £4/£15. Roast piquilla peppers (£5.50) and pipirrana de habichuelas chopped veg in oil (£3.95) stand out among the tapas.

Babies and children admitted (daytime only). Entertainment (flamenco shows, 9.30pm Tue-Sat; £2). Music (DJ 11pm Thur-Sat). Restaurant (available for hire, capacity 110). **Map p272 K5.**

Shochu Lounge ★

Basement, Roka, 37 Charlotte Street, W1T 1RR (7580 9666/www.shochulounge.com). Goodge Street or Tottenham Court Road tube. **Open** 5pm-midnight Mon, Sat; noon-midnight Tue-Fri; 6pm-midnight Sun. **Food served** 5.30-11.30pm Mon, Sat; noon-3.30pm, 5.30-11.30pm Tue-Fri; 6-10.30pm Sun. **Credit** AmEx, DC, MC, V. **Bar/restaurant**
Beneath the contemporary Japanese restaurant Roka, slap-bang in media central, is this buzzy, evening-only basement whose approach is part 21st-century cosmopolitan, part feudal Japan. Shochu bases many of its concoctions on the titular vodka-like spirit made from grains such as rice, barley and buckwheat; here it's put to use in tonics and cocktails, the former (£6.90) a 75ml measure in an unusual range of flavours (rhubarb, blood orange, sharon fruit). The jasmine variety 'produces feelings of optimism and euphoria'. This may also be said of the cocktails (£8), not least the combination of shochu and saké with cucumber garnish in a Noshino martini. Shochu can also be taken neat in 50ml measures; ikkomon is from potatoes, heyhachiro from sweet potatoes. Saké is served hot or cold by the carafe or by the bottle (£16-£120). Vessels with wonderful Japanese labels and rustic instruments frame an otherwise contemporary, laid-back lounge.
Music (DJ 8.30pm Thur-Sat; free). **Map p272 J5.**

Social ★

5 Little Portland Street, W1W 7JD (7636 4992/www.thesocial.com). Oxford Circus tube. **Open/food served** noon-midnight Mon-Wed; noon-1am Thur-Sat; 6pm-midnight occasional Sun. **Credit** AmEx, MC, V. **Bar**
Nearly a decade young, the much-loved Social remains faithful to its mission to provide proper cocktails, decent global beers, fab jukebox tunes, cutting-edge DJs and beans on toast to the masses. The cocktails are 20 in number and around £6 in price: classics (cosmopolitans with Ketel One Citron, brambles with Plymouth gin) and a few inventions (the Social is a mix of Frangelico, Teichenné Butterscotch, cream and chocolate sprinkles). Shooters (£3, three for £7.50) suit the buzz in the cavernous basement DJ bar better than the more sedate, five-table affair upstairs. Beers draught (San Miguel, Beck's Vier) and bottled (Tsing Tao, Red Stripe, Brahma and Tiger) offer a global view, and the handful of wines sets the tone for the menu, a staunchly plate-on-your-knees approach to dining. Where else could you order spaghetti hoops on toast (£3.70) – grated cheese optional?
Babies and children admitted (until 5pm). Jukebox. Music (DJs/bands 7pm Mon-Sat, occasional Sun; free-£5). **Map p272 J5.**

Holborn

Bar Polski

11 Little Turnstile, WC1V 7DX (7831 9679). Holborn tube. **Open/food served** 4-11.30pm Mon; 12.30-11pm Tue-Thur; 12.30-11.30pm Fri; 6-11.30pm Sat. **Credit** MC, V. **Bar/café**
A neat, modern space that mutates from Polish café during the day into something resembling a crowded student bar at night. The likes of pierogis, bigos, sandwiches, Polish sausages and baked cheesecake are available anytime, but by the evening all anyone's interested in are the vodkas. These are divided into 'dry and interesting', which produced Zlota Jesien (a humdinger described as a Polish Calvados); 'clean and clear'; 'kosher'; and 'nice and sweet' – try Lancut rose petal (delicious if you like turkish delight). Most shots cost £2.50. Polish brandy, sliwowica and Polish lagers and ciders are further options.
Babies and children admitted. Bookings not accepted. Takeaway service. **Map p275 M5.**

Bountiful Cow ★

51 Eagle Street, WC1R 4AP (7404 0200). Holborn tube. **Open** 11am-11pm Mon-Sat. **Food served** noon-3pm, 5-10.30pm Mon-Sat. **Credit** AmEx, MC, V. **Bar/restaurant**
For review, *see p40.*
Disabled: toilet. Music (jazz, 8pm Sat; free). Restaurant (available for hire, capacity 80). TVs. **Map p274 M5.**

Central

Norfolk Arms ★

There are distinct Spanish touches to this once traditional, green-tiled boozer: the Iberian hams hanging behind the bar, the strings of peppers and garlic, and the staff. The menus are equally Hispanic: tapas (around £3.50) include chorizo in cider, and the cheeseboard (£10.50) features tetilla gallega, guadamur and blue cabrales. The 20-strong wine list has a Bajoz Cano tempranillo (£3.75/£15), as well as a standard Muro Blanco (£3/£12); there's San Miguel (plus John Smith's and Theakston) on tap, and the sherries (Manzanilla La Gitana, Bodegas Hidalgo) are also authentic. A better reason to strip down a sad old pub you could not imagine. *For listings, see p48.*

CC Bar

Renaissance Chancery Court Hotel, 252 High Holborn, WC1V 7EN (7829 9888/www. marriott.com). Holborn tube. **Open/food served** noon-11pm Mon-Sat; noon-10.30pm Sun. **Credit** AmEx, DC, MC, V. **Hotel bar**
There's a very welcoming atmosphere here, unusually so for a cocktail bar in an upmarket hotel. The high-ceiling room is beautiful, but the fittings and furniture, while comfortable (lots of upholstered sofas and plumped cushions), aren't. The cocktails are first rate. Expensive, yes, (£11.50), but they come with regularly replenished nibbles and attentive service, and there's no pressure to drink up and move on. A Spring Blossom was a heady mix of Absolut blackcurrant vodka, cassis liqueur, lemon juice and sugar, topped with Piper Hiedsieck champagne over ice. Across the courtyard is the hotel's other bar, Pearl (www.pearl-restaurant. com), which also serves cocktails but specialises in premium wines by the glass.
Babies and children admitted. Bar available for hire. Disabled: toilet. Function room (capacity 15). Restaurant (in hotel; capacity 150). Tables outdoors (6, courtyard). **Map p275 M5**.

to create a rather confusing warren of snugs and alcoves; the lavish lavs and Corinthian columns are especially impressive. The beer is all from Samuel Smith and sold for around £2 a pint: astonishing, given the fancy furnishings and central location. If on form, the Old Brewery Bitter can be a top drop; the bottled cherry beer, when poured in with the Extra Stout, is the nearest you'll get to liquid black forest gateau. *No piped music or jukebox.* **Map p272 L5.**

King's Cross

Big Chill House
257-259 Pentonville Road, N1 9NL (7427 2540/www.bigchill.net). King's Cross tube/rail. **Open** noon-midnight Mon-Thur, Sun; noon-3am Fri, Sat. **Food served** noon-11pm daily. **Admission** £5 after 10pm Fri, Sat. **Credit** MC, V. **Bar**
Beside the King's Cross Thameslink station, the N1 branch of the multi-tentacled and laudable Big Chill festival and music bar operation made an impressive debut in 2007. Easy-to-share dishes, platters, sandwiches and burgers are consumed by a music-savvy daytime crowd, as are Tiger, Budvar and Leffe by the bottle. Wines run from a house Oléa de Comté (£3.25/£12.50) to a £24.50 Sancerre. After dark, cocktails appear, including house varieties by the glass or jug (Big Chill Punch with Finlandia and white peach purée, £6.50/£19.50), accompanying an adventurous live music programme. Above the main bar area are an upstairs bar and terrace. *Babies and children admitted (until 6pm). Disabled: toilet, access ramp. Games (board games). Music (DJs/bands daily). Tables outdoors (12, terrace).*

Harrison
28 Harrison Street, WC1H 8JF (7278 3966/ www.harrisonbar.co.uk). King's Cross tube/ rail. **Open** 11am-11pm Mon-Fri; 1-10.30pm Sun. **Food served** noon-3pm, 6-9.30pm Mon-Fri; 2-6.30pm Sun. **Credit** AmEx, MC, V. **Gastropub**
A swift refurbishment in January 2008 has accentuated this corner pub's status as a smart but unpretentious spot for a pint, a natter and a Sunday roast. In Clerkenwell this place would go almost unnoticed; here, amid a Legoland of unappealing housing estates, it's practically miraculous. Früli, Timothy Taylor Landlord, Erdinger, Amstel, Staropramen and London Pride taps line the main bar that occupies one side of a simply furnished room; tables out offer extra seating on sunnier days. Star gastropub fare (steamed mussels,

Princess Louise ★ NEW
208-209 High Holborn, WC1V 7BW (7405 8816). Holborn tube. **Open** 11am-11pm Mon-Fri; noon-11pm Sat; noon-10.30pm Sun. **Food served** noon-2.30pm, 6-8.30pm Mon-Thur; noon-2.30pm Fri, Sat. **Credit** AmEx MC, V. **Pub**
Following an eight-month refurbishment, the Grade II-listed Princess Louise has scrubbed up something wonderful. Decorated tiles, stained-glass windows, finely cut mirrors and ornate plasterwork have all been given a polish, and Victorian wood partitions have been put back

Central

cheeseburgers with potato wedges) is well put together and fairly priced.
Bar available for hire (Sat). Games (backgammon, chess). Music (DJs 7.30pm Fri; bands, fortnightly Sun; free-£5). Tables outdoors (7, pavement).

King Charles I ★
55-57 Northdown Street, N1 9BL (7837 7758/www.kingcharles1st.co.uk). King's Cross tube/rail. **Open** noon-11pm Mon-Thur; noon-1am Fri; 5-11pm Sat, Sun. **Credit** MC, V. Pub
The King Charles is frequented by loyal (mainly male) regulars who are pleased as punch to partake of great beers in such a conspiratorial setting. Thwaites Original, Bishops Tipple, Deuchars IPA and a global range of bottled beers (Baltika, Deus, even Stiegl, rarely seen outside its native Salzburg) baffle the first-time visitor, as might the quirky decor touches: an old bar billiards table, unusual advertising for the Leu Family Tattoo Parlour, ethnic figures and carnival masks. If there was a pianist, he would stop as you walked in; instead, Johnny Cash sings from a Heritage Selection jukebox. To help the drinking along, you can phone for food from nearby takeaways.
Bar available for hire. Games (bar billiards, board games). Jukebox. Tables outdoors (5, pavement).

Norfolk Arms ★
28 Leigh Street, WC1H 9EP (7388 3937/ www.norfolkarms.co.uk). Russell Square tube/ King's Cross tube/rail. **Open** 11am-11pm Mon-Sat; noon-10.30pm Sun. **Food served** 12.30-3.30pm, 6.30-10.15pm Mon-Fri; 12.30-10.15pm Sat, Sun. **Credit** AmEx, MC, V.
Gastropub
For review, *see p46.*
Babies and children admitted. Function room (capacity 30).Tables outdoors (10, pavement).

06 St Chad's Place
6 St Chad's Place, WC1X 9HH (7278 3355/ www.6stchadsplace.com). King's Cross tube/ rail. **Open** 8am-11pm Mon-Wed; 8am-1am Thur, Fri. **Food served** 8-10am, noon-2.30pm, 6-9.30pm Mon-Fri. **Credit** MC, V. Pub
This weekday-only converted warehouse echoes the working environment with its bare bricks, low industrial lights and train rattle from the nearby Thameslink platforms; even the menus are on clipboards. Signposted from Pentonville Road and tucked down a narrow alleyway, it also feels rather underused. A shame, really, what with its 30 wines, Peroni, Paulaner and Maisel's Weisse on draught, and fine charcuterie

platters. There's even free Wi-Fi. Still, perhaps a working environment is the one thing drinkers and diners want to get away from.
Babies and children admitted (until 6pm). Bar available for hire (Sat). Disabled: toilet. Music (DJ 7pm Thur, Fri; free). Tables outdoors (3, pavement). Wi-Fi (free).

Ruby Lounge
33 Caledonian Road, N1 9BU (7837 9558/ www.ruby.uk.com). King's Cross tube/rail. **Open** 5-11pm Mon-Wed; 5pm-midnight Thur; 5pm-2am Fri, Sat; 5-10.30pm Sun. **Credit** MC, V. Bar
The froth and sediment of King's Cross street life washes past this classy DJ and cocktail bar – opened long before the area's grime-to-gloss transformation began to gather force. At the pentagonal island bar, whose shape forms the logo on the menu and in the windows, the 50-strong cocktail list includes 14 'Ruby Lounge Favourites' (£6) such as a Strawberry Nemesis of Stoli Raspberry, Bison vodka and framboise. Draught beers, Leffe and San Miguel, and reasonable merlot and shiraz wines underscore a powerful music agenda, 'fundamental to what Ruby is all about'. Resident DJs give way to live jazz every other Thursday.
Bar available for hire (Mon-Thur). Music (DJs 9pm Fri, Sat; jazz 8pm alternate Thur; free). Tables outdoors (3, pavement).

St Pancras Champagne Bar
★ NEW
St Pancras International Station, Pancras Road, NW1 2QP (3006 1550/www.searcy stpancras.co.uk). King's Cross tube/rail/ St Pancras International rail. **Open** 8am-11pm daily. **Food served** 8am-11pm. **Credit** AmEx, MC, V. Champagne bar
Part of the impressive £800 million refurb of St Pancras station is the 'longest champagne bar in Europe': 300ft of booth tables and ice buckets. Here you can ponder life's inessentials: is a glass of Pommery Brut Royal (£9.50) nicer than one of Henriot Rosé (£9.50)? Is the new St Pancras as impressive as New York's Grand Central Station? Does it matter? The selection is a bit predictable, but it's none the worse for that. There are old standards such as Moët et Chandon and, at the other end of the scale, classics such as Paul Roger Cuvée Sir Winston Churchill 1998. Perfect for toasting new romances or celebrating the departure of the in-laws. But the second you leave the station, you're smack bang back in the teeth of reality.
Babies and children admitted (seating area only). Disabled: toilet (in station).

Knightsbridge

Mandarin Bar

Mandarin Oriental Hyde Park, 66 Knightsbridge, SW1X 7LA (7235 2000/ www.mandarinoriental.com). Knightsbridge tube. **Open/food served** 10.30am-1.30am Mon-Sat; 10.30am-11.30pm Sun. **Admission** £5 after 10.30pm Mon-Sat. **Credit** AmEx, DC, MC, V. **Hotel bar**

This isn't the place to come to for a quiet drink. It's not that the music is too loud – though there are small-scale bands here nightly – and it's not that the acoustics are unforgiving. It's simply that the open spaces and the usually too bright lighting prevent any sort of intimacy from developing. Despite the slick decor, the atmosphere is halfway between a nightclub and the business-class lounge at an airport. The drinks are perfectly OK, although for £14, we'd expect at least to be offered egg white for our whisky sour, and for it to be made as requested (we asked for it straight up; it was served on the rocks).
Disabled: toilet (in hotel). Music (jazz trio 9pm Mon-Sat, 8pm Sun).

Swag & Tails

10-11 Fairholt Street, SW7 1EG (7584 6926/ www.swagandtails.com). Knightsbridge tube. **Open** 11am-11pm Mon-Fri. **Food served** noon-3pm, 6-10pm Mon-Fri. **Credit** AmEx, MC, V. **Pub**

Tucked away in an astonishingly posh maze of mews, the Swag & Tails feels like a cosy village local, at least if the village in question is somewhere deep in the Surrey stockbroker belt. The stripped pine and heavy curtains are plummy, and the ostentatious displays of champagne make it practically a period piece. Still, despite its dated feel and the inevitably too-high prices (burgers are £11.25), we rather like it. The welcome is usually warm, the music is hand-picked (Dylan's last album when we visited) and the beer decent, and you can't fake the rare sensation that, somehow, you shouldn't be in here.
Babies and children admitted (restaurant only). Restaurant available for hire (Sat, Sun; capacity 34). Tables outdoors (6, conservatory). TV.

Townhouse

31 Beauchamp Place, SW3 1NU (7589 5080/ www.lab-townhouse.com). Knightsbridge tube. **Open/food served** 4pm-midnight Mon-Sat; 4-11.30pm Sun. **Credit** AmEx, MC, V. **Bar**

You'll need to pick your night at this bijou cocktail bar tucked into a Georgian townhouse.

When it's busy, it retains the exclusive yet accessible vibe that once defined it. When it's not, as on the night we visited, it's quite a forlorn place: too many staff with too little to do, over-bright lighting, iffy music, and, for no good reason, a big screen showing what appeared to be David Attenborough's *The Life of Birds*. The cocktails are very good and fairly priced, but the dated menu design only reinforces the feeling that the place could do with a spring clean.
Booking advisable. Dress: smart casual. Function room (capacity 50). Music (DJs 8.30pm Tue-Sat; free). Over-21s only.

Zuma

5 Raphael Street, SW7 1DL (7584 1010/ www.zumarestaurant.com). Knightsbridge tube. **Open** noon-11pm Mon-Fri; 12.30-11pm Sat; noon-10pm Sun. **Food served** noon-2.15pm, 6-10.45pm Mon-Thur; noon-2.45pm, 6-10.45pm Fri; 12.30-3.15pm, 6-10.45pm Sat; 12.30-3.15pm, 6-10.15pm Sun. **Credit** AmEx, DC, MC, V. **Bar/restaurant**

This capacious, Japan-themed bar-restaurant has an open-plan design that one suspects would make the place terribly sad and terribly dated if there were no one in it. Good thing, then, that Zuma is always packed: at 10pm on a Monday night in February, the bar and the restaurant were both absolutely rammed. In spite of the crowds, the impressive staff took plenty of time over our drinks: a gentle old-fashioned made with a Japanese single malt, and a saketini that blended Tanqueray Ten with Tosatsuru Azure saké to potent effect. If you can bag a couple of stools, the people-watching is terrific.
Babies and children welcome: high chairs. Disabled: toilet. Function rooms (capacity 14). Restaurant. Tables outdoors (4, garden).

Leicester Square

Cork & Bottle ★

44-46 Cranbourn Street, WC2H 7AN (7734 7807). Leicester Square tube. **Open/food served** 11am-11.30pm Mon-Sat; noon-10.30pm Sun. **Credit** AmEx, MC, V. **Wine bar**

Kiwi Don Hewitson's worldly but down-to-earth passion for wines is clear to see in this wonderful wine cellar hidden amid kebab joints on a tacky corner of Leicester Square. Having just celebrated its 40th birthday, the Cork & Bottle stocks Don's hand-picked choices from a lifetime of visiting vineyards, all enthusiastically and knowledgeably described in his encyclopedic menu (part directory, part fanzine), published quarterly. In homely surroundings, you can sip

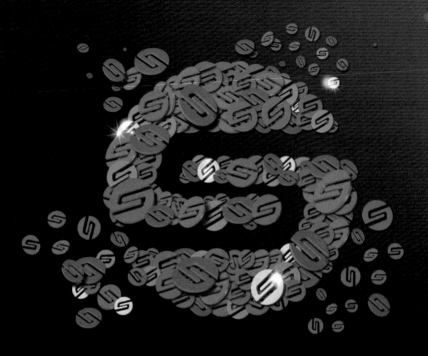

Winner of the Smirnoff BEDA London Club of the Year Award

THE SHADOW LOUNGE
LONDON SOHO

THE SHADOW LOUNGE CONTINUES TO REIGN NOT ONLY AS LONDON'S NO.1 GAY MEMBERS CLUB, BUT ALSO AS ONE OF THE MOST STYLISH, FASHIONABLE AND SUMPTUOUS EXPERIENCES IN THE CAPITAL.

FOR MEMBERSHIP BENEFITS AND FURTHER DETAILS CONTACT **020 7255 8611** OR DOWNLOAD AN APPLICATION FORM FROM **WWW.THESHADOWLOUNGE.COM**

5 BREWER STREET
LONDON, SOHO W1F 0RF
WWW.THESHADOWLOUNGE.COM

OPENING HOURS:
MON TO SAT
9PM - 3AM.

I ♥ SOHO
www.ilovesoho.co.uk

DOWNLOAD EXCLUSIVE MEMBER MIX CD'S FROM WWW.THESHADOWLOUNGE.COM

'simply the greatest dry chenin in the world' or 'Oliver Tricon's finest vintage ever', the first of 308 steps on a world tour of wines.
Babies and children admitted. **Map p273 K7**.

De Hems
11 Macclesfield Street, W1D 5BW (7437 2494). Leicester Square tube. **Open/food served** 10am-midnight Mon-Sat; noon-10.30pm Sun. **Credit** AmEx, DC, MC, V. **Pub**
Benelux beers are ubiquitous these days, but there was a time when few venues purveyed pilsners and lagers from the Low Countries. This ornate-fronted hostelry on the edge of Chinatown was always the historic exception. First a refuge for homesick Dutch sailors, then an overseas base for the wartime Resistance, De Hems is now a convivial two-floor pub whose dark wood interior and sturdy bar counter, lined with Grolsch Weizen, Maredsous and Bellevue Kriek taps, are unmistakably Netherlandish. More unusual beers such as Orval, Vedett, Kwak and many other bottled varieties are stored behind the bar, and a menu board alongside offers bitterballen, frikadellen and other Dutch snacks.
Babies and children admitted (until 7pm). Disabled: toilet. Function room (capacity 90). Games (fruit machine). Music (DJ, 8pm Fri, Sat; free). Tables outdoors (3, pavement). TVs. **Map p273 K6**.

Harp
47 Chandos Place, WC2N 4HS (7836 0291). Charing Cross tube/rail. **Open** 11am-11pm Mon-Sat; noon-10.30pm Sun. **Food served** 11.30am-4pm daily. **Credit** MC, V. **Pub**
This honest little boozer diagonally opposite Charing Cross Post Office brings in blokey regulars who like to mull over the racing form. Apart from the engaging company, attractions include a wide range of interesting ales (Arundel Sussex Gold, Sharp's Eden, Bishop's Tipple, Harveys Best, Black Sheep) and white china dishes of award-winning sausages by O'Hagan's (including venison with redcurrant and pork and bitter) sizzling in a pot near the beer taps. Obscure portraits and ill-matched paintings are offset by the careful blue-and-green glazed harp motifs in the window.
No piped music or jukebox. **Map p273 L7**.

International
116 St Martin's Lane, WC2N 4BF (7655 9810/www.theinternational.co.uk). Leicester Square tube/Charing Cross tube/rail. **Open/food served** noon-2am Mon-Sat; noon-10.30pm Sun. **Credit** AmEx, MC, V. **Bar**

Insider Knowledge
Brumus Bar

And you are?
Marianne Clave, general manager of the Haymarket Hotel and Brumus Bar (*see p60*). We opened in May 2007.
Deep pink is quite an unusual colour for a bar, isn't it?
It's very bold, yes, especially as the wallpaper goes over the ceiling and the furniture is pink too.
You have quite a few unusual ornaments in here too...
There's a big horse made out of engine parts, and we have two antique metal umbrella lights, which are beautiful.
What kind of people come here?
We have the Theatre Royal opposite, so we get a lot of theatregoers in the evening, as well as people from local businesses. Burberry uses us a lot because it's next door.
Do you think hotel bars tend to be better than other types of bars?
I think you get better service. If you're in a five-star hotel, you'll get five-star service in the bar as well, because that culture is engrained everywhere.
How is yours different from other London hotel bars?
We want it to be comfortable here, not pretentious. We never want to intimidate people when they come in, so there's no dress code. As long as you're wearing clothes, it's OK.
Do you get many celebrities in here, being near theatreland?
David Beckham was staying here and he came in for a drink. But we're not going for the 'celebrity haunt' thing

Central

St Pancras Champagne Bar. *See p48.*

Surrounded by dismal chains, this chic and cosmopolitan bar-eaterie easily stands out. With abstract paintings on the walls and the salon feel of the burgundy divans, you're in suitably decadent surroundings for the choice of seven original International Special cocktails (£7.95) or those made according to spirit (£6.95). Try a Ketel One cosmopolitan with Cointreau, fresh lime and cranberry, French martinis with Rain vodka, or a Weekend Away of Wokka Saki, amaretto and fresh watermelon. Throw in 20 wines, bar food (£2.50-£6.95) and seafood platters (£12.95-£14.95) and you have a classy combination.
Babies and children admitted (restaurant). Disabled: toilet. Function rooms (capacity 110). Restaurant (available for hire, capacity 50). Tables outdoors (3, pavement). TV.
Map p273 L7.

Salisbury
90 St Martin's Lane, WC2N 4AP (7836 5863). Leicester Square tube. **Open** 11am-11.30pm Mon-Thur; 11am-midnight Fri; noon-midnight Sat; noon-10.30pm Sun. **Food served** noon-9.30pm daily. **Credit** AmEx, DC, MC, V. **Pub**
There's now a cashpoint by the door and a rainbow of WKDs in the fridge, but glimpses of modernity are still largely absent from this Victorian landmark. All cut-glass mirrors, mahogany fittings and ornate lamps, the breathtaking interior is the star. The five or so ales are in similarly fine nick, and the friendly efficiency of the staff surprises and delights. The pub's location on a busy corner near Leicester Square means that it inevitably attracts the sort of people who choose to meet in pubs on busy corners near Leicester Square. Still, if you must go drinking in this neck of the woods, it's a good bet.
Babies and children admitted (until 5pm). Function rooms (capacity 40). Games (board games, chess). Tables outdoors (4, pavement).
Map p273 L7.

Marylebone

Artesian ★

Langham Hotel, 1C Portland Place, W1B 1JA (7636 1000/www.artesian-bar.co.uk). Oxford Circus tube. **Open/food served** 5pm-1.30am daily. **Admission** (non-guests) £5 after 11pm Mon-Thur, Sun; £7 after 11pm Fri, Sat. **Credit** AmEx, DC, MC, V. **Hotel bar**

Even in this city of the three-quid pint and ten-quid cocktail, it's hard not to gasp at Artesian's list of cocktails: order any three and add service, and you won't get much change from a £50 note. At least you'll be drinking them in some style. David Collins has done a fine job regenerating this kidney-shaped, high-ceilinged room at the Langham: lit by huge hanging lamps, the back bar is immeasurably dramatic; the chairs and tables are less eye-catching but still very handsome. The drinks almost live up to the setting. Our Essence of Shinjuku, rooted in Nigori saké and Yamazaki 18-year-old malt whisky, was a bit too subtle for its own good; the Cobbled Toddy, a tall mix of Monkey Shoulder whisky with orange, honey and a suspicion of port, was inspired.

Babies and children admitted (until 8pm). Disabled: toilet (in hotel). Games (dominoes). Restaurant. **Map p270 H5.**

Duke of Wellington

94A Crawford Street, W1H 2HQ (7723 2790). Baker Street tube/Marylebone tube/ rail. **Open** noon-11pm Mon-Sat; noon-10.30pm Sun. **Food served** noon-3pm, 6.30-10pm Mon-Fri; 12.30-4pm, 6.30-10pm Sat; 12.30-4pm, 7-9pm Sun. **Credit** AmEx, MC, V. **Gastropub**

Since its makeover by the owners of the Brown Dog in Barnes, the Duke has attracted a moneyed clientele happy to splash out £30 on a decent Pouilly-Fumé or £55 on a better red from Pauillac. They're mostly here, though, for the food: for the roast guinea fowl with a puy lentil casserole (£16) and the lasagne of ceps and jerusalem artichokes (£13). There's still a small bar, with three stools and taps of London Pride, Adnams, Leffe, Guinness and Beck's Vier, but this is definitely a sit-down-to-dine place. Unlike the wines, the decor is spectacularly and bizarrely ill-chosen: a framed Falklands-era *Sun* splash here, fading boxing posters there and some fairly awful art dotted about the place.

Babies and children admitted (until 7pm). Function room (capacity 25). Tables outdoors (5, pavement). **Map p270 F5.**

Golden Eagle ★

59 Marylebone Lane, W1U 2NY (7935 3228). Bond Street tube. **Open** 11am-11pm Mon-Sat; noon-7pm Sun. **No credit cards.** **Pub**

Every year, we like this pub a bit more. And every year, it seems a bit more agreeably out of place. Sure, a paint job has brightened it up, but the Golden Eagle remains what it's been for years: an unpretentious little boozer (and we mean little – there's just a clutch of bar stools lined up by the window), not hugely charismatic, but pleasingly untouched by corporate hands and always serving two or three well-kept ales (St Austell Tribute, say, or London Pride). Try to make it for one of the thrice-weekly piano singalongs, which make a jolly counterpoint to the barman's amusingly weary demeanour. You'd like it if this place was in your neighbourhood; tucked away in this increasingly chi-chi corner of Marylebone, it's an absolute peach.

Music (pianist 8.30pm Tue, Thur, Fri; free). TV. **Map p270 G5.**

Mason's Arms

51 Upper Berkeley Street, W1H 7QW (7723 2131). Marble Arch tube. **Open** noon-11pm Mon-Thur, Sun; noon-11.30pm Fri, Sat. **Food served** noon-2.30pm, 6-9pm Mon-Thur; noon-3pm, 6-9pm Fri-Sun. **Credit** MC, V. **Pub**

One of just three London pubs operated by the Dorset brewery Hall & Woodhouse, the Mason's Arms isn't one for showing off. There's no stripped pine and no farmer's market menu, just an assortment of very decent Badger ales (notably Best Bitter and Golden Ale) and some less interesting Hofbräu lagers, poured for the benefit of talkative punters who cluster around a central bar and a couple of gas-powered 'open' fires, or else tuck themselves away in a pleasingly bizarre, one-table snug. It's nothing more or less than a tidy, welcoming and likeably old-fashioned little local in a part of town where you might not expect to find one.

Function room (capacity 20). Games (quiz machine). Tables outdoors (7, pavement). TV. **Map p270 F6.**

Occo Bar & Kitchen

58 Crawford Street, W1H 4NA (7724 4991/ www.occo.co.uk). Edgware Road tube. **Open** noon-midnight Mon-Fri; 10am-midnight Sat, Sun. **Food served** noon-3pm, 6.30-11pm Mon-Fri; 10am-4pm, 6.30-11pm Sat, Sun. **Credit** AmEx, MC, V. **Bar/restaurant**

This quiet Moroccan-inspired venue, subtly lit by flickering lanterns, is more of a restaurant than

Central

a boozer, which is in keeping with its laid-back feel. There's an impressive list of cocktails: six sparkling varieties, including a Fez Flute of Tanqueray gin, Lanique rose petal vodka, strawberry purée and prosecco; ten long drinks (£7.50) featuring a Moroccan Rose of Wyborowa Rose, triple sec and pomegranate; a rather odd Pimm's called Marrakech Mystery (Smirnoff Black, Drambuie and muddled strawberries); and a dozen or so short drinks (£6.50) and martinis (£8). There are standard Moroccan dishes on the menu and a beer called, appropriately enough, Casablanca in the fridge.
Babies and children admitted (daytime only). Disabled: toilet. Function rooms (capacity 50). Restaurant (available for hire, capacity 20). Tables outdoors (6, pavement). **Map p270 F5.**

Queen's Head & Artichoke
30-32 Albany Street, NW1 4EA (7916 6206/ www.theartichoke.net). Great Portland Street or Regent's Park tube. **Open** 11am-11pm Mon-Sat; noon-10.30pm Sun. **Food served** 12.30-3.30pm, 6.30-10pm Mon-Fri; 12.30-10pm Sat, Sun. **Credit** AmEx, MC, V. **Gastropub**
A tidy gastronomic operation on a quiet corner near Regent's Park. Most of the patrons at this light-flooded, converted Victorian pub come for the food, though the place does also get busy with after-work drinkers during the week. A daily menu of eight starters and eight mains,

served in the ground floor bar or the grander first floor dining room, runs the gamut of gastropub favourites from pumpkin soup to pan-fried salmon, and a 20-strong selection of tapas includes many Middle Eastern standards. The 40 wines on the list begin with a basic El Muro from La Mancha (£3.10 for a glass, £12 the bottle) and run up to a Meursault Domaine Michelet burgundy (£45). By contrast, the range of beers on tap is slightly disappointing: there's Löwenbräu, Marston's Pedigree and San Miguel.
Babies and children admitted. Disabled: toilet. Restaurant available for hire (capacity 50). Tables outdoors (4, garden; 8, pavement). **Map p270 H4.**

Salt Whisky Bar & Dining Room
82 Seymour Street, W2 2JE (7402 1155/ www.saltbar.com). Marble Arch tube. **Open** 10am-1am Mon-Sat; 10am-12.30am Sun. **Food served** 11am-3pm, 5-11pm daily. **Credit** AmEx, MC, V. **Bar**
If you can find a better selection of whisky anywhere, the chances are you're seeing double, such is the overwhelming array of malts, bourbons and blends here. However, once you get over this staggering choice there is nothing much left to impress you at what is an otherwise conventionally trendy, single-room bar on the corner of Edgware Road – though at £8 to £10 for cocktails the prices leave an impression. This place is in need of something extra and though

the weekly live music nights are a good start, the rest of the time the cool back-lit bar, dim lighting and leather upholstery are simply not enough in themselves to create a winning drinking environment, while the two screens playing music videos positively detract from it. *Bar available for hire. Music (DJs 8.30pm Thur, 8pm Fri, Sat; free). Restaurant (available for hire, capacity 75). Tables outdoors (8, pavement). TVs.* **Map p270 F6.**

Temperance

74-76 York Street, W1H 1QN (7262 1513/ www.thetemperance.co.uk). Baker Street or Marble Arch tube. **Open** noon-11pm Mon-Sat; noon-10.30pm Sun. **Food served** noon-3pm, 6-10pm Mon-Sat; noon-4pm Sun. **Credit** AmEx, MC, V. **Gastropub**

The Temperance exudes a welcoming calm from its large, dark wood interior. Wine is the top drink, with a range that includes a humble Portuguese Santo Isidro de Pegões (£3.60/£13.50) and a Red Dot shiraz viognier (£24); but there's also Greene King IPA, Adnams, Leffe and San Miguel on tap. Standard tapas (three for £10) are available, but most people come for the five-strong starter and ten-strong main menus, the former offering rabbit terrine (£5.50) and merguez sausage (£5.95), the latter baked darne of Scottish salmon (£11.50) and duck-leg confit (£11.50). Specials include cassoulet (£12.50) on Wednesdays and boeuf bourguignon (£10.95) on Thursdays.

Artesian. *See p53.*

Babies and children welcome: high-chairs, toys. Function room (capacity 120). Tables outdoors (4, pavement). **Map p270 F5.**

Windsor Castle

27-29 Crawford Place, W1H 4LJ (7723 4371). Edgware Road tube. **Open** 11am-11pm Mon-Thur; 11am-midnight Fri, Sat; noon-10.30pm Sun. **Food served** noon-3pm, 6-10pm Mon-Fri, Sun; 6-10pm Sat. **Credit** MC, V. **Pub**

Landlord Michael Tierney's obsession with British history and the royal family manifests itself in this absurd pub, apparently popular with every minor celebrity you can think of. Did Joe Brown, Keith Chegwin and Dennis Waterman come here, see the laughably bad portrait of Prince Charles with a huge poppy and decide they should dish out autographs, or did Tierney buy their signed pictures with the china sets and Toby jugs? In any case, beers (Bombardier, Wadworth 6X, Adnams) have an unsurprisingly British bent, although the food is pub Thai and there's a German Blue Max Liebfraumilch (£3.30/£12) on the wine list. The fantastic Handlebar [moustache] Club has its monthly meeting here. *Babies and children admitted. Restaurant (available for hire, capacity 24). Tables outdoors (5, pavement).* **Map p270 F5.**

Wonder Bar ★ NEW

Selfridges, 400 Oxford Street, W1A 2LR (7318 2476/www.selfridges.com). Bond Street tube. **Open/food served** 9.30am-8pm Mon-Wed, Fri, Sat; 9.30am-9pm Thur; noon-6pm Sun. **Credit** AmEx, MC, V. **Wine bar**

It fell foul of the law for serving small measures last year, but Selfridges' Wonder Bar is still one of London's best wine showcases. Wrapped around the store's wine shop with Muji-esque beige wood panelling rising high, it fills up rapidly. There's a feeling – and a pleasant one – that people have come here to be educated. They buy a card, then run through a preserving machine on one wall with measures as low as 125ml – not as small as they once were, but at least not as headache-inducing as those in some bars. Meat platters like flavoursome Spanish pata negra ham and celeriac remoulade go well with the carefully selected wines; new wave Spain is well represented via 2004 Alvaro Palacios' Petalo del Bierzo, and there's a taste of what passé Châteauneuf du Pape ought to be like in the rich, dense and spice-inflected Vieux Telegraphe's 2003. There are some quality champagnes available by the glass too. *Bar available for hire. Babies and children admitted. Wine shop.* **Map p271 G6.**

Central

wagamama

delicious noodles ׀ rice dishes
freshly squeezed juices
wine ׀ sake ׀ japanese beers

bloomsbury ׀ borough / london bridge ׀ brent cross ׀ camden
canary wharf ׀ covent garden ׀ croydon ׀ earls court ׀ fleet street
haymarket ׀ islington ׀ kensington ׀ knightsbridge ׀ leicester square
mansion house ׀ moorgate / citypoint ׀ old broad street / bank ׀ putney
royal festival hall ׀ soho ׀ tower hill ׀ victoria ׀ wigmore ׀ wimbledon

Mayfair

Absolut IceBar/BelowZero

29-33 Heddon Street, W1B 4BN (7287 9192/www.belowzerolondon.com). Oxford Circus or Piccadilly Circus tube. **Open** 3.30pm-midnight Mon-Wed; 3.30pm-12.30am Thur; 3.30pm-1am Fri; 12.30pm-1am Sat; 3.30-11pm Sun. **Admission** (IceBar) £12-£15. **Credit** AmEx, MC, V. **Bar**

IceBar, a collaboration between Absolut and the designers at Ice Hotel, is probably not a place at which to settle in for a long night's drinking: that's because the temperature inside is a constant five degrees below zero, and everything (tables, chairs, glasses) is hewn from ice. Twice a year, the design is changed: when we visited, there was a 'disco' theme and people were shuffling uncertainly across a frozen 'dancefloor'. You pay a £12 fee (£15 at weekends), don a poncho and mittens (which are surprisingly warm and effective against the ambient chill) and claim your drink (refills after the first 'free' drink cost £6). The drinks list is vodka-based, unsurprisingly, with cocktails and 20 different flavours to add to your slug of Absolut. BelowZero next door is a more temperate environment, with an excellent range of 'grazing' snacks, as well as a formal Modern European menu, served in the 'Moose' dining room.
Babies and children admitted (until 7pm). Bar available for hire (capacity 60). Disabled: toilet (in restaurant). Music (DJs 9pm Thur-Sat, in restaurant). Restaurant. **Map p273 J7.**

Audley

41-43 Mount Street, W1K 2RX (7499 1843). Bond Street or Green Park tube. **Open** 11am-11pm Mon-Sat; noon-10.30pm Sun. **Food served** 11am-10pm Mon-Sat; noon-9pm Sun. **Credit** AmEx, MC, V. **Pub**

This Mayfair institution has a lot going for it: a splendid, high-ceilinged Victorian interior with the requisite panelling and chandeliers, cask ales (Young's, London Pride, Greene King IPA), Leffe and Hoegaarden on draught, an imaginative wine list that mixes Old World and New, and solid pub grub. A pity, then, that our pints of Young's Ordinary were served too cold and the piped music played too loudly. They don't need to manufacture atmosphere here: the place is usually heaving with boisterous office workers, wide-eyed tourists and the odd louche resident of the nearby mansion blocks.
Babies and children admitted (restaurant, until 6pm). Games (fruit machine). Restaurant. Tables outdoors (6, pavement). TV.
Map p271 G7.

Claridge's Bar

Claridge's Hotel, 49 Brook Street, W1K 4HR (7629 8860/www.claridges.co.uk). Bond Street tube. **Open** noon-1am Mon-Sat; noon-midnight Sun. **Food served** noon-11pm daily. **Credit** AmEx, DC, MC, V. **Hotel bar**

When we visited Claridge's on a Thursday night, they were standing three-deep at the bar – eager, it seems, to pay, as we did, £19 and £20 respectively for glasses of Puligny Montrachet and St Emilion Grand Cru. The cocktail list is no less wallet-lightening, though it's spectacularly comprehensive – and the mixologists exude the kind of insouciant expertise that goes with the territory in an upmarket joint like this. The clientele divides more or less evenly between post-work PR-girl gangs pushing the boat out and rich Europeans in loafers and pastel knits, and there's a good deal of anthropological entertainment to be had from observing these two tribes at play. On a quiet night, relax in one of the leather armchairs and luxuriate.
Babies and children admitted (restaurant). Disabled: toilet (hotel). Restaurant.
Map p271 H6.

Donovan Bar ★

Brown's Hotel, 33-34 Albemarle Street, W1S 4BP (7493 6020/www.roccofortehotels.com). Green Park tube. **Open/food served** 11am-1am Mon-Sat; noon-midnight Sun. **Credit** AmEx, DC, MC, V. **Hotel bar**

To get to the Donovan, you have to pass through an anonymous, standard-issue hotel bar, with acres of grey carpet and a pianist tinkling away in a corner. But don't let the unpromising approach put you off: this cosy little room is an altogether more attractive proposition. Lined with lovely black-and-white shots by the eponymous Swinging Sixties snapper, the Donovan mixes sophistication and buzz in more or less equal measures. Traditional cocktails are flawlessly executed (mojitos and manhattans, for example, cost £13.50), and the extravagantly long drinks menu offers some interesting contemporary variations on the classics (including the 'Appletini'), and a wide range of non-alcoholic 'mocktails'. The free snacks are frequently replenished, and the staff are solicitous without being over-attentive. The place isn't very big, and it's understandably popular, so you may have to wait at the bar for a table.
Disabled: toilet (hotel). Music (jazz 9pm Mon-Sat; free). Restaurant. **Map p273 J7.**

Galvin at Windows ★ [HOT 50]

28th floor, London Hilton, 22 Park Lane, W1K 1BE (7208 4021/www.galvinatwindows.com).

Hyde Park Corner tube. **Open** 10am-1am Mon-Wed; 10am-3am Thur-Sat; 10am-11pm Sun. **Food served** 6pm-1am Mon-Sat; 6-10.30pm Sun. **Credit** AmEx, DC, MC, V.
Hotel bar
There's no more remarkable site for a bar in London than Windows: 28 floors up, at the top of the Park Lane Hilton, with an extraordinary panoramic view of the capital. Add to that a sleek interior that mixes art deco glamour with a hint of '70s petrodollar kitsch, and you can't go wrong. Admittedly, it's not cheap – £11.95 for a cocktail – but the drinks are assembled with care, and service is attentive without being obsequious. Our Heavenly Flower – a mix of gin, elderflower cordial, blueberry purée and Campari – was, yes, heavenly.
Babies and children admitted (restaurant). Disabled: toilet (in hotel). Restaurant.
Map p271 G8.

Guinea NEW

30 Bruton Place, W1J 6NL (7409 1728/ www.theguinea.co.uk). Bond Street or Oxford Circus tube. **Open** 11.30am-11.30pm Mon-Fri; 6-11.30pm Sat. **Food served** *Bar* noon-2.30pm Mon-Fri; *Restaurant* noon-2.30pm, 6-10.30pm Mon-Fri; 6-10.30pm Sat. **Credit** MC, V.
Pub/restaurant
Tucked away in an attractive West End mews, the Guinea is a proper boozer – and there aren't many of those in this part of town. The largely besuited punters sup from a limited but well-kept range of ales (Young's Ordinary and Special, Bombardier) and an impressively long wine list. There's a battered charm about the interior – worn carpets, heavy curtains, wooden booths – that's clearly the effect of longevity rather than retrofitting. The steak and kidney pies, served on weekday lunchtimes, have won awards, and for more refined palates there's a proper restaurant, the Guinea Grill, next door.
Babies and children admitted (over 12s, restaurant dinner only). Function room (capacity 28). Restaurant. **Map p271 H7**.

Mahiki

1 Dover Street, W1S 4LD (7493 9529/ www.mahiki.com). Green Park tube. **Open** 5.30pm-3.30am Mon-Fri; 7.30pm-3.30am Sat. **Food served** 5.30-10.30pm Mon-Fri; 7.30-10.30pm Sat. **Admission** £10 after 9.30pm Mon, Tue; £15 after 9.30pm Wed-Sat. **Credit** MC, V. **Cocktail bar**
Regular and much-publicised patronage by junior members of the Royal Family means you'll have to queue to get in here, even midweek; though when you're in this Mayfair basement,

you're as likely to find yourself sharing a booth with thirtysomething IT contractors on expenses as with rock star brats or blue bloods. Still, there's a nicely unbuttoned, relaxed feel to the place (encouraged by the faux-Hawaiiana, which extends to the grass-skirted bar staff), and the cocktails are excellent. Our zombie wasn't cheap (£12), but worth it for the dash of absinthe added to the rum and grapefruit juice.
Bar available for hire. Music (DJs 10.30pm nightly). **Map p273 J7**.

Mô Tea Room

25 Heddon Street, W1B 4BH (7434 4040/ www.momoresto.com). Oxford Circus tube. **Open** noon-midnight daily. **Food served** noon-11.30pm Mon-Sat; noon-11pm Sun. **Credit** AmEx, DC, MC, V. **Bar**
A small corner of the West End that is forever Marrakech. That, at least, is the idea, though the casbah chic (or is it kitsch?) here may be a little rich for some tastes: it's all ornate flickering lanterns and whitewashed walls (one has a slightly disconcerting transliterated Arabic sign reading simply 'Sharia'), and a soundtrack that alternates between rai and French chanson. The cocktails are reasonably priced (£8-£8.50) compared to other places nearby. A Marrakech O'Marrakech, mixing rum, mint and champagne, was delightfully refreshing, though a baby bellini overdid the mango juice. There's also an extensive wine list, which includes a dizzying choice of champagnes.
Babies and children admitted. Bar available for hire. Function room (capacity 30). Tables outdoors (6-15, terrace). **Map p273 J7**.

Only Running Footman ★ NEW

5 Charles Street, W1J 5DF (7499 2988/ www.themeredithgroup.co.uk). Oxford Circus tube. **Open/food served** 7.30am-midnight daily. **Credit** AmEx, MC, V. **Pub/restaurant**
For review, *see p63*.
Babies and children admitted. Disabled: toilet. Function rooms (capacity 35). Restaurant (available for hire, capacity 30). Tables outdoors (10, pavement). TVs. **Map p271 H7**.

Polo Bar ★ HOT 50

Westbury Hotel, New Bond Street, W1S 2YF (7629 7755/www.westburymayfair.com). Bond Street or Oxford Circus tube. **Open** 11am-midnight Mon-Sat; noon-midnight Sun. **Food served** 11am-10.30pm daily. **Credit** AmEx, DC, MC, V. **Hotel bar**
Polo eschews the bland international style of so many hotel bars in favour of gorgeous art deco fittings that are just the right side of opulent;

Central

Duke of Wellington. *See p53.*

that's one reason it's such a hit with post-work revellers as well as discerning solo drinkers. Another is the cocktails: the barman here will knock you up a flawless version of one of the classics – in our case, a perfect moscow mule – or something a little more idiosyncratic: our De Vigne (£11) was a heady confection of vodka, lime and champagne. There's superior (and reasonably priced) bar food too: tapas, the usual club sandwiches and caesar salads.

Babies and children admitted (until 6pm). Bar available for hire. Disabled: toilet (hotel). Restaurant. **Map p273 J7**.

Trader Vic's

London Hilton, 22 Park Lane, W1K 4BE (7208 4113/www.tradervics.com). Hyde Park Corner tube. **Open/food served** noon-1am Mon-Thur; noon-3am Fri; 5pm-3am Sat; 5-11pm Sun. **Credit** AmEx, DC, MC, V. **Hotel bar**

It's hard to know quite who this place is aimed at: it's too far from any of the major rail terminals or theatres for the bridge-and-tunnel crowd, and hardly somewhere you'd come to for a relaxing drink if you're actually staying at the Hilton. The interior is uncompromising South Pacific kitsch, down to the waitresses swathed in batik (who didn't look especially happy about it on our visit). The cocktail list is acceptably long

and, for this part of town, reasonably priced: our mai tai came in at £8.50, though it was on the sickly sweet side.

Babies and children admitted (restaurant). Disabled: toilet (hotel). Function room (capacity 70). Music (band 10.30pm Mon-Sat; free). Restaurant available for hire (capacity 170). **Map p271 G8**.

Piccadilly

Brumus Bar ★ NEW

Haymarket Hotel, 1 Suffolk Place, SW1Y 4BP (7470 4000/www.firmdale.com). Piccadilly Circus tube. **Open/food served** 11am-midnight daily. **Credit** AmEx, MC, DC, V. **Hotel bar**

As you'd expect of the main bar at London's most talked-about new hotel, Brumus is a handsome chap. More surprising, it isn't a bit snobbish – in fact, on a Saturday night, at least half the attendees were decidedly unhip, somewhat elderly post-theatre types. The wallpaper and ceiling bear vaguely geomantic motifs on a mollifying maroon backing, matched by upholstered bar stools and comfy mini furniture (think low easy chair rather than sloppy couch), fully accessorised by a horse made of cogs and delicious standing tea-light chandeliers. The

Electric Bird Cage

pricey cocktails are imaginative, if a little too solicitous; we expected more bite from an intriguing Blazing Apple martini (feijoa and red chilli, feijoa vodka, Apple Sourz, lychee juice). There are good wines and, although not explicitly mentioned on the list, bottled beers like Peroni. *Babies and children admitted. Disabled: toilet. Entertainment (cabaret, 6pm Fri; free). Function rooms (capacity 50). Restaurant. Tables outdoors (5, pavement).* **Map p273 K7**.

Electric Bird Cage NEW

11 Haymarket, SW1Y 4BP (7839 2424/ www.electricbirdcage.com). Piccadilly Circus tube. **Open** noon-4am Mon-Fri; 7pm-4am Sat. **Food served** noon-10pm Mon-Fri; 7-10pm Sat. **Admission** £15 after 10pm Fri, Sat (guest list £10). **Credit** AmEx, MC, V. **Cocktail bar**

With its yen for contemporary chinoiserie and Jeff Koons-ish kitsch, the theatrical hand of designer Shaun Clarkson – responsible for Covent Garden's Denim and La Pigalle – is strikingly evident in the latest incarnation of this venue. The main room is dominated by a dramatic, black and cream carousel bar under an elegant red stucco ceiling, and matching banquettes line the walls. The drinks run from green tea to cocktails, the Frozen Vanilla Honey Bee (Absolut Vanilla, Kahlúa, Baileys, honey liqueur Bärenjäger and vanilla ice cream) proving that the venue's eccentricity isn't restricted to the decor. One sour note is struck by the music: a grisly (if quiet) array of 'chill-out' and Chinese coffee-table pop. *Bar available for hire. Disabled: toilet. Music (DJs 8.30pm Thur-Sat).* **Map p273 K7**.

5th View

5th floor, Waterstone's, 203-206 Piccadilly, W1J 9HA (7851 2468/www.5thview.co.uk). Piccadilly Circus tube. **Open** 10am-9pm Mon-Sat; noon-5pm Sun. **Food served** noon-3pm, 5-9pm Mon-Fri; noon-4pm, 5-9pm Sat; noon-4pm Sun. **Credit** AmEx, MC, V. **Bar**

There are few more indulgent pleasures than whiling away a couple of hours in a pub with a good book. But what about drinking in a bookshop? Set on the fifth floor of Waterstone's, this unexpected establishment offers weary readers the chance to find out. The views are pretty good, if not quite as good as you'd expect given the name; the cocktails are decent; and the list of beers is admirably long, running from Negra Modelo to Special Brew ('enjoyed by those who pursue the park life', jests the menu). Despite this, though, the atmosphere doesn't amount to much: this might be a nice novelty, but it's a novelty all the same.

Babies and children admitted (until 5pm). Bar available for hire. Disabled: toilet. Function rooms (capacity up to 120). **Map p273 J7**.

Glass

9 Glasshouse Street, W1R 5RL (7439 7770/ www.paperclublondon.com). Piccadilly Circus tube. **Open** 5-11pm Mon-Thur; 5pm-1am Fri; 7pm-1am Sat. **Food served** 5-11pm Mon-Fri; 7-11pm Sat. **Credit** AmEx, MC, V. **Bar**

Part of an enterprise that includes a restaurant and a swanky club, Glass appears to lead something of a double life. When it's busy, this shiny, happy room is popular with the kind of cash-happy gents whose tie knots are bigger than your fist. And when it's quiet, it's a large and slightly sad room haunted by the ghosts of the party you've managed to miss. The cocktails are actually pretty decent, especially a black mamba made with Glenmorangie 10-year, blackberries and lime juice; but as we drank, the music lurched from '20s jazz via bangin' electro to Lenny Kravitz, trying desperately to create an atmosphere that had slipped out the door. *Bar available for hire. Disabled: toilet. Music (DJs 7pm daily).* **Map p273 J7**.

Rivoli at the Ritz

Ritz Hotel, 150 Piccadilly, W1J 9BR (7493 8181/www.theritzlondon.com). Green Park tube. **Open** 11.30am-1am Mon-Sat; noon-11.30pm Sun. **Food served** noon-10pm daily. **Credit** AmEx, DC, MC, V. **Hotel bar**

The Ritz's landmark bar was refurbished a few years ago, apparently tarted up to something like its 1920s glory. We've not seen photographs of how it looked in its heyday, but we can say with some certainty that it probably looked a lot more tasteful in black and white. The ostentatiousness is astonishing, with the handsome curved art deco furniture totally overshadowed by the garish accents and the hideous leopard-print chairs. The drinks are suitably expensive and the atmosphere suitably prickly (jackets and ties, gents). Everyone likes a bit of needless luxury from time to time, but there are more appealing and places than this in which to find it. *Babies and children admitted (lounge area). Disabled: toilet (hotel). Dress: jacket and tie, no jeans or trainers. Restaurant.* **Map p273 J8**.

1707 ★

Fortnum & Mason, 181 Piccadilly, W1A 1ER (7734 8040/www.fortnumandmason.com). Piccadilly Circus tube. **Open/food served** noon-11pm Mon-Sat; noon-6pm Sun. **Credit** AmEx, MC, V. **Wine bar**

Central

Strange that this most traditional of London shops should have decided to import a flavour of the New World: its revamp has created a bar that wouldn't be out of place in Melbourne or San Francisco. Making a feature of a temperature-controlled, walk-in wine cellar, having style bar-esque slatted wood surrounds, 1707 follows through with the store's great Bordeaux and Burgundy range omitted in favour of New World beauties such as Grosset's Polish Hill 2007 riesling from Australia; Santa Maria pinot noir from California's Au Bon Climat is another excellent bottle. The food to accompany all this is stronger on turf than surf, a pork pie with scotch egg far superior to potted shrimp lacking in mace and overdoing the butter. But overall this is one of the snazzier places for drinking wine in the city.
Babies and children admitted. Bar available for hire. Disabled: toilet. Restaurants (available for hire). **Map p273 J7**.

St James's

Dukes Hotel ★
35 St James's Place, SW1A 1NY (7491 4840/ www.dukeshotel.co.uk). Green Park tube. **Open** noon-11pm Mon-Sat; noon-10.30pm Sun. **Food served** noon-5pm daily. **Credit** AmEx, DC, MC, V. **Hotel bar**
This centenarian hotel was renovated top to bottom in 2007 by hotelier Campbell Gray (he of One Aldwych fame) and designer Mary Fox Linton, transforming its discreet, highly regarded but old-fashioned bar into a swish landmark destination for connoisseurs of life's good things. Ian Fleming was a regular and it's believed that Dukes' martinis, flamboyantly made at guests' tables, played a part in shaping the legendary Bond character. You can get the Vesper martini here, but Dukes' own versions are stirred, not shaken. Choose from frozen Potocki vodka (a Polish rye variety) or Plymouth gin. The extra-dry vermouth is spritzed into the chilled glasses with a perfume-style atomiser and there's a veritable rumba of lemon peel over the rims. With the expert barmen performing theatrically for each group of customers, there's a definite buzz about the place. And though the bill at the end of the night may well be best approached with your eyes closed, the payload is probably the best martini in the world. Trendy flavours (balsamic vinegar, chocolate, passion fruit, rose petal) and other such concoctions are available – but best leave those to the inevitable stream of well-heeled tourists. Drinking Dukes-style is really all about the Way of the Dry Martini.

Dress: smart casual. Restaurant. Tables outdoors (4, garden). **Map p281 J8**.

Golden Lion
25 King Street, SW1Y 6QY (7925 0007). Green Park or Piccadilly Circus tube. **Open** 11am-11pm Mon-Fri; noon-6pm Sat. **Food served** noon-3pm Mon-Sat. **Credit** AmEx, MC, V. **Pub**
With its site opposite Christie's, in a district full of gentlemen's clubs, you might expect the Golden Lion to have an exclusive air about it. In fact, the staff at this splendidly traditional pub, with its frosted lattice windows and elegantly curved, columned and balconied façade, are entirely without pretension. The punters, a predominantly liquid lunch and post-work crowd, are mainly concerned with sinking ales (London Pride or Hogs Back Brewery TEA) or bottled lager (Kirin Ichiban or San Miguel) before returning to the grindstone. There's a cramped little bar on the ground floor, and a slightly more spacious dining room and bar upstairs that serves bog-standard pub-grub.
Function room (capacity 50). Games (quiz machine). Restaurant. Tables outdoors (3, pavement). TV. **Map p273 J8**.

Red Lion
23 Crown Passage, off Pall Mall, SW1Y 6PP (7930 4141). Green Park or St James's Park tube. **Open/food served** 11am-11pm Mon-Sat. **Credit** MC, V. **Pub**
Hidden down a dark and narrow passageway, this traditional pub is an in-the-know location for local workers, and would doubtless excite overseas tourists looking for something quaintly English. The small ground-floor room, with china plates lining the walls and an attractive little bar tucked in one corner, offers nowhere to hide, in keeping with the sense that most of the clientele are familiar to one another. The musty upstairs room is often empty, but it's worth a peek for its cluttered and dated decor and gentlemen's club feel. On tap are Adnams, Guinness, Kronenbourg and Stella, but one of the ample selection of whiskies seems the most appropriate tipple here.
Babies and children admitted (until 7pm). Function room (capacity 30). No piped music or jukebox. TV. **Map p273 J8**.

Soho

Admiral Duncan
54 Old Compton Street, W1V 5PA (7437 5300). Leicester Square tube. **Open** noon-11pm Mon-Thur; noon-11.30pm Fri, Sat; noon-10.30pm Sun. **Credit** MC, V. **Bar**

Only Running Footman ★ NEW

There's something gracious about many Mayfair pubs: disinclined to lay on satellite sport and all-night happy hours, the best retain an old-world charm. This is one such pub, already looking as if it's been here forever, although it actually reopened in 2007 after a huge refurb. The ground floor is a proper boozer, with jolly chaps propping up the mahogany bar, three decent ales (London Pride, Young's and Bombardier) on draught and an extensive menu of enticing bar food: burger and ploughman's alongside potted shrimp and eton mess. On the first floor, there's a more formal dining room, serving a mostly British menu. The wine selection is good, with more than a dozen by the glass at around the £5-£8 mark. *For listings, see p58.*

In Soho's trendier gay bars, cruising takes second place to posing. Not so at the Admiral Duncan, which still flies the rainbow flag of unashamed Friday night fun. Indeed, the Duncan is one of the scene's most 'unpretentious' (downmarket) pubs. The naff drinks set the tone: sex on the beach, screaming orgasm and blow job; the decor is butch, cosy and camp all at once (beige brick walls, beamed ceilings, fuchsia walls and a fluorescent pink sign outside). The crowd is just as mixed: screaming queens with drunken female friends, and balding geezers. Despite its raucous spirit, the Admiral has known tragedy: in 1999, three people were killed by a bomb, and in 2004, bar manager David Morley was murdered. *Games (fruit machines, quiz machine).* **Map p273 K6**.

Ain't Nothin' But... The Blues Bar

20 Kingly Street, W1B 5PZ (7287 0514/ www.aintnothinbut.co.uk). Oxford Circus tube. **Open** 6pm-1am Mon-Wed; 6pm-2am Thur; 6pm-3am Fri; 2pm-3am Sat; 3pm-midnight Sun. **Admission** free before 8.30pm. Varies after 8.30pm. **Credit** MC, V. Music bar
The current revival in live music has done nothing but benefit the honest-to-goodness Ain't Nothin' But... The Blues bar. As basic as the similarly titled 78 by Georgia White, which is mounted opposite the pleasingly cluttered front bar counter, Ain't Nothin' But... comprises a scuffed wooden room with dining at the back (beef stroganoff £7.95, Thai green chicken curry £6.95) and live music every night. A significant number of foreign enthusiasts on return visits join musos and shoppers over pints of Adnams, Red Stripe or Aspall Suffolk cider, perhaps chased with a shot or two of Jack Daniel's, Jim Beam or Maker's Mark.
Music (blues/jazz nightly; open mic, 3-7pm Sat; blues 3-7pm Sun). **Map p273 J6**.

Akbar

77 Dean Street, W1D 3SH (7437 2525/ www.redfort.co.uk/akbar). Leicester Square, Piccadilly Circus or Tottenham Court Road tube. **Open** 5pm-1am Mon-Sat. **Food served** 5-11pm Mon-Thur; 5-11.30pm Fri, Sat. **Credit** AmEx, MC, V. Cocktail bar
Downstairs from the Red Fort Indian restaurant of some renown, the equally superior Akbar basement cocktail lounge also sources its ingredients from far and wide. The Stolichnaya used in some of the 30 martinis, long drinks and shorts (all £7) can be infused with lemongrass or ginger; a Ruby adds a dusting of nutmeg to the Stoli, fresh watermelon and mango purée; and fresh pomegranate is mixed with basil-

infused Bombay Sapphire, Maraschino and apricot purée to create a Garden of Earthly Delights. The five fresh fruit lassis (£5) are similarly well sourced, and the bar snacks (minced lamb goolar with fresh orange rind, £7) are reliably good. All the above are served in an understated, candlelit space.
Bar available for hire. Music (DJs 8pm Thur-Sat; free). Restaurant (available for hire, capacity 77). TV (big screen). **Map p273 K6**.

Alphabet

61-63 Beak Street, W1F 9SS (7439 2190/ www.alphabetbar.com). Oxford Circus or Piccadilly Circus tube. **Open** noon-11pm Mon-Sat. **Food served** noon-4pm, 5-9pm Mon-Fri; noon-9pm Sat. **Credit** AmEx, MC, V. Bar
At the forefront of London's bar revolution in the late 1990s, Alphabet still does little wrong; but it could, perhaps, do with a little contemporary competition. Having cornered the market in bar floor designs – although the street names are fading from the downstairs A-Z map – Alphabet is going big on Amazonian antioxidants. Acerola and acel berry are blended with various flavours (guava, papaya, mango) to create a Latin Passion (£6.50) or a Batida (£6.50), and Sagatiba Puro Velho cachaça and Boru vodka are used with abandon. Sixteen varieties of wine (eight by the glass), quality bites (Alphabet platter, £10.50) and bottled continental lagers (Warsteiner, Peroni) attract a savvy, urban clientele.
Babies and children admitted (until 5pm). Bar available for hire. Music (DJs 7.30pm Wed-Sat; free). **Map p273 J6**.

Argyll Arms

18 Argyll Street, W1F 7TP (7734 6117). Oxford Circus tube. **Open** 10am-11pm Mon-Sat; 10am-10.30pm Sun. **Food served** 10am-10pm daily. **Credit** AmEx, MC, V. Pub
The clientele at the impressive, historic, frosted-glass-and-mahogany Argyll Arms is almost as transitory as Oxford Circus, a stone's throw away. The pub was just as popular in 1895, when Robert Sawyer saw fit to divide the interior into sections according to social classes, and these days you can be quite intimate while the world and its shopping bags shuffle past outside. It's a Nicholson's pub, so traditional fare includes pies, fish and chips, and draught ales Shepherd Neame Spitfire, Adnams, London Pride, Black Sheep and Timothy Taylor Landlord. The upstairs Palladium Bar, diagonally opposite the theatre of the same name, is an old luvvies' favourit
Babies and children admitted (restaura Games (fruit machines). Restaurant. outdoors (5, pavement).* **Map p27?**

Blue Posts

28 Rupert Street, W1D 6DJ (7437 1415).
Leicester Square or Piccadilly Circus tube.
Open 11am-11.30pm Mon-Thur; 11am-
midnight Fri, Sat; noon-10.30pm Sun. **Food
served** noon-9pm Mon-Fri; noon-6pm Sat,
Sun. **Credit** MC, V. **Pub**
One of several in central London, this particular
Blue Posts in the heart of Soho's gay quarter is
professionally run and amiably staffed. Guests,
gay and straight, old and young, enjoy a choice
of Timothy Taylor Landlord, Old Speckled Hen,
Peetermans Artois, London Pride, Hoegaarden
and Leffe on draught, with £3.50 baguettes and
£5 omelettes (try the hangover-killing Blue Posts
special, with minced beef and onion). Other
mains (fish and chips, curry) are also reasonably
priced. Rooms upstairs and in the back
accommodate the late-week overflow of punters
from the cabin-like main space.
*Babies and children admitted (restaurant,
until 6pm). Music (jazz 4-7pm Sun; free).
Restaurant (available for hire, capacity
30). Tables outdoors (2, pavement).*
Map p273 K7.

Candy Bar   `HOT 50`

*4 Carlisle Street, W1D 3BJ (7494 4041/
www.candybarsoho.com). Tottenham Court
Road tube.* **Open** 5-11.30pm Mon-Thur;
5pm-2am Fri, Sat; 5-11pm Sun. **Admission**
£5 after 9pm Fri; £6 after 9pm Sat. **Credit**
MC, V. **Bar**
A recent facelift has left Candy Bar working the
glam princess look with pink disco balls
adorning the skinny main bar – but still
(annoyingly) too few seats. Cruisier than the
QM2 on Friday and Saturday nights, with pole
dancing in the bijou basement, the original
lesbian bar really does take its sexuality
seriously. Drink prices are fairly average, with
Candy Classic cocktails (£6) the tipple of choice
and one of London's longest happy hours (Thur-
Sat 5-7pm, Sun-Wed all night) boasting shots at
£2. An 'anytime offer' dishes up two double
vodka and Red Bulls for £12.50. Perhaps they
should have called it the 'anyone's for £12.50
offer'… Yep, it's a definite booze-fest. Wear flats
for the stagger home.
*Music (DJs 9pm nightly; £5 Fri, £6 Sat after
9pm).* **Map p272 K6.**

Coach & Horses

29 Greek Street, W1D 5DH (7437 5920).
Leicester Square or Piccadilly Circus tube.
Open/food served 11am-11pm Mon-Thur;
11am-11.30pm Fri, Sat; noon-10.30pm Sun.
Credit AmEx, MC, V. **Pub**

So steeped in its own legend that it has the word
'Norman's' above its own pub sign, the Coach is
nonetheless moving away from the era of the
famously rude landlord Norman Balon and the
associated cast of louche, literary regulars. These
days, breakfasts, Beck's Vier, Wi-Fi access, Illy
coffee and an upstairs dining room are main
features. Still, landlord Alistair Choat also knows
the value of nostalgia, so Peter O'Toole and
Jeffrey Bernard appear on the walls in mounted
handbill and caricature form, and the Beatles-era
Double Diamond, Ind Coope and Skol Lager signs
still glow in lollipop colours from the back bar.
No piped music or jukebox. **Map p273 K6.**

Crown & Two Chairmen ★

31 Dean Street, W1D 3SB (7437 8192).
Tottenham Court Road tube. **Open** noon-
11pm Mon-Thur; noon-11.30pm Fri, Sat;
noon-10.30pm Sun. **Food served** noon-
10pm Mon-Sat; noon-9pm Sun. **Credit**
AmEx, MC, V. **Pub**
The Mitchell Brothers' overhaul of this Soho
corner boozer has proved a great success, with
punters flooding in to take their pick of an array
of global beers ('19 and counting'). The colourful
continental taps – Belle-Vue Kriek, Paulaner,
Maredsous Blonde, Schneider Weisse, Küppers
Kölsch and even Budvar Dark – stand in line
with more familiar ones for Wadworth 6X and
Guinness. Such variety comes in a more downbeat,
open-plan interior, with plenty of space for you
to tuck into your West Country Casterbridge beef
burger with chips (£6.90). For intimacy, head to
the refurbished space upstairs.
Babies and children admitted (until 5pm). TV.
Map p273 K6.

Dog & Duck ★

18 Bateman Street, W1D 3AJ (7494 0697).
Tottenham Court Road tube. **Open** 10am-
11.30pm Mon-Sat; noon-10.30pm Sun. **Food
served** noon-10pm Mon-Sat; noon-9pm Sun.
Credit MC, V. **Pub**
This cosy, century-old Nicholson's corner pub has
changed little since Orwell hung out here in the
1940s. Today's regulars take their tipples
seriously; there are even ale tasting sessions on
Monday evenings. Quality Timothy Taylor
Landlord, Black Sheep and Bombardier ales
aside, there are 'finest British sausages' from John
Pettit, butcher to Harrods and Fortnum & Mason,
as well as an array of hearty mains. Head
upstairs for table service in the comfort of the
George Orwell Bar & Dining Room (he once hired
it to celebrate the success of one of his books).
*Babies and children admitted (until 5pm).
Function room (capacity 30).* **Map p273 K6.**

Edge

*11 Soho Square, W1D 3QE (7439 1313/
www.edgesoho.co.uk). Tottenham Court Road
tube.* **Open/food served** noon-1am Mon-Sat;
2-11.30pm Sun. **Credit** MC, V. **Bar/club**
Don't be misled by the name: gay bar the Edge
is anything but edgy. The buzzing ground-floor
café is a muted mix of beige and grey with an
overstuffed vase of flowers adorning a copper
bar. Fashionably clad hipsters sip one of ten
wines by the glass (South African chenin blanc,
say, or Chilean sauvignon merlot, £3.40), swill
cocktails (margarita, cuba libra, cosmopolitans
and lime daiquiris, £6.50) or nibble on crab
cakes with garlic aïoli. The next two floors,
designed by Saatchi & Saatchi, are chic and
loungey – all funky sofas and arty lighting –
but, annoyingly, these rooms are often reserved
for private parties, as is the clubby top-floor bar
with its great views over Soho Square.
*Disabled: toilet. Function rooms (capacity
50-100). Music (pianist 9pm-midnight Wed,
Sun; DJs 9pm Thur-Sat; free). Tables outdoors
(6, pavement). TV (big screen, satellite).*
Map p272 K6.

Endurance ★

*90 Berwick Street, W1F 0QB (7437 2944).
Leicester Square, Oxford Circus or Tottenham
Court Road tube.* **Open** noon-11pm Mon-
Wed; noon-11.30pm Thur-Sat; 1-6pm Sun.
Food served noon-4pm Mon-Sat; 1-4pm
Sun. **Credit** AmEx, MC, V. **Gastropub**
Berwick Street's finest, the Endurance attracts
the vinyl junkies, market traders and sparky
Soho street life that keep this locality lively and
totally authentic. Quality wines (Chablis £26,
Fleurie Reserve £26), decent draught ales
(Deuchars IPA, London Pride) and Dutch lagers
(Amstel, Heineken) are served at the hexagonal
bar counter while crowd-pleasing tunes (the
Doves, Lily Allen, the White Stripes) blast out
from a fantastic retro Silver City jukebox.
Superior daytime food (stews, steaks, pan-fried
fish) fuels constant custom, the air filled with
busy Soho chatter, while the dark interior with
its black banquettes and stuffed boar's head lends
gravitas to the otherwise fun surroundings.
*Babies and children admitted (until 5pm).
Jukebox. Tables outdoors (9, garden).*
Map p273 J6.

Floridita ★

*100 Wardour Street, W1F 0TN (7314 4000/
www.floriditalondon.com). Tottenham Court
Road tube.* **Open** 5.30pm-2am Mon-Wed;
(members or guest list, or doorman's
discretion) 5.30pm-3am Thur-Sat. **Food
served** 5.30pm-1am Mon-Wed; 5.30pm-
1.30am Thur-Sat. **Admission** (after 7pm
Thur-Sat) £15. **Credit** AmEx, DC, MC, V.
Cocktail bar

For review, *see p72.*
*Babies and children admitted. Booking
advisable. Disabled: toilet. Music (DJ & Cuban
band 7.30pm Mon-Sat). Function rooms
(60-80 capacity).* **Map p273 K6**.

Freedom

*66 Wardour Street, W1F 0TA (7734 0071/
www.freedombarsoho.com). Leicester Square
or Piccadilly Circus tube.* **Open** 5pm-3am
Mon-Sat; 5-11.30pm Sun. **Food served** 5pm-
2am Mon-Sat; 5-9.30pm Sun. **Admission** £5
after 10pm Fri, Sat. **Credit** MC, V. Bar

At Freedom, gay liberation equals glamour. If
Liberace were alive today, and had better taste,
he might pop in for a glass of bubbly. Chandeliers
line the bar and zebra-print banquettes, and
venetian mirrors up the glitz factor. The drinks
list includes bellinis (£8), flavoured martinis
(butterscotch, chocolate, strawberry, £7) and fab
cocktails (caipirinhas, cosmopolitans, mojitos,
£7.50), all sipped by designer-clad men with
slicked-back hair. Fosters and Kronenbourg
Blanc are also on tap but the girlie drinks attract
their fair share of women: perhaps explaining
why Freedom seems friendlier than Rupert Street
(*see p72*), its trendy neighbour. And if the
Dynasty decor feels too formal, you can let your
hair down in the basement disco till 3am.
*Bar available for hire. Disabled: toilet. Function
room (200 capacity). Music (shows 9pm Thur;
DJs 9pm Fri, Sat).* **Map p273 K6**.

French House ★ HOT 50

*49 Dean Street, W1D 5BG (7437 2799).
Leicester Square or Piccadilly Circus tube.*
Open noon-11pm Mon-Sat; noon-10.30pm
Sun. **Food served** *Bar* noon-3pm Mon-Sat.
Restaurant noon-3pm, 5.30-11pm Mon-Sat.
Credit AmEx, DC, MC, V. Pub

Brumus Bar. *See p60.*

Central

Through the door ('Poussez') of this venerable Gallic establishment have passed many titanic drinkers of the pre- and post-war era, the Bacons and the Behans, the venue's French heritage also enticing De Gaulle to run a Resistance operation from upstairs. His snozzle still fills the photograph behind the bar, beer is still served in half pints and litre bottles of Breton cider (£7) are still plonked on the famed back alcove table of this small but significant establishment. History aside, the squeeze and the smoking ban force post-work crowds out of the door ('Tirez') summer and winter to congregate under the tricolour and merge with today's busier, blander Soho.
Babies and children admitted (restaurant). No piped music or jukebox. Restaurant.
Map p273 K6.

Green Carnation NEW

5 Greek Street, W1D 4DD (7434 3323/ www.greencarnationsoho.co.uk). Tottenham Court Road tube. **Open** *4pm-2.30am Mon-Sat; 4pm-midnight Sun.* **Credit** *MC, V.* Bar
Few gay venues in Soho attract quite as diverse a crowd as the Green Carnation. Downstairs is your standard Soho gay bar, complete with house music and beautiful Brazilian bar staff. Upstairs is where it gets really interesting. The venue is dedicated to the spirit of Oscar Wilde, whose quotes adorn the green and gold lacquered walls. Against this decadent backdrop you'll find pianists, singers and even a gay literary salon night called Polari (second Tuesday monthly). Fridays is Wilde Ones with music producer Tris Penna providing 'music for aesthetes'.
Bar available for hire. Entertainment (cabaret, 10.30pm Wed; literary group 8pm 2nd Tue of mth; free). DJs (9pm Fri, Sat; £5 after 10pm). Music (jazz 10pm Mon; pianist 10pm Thur; free). **Map p272 K6.**

Kettners ★

29 Romilly Street, W1D 5HP (7734 6112/ www.kettners.com). Leicester Square tube. **Open** *11am-midnight Mon-Wed; 11am-1am Thur-Sat; 11am-10.30pm Sun.* **Food served** *noon-midnight Mon-Wed; noon-1am Thur-Sat; noon-10.30pm Sun.* **Credit** *AmEx, DC, MC, V.* Champagne bar
Devoid of the hen nights so familiar to its neighbours, old-timer Kettners maintains an air of true elegance. A bar straight out of the jazz age manned by smart and efficient staff leads on to a low-lit room full of sofas and well-heeled souls enjoying a sophisticated tipple after work. And sipping champagne beneath the looming portraits of various Mr Darcy

types doesn't come much more sophisticated: the selection is vast with bottles ranging from £45 for a delicious Ayala Brut Majeur NV to £1,400 for Bollinger's Nebuchadnezzar. The atmosphere is never better than when one of the live lounge acts is in full swing. Class in a flute-shaped glass.
Babies and children admitted (restaurant). Entertainment (live music 1pm daily & 7pm nightly; free). Function rooms (up to 80 capacity). Restaurant. **Map p273 K6.**

LAB

12 Old Compton Street, W1D 4TQ (7437 7820/www.lab-townhouse.com). Leicester Square or Tottenham Court Road tube. **Open** *4pm-midnight Mon-Sat; 4-10.30pm Sun.* **Food served** *6-11pm Mon-Sat; 6-10.30pm Sun.* **Credit** *AmEx, MC, V.* Cocktail bar
As the painstakingly conceived sections of its encyclopedic drinks menu suggest, LAB is streets ahead, high and mighty, as well as being short and sexy. Certainly small and sexy, its two-floor space is invariably packed with Sohoites fuelled by London's freshest mixologists. Straight out of LAB (London Academy of Bartending) school, graduates are aided by colleagues of considerable global experience, and can fix some 30 original concoctions (most around £7) or 50 classics, using high-end spirits and fresh ingredients. A contemporary retro decorative and aural backdrop does the rest. A Sri Thai menu (royal Thai platter for two, £13.95) is offered by the restaurant next door.
Bar available for hire. Dress: no ties. Music (DJs 8pm Mon-Sat). **Map p273 K6.**

Lucky Voice

52 Poland Street, W1F 7NH (7439 3660/ www.luckyvoice.co.uk). Oxford Circus tube. **Open/food served** *6pm-1am Mon-Thur; 3pm-1am Fri, Sat; 3-10.30pm Sun.* **Credit** *AmEx, MC, V.* Karaoke bar
This post-work novelty, a karaoke bar with private rooms, has proved a great success since opening in 2007. The drinks menu is equally Japanese-themed, with a dozen or so drinks short and long (£7), including a Kimono of light rum, lychee and soda, and a Sakkapolitan of saké, Citron vodka, Cointreau and cranberry juice. Beers include Kirin and Asahi, sakés Samurai (£23) and Hanufugestu Ginjo (£26), but there is little point in coming here unless you're up for a serious sing-song – the bar feels like a waiting room. Decent sushi boxes (£10-£32) are available too.
Entertainment: karaoke pods; £5-£10 per hr. Over-21s only. **Map p272 J6.**

Central

Milk & Honey ★ HOT 50

*61 Poland Street, W1F 7NU (7292 9949/
www.mlkhny.com). Oxford Circus tube.* **Open**
Non-members 6-11pm Mon-Fri; 7-11pm Sat.
Members 6pm-3am Mon-Fri; 7pm-3am Sat.
Food served 6pm-2am Mon-Sat. **Credit**
AmEx, DC, MC, V. **Cocktail bar**
The house rules here include 'No name-
dropping, no star fucking. No hooting, hollering,
shouting or other loud behaviour'. This
admirable restraint continues in the low-key
speakeasy-style decor and in the lighting – so
dim that you may have trouble reading the menu
– but who cares, everyone looks fantastic. Milk
& Honey is a members-only bar that is also open
to all comers at certain times, and it's worth
reserving a table here for the cocktails alone.
Staff know their business, and drinks (a long
list includes sours, swizzles, punches and fizzes)
are first rate and not greedily priced (most cost
£7.50). A grown-up place and all the better for
it. Sister bars are the Player (*see below*) and the
newly opened East Room (*see p187*).
*Booking essential for non-members. Dress:
smart casual; no sportswear. Function rooms
(capacity 25).* **Map p273 J6.**

Old Coffee House

*49 Beak Street, W1F 9SF (7437 2197).
Oxford Circus or Piccadilly Circus tube.*
Open 11am-11pm Mon-Sat; noon-10.30pm
Sun. **Food served** noon-3pm Mon-Sat.
Credit MC, V. **Pub**
Slap in Soho bar central, this conspiratorially dark
drinking den seems to have changed little since it
first offered the eponymous coffee and idle chatter
in the 18th century. Draught Wadworth 6X,
Marston's Pedigree, John Smith's and San Miguel
now pull in the punters, who gather beneath the
stuffed fish and birds, and promotional mirrors
from the days of guineas and shillings. The
merlots, muscadets and chardonnays are cheap,
from £3/glass, £12.50/bottle, should a stray
female waltz in, while lunchtime grub is of the
ketchup-with-everything variety. An anomaly,
then, that no-one has yet seen fit to rectify by
turning day-glo or retro or something.
*Babies and children admitted (restaurant).
Function room (50 capacity). Restaurant.
TV (big screen, satellite).* **Map p273 J6.**

Phoenix Artist Club

*1 Phoenix Street, WC2H 0DT (7836 1077/
www.phoenixartistclub.com). Leicester Square
or Tottenham Court Road tube.* **Open** 5pm-
3am Mon-Sat. *Members only* after 8pm. **Food
served** 5-9.30pm Mon-Sat. **Membership**
£50-£120/yr. **Credit** AmEx, MC, V. **Bar**

Kitsch, louche and very late-night, the Phoenix
attracts a regular crowd of debauched luvvies
and miscreants to its basement den. Decked out
in framed handbills, publicity shots and gaudy
art, the bar offers a decent range of draught
lagers (Red Stripe, Kirin, Budvar), plus
Bombardier and Bellevue Kriek, to all comers
during the day and to members after 8pm (non-
members can stay after 8pm but must arrive
before). As well as a dozen wines (Crystal
Brook chardonnay or shiraz, £4.20/£14.95), the
Phoenix offers platters (Greek or Asian, £5.95),
combos (Tex-Mex for two, £10.95) and ten
mains (sirloin steak, £9.95). Most, though, are
here for the post-midnight banter in a reliably
upbeat and lively space.
*Bar available for hire (members only).
Function room (members only; 100 capacity).*
Map p273 K6.

Pillars of Hercules

*7 Greek Street, W1D 4DF (7437 1179).
Tottenham Court Road tube.* **Open** 11am-
11pm Mon-Sat; noon-10.30pm Sun. **Food
served** noon-9pm daily. **Credit** MC, V. **Pub**
Its mock Tudor frontage spanning the entrance
to Manette Street, the traditional Pillars is a
popular Soho pit stop for tourists, but is a
quality destination nonetheless. Theakston's
Old Peculier, Adnams, Bombardier, Young's and
Deuchars are the ales that attract regular locals
to this narrow, intimate space decorated with
black-and-white photographs of Hyde Park and
fog-bound open-topped omnibuses. Russian
Baltika and Portuguese Sagres stand out
among the international bottled lagers but the
management is at pains to point out that all its
food 'is seasonal and sourced from excellent
British suppliers', so the ribeye steak (£9.95) is
21-day hung, the sausages (bangers and mash
£5.95) obtained from Smithfield Market. Spotted
dick and custard (£3.25) for afters, of course.
*Games (fruit machine). Music (DJs 6.30pm
Wed; free). TV.* **Map p272 K6.**

Player

*8 Broadwick Street, W1F 8HN (7292 9945/
www.thplyr.com). Oxford Circus or Tottenham
Court Road tube.* **Open** 5.30pm-midnight
Mon-Wed; 5.30pm-1am Thur, Fri; 7pm-1am
Sat. **Food served** 6-11pm Mon-Fri; 7-11pm
Sat. **Credit** AmEx, MC, V. **Cocktail bar**
A drinks menu unchanged since 2005 and
several head bartenders since the days of Dick
Bradsell in 1999, of late the Player hasn't been
trying too hard to keep a buzz in this sexy
basement space. True, as the cocktail menu says,
'don't fix what ain't broke'; it's a philosophy ably

Central

Floridita ★

For a proper night out in the heart of Soho, take your beloved to Floridita, on the former site of Conran's Mezzo. Named after the famous Hemingway haunt in Havana, this glitzy but tasteful basement strives to get the drinks and entertainment just right. Actually it's a two-floor operation; the cavernous bar space down a stunning staircase is called the Constante (after Ern's barman). In common parlance and on the logos, however, it's Floridita, like the restaurant upstairs. After your entrance and escorted sashay to table, you negotiate a cocktail menu categorised in Spanish. Most, priced at £8, involve Havana Club Anejo Blanco expertly shaken with fresh mint, fresh lime, sugars and various dashes by a vivacious barman. The Hemingway Special also contains fresh grapefruit and Maraschino; the Presidente sweet Vermouth and orange Curaçao; and the Chicago Flip, one of 14 *nuevo cubano* choices, vintage port shaken with egg yolk. As well as these 70, there are specials including an aged margarita (£15) using Jose Cuervo 1800. Bar snacks (deep-fried suckling pig with bacon, £3) are reasonable, the mains (grilled swordfish, £18) less so, and live music comes courtesy of Salsa Unica every evening. *For listings, see p69.*

demonstrated by the immaculately conceived drinks: ten Player Favourites (£6.50-£8), In Flight martini Upgrades (from £6.50 Economy to £11 First) using Wyborowa, Grey Goose and Wyborowa Single Estate vodkas. True, the food (grilled tiger prawns £6, imam bayildi spiced aubergine £4) is still superior. Yet the disco balls over the DJ booth have faded, the button stools are tatty and the atmosphere somewhat jaded. Time again to roll the dice?
Bar available for hire. Disabled: toilet. Music (DJs 8pm Thur-Sat; £5 after 9pm). **Map p273 K6.**

Polka

58-59 Poland Street, W1F 7NB (7287 7500/ www.polkasoho.co.uk). Oxford Circus tube. **Open/food served** 4.30pm-midnight Mon-Thur; noon-midnight Fri, Sat. **Credit** AmEx, MC, V. **Bar**
W'' h the dimming of Amber and the opening ucky Voice (*see p70*), it's all change on d Street. Polka, a Jamies chain venue, still

attracts regulars to its intimate, candlelit, two-floor interior, the upstairs open from Wednesday to Saturday. Half the two-dozen cocktails (£6-£6.50) are inventions of the (mainly Italian) staff, including an Azzurro (Bombay Sapphire gin, juniper, anise syrup and fresh basil), and a Polka (raspberry cosmopolitan with Belvedere Pomarancza). The wine list numbers two dozen reds and whites, half of which are available by the glass, with the Babich Black Label Marlborough sauvignon blanc or the Grant Burge Barossa Vines shiraz offering sound Antipodean choices. Substantial meze boards (£16.95) and booze-soaking snacks (chicken and red pepper skewers, falafels and the like, from £4.50) complete the picture.
Bar available for hire. Disabled: toilet. Music (DJs 8pm Thur-Sat; free). **Map p272 J6.**

Rupert Street

50 Rupert Street, W1D 6DR (7292 7141/ www.rupertstreet.com). Leicester Square or Piccadilly Circus tube. **Open** noon-

11pm Mon-Thur; noon-11.30pm Fri, Sat; noon-10.30pm Sun. **Food served** noon-10pm daily. **Credit** AmEx, MC, V. **Bar**
Soho's original S&M (stand-and-model) bar, Rupert Street attracts pretty boys and their well-groomed admirers. Calling to mind *Queer as Folk*, the 1990s decor is glossy and shiny, and so is the clientele. The exposed pipes on the ceiling add the requisite touch of industrial, boiler-room chic while the glass wraparound windows and the large mirror on the back wall enhance the somewhat chilly see-and-be-seen vibe. The way men flash their cash at the bar, you'd expect pricier drinks but specials include flavoured vodka shots (£1.50), double Smirnoff and Red Bull (£5), and frozen Cuervo margaritas (£3). In the summer, tables spill out onto the pavement with a view of the neighbouring clip joints, their seediness jarring with Rupert Street's glossy sheen.
Disabled: toilet. Music (DJs 8pm Fri, Sat, Sun; free). Tables outdoors (5, pavement). TV (big screen, satellite). **Map p273 K6**.

Spice of Life
37-39 Romilly Street, W1D 5AN (7437 7013/ www.spiceoflifesoho.com). Leicester Square or Tottenham Court Road tube. **Open** 11am-11pm Mon-Sat; noon-10.30pm Sun. **Food served** noon-10pm daily. **Credit** AmEx, DC, MC, V. **Pub**
The landmark Spice, towering beside a mess of building work that will eventually transform Cambridge Circus, has laudably reconnected with its past to provide a regular live music programme complemented by quality ales, decent wines and proper pub grub. The then Scots House hosted Bob Dylan and Paul Simon back in the day; now it's indie, jazz and BYO sax on Tuesdays. A McMullen ale (AK or Country), a Spy Valley sauvignon blanc or a Criadores Rioja, all well priced, may accompany your Moroccan roasted snapper with cumin (£9.95) or a beef 'Spice' burger (£6.95).
Bar available for hire. Disabled: toilet. Games (backgammon, Connect 4, Jenga). Music (open-mic 6.30pm Mon, free; blues 8pm

Tue, free; jazz 8pm Wed, Thur, lunch Fri,
Sun, £5-£10; acoustic guitar/bands 7.30pm
Fri, Sat, £6). Tables outdoors (5, pavement).
Map p273 K6.

Sun & Thirteen Cantons

21 Great Pulteney Street, W1F 9NG (7734
0934). Oxford Circus or Piccadilly Circus
tube. **Open** noon-11pm Mon-Fri; 6-11pm Sat.
Food served noon-3pm, 6.30-10pm Mon-Fri.
Credit AmEx, DC, MC, V. **Pub**
Built way back in 1882, with links to Soho's
Swiss heritage (hence the name – there's still a
Helvetic map on the wall), this Soho boozer has
opted to attract a middle-aged music crowd
with laid-back, sleek comfort, quality lagers,
Thai food and decorative references to the
1970s. Check out the Bonds-era Clash posing on
a New York rooftop that sits above the taps of
Fuller's London Pride, Kirin, Peetermans and
Grolsch, and fridges of Tiger, Sol, Budvar and
decent pinot grigio. Asian standards are served
at mealtimes in a back room of similar shiny
wood to the neat front bar.
Function room (capacity 80). Music (DJs 7pm
occasional Thur, Fri; free). **Map p273 J6**.

Toucan

19 Carlisle Street, W1D 3BY (7437 4123/
www.thetoucan.co.uk). Leicester Square or
Tottenham Court Road tube. **Open** 11am-
11pm Mon-Fri; noon-11pm Sat. **Food served**
11am-3.30pm Mon-Sat. **Credit** MC, V. **Pub**
This two-floor Irish hostelry off Soho Square
hasn't always been Guinness-themed. Amid
the striking vintage publicity material (seals,
toucans and suchlike) for stout, Jimi Hendrix is
commemorated, as the basement (then known
as Knuckles) was once the venue for an early
London show. Today Toucan is a post-work
oasis of jovial pub banter, generally engaged
in over a pint of the black stuff, although black
velvets (laced with champagne, £6) and red
witches (with Pernod, cider and blackcurrant,
£6) are also available. An impressive 50-strong
selection of little-found Irish whiskeys –
Knappogue Castle, Hewitts, Clontarf Reserve
– complements a 20-strong list of very rare
ones, 42-year-old Tullamore, Old Midleton, and
so on. There's decent lunchtime pub grub too.
TV (satellite). **Map p272 K6**.

Two Floors ★

3 Kingly Street, W1B 5PD (7439 1007/
www.barworks.co.uk). Oxford Circus or
Piccadilly Circus tube. **Open** noon-11.30pm
Mon-Thur; noon-midnight Fri, Sat. **Food**
served noon-4pm Mon-Sat. **Credit** MC, V. **Bar**

Sparse, laid-back and bohemian, the two-floor
Two Floors is understated and quite wonderful.
Beers here are mainly bottled (Modelo Especial,
Red Stripe, Brooklyn), ales (St Peter's, Sierra
Nevada) too, with draught Kirin and £6
caipirinhas, caipiroskas (plain, vanilla and
cinnamon) and cosmopolitans thrown in. There
are £4 lunchtime ciabattas too – chorizo and
emmental or mozzarella, tomato and basil
perhaps? Though even the laziest daytime
rendezvous might well spark into a raging
evening session along the new bar hub of
Kingly Street. Alexandra Carpenter and
Richard Hubner's strikingly graphic depictions
of people interacting should survive a major
paint job scheduled for early 2008.
Babies and children admitted (daytime only).
Bar available for hire. Tables outdoors
(2, courtyard). **Map p273 J6**.

Yard

57 Rupert Street, W1D 7PL (7437 2652).
Piccadilly Circus tube. **Open** 4-11pm Mon-Sat;
4-10.30pm Sun. **Credit** AmEx, MC, V. **Bar**
Summer sees the Yard's courtyard buzzing
with a relaxed, thirtysomething crowd of gay
men supping pints beneath the evening sky.
Though drinking in the open air is the draw,
the setting isn't exactly bucolic: barren white
brick walls, stone floors and ventilation boxes
give the place an institutional feel. Inside, the
ground-floor bar is a somewhat characterless
affair, marred by unflattering lighting and
cheesy dance music. A few lone tables offer a
depressing place for a heart-to-heart, washed
down by the usual suspects on tap. By contrast,
the Loft, the upstairs bar, is comfy, cosy and
convivial. The brown leather love seats are
good for canoodling and the small balcony has
an urban, fire escape vibe – think steamy
summer nights and *A Streetcar Named Desire*.
Function room (110 capacity). Music
(DJs 8pm Fri, Sat; free). Tables outdoors
(4, courtyard). **Map p273 K6**.

South Kensington

Admiral Codrington

17 Mossop Street, SW3 2LY (7581 0005/
www.theadmiralcodrington.co.uk). South
Kensington tube. **Open** 11.30am-midnight
Mon-Thur; 11.30am-1am Fri, Sat; noon-
10.30pm Sun. **Food served** noon-2.30pm
Mon-Fri; noon-3.30pm Sat; noon-4pm Sun.
Credit AmEx, MC, V. **Pub**
From the outside, the Cod appears to be a
friendly old boozer, but inside the look has been
cleaned up with cream walls, spot lighting and

Central

varnished pine furniture, leaving it somewhat soulless except for the beautiful old island bar in the centre. Pictures of carefree cricketers and jolly huntsmen hint at the venue's former Sloane Ranger reputation, but these days it's better known for the unpretentious pub food on offer in the adjacent fish restaurant. Dishes such as crispy salmon and smoked haddock fish cakes (£10.95) and the Admiral's fish and chips (£11.95) were in such demand on our recent visit that we had to wait an hour for a table. A 30-strong fine wine list can be enjoyed by diners and drinkers alike and starts at around £13; an unusually well-heated courtyard is relished by smokers in the winter months. *Babies and children welcome. Function room (capacity 60). Games (backgammon). Restaurant (available for hire). Tables outdoors (4, garden).* **Map p280 D3.**

Anglesea Arms ★

15 Selwood Terrace, SW7 3QG (7373 7960/www.capitalpubcompany.com). South Kensington tube. **Open** 11am-11pm Mon-Sat; noon-10.30pm Sun. **Food served** noon-3pm, 6.30-10pm Mon-Fri; noon-5pm, 6-10pm Sat; noon-5pm, 6-9.30pm Sun. **Credit** AmEx, MC, V. **Pub**
The 180-year-old Anglesea was Dickens' and DH Lawrence's local (a photo on the wall shows the latter in Selwood Terrace on his wedding day in 1914) and where the Great Train Robbery was plotted. The ghost of a rather mysterious woman called Fifi, depicted in naked splendour in a painting on the wall, apparently roams the basement at night. Hoards of aristocratic etchings and late 19th-century London photographs adorn the dark, panelled wood walls, adding to the feel of a place lost in time. Real ales are the speciality here – Brakspear Oxford Gold, Hogs Back and Adnams among them – but there's Kirin and San Miguel on draught for the young 'uns. Food, served in a dining area with roaring fire, is traditional English; an outdoor terrace bedecked with hanging baskets completes the time warp in summer. *Babies and children admitted. No piped music or jukebox. Restaurant (available for hire). Tables outdoors (12, terrace). TVs.* **Map p280 B4.**

Collection

264 Brompton Road, SW3 2AS (7225 1212/www.the-collection.co.uk). South Kensington tube. **Open** 5pm-midnight daily. **Food served** 5-11.30pm daily. **Credit** AmEx, MC, V. **Bar/restaurant**

This fashion-themed bar is an irony-free shrine to celebrity culture. Your journey to fantasy land commences with a trip down a *Big Brother*-style raised walkway, with giant screens blasting fashion TV, while a red carpet that is frequently used for catwalk shows runs the length of the bar. Flaming torches, stuffed giraffes and bamboo panelling add a rather incongruous colonial twist, but the fame game continues with the name-dropping drinks menu. The Hollywood champagne cocktail (£11) is allegedly Prince William's favourite, while the mojito Especial is the Chelsea football team's choice of tipple (£10). There's an impressive range of bubbly, from £10 a glass to a Bollinger jereboam at £1,100. The wine list plays it safe, but there's a more extensive range on offer in the mezzanine-level restaurant, which does a mix of Mediterranean and Asian-inspired dishes. *Babies and children admitted (restaurant). Bar available for hire. Booking advisable. Disabled: toilet. Function room (capacity 70). Music (DJs 8pm daily; £10 after 10pm Sat, Sun). TVs (big screen, satellite).* **Map p280 C3.**

Drayton Arms

153 Old Brompton Road, SW5 0LJ (7835 2301). Earl's Court or Gloucester Road tube. **Open** noon-midnight daily. **Food served** noon-4pm, 6-10pm Mon-Fri; noon-10pm Sat; noon-9pm Sun. **Credit** AmEx, DC, MC, V. **Pub**
Scuffed leather sofas, faux-Gothic light fittings and dark burgundy walls lend an air of urban trendiness to this traditional corner pub. A correspondingly hip and extensive range of draught beers includes Küppers Kölsch (£3.40) and strawberry Früli (£3.80), while the list of fourscore wines ranges from a South African chenin blanc at £11.10 to St Emilion Grand Cru for £25.20 a bottle. The Drayton really comes to life on weekend evenings when the music is loud and the large windows of the beautiful Victorian frontage get misted up with the breath of twentysomethings in turned-up collars spouting their best chat-up lines. The same crowd returns for the generous, hangover-fixing Sunday roasts and a nice line in warm hair of the dog – Baileys latte, anyone? *Babies and children admitted. Disabled: toilet. Music (DJs 8pm Fri; free). Quiz (8.30pm Mon; £2). Tables outdoors (6, pavement). TVs.* **Map p280 A4.**

Enterprise

35 Walton Street, SW3 2HU (7584 3148/ www.theenterprise.co.uk). Knightsbridge or South Kensington tube. **Open** noon-11pm Mon-Sat; noon-10.30pm Sun. **Food served**

Central

RUMI

> "At every **instant** and from every side,
> resounds the **call of Love**:
> We are **going** to sky, who wants to **come with us?**
> We have **gone to heaven**,
> we have been the **friends** of the angels,
> And **now** we will **go back** there,
> for there is **our country**."
>
> - Rumi (1207-1273)

CORPORATE EVENTS · LAUNCH PARTIES
LEAVING PARTIES · BIRTHDAYS · REUNIONS
ANNIVERSARIES · CHRISTMAS PARTIES

Rumi, 531 Kings Road, London SW10 0TZ
Tel: 020 7823 3362 · E-mail: info@rumibar.com

www.rumibar.com

noon-3pm, 6-10pm Mon-Fri; noon-3.30pm, 6-10.30pm Sat, Sun. **Credit** AmEx, MC, V. **Bar/restaurant**
With faded-chic furniture and windows draped in swathes of fabric, Enterprise works the French bistro look well. Most of the diminutive floor space is taken up with diners, but there are a few places for late thirtysomething sophisticates to perch at the bar and admire their reflections in an impressive floor-to-ceiling mirror. The staff here are a cut above, and extremely knowledgeable about their vino. Choose from a list of 80 (mainly French) wines, including an amazing 2002 Château Senailhac Bordeaux (£6.50/£26), a decent 2006 Chablis Laroche (£7/£27) and seven sauvignon blancs. The continental approach extends to the draught beer, which is only available in half pints, while the food menu puts a Mediterranean spin on traditional British pub staples – a delicious slow braised beef served with parmesan pudding (£14.75), for example. Shame about the TV in the corner showing sports.
Babies and children welcome. Restaurant. Tables outdoors (4, pavement). TV (big screen, satellite). **Map p280 D3.**

190 Queensgate

The Gore Hotel, 190 Queensgate, SW7 5EX (7584 6601/www.gorehotel.co.uk). Gloucester Road or South Kensington tube. **Open/food served** noon-1am Mon-Wed, Sun; noon-2am Thur-Sat. **Credit** AmEx, MC, V. **Hotel bar**
Located just around the corner from the Royal Albert Hall, this annexe of the Gore Hotel draws an eclectic mix of concert-goers, businessmen and local Imperial College and Royal College of Music students. The heavy, mahogany-panelled walls and oil paintings of grand old dukes make for a comical backdrop to the Euro-dance soundtrack, DJ nights and hip young bartenders showing off their knowledge of the 53-strong cocktail menu (£9.50 upwards). Vodka lovers will be in heaven with 28 varieties to choose from, including six flavours of Stolichnaya (£6-£11); ditto whisky aficionados. A velvet-draped 'Cinderella's Carriage' alcove at the back can be hired by those seeking further inebriated pomp and circumstance.
Music (DJs 10pm Sat; free). Function room (capacity 100).

Oratory

234 Brompton Road, SW3 2BB (7584 3493/ www.brinkleys.com). Knightsbridge tube. **Open** 11am-11pm Mon-Sat; 11am-10.30pm Sun. **Food served** noon-4pm, 6-11pm Mon-Sat; noon-4pm, 6-10.30pm Sun. **Credit** AmEx, MC, V. **Bar/brasserie**

With its high ceilings, gilt mirrors, chandeliers and swirling gold leaf-painted walls the Oratory wants to give the illusion of opulence, but lacks the polished feel of other Kensington brasseries. No bad thing. During the day, the interior is light and airy thanks to the huge glass frontage – open to the street in summer. Staff kick back a little, and tables and chairs outside become the place to people-watch. Being part of the Brinkley's chain, the Oratory can afford to supply wines at less of a mark-up than many bars in these parts – a bottle of pinot grigio comes in at £11, Norton malbec at £10 and a half bottle of house fizz is just £13.50. There is a limited beer selection (bottled Tiger, Peroni and Bud only). Food is informal British and Mediterranean favourites, with mains such as the Oratory burger and chips or moules marinière for under a tenner.
Babies and children admitted (restaurant). Tables outdoors (6, pavement). **Map p280 C3.**

Strand

Gordon's [HOT 50]
47 Villiers Street, WC2N 6NE (7930 1408/ www.gordonswinebar.com). Embankment tube/ Charing Cross tube/rail. **Open** 11am-11pm Mon-Sat; noon-10pm Sun. **Food served** noon-10pm Mon-Sat; noon-9pm Sun. **Credit** AmEx, MC, V. **Wine bar**
Gordon's specialises in sweaty, tobacco-stained, tucked-away alcoves – and still the hordes come. Wall hangings are of the Queen and Duke of Edinburgh in a clinch at their Silver Jubilee, and Lord Kitchener exhorting 'More troops please'. It's hardly à la mode, but while a few buttoned-up gents find their way into this basement bar, you're more likely to find shaved-headed chaps in baggy jeans drinking with girls in Top Shop dresses: surprising for somewhere that's been serving drinks since 1890 (and looks like it). The wine list doesn't bear much scrutiny, and food is buffet-style (salads, poached salmon, pâté and bread), so focus on the assorted ports, sherries and Madeiras. A drier style of Madeira, the sercial from Blandy's was a glorious sweet and sour mix of dried prunes and hazelnuts, with biting acidity to cut through the excess. A place for assignations or laying down furtive plans.
Babies and children admitted. No piped music or jukebox. Tables outdoors (20, terrace). **Map p273 L7.**

Retro Bar ★ [NEW] [HOT 50]
2 George Court WC2N 6HH (7321 2811). **Open** noon-11pm Mon-Fri; 5-11pm Sat; 5-10.30pm Sun. **Credit** MC, V. **Bar**

Central

Hidden down a quaint alley, and seemingly frozen in 1984, the Retro Bar is one of London's most eccentric gay bars. A framed black and white photograph of Boy George, circa *Colour by Numbers*, hangs above the jukebox. And what a jukebox: Grace Jones, the Buzzcocks, Visage, the Associates and a smörgåsbord of 1980s compilations. If the nostalgic soundtrack gives you a warm glow, so will the cosy decor: red and gold flock wallpaper, creaky wood floors, red leather love seats and more pop icons lining the walls (Adam Ant, Marc Bolan, Siouxsie Sioux, Sid Vicious). On our visit, Duckie hostess Amy Lamé held court at a table in a corner, white beret tilted just so. The themed nights are appropriately offbeat: there's a poptastic music quiz on Tuesdays (on one evening, the entire pub joined in to sing the chorus to the Carpenters' 'Yesterday Once More'); on Thursdays, amateur DJs can show off their record collection; every year there's a tongue-in-cheek Eurovision night. Upstairs, there's a quiet bar with more sofas and tables – an excellent venue for dates, catch-ups or reminiscing about the good old days when Boy George preferred a cup of tea to sex.
Games (games night, 5pm Sun, board games, Xbox). Jukebox. Music (DJs 8pm Thur, Sat; free). Quiz (9pm Tue; £1 per team).
Map p273 L7.

Trafalgar Square

Albannach

66 Trafalgar Square, WC2N 5DS (7930 0066/ www.albannach.co.uk). Charing Cross tube/rail.
Open/food served noon-1am Mon-Sat.
Credit AmEx, DC, MC, V. **Bar/restaurant**
Impressively located slap on Trafalgar Square, Albannach (as opposed to 'sassanach') specialises in Scotch whiskies and cocktails thereof. A map in the menu explains where these Highland and Island malts come from, the pages brimming with 17-year-old Glengoynes (£9.50), 12-year-old Cragganmore (£7.50) and 29-year-old Auchentoshan (£50). The imaginative cocktail list (£7.50-£8) includes a Shetland Pony of Blackwood's Shetland gin, citrus, peach and passion fruit, and an Islay Punch with Bowmore Darkest, lime and bitters. Among the native dishes are organic Scottish salmon fish cakes (£6.50), shallow-fried haggis parcels (£4.50) and, improbably, a meat-free scotch egg (£5.50). Kilted staff, illuminated reindeer and too many loud office groups detract from the quality on offer.
Disabled: toilet. Function rooms (capacity up to 150). Tables outdoors (3, pavement). TV (projector). **Map p273 K7.**

ICA Bar ★

The Mall, SW1Y 5AH (7930 3647/ www.ica.org.uk). Charing Cross tube/ rail. **Open** noon-11pm Mon; noon-1am Tue-Sat; noon-11pm Sun. **Food served** noon-2.30pm, 5-10.30pm Mon; noon-2.30pm, 5-11pm Tue-Fri; noon-4pm, 5-11pm Sat; noon-4pm, 5-10pm Sun. **Admission** *(non-members)* £2 Mon-Fri; £3 Sat, Sun.
Credit AmEx, MC, V. **Bar**
Having paid the £2 day membership fee (and thus skirting a local law concerning alcohol sales and nearby Buckingham Palace), walk through the ICA gallery to what at first appears to be a rather modest, raised café area of institutional atmosphere. But the ICA is in fact very much a bar, and a well-stocked, artily cool, late-opening one at that. Draught Budvar, Beck's Vier and Leffe and bottled Budvar Dark are complemented by a list of ten cocktails (£6-£7) – mojitos, manhattans and margaritas and the like. Some surprisingly decent wines are available by the glass, including a Chablis St Martin Domaine Le Roche (£8/£31), although if you're after a Châteauneuf du Pape Cuvée des Sommeliers, you'll have to buy the bottle (£41). Sandwiches, pies, platters and specials comprise a substantial food selection.
Babies and children welcome (until 9pm). Cinema. Disabled: toilet. Function rooms (capacity up to 100). Internet access (free). Music (bands/DJs weekly; check website for details). **Map p273 K8.**

Ship & Shovell

1-3 Craven Passage, WC2N 5PH (7839 1311). Charing Cross tube/rail. **Open** 11am-11pm Mon-Sat. **Food served** noon-3.30pm Mon-Fri; noon-4pm Sat. **Credit** AmEx, MC, V.
Pub
Sir Cloudesley Shovell is a strange enough character to name a pub after, let alone two facing each other prow to prow at the Thames end of the Arches. Both taverns bear the decorative nautical traces of the 18th-century captain whose ship ran aground in the Scilly Isles. Each also offers the same praiseworthy range of draught beers: Badger, Tanglefoot and Sussex in terms of British bitters; HB and HB Export the German lagers. Food is served in both, in the case of the smaller, more intimate branch, via a dumb waiter. The selection ranges from bacon sarnies (£3.95) to a 'famous' Sussex smokie (£7.95) – smoked fish in a savoury crumble.
Babies and children admitted (Sat only). Bar available for hire. Function room (capacity 35). Games (darts, fruit machine). TV.
Map p273 L7.

Boisdale. *See p80.*

Central

Victoria

Albert

52 Victoria Street, SW1H 0NP (7222 5577).
St James's Park tube/Victoria tube/rail. **Open**
10am-11pm Mon-Sat; 10am-10.30pm Sun.
Food served 10am-10pm daily. **Credit**
AmEx, DC, MC, V. **Pub**

The former Blue Coat Boy was rebuilt in ornate
Victorian style in the mid-19th century, its
parliamentary connections illustrated by the
portraits of past PMs up the staircase to the
carvery. Downstairs in the main bar, a
spacious, wooden interior accommodates many
a hungry tourist happy to tuck into the likes of
organic beef and Bombardier pie (£7.99) but
somewhat confused by the draught beer of the
same name and its various counterparts:
Greene King IPA; Fuller's London Pride;
Adnams Broadside and Courage Directors.
Treacle sponge (£3.19) may also require some
explanation. Most seem happy, though, some
even parting with pounds, euros or dollars for
a beer mug or T-shirt souvenir.
Babies and children welcome: children's room.
Games (fruit machines, quiz machine). Dining
room. **Map p281 J9**.

bbar

43 Buckingham Palace Road, SW1W 0PP
(7958 7000/www.bbarlondon.com). Victoria
tube/rail. **Open** 11am-11pm Mon-Fri. **Food**
served noon-10.30pm Mon-Fri. **Credit**
AmEx, DC, MC, V. **Bar/restaurant**

The choice at this South African bar is
staggering. Some 75 cocktails, more than 100
wines (a third of which are available by the
glass) and 20 beers (nearly all bottled) are
offered in a contemporary interior decorated
with safari images. Behind is the restaurant
proper, but decent bar food includes lunchtime
salads and sandwiches (chicken caesar wraps,
£7) and booze-soaking evening snacks (satays,
spring rolls, koftas, £9). As well as all the
classics, slick and professional staff fix
excellent cape martinis (£7.50) of cape
gooseberries mixed with apricot jam, sultana-
infused Whitley Neill gin, orange bitters and
cranberry. Beers (£3.50) include Windhoek,
Savanna and Castle from southern Africa,
wines an Ormer Bay fair trade chenin blanc
(£4.70/£17.50) and a Brampton shiraz/viognier
(£29) of similar provenance.
Babies and children admitted (daytime only
in bar, all day in restaurant). Bar available
for hire. Disabled: toilet. Function room.
Restaurant. Tables outdoors (4, pavement).
Map p281 H9.

Boisdale ★ HOT 50

13 Eccleston Street, SW1W 9LX (7730 6922/
www.boisdale.co.uk). Victoria tube/rail. **Open/**
food served noon-1am Mon-Fri; 7pm-1am
Sat. **Admission** £12 (£4.50 before 10pm) after
10pm Mon-Sat. **Credit** AmEx, DC, MC, V. **Bar**

From the labyrinthine variety of bar and
restaurant spaces to the overstated tartan
accents, there's something faintly preposterous
about this entire operation. Rest assured, though,
that we write this with the utmost affection:
there's nowhere quite like this posh, Scottish-
themed enterprise, and that includes its sister
branch in the City. If you're here to drink, you're
drinking single malts, a terrific range perhaps
matched in London only by the members-only
Scotch Malt Whisky Society in Clerkenwell;
another very nice touch is the new heated cigar
terrace (reservations may be required). Oh, and
Boisdale is actually a Hebridean port, and it's
pronounced 'boys-dale'. So now you know.
Function room (capacity 34). Music (jazz 10pm
Mon-Sat). Restaurant. **Map p281 H10**.

Cask & Glass

39-41 Palace Street, SW1E 5HN (7834 7630).
Victoria tube/rail. **Open** 11am-11pm Mon-Fri;
noon-9pm Sat; noon-4.30pm Sun. **Food served**
noon-2.30pm Mon-Fri. **Credit** AmEx, DC,
MC, V. **Pub**

Hanging baskets of flowers and the kind of pub
frontage usually associated with villages in Kent
compose a very pretty picture here, especially
when incongruously compared to the raging
commerce around this stretch between Victoria
and Westminster. It's a Shepherd Neame pub, and
a cosy one at that, with taps of brewery
standards (Master Brew, Bishops Finger, Kent's
Best and Spitfire, and stablemates Holsten and
Oranjeboom) set on an equally modest bar
counter. Recent restoration has uncovered a series
of old caricatures and black and white
photographs that lend a suitably charming touch
– although the wine list could be a little more
ambitious than the unadventurous half-dozen
bottles currently on offer.
Bar available for hire. No piped music or
jukebox. TV. **Map p281 J9**.

Ebury ★ NEW HOT 50

139 Ebury Street, SW1W 9QU (7730 5447/
www.eburywinebar.co.uk). Victoria tube/rail.
Open/food served noon-11pm Mon-Sat;
6-10pm Sun. **Credit** AmEx MC, V. **Wine bar**

Not to be confused with the popular Ebury
gastropub in Pimlico, this place has many charms
of its own. It's a classic wine bar with brass and
hunting prints and *Old Curiosity Shop* look to

Central

the front. Families and couples head straight for well-prepared dishes in the restaurant at the back, such as rich, tasty rabbit terrine or succulent rack of lamb with sliced potatoes, garlic and thyme sauce. The selection of 100 wines is to be commended for having nearly half of the total by the glass, including every dessert wine: rare is it that you want a whole bottle at the end of dinner. The selection also manages to take in some good Italian whites, such as Piedmont's Andelasia. Ebury is slick and well-mannered without any kind of style-bar fireworks.

Babies and children admitted (lunchtime only). Bar available for hire. Restaurant. TV.
Map p281 H10.

Plumbers Arms
14 Lower Belgrave Street, SW1W 0LN (7730 4067). Victoria tube/rail. **Open** 11am-11pm Mon-Fri. **Food served** 11am-10pm Mon-Thur; 11am-2.30pm Fri. **Credit** AmEx, DC, MC, V. **Pub**
Good ales attract a slew of regulars to this unassuming pub in a quiet Victoria street. Quiet, that is, except for one night in 1974 when Lady Lucan burst in to tell of the murder of the family nanny; the subsequent manhunt for her husband is related by the news splashes framed and mounted here. Three decades on, workmen peacefully sip Oakham Inferno, Geordie Pride and a changing guest ale, as well as Young's, Fuller's London Pride and Hoegaarden. It's a Punch Tavern, so the food selection bears similarities to establishments such as the Red Lion (*see p82*) in Westminster: roast beef (£7.59); fish and chips (£8.59) and decent Aberdeen Angus burgers (£6.99).
Function room (capacity 25). Games (board games, darts, quiz machine). Tables outdoors (3, pavement). TV. **Map p281 H10**.

Thomas Cubitt
44 Elizabeth Street, SW1W 9PA (7730 6060/ www.thethomascubitt.co.uk). Victoria tube/rail. **Open/food served** noon-10pm daily. **Credit** AmEx, MC, V. **Bar/brasserie**
Two years after its opening, this upmarket brasserie still fills up every mealtime with a civilised Belgravia clientele. They're happy to venture in the direction of less civilised Victoria coach station to partake of dishes like chargrilled quail (£9.50), slow-braised Welsh lamb shank (£13) and steamed Shetland mussels (£10.50). Sunday roasts (£13.95) are unsurprisingly popular too. As for drinks (although the layout of the main bar lends itself more to dining), a 30-strong wine selection includes a dozen by the glass (Chilean Alameda

Insider Knowledge
Boisdale

You are?
Ranald Macdonald, founder of Boisdale, Victoria (*see p80*).
You're famous for your extensive whisky menu. How many varieties do you have?
We have a couple of hundred whiskies and a lot of them are very hard to get hold of anywhere else. The Macallan '46 is really delicate. You can feel a whole orchestra playing lightly as you walk through the glen. It's also £625 a shot so it's rather expensive.
What makes a good whisky?
The water must be soft and pure. Then, if you're using malted barley, the way you germinate the barley as you warm it is significant. The next thing is the cask conditioning – the flavour of the whisky comes from the cask it's been stored in.
You also claim to have London's best selection of Cuban cigars. Do whisky and cigars go well together?
Whisky and cigars are a marriage made in heaven. We now have a cigar terrace at the top of the building which is heated through the winter.
There's a members' club at the heart of Boisdale – what kind of people join it?
There are a lot of businessmen, some royals, City people, artists – all sorts. We're getting a lot of new, younger members. What all the members share in common is that they love Boisdale.

Central

sauvignon blanc £3.50/£14, Henri Pellé Sancerre £7/£27, Domaine Heresztyn Bourgogne rouge £7.50/£29). Cocktails include an 'English mojito' (£8) made with Hendrick's gin (isn't that Scottish?), and house bloody mary (£7) with Godminster organic horseradish vodka, while Bitburger, Weizen and Adnams come on tap. *Babies and children welcome. Bar available for hire. Function rooms (capacity 50). Tables outdoors (8, pavement).* **Map p281 H10.**

Zander Bar
45 Buckingham Gate, SW1E 6BS (7379 9797/www.bankrestaurants.com). St James's Park tube/Victoria tube/rail. **Open** 11am-11pm Mon-Wed; 11am-1am Thur, Fri; 5pm-1am Sat. **Food served** noon-2.45pm, 5.30-11pm Mon-Fri; 5.30-11pm Sat. **Credit** AmEx, DC, MC, V. **Cocktail bar**
Sister to the Bank Aldwych restaurant, this cocktail bar was all the rage in the early 1990s. Times have changed but not the long, gleaming zinc counter and service behind it. The quality is illustrated by the five immaculate champagne cocktails (£9) including a Bank Spring Punch of Ketel One Citron, passion fruit purée and champers, and the 15 Bank signature cocktails (£7-£7.50), such as a De-Congestion Charge of Matusalem Platino, Chambord, watermelon, passion fruit and raspberry purée. Caribbean rarities hide amid the high-end spirits – Gosling Black Seal and Clement Première Canne Bleue rums from Bermuda and Martinique, for example – and twice-weekly DJ sessions make a valiant attempt to reduce the average age of the clientele. *Babies and children admitted (restaurant only). Bar available for hire. Disabled: toilet. Restaurant. Tables outdoors (30, terrace).* **Map p281 J9.**

Westminster

Cinnamon Club
The Old Westminster Library, 30-32 Great Smith Street, SW1P 3BU (7222 2555/ www.cinnamonclub.com). St James's Park or Westminster tube. **Open** *Library bar* 11am-11.45pm Mon-Sat. *Club bar* 6-11.45pm Mon-Sat. **Food served** noon-2.30pm, 6-10.45pm Mon-Sat. **Credit** AmEx, DC, MC, V. **Cocktail bar/restaurant**
Divided between an upscale Indian restaurant, a buzzy DJ basement and sedate, study-like cocktail bar by the main entrance, this former local library has a contemporary but distinctly grown up Asian flavour. The drinks menu, shared between the two bars, features a dozen signature cocktails (around £10), including a

Rupee Rush of Manor Farm sloe gin and microbrewed ginger beer, and a Four C Vodka of house-infused cardamom and cinnamon vodka. Cardamom also mingles with edible gold leaf and Gabriel Boudier Saffron gin in a Fool's Gold (£12), while lychee and rose petal, pomegranate and wild Scottish blueberries come to the fore in the half-dozen martinis (£8). Beers include Moritz, Lao and Sierra Nevada. *Babies and children welcome. Bars available for hire. Disabled: toilet. Function rooms (capacity 35-90). TVs.* **Map p281 K10.**

Red Lion
48 Parliament Street, SW1A 2NH (7930 5826). Westminster tube. **Open** 10am-11pm Mon-Fri; 10am-9.30pm Sat; noon-9pm Sun. **Food served** noon-8.30pm Mon-Fri; noon-8pm Sat, Sun. **Credit** AmEx, MC, V. **Pub**
'A Great British Tradition' runs the wording around this 600-year-old pub between the Cenotaph and Big Ben. And with Spitfire, Courage Directors, Fuller's London Pride, Theakston Old Peculiar, Old Speckled Hen, Black Sheep bitter and John Smith's poured in wood-panelled surroundings, while sideburned politicians from Gladstone's day look down, who could gainsay such a statement? Continental Zywiec, Budvar and Peroni hide among the bottles in the fridge, as do a few New World wines (Cape Province chenin blanc, £3.25/£12.35) – although they accompany the distinctly British fish and chips (£7.99) and steaks (£7.25) served in the restaurant upstairs. *Babies and children admitted (until 5pm). Bar available for hire. Comedy (7.30pm Mon; £2). Tables outdoors (5, pavement). TV.* **Map p281 K8.**

Speaker **NEW**
46 Great Peter Street, SW1P 2HA (7222 1749/www.pleisure.com). St James's Park tube. **Open** noon-11pm Mon-Fri. **Credit** MC, V. **Pub**
It's a while since we've heard such compelling bar banter as here, where the Friday lunch barflies – some suited, some in high-visibility vests – kept up an effortlessly cheery running commentary on all the comings and goings. The Speaker does all the important things right – four real ales (Spitfire, Young's Bitter and excellent rare guests), racks of wine, jacket spuds or £2.50 sarnies – and defiantly ignores pretty much anything else, including the anticipated House of Commons schtick (instead, there's a case of quarrying dynamite) and any entertainment except conversation. As they say themselves: this is a real pub. We're glad. *No piped music or jukebox.* **Map p281 K10.**

City

City

Money talks in the City, and the Square Mile's drinking holes offer movers, shakers and bewildered tourists ample opportunity to spend it. Sip martinis in swanky surrounds at **1 Lombard Street** or newcomer **Mustard**, clink champagne glasses on top of the world at **Vertigo 42** or join E1 cool kids for juleps at Commercial Street's **Hawksmoor**. Should a pub vibe hold more appeal, there are plenty of those too: try the small but perfectly formed **Seven Stars**, the historic **Ye Olde Mitre**, refreshingly fuss-free **Bell** or the legendary **Golden Heart**. Many venues close at weekends in Bank and Mansion House (less so around Liverpool Street and Chancery Lane), but the raucous Friday night crowd really knows how to party. The City also boasts a swathe of chain wine bars run by Davy's (www.davy.co.uk) and Balls Brothers (www.ballsbrothers.co.uk), where you'll find fine wines and solid pub fare. Corney & Barrow (www.corney-barrow.co.uk) is a slightly sleeker and sexier option.

Chancery Lane

Cittie of Yorke
22 High Holborn, WC1V 6BN (7242 7670). Chancery Lane tube. **Open** 11.30am-11pm Mon-Sat. **Food served** noon-3pm, 5-9.30pm Mon-Sat. **Credit** (over £10) AmEx, MC, V.
Pub
It's big, it's beery, but above all it's brown: the cleaners here must get through a month's worth of furniture polish in one night. There's a cosy front area, a cavernous back room and a spacious downstairs. You can be sure of getting a table even at post-work peak hours, and you'll certainly never be forced to scream into each other's ears. While Samuel Smith pubs are often a magnet for people who resent paying more than £2 a pint, the Cittie's regulars just love it for what it is – a provider of reliable booze in a convenient point between City and West End. *Babies and children admitted (downstairs, until 5pm). Bar available for hire. Games (darts, fruit machine).* **Map p274 M5**.

Seven Stars ★ HOT 50
53 Carey Street, WC2A 2JB (7242 8521). Chancery Lane or Holborn tube. **Open** 11am-11pm Mon-Fri; noon-11pm Sat; noon-10.30pm Sun. **Food served** noon-3pm, 5-10pm Mon-Fri; 1-9pm Sat, Sun. **Credit** AmEx, MC, V.
Pub/Restaurant
The TV career of landlady Roxy Beaujolais may have stuttered, but her flagship pub goes from strength to strength. People pile down here on weekday evenings, knowing full well they'll probably be forced to drink on the pavement outside – but they don't care. It's a fantastic social hub for London characters, from eccentric lawyers to burlesque babes. If you can squeeze into the small but perfectly proportioned interior, you'll get a slice of low-rent, bohemian London: archive film posters, checked tablecloths and an antique dumb waiter bringing food down from the tiny kitchen upstairs. The grub is top-class but unpretentious; there are no extensive menus to browse, just a few words chalked on the blackboard, which invariably promise high quality. It's one of the few London pubs where you're happy to pay £6 for a large glass of burgundy because you know you aren't being ripped off; the beers are also wonderfully kept, and the house martini a must-try. It's higgledy, it's piggledy, and if you want to go to the toilet you'll have a nail-biting clamber up some rickety stairs – but at the weekend, when it's less hectic, this is one of the most perfect pubs in town.
No piped music or jukebox. **Map p275 M6**.

Ye Olde Mitre ★ HOT 50
1 Ely Court, Ely Place side of 8 Hatton Garden, EC1N 6SJ (7405 4751). Chancery Lane tube/Farringdon tube/rail. **Open** 11am-11pm Mon-Fri. **Food served** 11am-9.30pm Mon-Fri. **Credit** AmEx, MC, V. **Pub**
Consistently voted one of the best pubs in London by self-proclaimed experts on internet forums – and you'd have to say they've got this one spot on. Its secluded location requires you to slink down an alleyway just off Hatton Garden, and as you do so you're transported to a parallel pub universe where the clientele are

City

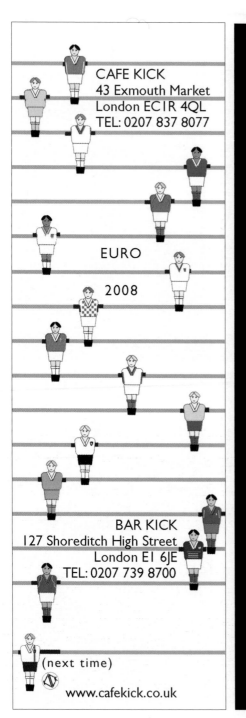

CAFE KICK
43 Exmouth Market
London EC1R 4QL
TEL: 0207 837 8077

EURO

2008

BAR KICK
127 Shoreditch High Street
London E1 6JE
TEL: 0207 739 8700

(next time)

www.cafekick.co.uk

disconcertingly friendly and the staff (clad in pristine black and white uniforms) briskly efficient. A Monday-to-Friday joint, it opens for just one weekend a year to coincide with the British Beer Festival. Ales are certainly the speciality – Deuchars and Adnams are regulars, with frequently changing guest beers beside them – but the proprietors don't turn their noses up at wine (a mistake many real ale pubs make). Snacks – pork pies, scotch eggs, sausage rolls – go down a treat, and the whole pub is suffused with the agreeable aroma of cheese on toast, rounds of which are regularly brought out from behind the bar. With two small ground-floor rooms, another less characterful room upstairs, and 'Ye Nook' tacked on the side, it's a pint-sized pub that's earned its top-notch reputation. *Function room (30 capacity). No piped music or jukebox. Tables outdoors (12 barrels, pavement).* **Map p274 N5**.

Fleet Street & Blackfriars

Black Friar ★
174 Queen Victoria Street, EC4V 4EG (7236 5474). Blackfriars tube/rail. **Open** 10am-11pm Mon-Wed, Sat; 10am-11.30pm Thur, Fri; noon-10.30pm Sun. **Food served** 10am-10pm Mon-Sat; noon-10pm Sun. **Credit** AmEx, MC, V. **Pub**
This curiously wedge-shaped pub at the north end of Blackfriars Bridge lures significant numbers of people away from their desks at 6pm – particularly in summer, when they spill out across the adjoining gardens. A handful of real ales, a dozen or so wines by the glass and the standard lagers quench the thirst, while the pub nosh (from steak pie to goat's cheese tart) is more than adequate. If you can manage to push your way inside, you'll find an extraordinary interior resplendent with wooden carvings of Dominican monks. It's loopy, but it works. *Babies and children admitted (until 9pm). Tables outdoors (10, pavement). TV.* **Map p275 O6**.

Castle NEW
26 Furnival Street, EC4A 1JS (7405 5470). Chancery Lane tube. **Open** 11am-11pm Mon-Fri. **Food served** noon-3pm Mon-Fri. **Credit** MC, V. **Pub**
There's nothing immediately special about this corner boozer, either from the outside – big glass windows and a few hanging baskets – or inside (in spite of the refit: dark stripped boards, couple of mirrors, blood-red walls, and swathes of pinstripe; sorry, that's the clientele), so it hardly seems worth the detour off High Holborn, until

you check the drinks list. This is one of the only pubs in the city to serve such an extensive range of cask ales: eight on pump, and, written on the blackboard, a list of eight to come. On our visit there was Nethergate's Redcar Best (3.0%) and Elgood's Greyhound (5.2%), with Tower Pale Ale and Stonehenge Pig Swill expected soon. There are eight decent whites and reds (from £4.50 by the glass). Then there's the food: quality door-stop sarnies, toasties, ploughman's and several roasts, plus free finger food from 6pm on Monday and Tuesday. *Function room (up to 60 capacity). Games (darts). Quiz (7.45pm Tue; free). TVs.* **Map p275 N6**.

El Vino
47 Fleet Street, EC4Y 1BJ (7353 6786/ www.elvino.co.uk). Blackfriars tube/rail. **Open** 8.30am-9pm Mon; 8.30am-10pm Tue-Fri. **Food served** 8.30am-9pm daily. **Wine bar**
You feel the weight of history when you're warmly welcomed into this old wine bar. The scene of untold boozy lunches when Fleet Street was still the epicentre of journalism, it's lost very little of its character over the years. At the front, there's a shabby bar perfect for propping up, and at the back, neat rows of wooden tables, with everyone (from City suits to 1980s media derelicts) happily knocking back the plonk. Dip into the red menu – great house selections, with six by the glass – or explore the fearsome green alternative, with hundreds of bottles on offer. *Booking advisable for restaurant. Function room (50 capacity). Tables outdoors (4, courtyard).* **Map p275 N6**.

Mustard Bar & Lounge NEW
2 Old Change Court, Peter's Hill, EC4M 8EN (7236 5318/www.mustard-bar.com). St Paul's tube. **Open** 11am-10pm Mon-Wed; 11am-midnight Thur, Fri. **Food served** noon-3pm, 5-10pm daily. **Credit** AmEx, MC, V. **Bar/Restaurant**
The sleek, black interior of this swish City bar – all sweeping banquettes, beaded curtains and globe lights – conjures up images of '60s sci-fi classic *Barbarella*. Fun, frivolity and glamour are firmly on the menu, though there's also John Smith's on tap for when you drag the accounts manager here against his will at Christmas. Cocktails rather than ales are the drink of choice (myriad beers jostle for fridge space) and the cheery bar staff are adept mixers. A big screen pulls in the after-work crowd for key sporting fixtures. It feels somewhat at odds with the slick decor but folds discreetly away into the wall at the end of the match. Groovy, baby.

City (margin)

Bar available for hire. Disabled: toilet. Function room (up to 100 capacity). Music (DJs 8pm Thur, Fri; free). Restaurant. Tables outdoors (30, garden). TVs (big screen, satellite). **Map p277 P7**.

Ye Olde Cheshire Cheese
145 Fleet Street, EC4A 2BU (7353 6170).
Blackfriars tube/rail. **Open** 11am-11pm Mon-Sat; noon-6pm Sun. **Food served** noon-9.30pm Mon-Fri; noon-8.30pm Sat; noon-5pm Sun. **Credit** AmEx, DC, MC, V. Pub
If you were to put a branch of All Bar One at one end of the drinking den spectrum, you'd find this pub leering at it with yellowing teeth from the other. Gloriously musty, it's a 16th-century boozer laid out across several floors, and retaining much of the dinginess that is said to have inspired scenes in Dickens' novels. Take away the history, though, and what do you have? A straightforward Samuel Smith pub, with all the usual own-brand simulacra of well-known alcohol types and run-of-the-mill grub.
Babies and children admitted (restaurant). No piped music or jukebox. Restaurant. **Map p275 N6**.

Liverpool Street & Moorgate

Commercial Tavern
142 Commercial Street, E1 6NU (7247 1888).
Aldgate East tube/Liverpool Street tube/rail. **Open** 5-11pm Mon-Fri; noon-11pm Sat, Sun. **Credit** MC, V. Pub/Bar
It's hard not to like the current incarnation of this landmark flatiron corner pub, with its inspired chaos of retro-eccentric decor and warm, inclusive atmosphere. It seems to have escaped the attentions of the necking-it after-work masses: we can't help wondering if this is something to do with the absence of wall-to-wall lager pumps. Instead, there are four hand pumps offering the likes of Black Sheep and Old Rosie scrumpy, an esoteric bottled collection including Weston's organic cider and a fine collection of sprits (though no cocktail list). The bar itself celebrates the senses rather than sousing them: it's made up of colourful art deco tiles; there's a distinct decorative playfulness throughout, most obvious in stagey lighting, a multiplicity of wallpapers and, upstairs (a lovely room with its own bar), a wall of teacups and saucers. A great example of how a historic pub can be quite lit up with new life.
Disabled: toilet. Games (pool table). Tables outdoors (3, pavement). **Map p276 R5**.

George
Andaz, 40 Liverpool Street, EC2M 7QN (7618 7300). Liverpool Street tube/rail. **Open** 10am-11pm Mon-Wed; 10am-midnight Thur, Fri; 11am-11pm Sat; noon-10.30pm Sun. **Food served** noon-2.30pm, 6-9.30pm Mon-Fri; noon-5pm, 6-9pm Sat, Sun. **Credit** AmEx, DC, MC, V. Hotel pub
A vaulted banqueting hall ceiling, leaded windows, wooden panels and a framed Bishopsgate scene from 1602. Surely the markings of the dreaded historical theme pub? Mercifully not. This bar, attached to the Andaz (formerly Great Eastern) hotel, adds up to far more than the sum of its parts. The space takes light well by day, and at night shrouds thirsty City types in atmosphere. Catering to workaday lager needs, with Bombardier and London Pride also on parade, this well-executed if plain venue wouldn't be the first choice in which to celebrate that big deal. But to celebrate, say, the end of a particularly bloody Tuesday, there is no more welcoming place.
Disabled: toilet. Function room (50 capacity). TVs. **Map p277 R6**.

Golden Heart ★ HOT 50
110 Commercial Street, E1 6LZ (7247 2158). Liverpool Street tube/rail. **Open** 11am-midnight Mon-Sat; 11am-10.30pm Sun. **Credit** AmEx, MC, V. Pub
Landlady Sandra Esqulant has been the hand on the pump at this classic east London boozer for 30 years, and if it's gained a reputation in the last ten or so of them as a home from home for the Brit Art crowd, they're no more feted inside its wood-panelled walls than any of the other locals. There's a proper community vibe here with old blokes propping up the bar alongside market geezers and tattooed foreign exchange students. Stand outside (the favoured option since the smoking ban took hold) on a sunny Sunday and it can sometimes feel like you've accidentally gatecrashed a fancy dress party – nu-rave kids hiding behind '80s Ray-Bans, vintage-clad thirtysomethings sipping cheap wine and – last time we were in – a bearded artist clutching a pint in one hand and a cardboard box containing the antique corpse of a small dog in the other. Oddball style credentials aside, this is a pub where old fashioned manners and old-school decor rules – small rooms, crowded tables, open fires and pub-industry memorabilia. A neon sign flashing out 'Stand still and rot' offers a more modern vibe. The regulars can't get enough of the place but it's hard to tell if its popularity with the younger crowd is a result of its own virtues or just

cultish nostalgia. Sometimes – when the fluoro jukebox is belting out a guilty pleasure – the two are inseparable. As for Esqulant, she's in it for the long haul: 'I want to be laid out in here when I die,' she says.

Babies and children welcome. Function room (45 capacity). Jukebox. Tables outdoors (4, pavement). TVs (big screen, satellite).
Map p276 R5.

Gramaphone

60-62 Commercial Street, E1 6LT (7377 5332/ www.thegramaphone.co.uk). Aldgate East tube/ Liverpool Street tube/rail. **Open** noon-midnight Mon-Thur; noon-3.30am Fri; 9pm-3.30am Sat; noon-midnight Sun. **Food served** noon-10pm Mon-Fri; noon-8pm Sun. **Credit** AmEx, MC, V. **Bar**

This cavernous bar-club is owned by the same people as the Rhythm Factory on Whitechapel Road (*see p178*), which explains the quality of the nights put on in the ground-floor room – Upset the Rhythm, in particular, stands out as one of the capital's best indie showcases. The upstairs bar is roomy and entirely lacking in trendy decor pretensions – a fine break from the weirdo art installation and beheaded Barbie doll norm round these parts. Bag a sofa, a Guinness and a plate of decent-value Thai food before heading for a rummage on Brick Lane or back to your desk in the City.

Babies and children admitted (until 7pm). Disabled: toilet. Function room (150 capacity). Music (DJ 7pm Thur-Sat; bar free; club £5-£7). **Map p278 S6.**

Hawksmoor ★ HOT 50

157 Commercial Street, E1 6BJ (7247 7392/ www.thehawksmoor.com). Liverpool Street tube/rail. **Open** noon-1am Mon-Sat. **Food served** noon-3pm, 6.30-10.30pm Mon-Fri; 6.30-10.30pm Sat. **Credit** AmEx, DC, MC, V. **Cocktail bar/Restaurant**

As a restaurant, Hawksmoor succeeds despite the unprepossessing room it inhabits, of undistinguished proportions and uninteresting beige, brick and wood decoration. As a bar, it succeeds despite being stuck at one side of said room, with no dedicated seating of its own beyond a few barstools. Those stools are among London's finest ringside seats, however, for Hawksmoor's laid-back bartenders are cocktail intellectuals. The menu tracks classics such as juleps and 'aromatic cocktails' from their inception; Gin and Pine (conceived in 1862) was served in a cold glass of perfect proportion; Scoff Law (1924; whisky, Noilly Prat, pomegranate and lemon) was a smooth,

1 Lombard Street ★

This converted corner bank houses one of the City's most celebrated eating and drinking holes. The Michelin-starred restaurant is, of course, the raison d'être of the whole operation. But even if you're not going to tarry here all night, the bar is well worth a visit on its own. The cocktails are tremendous, from frivolous, fruity bellinis to perfectly pitched classics. And really, don't hold back: you're unlikely to catch out the bar's efficient mixologists with a bespoke request. There's plenty of imagination on the non-alcoholic drinks front too – try the Coconut Fizz with fresh pineapple, cream, coconut cream and soda. Grazing fare doesn't let the side down either, with tasty tapas clocking in at the £12 mark. *For listings, see p92.*

Will you dine with a
Blonde or Brune tonight?

At last, Speciality Beers such as Leffe are finding their rightful place at the dinner table

A beer with dinner?

It's not such a strange question. The parallels between Speciality Beers and wine are plenty. Both have a rich tradition stretching back through generations and can be favourably paired with many culinary delights. But with such a tempting array of beers to choose from, how can you recognise a brew that's really special?

The clue is in the name. Speciality Beers really are special. Brewed in their country of origin, these authentic beers are made from age-old recipes. Each has its own unique taste and style, enhanced by the flavours of natural ingredients such as coriander, curaçao, roasted barley or morello cherries. They are brewed rather differently to your average lager, too. Abbots, at the Abbey de Leffe in Belgium, have been brewing Leffe for almost 800 years.

The beer is fermented at a higher temperature, producing the aromatic qualities. Any beer brewed with such care and attention deserves to be savoured and enjoyed. Drinking it is a

ritual, never to be rushed. The perfect Leffe should be served in the unique Leffe Chalice glass, crafted to heighten the drinking experience. Master Beer Sommelier and Belgian Beer Ambassador, Marc Stroobandt says, "Speciality Beers such as Leffe are full of tantalising flavours and stimulating aromas. They are great with food and enjoyed by wine and beer drinkers alike." Similar to wine pairing, Speciality Beers can add a whole new depth to the gastronomic experience.

Leffe Blonde and Leffe Brune each have their own distinct character. Blonde has a well-balanced, fruity flavour, while Brune is a darker and maltier brew. Whichever brew you choose, Leffe is an ideal introduction to the world of Speciality Beers. So why not discover Leffe with your dinner tonight?

For more information on Leffe and other Speciality Beers visit: **www.specialitybeerselection.com**

Discover Life. Discover Leffe

unfussy blend. Purist means neither severe – there are also more frivolous daquiris, tikis and punches – nor expensive, with much at £6.50. American beers (Anchor Steam, Brooklyn Lager) and well-chosen international wines provide further options. Recommended. *Babies and children admitted. Bar available for hire. Disabled: toilet. Function room (30 capacity).* **Map p276 R5**.

Ten Bells

84 Commercial Street, E1 6LY (7366 1721). Liverpool Street tube/rail. **Open** noon-midnight Mon-Thur, Sun; noon-1am Fri, Sat. **Credit** MC, V. **Pub**
The Ten Bells' location, between Liverpool Street and Brick Lane, and dishevelled scruff-bag charm ensures it's packed to within an inch of its life with fashionable young locals, after-work creatives and the odd on-the-up rock star most nights – suffice to say it's not a poser-free zone. On the whole, though, the crowd is a friendly bunch, though bore them with Jack the Ripper pick-up joint stories at your peril. The usual suspects are all on tap, with more adventurous bottled imported lagers also on offer. Summer sees the street outside packed with drinkers and boho bonhomie. *Quiz (7pm 1st Mon of mth; £5). Tables outdoors (4, pavement).* **Map p278 S5**.

Vertigo 42 `HOT 50`

Tower 42, 25 Old Broad Street, EC2N 1HQ (7877 7842/www.vertigo42.co.uk). Bank tube/DLR/Liverpool Street tube/rail. **Open** noon-3pm, 5-11pm Mon-Fri. **Food served** noon-2.15pm, 5-9.30pm Mon-Fri. **Credit** AmEx, DC, MC, V. **Bar**
Short of introducing iris-recognition scanning, the process of going for a drink at Vertigo 42 (book in advance, then get X-rayed and metal-detected on arrival) could scarcely be any more MI5. But jumping through the bar's security hoops is worth it – its 42nd floor location delivers the kind of stupendous views that render sparkling conversation redundant. Mixed drinks aren't the strong suit here – our less-than-generous serving of the £11.50, fizz-based house cocktail arrived both flat and lukewarm. Far better to concentrate on the champagne list, which ranges from an accessible £44 bottle of Veuve Delaroy through to a cold-sweat inducing £795.50 magnum of 1990 Krug; eight of the bottles are available by the flute. *Bar available for hire. Booking advisable. Disabled: toilet. Dress: smart casual.* **Map p277 Q6**.

Mansion House, Monument & Bank

Bar Bourse

67 Queen Street, EC4R 1EE (7248 2200/2211/www.barbourse.co.uk). Mansion House tube. **Open** 11.30am-11pm Mon-Fri. **Food served** 11.30am-3pm Mon-Fri. **Credit** AmEx, MC, V. **Wine bar**
Unexpected delights await at Bar Bourse. The mood is elegant yet friendly, service is slick but fuss-free. Lunchtime crowds see the place filled with chummy banter and delicious aromas (organic salmon with fennel and citrus salads, £17.50). By night, the light wood and Regency stripe interior has its tables cleared away as the black-clad staff focus on relaxed attentiveness. There are no taps, but the bottled lager is intelligently selected (Tiger, Budvar) to chime with the tapas menu. The wine list offers 20 of each colour, with prices kicking off at the £16 mark. Cocktails are as professionally mixed as any in the Square Mile. *Booking advisable. Off-licence. TV.* **Map p277 P7**.

Bell `NEW`

29 Bush Lane, EC4R 0AN (7929 7772). Cannon Street tube/rail. **Open** 11am-10pm Mon-Fri. **Food served** noon-3pm Mon-Fri. **Credit** AmEx, MC, V. **Pub**
This may well be the oldest area of London, but it seems to embrace contemporary style like no other – something that's made an endangered species of the old-school City pub. The Bell, however, survives, half-hidden off Cannon Street and serving well-kept ales (including Sharp's Atlantic IPA and Courage Best) in a cosy room for which the term 'unpretentious' could have been coined. Plentiful perches and lots of standing room mean there's ample space for perusing the scenes of City life gone by that adorn the walls and the roll of honour listing every landlord since the Great Fire. A gem. *Babies and children admitted (lunchtime only). TVs.* **Map p277 P7**.

Bonds Bar & Restaurant

Threadneedle Hotel, 5 Threadneedle Street, EC4R 8AY (7657 8088). Monument tube/Bank tube/DLR. **Open** 11am-11pm Mon-Fri; 3-10.30pm Sat, Sun. **Food served** noon-2.30pm, 6-10pm Mon-Fri; 3-10.30pm Sat, Sun. **Credit** AmEx, DC, MC, V. **Bar/Restaurant**
The drinks list might occasionally favour phonetics over accuracy ('cachasa' and 'julip' are two cases in point), but idiosyncratic spelling is

City

the only area in which this slick City watering hole takes its eye off the ball. In every other respect, it's right on the money: carefully made cocktails (including some impressively freestyle offerings, such as the violet and lemongrass sour), a well-pitched wine list, plus exemplary tapas and bar snacks such as kikones (fried maize kernels). All this, and the kind of amber-hued glow (courtesy of large tawny lampshades and wood panelling) that makes even the tired and emotional look air-brushed.

Disabled: toilet. Function rooms (up to 15 capacity). Restaurant. **Map p277 Q6.**

Bow Wine Vaults

10 Bow Churchyard, EC4M 9DQ (7248 1121). Mansion House tube/Bank tube/DLR. **Open** 11am-11pm Mon-Fri. **Food served** noon-3pm Mon-Fri. **Credit** AmEx, DC, MC, V. **Wine bar**
Resting in the most atmospheric of all the Square Mile's nooks and crannies, Bow Wine Vaults has seen to City thirsts for more than a quarter of a century. That decor remains low on the list of priorities only adds to its substance-over-style charm. And my, what substance. The owners take their vino seriously and should your tipple of choice fail to appear on the menu, they will happily order it in for next time. As it stands, though, the list is globetrotting enough to suit all thirsts and pockets, from Chilean merlot and cabernet sauvignon at around the £15 mark, reaching up to Amarone Classico 2000 Guerrieri Rizzardi at £65.

Restaurant (available for hire). Tables outdoors (14, pavement). TV (satellite). **Map p277 P6.**

Counting House

50 Cornhill, EC3V 3PD (7283 7123). Bank tube/DLR. **Open** 11am-11pm Mon-Fri. **Food served** noon-10pm Mon-Fri. **Credit** AmEx, DC, MC, V. **Pub**
As the name might suggest, this pub was once a bank, but don't imagine a transformed local branch of HSBC: this is a grand, towering old building with ornate railings and colossal mirrors. The place is clearly geared up to serve a moneyed clientele; while it's essentially a Fuller's pub – London Pride and Discovery as standard – there are such strange offerings as a 'pie tasting plate' for an eye-watering £17 and racks of vintage wines. While the booze is high quality and the decor initially impressive, the atrium-style layout of the building gives you the nagging feeling that you're drinking in an airport departure lounge.

Bar available for hire. Disabled: toilet. Function room (110 capacity). Games (fruit machine, quiz machine). TV (big screen). **Map p277 Q6.**

Mercer Restaurant & Bar

34 Threadneedle Street, EC2R 8AY (7628 0001/www.themercer.co.uk). Monument tube/ Bank tube/DLR. **Open** 7.30am-11pm Mon-Fri. **Food served** 7.30-10am, noon-3pm, 5.30-9pm Mon-Fri. **Credit** AmEx, MC, V. **Bar**
Lofty ceilings, huge windows, banquettes of polished black leather and unadorned oak floorboards – the Mercer's spare but decidedly handsome interior is perfectly in tune with the stealth-wealth vibe of its heart-of-the-City location. The cocktail line-up shares the same restrained but confident line, with old-school classics (including a hand-grenade of a martini) sharing space with quietly innovative creations such as a pleasingly earthy rhubarb julep. But the star of the operation is the vast wine list, which, thanks to the presence of two wine preservation systems, always offers 18 reds and 18 whites, all from interesting producers, by the glass (£4-£45) or 250ml carafe.

Babies and children admitted. Bar available for hire. Restaurant (available for hire, 80 capacity). **Map p277 Q6.**

1 Lombard Street ★

1 Lombard Street, EC3V 9AA (7929 6611/ www.1lombardstreet.com). Bank tube/DLR. **Open** 11am-midnight Mon-Fri. **Tapas served** 5.30-10.30pm Mon-Fri. **Credit** AmEx, MC, V. **Bar/Restaurant**
For review, *see p89.*
Disabled: lift; toilet. Entertainment: pianist and singer 6.30pm Fri. Restaurant (available for hire). Function room (40 capacity). **Map p277 Q6.**

Prism

147 Leadenhall Street, EC3V 4QT (7256 3875/www.harveynichols.com). Monument tube/Bank tube/DLR. **Open** 11am-11pm Mon-Fri. **Food served** 8am-10am, 11.30am-3pm, 6-10pm Mon-Fri. **Credit** AmEx, DC, MC, V. **Bar/Restaurant**
Drinking in a subterranean corridor shouldn't really work. The reality, though, is that this oddly proportioned bar (plus restaurant) is one of the City's finest drinking experiences. The Harvey Nicks-owned space has all the elegance associated with the brand, plus an unexpected clandestine feel. The cocktail menu changes monthly – try a Robert Burns (Glenmorangie, sherry and Grand Marnier) in January, for example. A big screen and Wii console add a touch of frivolity to proceedings.

Babies and children admitted. Booking advisable. Disabled: toilet. Function rooms (up to 60 capacity). **Map p277 Q6.**

City

West

West

Whether you fancy swanking it up with an expertly shaken cocktail (**Lonsdale**, **Montgomery Place**), keeping it real with a proper pint (**Cow**, **Earl of Lonsdale**) or diving into a world of insanity (**Tiroler Hut**), W11 has got it covered – no wonder the locals look so pleased with themselves. Elsewhere in west London the gastro revolution continues apace. Chiswick is rather taken with the grown-up charms of Gordon Ramsay's **Devonshire**, while the **Swan** remains an oversubscribed and much-loved local favourite. Over in Ealing, the **Lodge Tavern** has answered the prayers of the neighbourhood's younger residents by offering somewhere hip to hang out. Meanwhile, Stamford Brook's **Carpenter's Arms** has impressed critics and punters alike with its fine food. New to Maida Vale is pub-restaurant **Idlewild**, while Bayswater's **Westbourne House** has got W2 residents in a spin with its proper martinis and glitzy buzz. It's back to gastro in Shepherd's Bush with the fantastic **Anglesea Arms** and foodie haven the **Havelock**.

Acton

George & Dragon ★
183 High Street, W3 9DJ (8992 3712). Acton Central tube/rail. **Open** 3-11pm Mon, Tue; noon-11pm Wed, Thur; noon-midnight Fri, Sat; noon-10.30pm Sun. **Food served** 5-9.30pm Mon, Tue; noon-2.30pm, 5-9.30pm Wed-Sat; noon-6pm Sun. **Credit** (over £10) MC, V. **Pub**
This beautiful dark wood and brass gem stands out on Acton's rough and ready High Street. The pub was impeccably restored with money from English Heritage in 2006. But it's not just a pretty face, with a strong range of beers – including Fuller's real ales, Leffe, Früli, Litovel, Honey Dew and Paulaner – which draws older professional drinkers as well as a young after-work crowd. It's also deceptively spacious with the low beamed front bar opening on to a huge double-height back room with art nouveau statues and large mirrors.
Babies and children welcome (until 9pm, restaurant only): high chairs. Bar available for hire. Games (board games). Quiz (8pm Mon; £2). Restaurant (available for hire, 40 capacity).

Grand Junction Arms
Acton Lane, NW10 7AD (8965 5670). Harlesden tube. **Open** *Front bar* noon-midnight Mon-Sat; noon-10.30pm Sun. *Back bar* noon-3pm, 6-9pm Mon-Fri; noon-10pm Sun. **Food served** noon-3pm, 6-9pm Mon-Fri; noon-6pm Sun. **Credit** AmEx, MC, V. **Pub**

The Grand Junction Arms belongs to a time when people would have passed out if you'd told them that in the future pubs would serve risotto. Tucked away in an industrial wasteland north of the A40 between warehouses and car parks, this boozer dishes out pints of Young's and Bombardier to young and old. Pictures of woodland animals and a dark red patterned carpet belong firmly to the old school. The front bar is spacious, with pool tables and fruit machines, and there's also a smaller lounge area and a more formal back bar. The Grand Junction comes into its own on warm days when the large beer garden with canal views can be enjoyed to the full.
Babies and children admitted (until 7pm). Bar available for hire. Disabled: toilet. Games (fruit machines, 3 pool tables, quiz machine). Music (2pm Sun; free). Tables outdoors (20, garden). TVs (widescreen).

Rocket NEW
11-13 Churchfield Road, W3 6BD (8993 6123/ www.therocketw3.co.uk). Acton Central tube. **Open** 5-11pm Mon; noon-11pm Tue-Thur; noon-midnight Fri, Sat; noon-10.30pm Sun. **Food served** 7-10.15pm Mon; noon-3.30pm, 7-10.15pm Tue-Sat; noon-6pm, 7-9pm Sun. **Credit** AmEx, MC, V. **Gastropub**
Rocket aimed to bring the gastropub revolution to Acton. Its airy dark red room ticks all the boxes, with mismatched wooden furniture, posh crisps, free Wi-Fi and board games. The impressive corner building has a fenced-in terrace running around the outside. Inside, the low-level chatter of

well-heeled twentysomethings enjoying after-work drinks shows it has hit its target audience; we eavesdropped on some fresh-faced media types having an animated conversation about UFOs in Acton. Drinkers have a choice of London Pride, Sharp's Doom Bar, Harveys Sussex Best, Leffe and Staropramen, plus a good range of wines available by the glass and bottle.
Babies and children welcome: high chairs. Games (board games). Restaurant. Tables outdoors (5, terrace). Wi-Fi (free).

Bayswater

Elbow Room

103 Westbourne Grove, W2 4UW (7221 5211/ www.theelbowroom.co.uk). Bayswater or Notting Hill Gate tube. **Open/food served** noon-11pm Mon-Sat; noon-10.30pm Sun. **Credit** MC, V. **Pool bar**
Part of the chain of bar-cum-pool halls, this is a well-designed and welcoming spot. The front third of the long L-shaped space is given over to a bar boasting a mix of comfy private side booths and high tables. The (bookable) pool playing area is surprisingly stylish – red curtains hang elegantly between tables while the walls are adorned by fetching rippled wood decoration. And the lighting is just right as is the level of the music. Prices are good too, with bottles of wine from £11.50, cocktails from under £6 and a hustler-friendly menu of burgers and salads from £8. The beer choice could stretch to some decent ales on draught, but otherwise this slots the black nicely.
Bar available for hire. Games (7 pool tables; call for details of competitions). Music (DJs 8pm Sat; free). TV (big screen, satellite). **Map p279 B6**.

Harlem

78 Westbourne Grove, W2 5RT (7985 0900/ www.harlemsoulfood.com). Bayswater or Notting Hill Gate tube. **Open** 5pm-1.30am Mon; noon-1.30am Tue-Fri; 10am-2am Sat; 10am-10.30pm Sun. **Food served** 5pm-midnight Mon; noon-midnight Tue-Fri; 10am-midnight Sat; 10am-10.30pm Sun. **Credit** AmEx, DC, MC, V. **Bar/diner**
There's a great bar hidden away in this corner hangout (part of the Match group) opposite the Elbow Room. The space is fine – dark wood and ornate ceiling, a pretty chandelier here, exposed brickwork there. The booze has an intriguing American bent: pale ale from Sierra Nevada and porter-style brew from California, or maybe a Boilermaker (Yank beer with a shot of tequila or bourbon). The wine focuses on the Americas

too, from California to Chile. Juicy burgers and soul food come in generous portions and cocktails are well-mixed. And yet certain things grate – tables are too close together, staff are lackadaisical and, on our visit, the toilets stank. Put those right, and this could be a real neighbourhood beacon.
Babies and children welcome (until 6pm): high chairs. Music (DJs 10pm Mon-Sat; £5 after 10pm Mon-Thur, £10 after 10pm Fri, Sat). Takeaway service. **Map p279 B6**.

Mitre

24 Craven Terrace, W2 3QH (7262 5240/ www.capitalpubcompany.co.uk). Lancaster Gate tube/Paddington tube/rail. **Open** 11am-11pm Mon-Sat; noon-10.30pm Sun. **Food served** noon-3pm, 6-10pm Mon-Fri; noon-9pm Sat; noon-8pm Sun. **Credit** AmEx, MC, V. **Pub**
This Victorian Grade II-listed local has an appealing conspiratorial air – the sort of place in which Regan might have drunk with a source in *The Sweeney* back in the '70s. The sweeping corner site offers numerous private nooks where chesterfields and well-worn wooden tables are overlooked by a mishmash of old hunting prints and oils. The pints are a changing mix of Adnams, Fuller's and Brakspear, and the wine list includes a malbec and Chablis (it scores extra for offering carafes). The food is thoughtful too, mixing thai fish cakes and beef and Guinness pie, with Greek and Italian themed platters – a nod to changing times in a place that clings to its past.
Babies and children admitted (separate room). Function room (70 capacity). Tables outdoors (8, pavement). TV.

Royal Exchange

26 Sale Place, W2 1PU (7723 3781). Paddington tube/rail. **Open** 11am-11pm Mon-Sat; noon-10.30pm Sun. **Food served** noon-10pm daily. **Credit** AmEx, MC, V. **Pub**
One of the best boozers within easy striking distance of Paddington, this is a cosy old school gaff with a dedication to fine beer and fine horses. By day, screens follow the Sport of Kings around the country, while the quiet atmosphere encourages thoughtful perusing of the form. To drink, Adnams, Brakspear, Timothy Taylor and Murphy's are all worth a flutter, though a big win clearly merits one of the giant bottles of champagne that decorate the tiny backroom. Food includes sandwiches such as Limerick ham (like the Murphy's, a nod to the pub's Irish owners) and, on Fridays, salt beef.
Babies and children admitted (outdoors). Jukebox. Tables outdoors (4, pavement). TV (satellite).

West

Victoria

10A Strathern Place, W2 2NH (7724 1191).
Lancaster Gate tube/Paddington tube/rail.
Open 11am-11pm Mon-Sat; noon-10.30pm
Sun. **Food served** noon-9.30pm Mon-Sat;
noon-9pm Sun. **Credit** AmEx, MC, V. **Pub**
Perched beside a mini-roundabout and posh Hyde
Park mews, it's easy to see why the Victoria has
drawn everyone from Dickens and Churchill to
the Dracula Society. A characterful interior is
bookended by a pair of ravishing period
fireplaces, along with ornate mirrors, old prints
and vintage wallpaper above panelled walls. The
L-shaped bar dispenses a quartet of Fuller's
offerings, while a superior menu mixes the likes
of steak and ale pie with butternut squash and
sage risotto, alongside a well-chosen wine list at
around £20 a bottle. Clientele range from older
locals to foreign language students who have
wisely chosen to brush up their English (drinking
habits, that is) here.
Babies and children admitted (until 6pm).
Function rooms (up to 50 capacity). Games
(board games). Quiz (9pm Tue; £1). Tables
outdoors (7, terrace). TV.

Westbourne House ★ NEW

65 Westbourne Grove, W2 4UJ (7229 2233/
www.westbournehouse.net). Bayswater or Royal
Oak tube. **Open/food served** 11am-11.30pm
Mon-Thur; 11am-midnight Fri, Sat; 11am-
11pm Sun. **Credit** AmEx, MC, V. **Bar**
For review, *see right.*
Babies and children admitted (until 5pm).
Bar available for hire. Function rooms (up to
45 capacity). Tables outdoors (4, pavement).
Map p279 B6.

West

Chiswick

City Barge

27 Strand-on-the-Green, Kew, Surrey W4
3PH (8994 2148). Gunnersbury tube/rail/
Kew Bridge rail. **Open** 11am-11pm Mon-Sat;
noon-10.30pm Sun. **Food served** noon-9pm
daily. **Credit** AmEx, DC, MC, V. **Pub**
Located on a gorgeous stretch of the north bank
of the Thames, this Fuller's pub is not as small
as it first seems. Loftier punters may have to
duck their heads as they enter from the riverside
into a tiny, cave-like bar. Go up the stairs to the
right however, and things are a much more
roomy affair, with large tables, wooden chairs,
leather sofas and another bar. There is also a
glass-roofed conservatory area, and tables out
in the car park area at the back (complete with
smoker-friendly heaters). The riverside terrace is

Westbourne House ★ NEW

A big, handsome pub (formerly the
Shakespeare) has swapped its nicotine
stains and pint glasses for something
altogether more glitzy. Westbourne
House has enough shiny surfaces
to attract a flock of magpies, and the
gilding on the mirrors and faux-French
furniture are made all the more twinkly
and glittery by low lighting and a
profusion of candles. Oh, and there's
a pole smack in the middle of the floor,
which is just dying to have a leg thrown
over it. This new bar has definitely got
its priorities in the right place – and
that's firmly, resolutely on the drinks
list. The cocktail list is the work of
drinks supremo Mat Perovetz. There
are seven 'proper' martinis, spirits
are premium (Buffalo Trace Bourbon,
Green Mark and Zubrówka Bison Grass
vodkas, Martin Miller's Westbourne
Strength gin) and the delivery is pristine.
Try a Great Pear (£8) of Glenfiddich
muddled with pear, or an Old Cuban
(£8) made with Havana rum and
champagne. The pisco sours (£7)
are also pleasingly unmucked-around-
with. The wine list is admirable, with
Trinity Hill pinot noir (not cheap at £49)
and two varietals from Trentham Estate
in Australia. The food is no afterthought
either. There's a bijou list of antipasti,
mezedes, daily specials, sandwiches
and salads. All in all, a fine bar. *For*
listings, see left.

packed out in summer. Nautical paraphernalia
adorns the walls, including an old mooring
charges sign. The bars offer three cask Fuller's
ales including Chiswick bitter. Good, honest pub
grub is on offer as well as a decent wine list.
Babies and children admitted (until 9pm).
Games (quiz machine). Tables outdoors
(6, riverside terrace).

Devonshire NEW

126 Devonshire Road, W4 2JJ (7592 7962/
www.gordonramsay.com). Turnham Green
tube. **Open** 11.30am-midnight Mon-Fri;
11.30am-1am Sat; noon-11pm Sun. **Food**
served noon-3pm, 6-11pm Mon-Fri; noon-
10.30pm Sat; noon-9.30pm Sun. **Credit**
MC, V. **Gastropub**
Gordon Ramsay opened this, his second
gastropub, in 2007. It follows the template
established by the hugely successful Narrow in
Limehouse. Inside, everything is brown, from

West

the ceiling beams to the wood floors and dark brown bar and bar stools. Black and white images of Chiswick in years gone past adorn the walls. In tribute to its previous life as a shabby local boozer (it used to be the Devonshire Arms), there's as much pub here as there is gastro. This can make it all the more difficult to get a table, although on our recent weekday night visit only half the dining tables were occupied. On tap are two cask ales, Deuchars IPA and London Pride. However the Devonshire's real strength lies in the extensive wine list, highlights of which include a 2005 Quinta do Crasto from Portugal (£21) and a 2006 riesling from New Zealand's Wairau River (£28). The bar staff are young, attractive and predominantly female. Upmarket bar snacks include scotch eggs and mini pails of chips. *Babies and children welcome: high chairs. Booking advisable. Restaurant available for hire.*

Duke of Sussex NEW

75 South Parade, W4 5LF (8742 8801). Chiswick Park or Turnham Green tube. **Open** noon-11.30pm Mon-Thur; noon-midnight Fri, Sat; noon-10.30pm Sun. **Food served** noon-10.30pm daily. **Credit** MC, V. **Gastropub**
Formerly a sports/TV pub with a pool table and Elvis nights in leafy, gentrified Chiswick, the new Duke of Sussex is now a gastropub from the people behind the Realpubs chain. Low lighting, ubiquitous rich woods and chandeliers make for a cosy, relaxed atmosphere. These gastro design staples are complemented by some more idiosyncratic features, including cherubic friezes up high in the dining room. And the cooking doesn't conform to the hackneyed, same-old gastropub template either. Some things are familiar (pea and celeriac soup; brawn with gherkins and toast; skate with white beans and salsa verde; 28-day-hung steak and chips). But you've also got some Spanish dishes to choose

from, such as salt-cod croquettes, fabada (white bean and pork stew), and Galician fish stew. They fit in perfectly. This is simple, hearty, rustic food: what gastropubs should be all about. Thumbs up too for a wine list that's diverse, interesting and very good value, offering most items by the carafe as well as the bottle. We tried two Portuguese wines (one white, one red) and would gladly order them again.
Babies and children admitted. Disabled: toilet. Restaurant (available for hire, 64 capacity). Tables outdoors (20, garden). TVs.

George IV

185 Chiswick High Road, W4 2DR (8994 4624/www.georgeiv.co.uk). South Acton rail/Turnham Green tube. **Open** 11.30am-11pm Mon-Thur; 11.30am-1am Fri, Sat; noon-11pm Sun. **Food served** noon-3pm, 5-10pm Mon-Thur; noon-10pm Fri, Sat; noon-3pm Sun. **Credit** AmEx, DC, MC, V. **Pub**
The George IV is without doubt Chiswick's liveliest pub, with a young clientele drawn here by the live music and the famous Headliners Comedy Club, which in the past has played host to the likes of Harry Hill and Bill Bailey. Week nights are popular with couples and young professionals, while Friday nights have a particular buzz and also a noticeable lack of available seats (but fortunately no sticky floors). The lively bar team are usually students and Australians. This Fuller's house offers London Pride, London Porter, Discovery, Old Winter Ale and ESB on draught, while an easy-drinking pinot grigio (£14.50 a bottle, £3.05 a glass) is the bestselling wine.
Babies and children admitted (until 6pm). Comedy (9pm Fri, Sat; £10). Disabled: toilet. Games (darts). Music (rock bands 8pm 3rd Sun of mth, £5; 9pm last Sat of mth, free; salsa 2nd Sun of mth, free; jazz monthly, £5). Salsa classes (8pm, 9pm Tue; £6). Tables outdoors (8, garden). TVs.

Mawson Arms

110 Chiswick Lane South, W4 2QA (8994 2936). Turnham Green tube. **Open** 11am-8pm Mon-Fri. **Food served** noon-3pm Mon-Fri. **Credit** MC, V. **Pub**
The Mawson Arms is not exactly user-friendly: it only opens until 8pm and closes completely at weekends, and it's a 15-minute trek from the nearest tube. But ale-lovers will find this mini-pilgrimage well worth the effort. The pub is within barrel-rolling distance of Fuller's HQ, the Griffin, the oldest brewery in London. On tap choose from a wide selection of Fuller's finest: Chiswick, Discovery, London Pride, Swing Low

and Honey Dew, all impeccably kept, or ESB and Old Winter Ale in bottles. The drinkers here are a mix of workers from the brewery, punters from the popular brewery tour and local residents, generally an older crowd. If you feel 8pm is a bit too early to end your night, you can even get two-pint cartons of your favourite ale to take away.
Babies and children admitted. Function room (capacity 16). TV.

Old Pack Horse

434 Chiswick High Road, W4 5TF (8994 2872). Chiswick Park tube. **Open** 11am-11pm Mon-Thur; 11am-midnight Fri, Sat; 11am-10.30pm Sun. **Food served** noon-10pm Mon-Sat; noon-9pm Sun. **Credit** AmEx, MC, V. **Pub**
There are plenty of Fuller's pubs to choose from in Chiswick, but the Old Pack Horse is among the finest. The unimposing frontage of this down-to-earth boozer doesn't do justice to the large bar area inside, which is divided into three main areas, with plenty of cosy corners to hide away in. Unlike many a Chiswick pub, the Pack Horse has resisted gastrofication, remaining a traditional, well-run boozer that just happens to serve great Thai food (out of the separately run restaurant at the back). The bar offers the usual array of well-kept Fuller's ales: ESB, Discovery, Swing Low and London Pride. The clientele here is more eclectic than other pubs in the area, a mix of local workers of all ages, families, couples and regulars enjoying a pint and the paper on their own at the bar. It's popular but not so crowded on a Friday night that it's impossible to get a seat. The traditional decor incorporates chintzy-kitsch curtains and carpets and stained-glass windows, with open fires and leather sofas. Old black and white photos of Chiswick High Road, alongside posters of the Empire, cover the walls.
Babies and children admitted (restaurant all times; pub until 7.30pm). Games (fruit machines). Tables outdoors (6, pavement; 5, garden). TV.

Pilot

56 Wellesley Road, W4 4BZ (8994 0828). Gunnersbury tube/rail. **Open** noon-11pm Mon-Sat; noon-10.30pm Sun. **Food served** noon-3pm, 6.-10pm Mon-Fri; noon-4pm, 6-10pm Sat; noon-4pm, 6-9.30pm Sun. **Credit** AmEx, MC, V. **Gastropub**
The Pilot is more gastro than pub. This is probably no bad thing, particularly for the locals who come to this small, residentially situated hostelry for a quiet pint or cosy meal. There seems to be a real emphasis on dining; on a Friday night about 80 per cent of punters were eating. The clientele is

largely corporate lunchers from the nearby Chiswick Business Park and well-heeled locals in the evening and weekends. The food is excellent and it shows; getting a table on a weekend night is no easy feat. The decor is modern yet rustic – large wooden tables, wooden pews and stripped wood floors, with a very popular beer garden out the back. On tap this Fuller's pub serves London Pride and Honey Dew.

Babies and children admitted (until 7pm). Disabled: toilet. Function room (80 capacity). Tables outdoors (12, garden).

Roebuck

122 Chiswick High Road, W4 1PU (8995 4392/www.theroebuckchiswick.co.uk). Turnham Green tube. **Open** 11am-11pm Mon-Sat; noon-10.30pm Sun. **Food served** noon-10.30pm Mon-Sat; noon-10pm Sun. **Credit** AmEx, MC, V. **Gastropub**

This is yet another west London gastropub, but the Roebuck's relaxed atmosphere and prime High Road location mean it has become a firm local favourite. The decor in the bar area is neutral and quintessentially English (leather sofas, mahogany bar and tables, dark wood floor), while the white-walled dining area at the back has a light, airy atmosphere. The scents wafting from the open kitchen next to the bar may well tempt you into ordering from the menu of comfort-food staples such as sausage and mash and roast chicken. Frequented during the week by large groups of twirties seeking an after-work tipple, at weekends the Roebuck is also popular with families. The 40-strong wine list is categorised by character, while beer drinkers can choose from guest ales such as Adnams Broadside and Wells Eagle.

Babies and children welcome: children's menu, high chairs. Disabled: toilet. Tables outdoors (14, garden; 3, pavement).

Duke of Sussex. *See p97.*

West

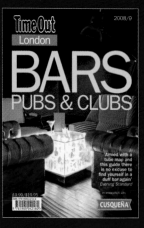

Sam's Brasserie & Bar

11 Barley Mow Passage, W4 4PH (8987 0555/ www.samsbrasserie.co.uk). Chiswick Park or Turnham Green tube. **Open** 9am-midnight Mon-Thur, Sun; 9am-12.30am Fri, Sat. **Food served** 9am-3pm, 6.30- 10.30pm Mon-Sat; 9am-3pm, 6.30-10pm Sun. **Credit** AmEx, MC, V. **Bar/brasserie**

Spearheaded by Sam Harrison, a protégé of Rick Stein, who is also an investor, this *Time Out* award-winning bar and brasserie has gone from strength to strength since its opening in 2005. Set in a stunning converted Victorian industrial space behind Chiswick Green, Sam's has a slightly corporate feel. The original structure of the paper factory it once was is still evident, from the concrete floor to the original beams in the roof. Seating comes in the form of wooden chairs around small, round tables, and one sofa tucked away in a corner. It's sleek and contemporary rather than cosy or comfortable. The well-groomed staff are mostly helpful and friendly, although during busy times service can be excruciatingly slow. There's an extensive list of cocktails, predominantly of the martini variety (try a raspberry/lychee one, £7). On the beer front there's little to get excited about on draught but a choice of ten bottles including Bitburger, Bohemia, London Pride, Chalky's Bite and Pilsner Urquell, all under £4. The wine list is also impressive, with around 30 by the glass, including a sauvignon blanc and Australian red (both £5.25 a glass) from Rick Stein's own Tower Lodge Estate in the Hunter Valley, Australia. A choice of tasty bar snacks includes a plate of cheese washed down with a carafe of merlot to share (£15).

Babies and children welcome: children's menu; high chairs; toys. Booking advisable Thur-Sat. Disabled: toilet. Music (jazz 7pm occasional Sun). Restaurant.

Swan

Evershed Walk, 119 Acton Lane, W4 5HH (8994 8262). Chiswick Park tube/94 bus. **Open** 5-11pm Mon-Fri; noon-11pm Sat; noon-10.30pm Sun. **Food served** 7-10.30pm Mon-Fri; 12.30-3pm, 7-10.30pm Sat; 12.30-4pm, 7-10pm Sun. **Credit** AmEx, MC, V. **Gastropub** For review, see p103.

Babies and children admitted (until 7pm). Tables outdoors (30, garden).

Ealing

Castlebar

84 Uxbridge Road, W13 8RA (8567 3819/ www.thecastlebar.co.uk). Ealing Broadway

Insider Knowledge
Westbourne House

You are?
Milos Popovic, general manager of Westbourne House (*see p96*). The owner, House Bars, specialises in taking old pubs and turning them into stylish bars. We opened in October 2007.

What was the place like before?
It was a pub called the Shakespeare, on what at that time was the wrong end of Westbourne Grove. There were pool tables, vending machines and big TV screens and it all smelled of beer. It took almost six months to turn it around, and a lot of money and effort, but now other places in the area are following suit and the whole road is going up.

What have you done with it?
We've turned it into a trendy cocktail bar. It's stylish but retro, with colours inspired by St Tropez, second-hand tables and chairs painted silver, and a big framed picture of our logo, a chandelier. There are three party areas people can hire.

What's special about the place?
We have one of the best-known bar managers in London, Mat Perovetz. He has an enormous drinks knowledge and a great palate, so he comes up with new cocktails every week. Watching him and his team at work is amazing – they spin the napkins around, roll bottles down their arms, throw straws in the air. It's very theatrical.

Your regulars must look very different now...
It's totally changed. The regulars from the old pub don't come here any more. It's a young crowd, 25- to 35-year-olds.

West

tube/rail/West Ealing rail. **Open/food served** 10am-10.30pm Mon-Wed, Sun; 10am-12.30am Thur-Sat. **Credit** AmEx, MC, V. **Gastrobar**
Part gastropub, part bar and part giant outdoor smoking area, the Castlebar has tried to be all things to all men. And judging by its loyal local following it's doing well. The huge terrace indulges rather than persecutes those who like a puff. It is decked, heated and covered, the blaring music pumped out almost makes you forget you're looking at an insalubrious stretch of the Uxbridge Road. Sweet staff do table service as well as manning the large square bar. A mammoth drinks menu boasts 22 whiskies, 13 vodkas and 14 rums, a comprehensive cocktail list and Adnams Broadside and Best, Leffe and Hoegaarden on tap.
Babies and children admitted. Disabled: toilet. Tables outdoors (45, garden). TV.

Drayton Court

2 The Avenue, W13 8PH (8997 1019). West Ealing rail. **Open** 11am-11pm Mon; 11am-midnight Tue-Thur; 11am-1am Fri, Sat; noon-11pm Sun. **Food served** noon-9pm daily. **Credit** MC, V. **Pub**
Tired of poky little London pubs? Then head down to this buttermilk-yellow west London landmark where space is definitely not at a premium. It's a Fuller's establishment (London Pride, ESB, Chiswick, Discovery) and sticks to the traditional mould with sepia-tinted gold-framed photographs showing off its former glory as a Victorian hotel. Good use of the space is made with a huge main bar and a separate cosier sitting room and sports bar. If you're still suffering from cabin fever, beautiful arched windows give out onto a terrace with stairs down to an enormous grassy beer garden surrounded by trees.
Babies and children welcome (until 9pm): children's menu. Comedy (8.30pm alternate Fri; £6-£9). Dance classes (lindy hop 8pm Mon; salsa 8pm Thur). Disabled: toilet. Function room (up to 92 capacity). Games (pool table). Music (acoustic bands 9pm Tue; jazz 8pm last Wed of mth; free). Quiz (9pm Sun; £1). Tables outdoors (40, garden). TVs (big screen, satellite).

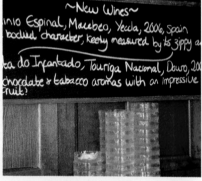

Ealing Park Tavern

222 South Ealing Road, W5 4RL (8758 1879). South Ealing tube. **Open** 5-11pm Mon; noon-11pm Tue-Sat; noon-10.30pm Sun. **Food served** 6-10pm Mon; noon-3pm, 6-10pm Tue-Sat; noon-3.45pm, 6-9.30pm Sun. **Credit** AmEx, MC, V.
Gastropub

Lovingly restored, this high-ceilinged Victorian pub buzzes all week long with punters slouching contentedly on its battered brown leather sofas. The vast space has been split into a dining room and main bar, with the kitchen doing a roaring trade in European gastropub fare. On the bar side there is a well-chosen wine list and Greene King IPA, Tribute and Leffe. Homely touches abound, with open fires, vintage lampshades and giant flower-filled vases which go down well with the young professional crowd who treat the Tavern as their own front room.
Babies and children welcome (until 8.30pm): high chairs. Restaurant. Tables outdoors (10, garden).

Swan

This locally lauded gastropub is not the sort of place you would just stumble across, given that it's about a 15-minute walk from Chiswick High Road, down a quiet residential lane. And yet it's always packed, with a wait of 20-30 minutes for a table on a weekday evening (you can't book). Its reputation has spread by word of mouth and it is regarded by many as the best gastropub in Chiswick (a high accolade in an area saturated with such establishments). Staff are very friendly, chatty, attentive, double-checking all food orders to avoid mistakes – and they even remember what their punters are drinking without being asked. There's no separate dining area in the medium-sized pub, which is divided into two main areas by the small square bar in the middle. On tap expect London Pride, Sussex Best Bitter, Timothy Taylor Landlord and Hoegaarden. The decor is basic but cosy: worn tables and chairs give it an air of scruffy chic. Locals make up the majority of the clientele; the Swan is very popular with couples and thirty- and fortysomethings. The huge wine list is impressive, especially the choice of reds, six of which are by the glass.
For listings, see p101.

Lodge Tavern **NEW**

53 The Mall, W5 3TA (8567 0173/www. thelodgetavern.co.uk). Ealing Broadway tube/rail. **Open** noon-1am Mon-Fri; noon-2am Sat; noon-midnight Sun. **Food served** noon-9pm Mon-Wed, Sun; noon-9.30pm Thur-Sat. **Credit** MC, V. **DJ bar**

The team behind Islington's Winchester bar brings its pub-cum-DJ lounge concept to Ealing in the shape of the Lodge Tavern. And the timber-clad walls, flock wallpaper, dark wood furniture and trophy antlers are exactly what the doctor ordered for W5's younger residents. Laid-back, unpretentious and quirky, with decent DJs at weekends and a large area for alfresco drinking, the Lodge has certainly made its mark. The bar staff know how to mix a decent cocktail, and alongside classic recipes there are seven house elixirs, including a refreshing Strazberi Sling (a Pimm's and vodka concoction). On tap are everyday beers like Kronenbourg, Guinness and Foster's – more effort has gone into selecting the short but diverse wine list.
Bar available for hire. Music (DJs 7pm Thur-Sat; jazz 7pm Sun; free). Tables outdoors (18, patio).

Red Lion

13 St Mary's Road, W5 5RA (8567 2541). South Ealing tube. **Open** 11am-11pm Mon-Wed; 11am-midnight Thur-Sat; noon-11pm Sun. **Food served** noon-3pm, 7-9.30pm Mon-Sat; 12.30-5pm Sun. **Credit** AmEx, MC, V. **Pub**

Sitting opposite Ealing Studios, the Red Lion was the pub of choice for cast and crew in its glory days, and apart from a distinct lack of famous drinkers not much has changed. Black and white photographs of celluloid stars line the walls and on our visit the handsome white fronted building boasted all the classic pub hallmarks, with Fuller's ales, an indefinable musty smell and colourful locals who would fit perfectly in an Ealing comedy. The bar has cosy nooks for quiet drinks and opens out onto a pretty high walled garden with tables and umbrellas for smokers and sunny days.
Babies and children admitted. Disabled: toilet. Tables outdoors (15, garden).

Hammersmith

Brook Green Hotel

170 Shepherd's Bush Road, W6 7PB (7603 2516/www.brookgreenhotel.co.uk). Hammersmith tube. **Open** 11am-midnight

West

Ladbroke Arms. *See p106.*

Mon-Thur, Sun; 11am-1am Fri, Sat. **Food served** 11am-10pm daily. **Credit** AmEx, DC, MC, V. **Pub**

This handsome Young's pub, located in the small leafy area between Hammersmith and Shepherd's Bush and attached to the small hotel of the same name, was tarted up in a re-vamp last year. Now the luxurious brown and green interior, complete with leather chairs and the odd chandelier, has a sort of regal elegance. Chill out music, dim lighting and a decent, well-priced cocktail menu draw a young crowd at weekends, while during the week there's an almost corporate feel, with a mix of business types and hotel guests. On tap are Young's,

Winter Warmer and Bombardier. There's also an excellent whisky selection. The extensive wine list is divided into bottles from Europe and Rest of the World.

Babies and children admitted (until 6pm). Disabled: toilet. Function room (90 capacity). Swing dancing (7pm Sun; £7). Tables outdoors (12, garden). TVs (big screen).

Carpenter's Arms ★ NEW

91 Black Lion Lane, W6 9BG (8741 8386). Stamford Brook tube. **Open** noon-11pm Mon-Sat; noon-10.30pm Sun. **Food served** 12.30-3pm, 7-10pm Mon-Sat; 12.30-4pm, 7.30-9pm Sun. **Credit** AmEx, MC, V. **Pub**

The Carpenter's Arms sounds like a pub and it looks like one too – a classic old corner boozer sandwiched between some typically delightful west London terraces. It also does a bloody good impression of a restaurant (the enticing English menu is well renowned). Inside, the decor is subtle, with white walls and wooden floors and furniture, though there's also a carefully chosen mishmash of paintings, lights and art objects that put the place squarely in the ever-so-slightly trendy gastropub bracket. The bar, however, is of the proper pub variety, with draught Guinness, Adnams and Addlestones cider (as well as Kronenbourg and Amstel). There's a decent beer garden for summer sessions too.
Babies and children admitted. No piped music or jukebox. Tables outdoors (8, garden).

Cumberland Arms NEW

29 North End Road, W14 8SZ (7371 6806/ www.thecumberlandarmspub.co.uk). West Kensington tube/Kensington (Olympia) tube/ rail. **Open** noon-11pm Mon-Sat; noon-10.30 Sun. **Food served** noon-3pm, 7-10.30pm Mon-Sat; noon-4pm, 7-10pm Sun. **Credit** MC, V. **Gastropub**

In an age of increasingly poncey gastropubs, this Olympia stalwart keeps it real, with its well-worn wooden tables and floorboards, real ales (London Pride, Timothy Taylor Landlord and Black Sheep on our visit) atop a lengthy wine list, and reasonably priced Mediterranean/North African menu. Drinkers and diners mingle happily, bar staff smile and the overflowing hanging baskets (a riot of colour come summer) lend rustic charm. Roast pork belly, Tunisian lamb and date tagine, pan-roasted wild salmon, spaghetti and meatballs are typical fare (the menu changes monthly); the cooking (and service) can be a bit slapdash, but the relaxed vibe aids digestion. The smattering of outside tables are useful come good weather.
Babies and children admitted (until 7pm). Games (board games). Tables outdoors (12, garden). TV.

Dove

19 Upper Mall, W6 9TA (8748 9474). Hammersmith or Ravenscourt Park tube. **Open** 11am-11pm Mon-Sat; noon-10.30pm Sun. **Food served** noon-3pm, 5-10pm Mon-Fri; noon-4pm, 5-9pm Sat; noon-5pm Sun. **Credit** AmEx, MC, V. **Pub**

This Fuller's gem enjoys a lovely location on the Thames near Hammersmith Bridge. But be warned that while cosy and romantic on a chilly winter's night (the perfect place for a date, in fact), in the summer, it and its neighbouring hostelries are packed out. The pub is divided into four distinct areas: a decent-sized riverside garden/terrace, a low-ceilinged lounge bar, a gorgeous conservatory area with vine leaves and fairy lights snaking across the ceiling, and the tiny front bar, which merits an entry in *Guinness World Records*. Real ales including London Pride, ESB and Chiswick are very well kept. The 17th-century building is also steeped in history: 'Rule Britannia' was penned in an upstairs room, and Charles II and Nell Gwynne once caroused here. Today, it's mostly twenty-to-fortysomethings and couples.
No piped music or jukebox. Tables outdoors (8, riverside terrace).

Queen's Arms

171 Greyhound Road, W6 8NL (7386 5078). Barons Court tube. **Open** noon-11pm Mon-Thur, Sun; noon-midnight Fri, Sat. **Food served** noon-3pm, 6.30-10pm Mon-Fri; noon-3.30pm, 6.30-10pm Sat; 12.30-4pm, 6.30-9pm Sun. **Credit** MC, V. **Gastropub**

Located in a residential area a short walk from the neon of Fulham Palace Road, this swish gastropub is not somewhere you are likely to happen upon by chance but the crowds it draws at weekends are testament to the quality of its food, cosy atmosphere and endlessly upbeat staff. Downstairs leather sofas, wooden tables and a rogue cow skin chair surround the black walnut bar, which stocks around 70 wines as well as Timothy Taylor and London Pride on tap. A wide staircase leads to an airy, modern dining area, with an open kitchen and retractable roof. Punters are largely well-to-do young professionals from Fulham and Hammersmith – strangely, on the weeknight of our recent visit they were almost all male.
Babies and children welcome: high chairs. Disabled: toilet. Quiz (8pm Mon; £1). Restaurant (upstairs available for hire, 50 capacity). TVs (satellite).

Ruby Grand NEW

225-227 King Street, W6 9JT (8748 3391/ www.ruby.uk.com). Hammersmith or Ravenscourt Park tube. **Open** 11am-11pm Mon-Wed; 11am-midnight Thur-Sat; 11am-10.30pm Sun. **Food served** noon-4pm, 6-10pm Mon-Wed; noon-4pm, 6-11pm Thur, Fri; 11am-4pm, 6-11pm Sat; 11am-9.30pm Sun. **Credit** AmEx, DC, MC, V. **Bar**

Part of the Ruby group (which includes Ruby Lounge in King's Cross), this newcomer has brought a touch of class to the Hammersmith drinking scene. The decor is tasteful and inviting and the clientele young and well-dressed. There

West

are no real surprises on the cocktail list, but they are competently prepared and a very reasonable £6.50 (£4.50 during happy hour). The large bar stocks over 40 rums, five proseccos and over 40 other wines, and on tap are Deuchars IPA and London Pride – you certainly won't run out of drink options. The bar is divided into three areas: a main bar with comfy leather seating, ornate, floral-motif wallpaper and giant Christmas-bauble type lampshades; a light, airy morning room and a sizeable dining area. There is also a great beer garden – a rarity around these parts. *Babies and children admitted (until 6pm). Bar available for hire. Disabled: toilet. Music (DJs 8pm Fri, jazz 8pm Sat; free). Function room (50 capacity). Restaurant (available for hire, 35 capacity). Tables outdoors (20, garden).*

Stonemason's Arms NEW

54 Cambridge Grove, W6 0LA (8748 1397). Hammersmith tube. **Open** 11am-11pm Mon-Sat; noon-11pm Sun. **Food served** noon-3pm, 6-10pm Mon-Fri; noon-10pm Sat; noon-9.30pm Sun. **Credit** AmEx, MC, V. **Gastropub**
Situated on a busy main road behind King Street, next to Kings Mall car park, the Stonemason's Arms does not enjoy the most tranquil of settings, but it's still very popular. The interior of this gastropub is light, clean and airy, with painted white brick walls, high ceilings, stone floors and well-spaced out wooden tables that create a rustic feel. Large mirrors and contemporary art adorn the walls. Punters are largely a young professional crowd. There's a cosmopolitan beer selection which includes London Pride, Litovel, Kirin, Hoegaarden, Leffe and Organic Honeydew, as well as Scrumpy on draught, and Boon Framboise, Boon Kriek, Franziskaner, Schneider Weisse, Fuller's Discovery, London Porter and ESB in bottles (all £3.10). Wine list choices include ten whites and nine reds, several reasonably priced. *Babies and children admitted (until 6pm). Function room (50 capacity). Tables outdoors (4, pavement).*

Holland Park

Julie's Wine Bar

135 Portland Road, W11 4LW (7727 7985/ www.juliesrestaurant.com). Holland Park tube. **Open/food served** 9am-11pm Mon-Sat; 9am-10.30pm Sun. **Credit** AmEx, MC, V. **Wine bar**
A testament to the glories of architectural salvage, Julie's is a happy mix of various intimate rooms decorated in styles ranging from Gothic chic to Victorian conservatory. During the day it's very wholesome, populated by families and ladies-who-lunch; in the evening it's a little more louche. A user-friendly menu of brasserie dishes is priced in keeping with the postcode. The well-stocked bar can provide most drinks, including a handful of classic cocktails, but as the name suggests, the emphasis is on wine, and with quite a few bottles available by the glass. Opened in 1969, the old girl has matured nicely into a local icon. *Babies and children welcome (crèche 1-4pm Sun, free for diners). Function rooms (up to 50 capacity). Restaurant (available for private hire, up to 100 capacity).* **Map p279 Z7**.

Ladbroke Arms

54 Ladbroke Road, W11 3NW (7727 6648/ www.capitalpubcompany.com/ladbroke). Holland Park tube. **Open** 11am-11pm Mon-Sat; noon-10.30pm Sun. **Food served** noon-2.30pm, 7-9.30pm Mon-Fri; 12.30-3pm, 7-9.30pm Sat, Sun. **Credit** AmEx, MC, V. **Gastropub**
The Ladbroke is well known for its floral displays (the beer garden at the front is wildly colourful) and – until it turned into a gastropub – as the drinking den of choice for local coppers. The balance has shifted firmly towards food these days (with a smart dining section at the rear and a wine list to match) but it's still popular with low-key middle-aged locals who pop in for a pint (Doom Bar from Cornwall's Sharp's brewery, say, or Adnams Broadside) and who appreciate the well-upholstered, carpeted interior and the efficient air-conditioning. *Babies and children admitted (dining only). No piped music or jukebox. Tables outdoors (12, terrace).* **Map p279 A7**.

Kensington

Churchill Arms

119 Kensington Church Street, W8 7LN (7727 4242). Notting Hill Gate tube. **Open** 11am-11pm Mon-Wed; 11am-midnight Thur-Sat; noon-10.30pm Sun. **Food served** noon-10pm Mon-Sat; noon-9.30pm Sun. **Credit** AmEx, MC, V. **Pub**
Tales of Churchill's drinking are legion: and so, too, should be the words of praise to this pub. Demijohns and hurling sticks swing from the beams, along with the obligatory Churchill ephemera, and the feel is immediately welcoming: by day, with Thai food as an accompaniment, as by night. Two roaring fires aid the low lighting and help you to read the narrow if affordable wine list (it never goes

West

north of the £20 mark). There's Caffrey's and Guinness on tap, with Fuller's Discovery and Pride in attendance too. We saw no vermouth behind the bar (Churchill liked this in his martini), with Pol Roger (his favourite champagne) available instead. We reckon the great man would have been pleased.

Babies and children admitted (until 1pm). Games (quiz machine). No piped music or jukebox. Restaurant. TV (satellite).

Elephant & Castle

40 Holland Street, W8 4LT (7368 0901). High Street Kensington tube. **Open** 11am-11pm Mon-Sat; noon-10.30pm Sun. **Food served** noon-10pm daily. **Credit** MC, V. Pub

This corner pub, just off the main Kensington drag of Church Street, has a much lovelier, more clandestine feel than at first suggested by the two sides of opaque glass windows. Inside, the combination of drawing room red walls and dark wood help to tame the daylight to cosy effect. A snug back corner, adorned with historic front pages from the *Evening Standard* and *Daily Mail* (the papers' offices are just down the road) provides the best spot of all to enjoy the short if affordable wine list (a trademark of a Nicholson's house) and the beer and fish and

Windsor Castle. *See p108.*

West

chips (a house speciality). London Pride is on duty, with (on our visit) Timothy Taylor guesting. *Games (fruit machine). Tables outdoors (8, pavement). TVs.*

Kensington Arms
41 Abingdon Road, W8 6AH (7938 3841/ www.kensingtonarms.com). High Street Kensington tube. **Open** 11am-11pm Mon-Sat; noon-10.30pm Sun. **Food served** noon-10pm Mon-Sat; noon-9pm Sun. **Credit** MC, V.
Gastrobar
Never judge a book by its cover. The pubby exterior of the Kensington Arms, replete with swinging pub sign, gives way to a space more like a café-bar inside, all pale wood and brightness. The initial shock wears off pretty quickly, however. The lunch menu, affordable gastro fare from caesar salad at £6 to fish and chips or steak at just under a tenner, is a gem. Beer includes Spitfire on tap and Cornish ale, Sharp's Doom Bar (perhaps a nod to the bar's Cornish cousin the Mariner's Rock). The jaunty, colourful decor, including 1930s travel destination posters, ensures this is more than a standard-issue, pale-wood gastro-joint.
Babies and children welcome: high chairs. Disabled: toilet. Tables outdoors (2, pavement). TV (satellite).

Scarsdale
23A Edwardes Square, W8 6HE (7937 1811). Earl's Court or High Street Kensington tube. **Open** noon-11pm Mon-Sat; noon-10.30pm Sun. **Food served** noon-10pm Mon-Sat; noon-9.30pm Sun. **Credit** AmEx, MC, V. **Pub**
Just as French House (*see p69*) in Soho was General De Gaulle's haunt, this hostelry was designed to appeal to the officers of Napoleon Bonaparte. These days the clientele are more likely to be rugby players than hussars, and the big fellas are kept in shape by peerless steak sandwiches (£9.95), and healed on Sundays with what may well be the best bloody mary in the west (west London, that is). For everyday tippling, Pride rubs shoulders with Old Speckled Hen and Arundel Sussex Gold. The small wine list dominated, naturally, by the French boasts such gems as a St-Emilion at under £16. The decor, a mix of materials and textures, achieves the symphonic, rather than the cacophonous, in the high ceilinged space.
Babies and children admitted (in restaurant). Restaurant. Tables outdoors (8, garden). TV.

Windsor Castle
114 Campden Hill Road, W8 7AR (7243 9551/ www.windsorcastlepub.co.uk). Notting Hill Gate

tube. **Open** noon-11pm Mon-Sat; noon-10.30pm Sun. **Food served** noon-3pm, 6-10pm Mon-Fri; noon-10pm Sat; noon-9pm Sun. **Credit** AmEx, MC, V. **Pub**
The Windsor Castle is so cutely historic, with its set of small interconnected rooms, wood panelling and open fires, that it looks more like a film set than the hard-working local it actually is. Given that the pub could get by on looks alone, it's admirable that the food is reasonable (sausage and mash with onion gravy, steak and big chips) and the drinks varied. Ales on tap include London Pride and Timothy Taylor Landlord plus a guest beer; there are lots of lagers, and a better-than-average choice of wines. Clientele are generally as you'd expect given the postcode. One gripe – the loos could do with more care and attention. The final plus: there's a lovely garden too.
Babies and children admitted (until 9pm). Games (board games). No piped music or jukebox. Tables outdoors (20, garden; 2, pavement). **Map p279 A8.**

Ladbroke Grove

Crescent House NEW
41 Tavistock Crescent, W11 1AD (7727 9250). Westbourne Park tube. **Open** noon-11pm Mon-Sat; noon-10.30pm Sun. **Food served** noon-10pm Mon-Sat; noon-4.30pm Sun. **Credit** MC, V. **Bar/restaurant**
For review, *see p111*.
Babies and children admitted. Bar available for hire. Disabled: toilet. Restaurant (available for hire, 60 capacity). Tables outdoors (4, garden; 2, pavement). **Map p279 Z5.**

Fat Badger
310 Portobello Road, W10 5TA (8969 4500/ www.thefatbadger.com). Ladbroke Grove or Westbourne Park tube. **Open** noon-11pm Mon-Thur; 11am-midnight Fri, Sat; noon-10.30pm Sun. **Food served** noon-3pm, 6.30-10pm Mon-Fri; 11am-5pm, 6.30-11pm Sat; noon-5pm Sun. **Credit** AmEx, MC, V.
Gastropub
Nearer multicultural Golborne Road than hip Notting Hill (its spiritual home), this Victorian corner boozer is the product of a suitably frayed gastropub conversion: all scuffed wooden flooring and bashed up sofas. Pink wallpaper depicting street muggings leavens an otherwise gloomy interior. Upstairs is a smarter dining room, though the diverting menu (brunch dishes plus the likes of venison and prune stew) can be eaten in the bar – as can posh snacks. Staff might be eccentrically slow, but there's plenty

to drink: draught Leffe, Staropramen, Amstel; Addlestones cider and two ales (Greene King IPA and Timothy Taylor Landlord). All of which goes down a treat with the trustifarian, coupley, business clientele.
Babies and children admitted (until 8pm). Bar available for hire. Games (board games). Restaurant (available for hire, 50 capacity). Tables outdoors (3, terrace). TV (big screen). **Map p279 Z5**.

Ruby & Sequoia
6-8 All Saints Road, W11 1HH (7243 6363/ www.ruby.uk.com). Ladbroke Grove or Westbourne Park tube. **Open** 6pm-12.30am Mon-Thur; 6pm-2am Fri; 11am-2am Sat; 11am-12.30am Sun. **Credit** AmEx, MC, V.
Bar/restaurant
Set back from the Portobello Road action, Ruby & Sequoia's slick black frontage and tinted windows scream style and inside the gorgeous gold-flocked wallpaper and olive leather booths don't disappoint. Cocktails are the main draw and well-mixed classics like cosmopolitans and caipirinhas (£7 each) hit the spot. Edgy art covers the walls but watching the boho babes and their beautiful boyfriends proved much more fun on our visit. Funky staff clad in black linen were sparky if a little clumsy – a third of one martini ended up on the table – and an extensive wine list plus 1664 Blanc and San Miguel on tap caters for those who prefer their refreshment neither shaken nor stirred.
Babies and children admitted (restaurant until 6pm Sat, Sun). Bar available for hire (Mon-Fri). Disabled: toilet. Music (DJs 9pm Thur-Sat, 6pm Sun; free). Restaurant. Tables outdoors (2, pavement). **Map p279 Z5**.

Maida Vale

Bridge House
13 Westbourne Terrace Road, W2 6NG (7432 1361). Warwick Avenue tube/Paddington tube/rail. **Open** noon-11pm Mon-Thur; noon-11.30pm Fri, Sat; noon-10.30pm Sun. **Food served** noon-10pm Mon-Sat; noon-9.30pm Sun. **Credit** (over £5) AmEx, MC, V.
Comedy pub
In keeping with its co-occupant the Canal Café Theatre upstairs, there is an arty look and bohemian feel at this laid-back local. The crowd who drink here are mostly dressed-down, give or take the odd chiffon-scarfed student, and the staff are nicely imperturbable and unflustered. Theatrical touches include the velvet curtain concealing the toilet doors, beads hanging over some of the windows and the cabaret-style red lampshades over the bar. As well as a standard set of draught beers, including London Pride, Stella and Hoegaarden, there's a good selection of teas and coffees.
Babies and children admitted (before 7pm). Comedy (7.30pm & 9.30pm Mon-Sat; 7pm & 9pm Sun; phone to confirm times; £5-£9). Disabled: toilet. Games (board games). Tables outdoors (8, terrace).

E Bar
2 Warrington Crescent, W9 1ER (7432 8455/ www.theetoncollection.com/restaurants/ebar). Warwick Avenue tube. **Open** 5pm-midnight Tue-Fri; noon-midnight Sat; noon-11.30pm Sun. **Food served** 5-10.30pm Tue-Fri; noon-10.30pm Sat; noon-10pm Sun. **Credit** AmEx, MC, V. **Bar**
Despite its pleasantly polished feel, subterranean E Bar never seems overrun with customers. In fact, if you're looking for a place to chat in relative peace and quiet, as well as a guaranteed seat on a Friday or Saturday night, you could do worse than descend the glass-lined steps to this tapas bar and cocktail lounge (there's alfresco seating available at ground level). Cocktails are of a high standard, the soft seating is abundant and the tasty tapas selection extensive – just don't expect to fall in love with the place.
Babies and children admitted (until 6pm). Games (backgammon, chess). Music (pianist 8pm Wed; DJs 8pm Thur; free). Tables outdoors (14, terrace).

Idlewild **NEW**
55 Shirland Road, W9 2JD (7266 9198/ www.ruby.uk.com/idlewild). Warwick Avenue tube. **Open** noon-11.30pm Wed, Thur; noon-midnight Fri, Sat; noon-10.30pm Sun. **Food served** noon-4pm, 7-10.30pm Wed-Sun. **Credit** MC, V. **Gastropub**
This artistically designed joint attracts a well-turned-out crowd looking for a bit more of a night out than most of the other local drinking holes can provide. There's quite a buzz here at weekends, particularly in the upstairs cocktail lounge. Inspired by the aristocratic high fashions of the 1920s, with an injection of contemporary cool and original touches, such as the collection of framed butterflies and moths on the staircase wall, this restaurant-pub is stylish without being poncey. There's a good wine list, a standard selection of well-prepared cocktails and a few bottled and draught beers.
Babies and children admitted (restaurant only, until 6pm). Function room (80 capacity). Music (DJ, 9pm Fri, Sat; acoustic 6.30pm Sun; free). Restaurant. Tables outdoors (2, garden).

West

Prince Alfred & Formosa Dining Rooms

5A Formosa Street, W9 1EE (7286 3287).
Warwick Avenue tube. **Open** noon-11pm
daily. **Food served** noon-3pm, 6.30-10pm
Mon-Sat; noon-4pm, 7-10pm Sun. **Credit**
MC, V. Pub/restaurant

The layout of this beautifully preserved 19th-
century pub reflects the divisions of Victorian
society: a series of partitions around the
magnificent central bar creates separate snugs
originally intended to keep the classes and the
sexes apart. Nowadays, though you can move
between snugs via waist-height hatchways,
these cramped compartments can be a slightly
awkward environment for socialising. They're
best for small groups, but may deter late
arrivals who might feel they are intruding on a
private party. The locals haven't been deterred
from flocking here, however, many of them
coming for the excellent standard of cuisine in
the modern restaurant at the back. The menu's
not for dieters, though, being made up
predominantly of rich, tasty dishes like chicken
breast with potato dauphinoise (£14) and
braised shin of beef with horseradish mash
(£15.50). The thoughtfully underdone finish in
the simple raftered dining room provides a
contrast with the pub, where drinkers down
pints of Erdinger, Bombardier, Staropramen or
Peroni safe in their snugs.
Babies and children admitted. Disabled: toilet.
Restaurant (available for hire, 60 capacity).
Tables outdoors (3, pavement).

Skiddaw

46 Chippenham Road, W9 2AF (7432 1341).
Westbourne Park tube. **Open** noon-midnight
Mon-Sat; noon-10.30pm Sun. **Food served**
noon-10.30pm Mon-Sat; noon-9.30pm Sun.
Credit MC, V. Gastropub

The combination of the original elements of a
decorative and detailed Victorian pub with the
added comforts of a contemporary update has
been pulled off to great effect here. The seating
revolves around a striking and beautifully
crafted wood and glass central bar which
divides the place in two. There are enough
angles in the handsomely wood-panelled walls
to provide an inviting set of nooks and crannies,
including a coffee-table corner tucked away
behind the bar and, most invitingly, the cushion-
heavy Bedouin-style private cubbyhole at the
back. Continental lagers dominate the pumps,
including Hoegaarden, Früli, Amstel and Peroni,
and on the varied food menu, which has a hint
of an Arabic slant, there are good deals on cross-
continental meze dishes (four plates for £11).

Babies and children welcome (until 7pm):
high chairs. Bar available for hire. Games
(board games). Music (DJs 9pm Fri; free).
Quiz (8.30pm Tue; £2). Tables outdoors
(9, terrace).

Warrington

93 Warrington Crescent, W9 1EH (7286 2929/
www.gordonramsay.com). Maida Vale tube.
Open noon-1am daily. **Food served** noon-
2.30pm, 6-10pm Mon-Thur; noon-2.30pm,
6-10.30pm Fri, Sat; noon-4pm, 6-10pm Sun.
Credit AmEx, MC, V. Gastropub

They don't come much grander than the
Warrington and though this perfectly restored
19th-century pub is a sight to behold, having a
drink here can feel more like visiting a museum
than unwinding with a pint. The cavernous
ground floor bar, with regal marble columns
supporting sculpted concrete arches, is not
exactly intimate, and unless the place is full,
which during the week it often isn't, this ornate
monster tends to overwhelm as much as
impress. There's no denying its magnificence
though, dripping with lavish art nouveau
decoration, interior stained-glass windows, an
ornately embossed ceiling, a floral red and gold
carpet and a semi-circular bar topped by what
looks like the back of an old galleon, complete
with cherubs gazing down at the bar staff. The
building once operated as a hotel and has now
come under the ownership of Gordon Ramsey
who has installed a relatively formal restaurant
on the first floor where the light colours and
clean cut finish are in complete contrast with the
grandiloquence downstairs. Well worth a visit
but you wouldn't want it as your local.
Babies and children welcome: children's menu.
Function room (16 capacity). Restaurant.

Warwick Castle NEW

6 Warwick Place, W9 2PX (7266 0921).
Warwick Avenue tube. **Open** noon-11pm
Mon-Sat; noon-10.30pm Sun. **Food served**
noon-9pm daily. **Credit** MC, V. Pub

One of the more straightforward boozers in
Maida Vale. There's nothing trendy about the
Warwick Castle, no gimmicks or any particular
claims to fame. But it does boast a reliably laid-
back atmosphere and, most reassuringly, often
at least one lonely old bloke propping up the bar.
Given how upmarket the area is, the punters are
a surprisingly and pleasantly mixed lot who,
along with the tables and chairs huddled tightly
around the bar counter, help to create the cosy,
chatty vibe. The place is in good nick throughout
with polished wood and an old grandfather
clock on the wall. There are no great surprises,

Crescent House `NEW`

Crescent House is on the site of the former Mother Black Cap pub, built in the 18th century. The blackboard outside advertises Spitfire (though it was off on our visit), but what staff do best here are cocktails. Our bloody mary was bloody good, with cream of horseradish and port added to the rich tomato mix. And quince sour was an elegant, well-judged blend of lemon juice, vodka and quince jelly with fine strips of apple floating on top; it disappeared very quickly. Non-alcoholic options include a delicious fizz made by mingling house-made gooseberry coulis with fresh mint leaves and organic Cox's apple juice, then topping with soda. As for the bar menu, chips (wonderful) are cooked in duck fat and served with marinated onglet, a beef cut that's best hung long and cooked swiftly to guarantee tenderness. The poultry is a great success too. Own-made potted shrimps and duck rillettes are similarly impressive. Most customers head straight to the decked 'herb garden' at the rear, but with Tavistock Crescent lying just next to the Hammersmith & City line, conversation is punctuated by trains rattling by. Upstairs is a fancy restaurant overseen by Daniel Ostler, who also designed the winning bar menu. *For listings, see p108.*

West

except perhaps on the taps where the Cornish St Austell brewery makes an appearance alongside more familiar brands.
Babies and children admitted (until 9pm). Quiz (9pm Thur; £1). Tables outdoors (4, pavement). TVs.

Waterway

54 Formosa Street, W9 2JU (7266 3557/ www.thewaterway.co.uk). Warwick Avenue tube. **Open/food served** noon-11pm Mon-Sat; noon-10.30pm Sun. **Credit** AmEx, DC, MC, V. **Bar/restaurant**
Right on the canal path, in view of the longboats moored along the banks, the Waterway makes good use of its location, with a decent sized decked area out front. Inside, the bar, which is separate from the restaurant, has a sloping wood-panelled ceiling and a minimalist decor making it look a bit like a trendy Alpine ski-lodge. This vaguely continental vibe conjures up a taste for coffee as much as for beer, and you can order either, with a standard set of bottled and draught lagers, plus London Pride and Adnams on the hand pumps. The bouncer on the door, relatively uptight staff and well-dressed drinkers hint at sophistication but the fireplace and chilled music policy help keep the tone relaxed.
Babies and children welcome: high chairs. Restaurant. Tables outdoors (40, terrace).

Notting Hill

Castle

225 Portobello Road, W11 1LU (7221 7103). Ladbroke Grove tube. **Open** noon-midnight Mon-Fri, Sun; 11am-midnight Sat. **Food served** noon-10pm Mon-Sat; noon-9.30pm Sun. **Credit** MC, V. **Gastropub**
Formerly the Warwick Castle, this pub was a pool hall and rowdy drinking den for market traders, musos (Rough Trade is close by) and Irish and Caribbean locals. Now, it's a seriously tidied-up gastropub, all anchovy mayo, chicken chermoula skewers and – on Saturdays at least – full of tourists looking for 'that blue door' from *Notting Hill* (it used to be on the house opposite). The pub may have lost a lot of character but the food's good (including perfect chips), the prices reasonable and the staff charming. Beers on tap include Greene King IPA, Gales Swing Low, Erdinger, Staropramen and Hoegaarden. The wine list is long too. Shame about the loos though – they could do with an overhaul.
Babies and children admitted (lunchtime Mon-Fri). Music (open mic 7.30pm Wed; free). Tables outdoors (3, pavement). TV.
Map p279 Z5.

Earl of Lonsdale

277-281 Westbourne Grove, W11 2QA (7727 6335). Ladbroke Grove or Notting Hill Gate tube. **Open** noon-11pm Mon-Fri; 10am-11pm Sat; noon-10.30pm Sun. **Food served** noon-9pm daily. **Credit** (over £10) MC, V. **Pub**
Opinion among regulars was divided when this large Sam Smith's pub in the heart of Portobello underwent a complete refurbishment around three years ago. Ironically, the owners have returned the bar to its original Victorian design. The main room is split into a maze of interconnected snugs with low, gated doorways that require most adults to bend double. It's certainly different – something akin to a gentlemen's club for elves. But if that's all a bit too much, there's a large backroom with sofas, banquettes and two open fireplaces. We were sad to see the old conservatory go, but its demise means the attractive beer garden is now even larger. The Lonsdale's far cheaper than other pubs in the vicinity and feels like a proper neighbourhood boozer once the Saturday tourists have gone. All this and beautifully maintained loos too.
Babies and children admitted (lounge room until 8pm). Games (fruit machine, quiz machine). Quiz (8.30pm Tue; £2). Tables outdoors (16, garden). **Map p279 Z6.**

Eclipse

186 Kensington Park Road, W11 2ES (7792 2063/www.eclipse-ventures.com). Ladbroke Grove or Notting Hill Gate tube. **Open/food served** 5pm-midnight Mon-Fri; 11am-midnight Sat; 11am-10.30pm Sun. **Credit** AmEx, MC, V. **Cocktail bar**
One of a small (five-strong) chain, Eclipse is a quietly groovy little joint, with a recessed fake-coal fire, exposed brick walls, leather banquettes and huge copper-coloured low hanging lamps. Lounge music plays, staff are on the ball and the cocktails are good, and nicely priced at £6. A milano (Hendricks gin and Aperol shaken with lemon juice and fresh raspberries) and a black and blue (fresh blackberries and blueberries crushed with limes and raspberry vodka) went down very nicely, though the latter would be too sweet for some tastes. A list of 25 cocktails includes four non-alcoholic mixes. The only duff note? The ladies loo could do with some TLC.
Babies and children admitted (lunchtime Sat, Sun). Bar available for hire. **Map p279 Z6.**

Electric Brasserie

191 Portobello Road, W11 2ED (7908 9696/ www.the-electric.co.uk). Ladbroke Grove tube. **Open** 8am-12.30am Mon-Wed; 8am-1am

Thur-Sat; 8am-midnight Sun. **Food served** 8am-10pm Mon-Fri; 8am-5pm, 6-11pm Sat; 8am-5pm, 6-10pm Sun. **Credit** AmEx, DC, MC, V. Brasserie

Though only opened a few years ago, the Electric has a classic brasserie look – right down to the beautiful mosaic tiled floor and long zinc bar. There's a fine array of bottles behind the bar, a lengthy wine list (available by the glass, bottle and carafe), plus Guinness on tap. Most tables are laid for eating (food, cooked in an open kitchen, is quality stuff), but there are lots of stools along the bar and some tables at the front of the premises for drinking; these are great for people watching. Set into the wall, near these tables, is the smallest TV screen we've seen in a bar. *Babies and children welcome: high chairs. Disabled: toilet. Tables outdoors (8, pavement).* **Map p279 Z6**.

First Floor

186 Portobello Road, W11 1LA (7243 0072/ www.firstfloorportobello.com). Ladbroke Grove tube. **Open** noon-11pm Mon-Thur; 11am-midnight Fri, Sat; noon-10.30pm Sun. **Food served** noon-5pm, 7-10pm Tue-Thur; noon-5pm Fri-Sun. **Credit** MC, V. Bar/restaurant

Buzzing night and day, this is the Notting Hill mix at its best: the crowd are a cross-section of locals straight out of central casting; the big, high-ceilinged room is decorated in plum colours and Cole & Son's 'Woods' wallpaper; squishy sofas and ramshackle furniture encourage slacking. The bar can answer most drink needs (though real ale-heads should look elsewhere), with cocktails (a blackberry caipirinha, £6.50, went down a treat), Guinness, Kirin and Konig Ludwig on tap, bottled beer galore and a well-tended selection of single malts, rums and bourbons. There's a restaurant on the first floor, which means decent bar food along the lines of prosciutto with fig and buffalo mozzarella. *Babies and children admitted. Function rooms (up to 40 capacity). Restaurant (available for hire, 50 capacity). Tables outdoors (7, pavement).* **Map p279 Z6**.

Lonsdale ★

44-48 Lonsdale Road, W11 2DE (7727 4080/ www.thelonsdale.co.uk). Ladbroke Grove or Notting Hill Gate tube. **Open** 6pm-midnight Mon-Thur; 6pm-1am Fri, Sat; 6-11.30pm Sun. **Food served** 6-10.30pm daily. **Credit** AmEx, MC, V. Cocktail bar

The beautifully over-designed main lounge (there are two more bars on different floors) is in 1970s sci-funk style, with brass 'bubble' walls and red leather seating. Dick Bradsell, undisputed king

of the London mixologists, no longer tends bar here but his spirits live on. A whole chapter of the 18-page drinks menu pays homage to Bradsell classics, such as the Rose Petal martini (£8) or the Bramble (Bombay Sapphire, crème de mure, £7). The menu is a sweeping historical tour of England's love affair with the mixed drink, from claret cups to sangarees to sours. The bar staff here are proud of this heritage and it shows – not in arch haughtiness, but in a real desire to make sure you enjoy a great drink, be it a vintage classic or something from London's cocktail renaissance. *Babies and children admitted (until 8.30pm). Disabled: toilet. Function room (60 capacity). Magician (9pm Wed; free). Music (DJs 9pm Fri, Sat; 8pm Sun; free). Tables outdoors (5, terrace).* **Map 279 A6**.

Montgomery Place ★

31 Kensington Park Road, W11 2EU (7792 3921/www.montgomeryplace.co.uk). Ladbroke Grove tube. **Open** 5pm-midnight Mon-Fri, Sun; 2pm-midnight Sat. **Food served** 6-11pm daily. **Credit** AmEx, MC, V. Cocktail bar

A dark, slinky bar, with low lighting, black leather banquettes and glam staff. Any bar that takes its inspiration from the likes of the Rat Pack and Hemingway (with a soundtrack to match) is setting the standard pretty high, but the cocktails here pass with flying colours. A watermelon fizz was a fabulously long and refreshing non-alcoholic option, while a rio bravo (fresh ginger mashed with almond syrup and shaken with lime and Sagatiba Pura cachaça, plus a lick of orange, £8) sorted the men from the boys. Substantial snacks are also worth ordering. Staff may look trendier-than-thou but are friendly and professional. A class act. *Babies and children admitted (afternoon Sat). Music (percussion 8pm Sun; free). Tables outdoors (2, pavement).* **Map p279 Z6**.

Negozio Classica

83 Westbourne Grove, W11 2QA (7034 0005/ www.negozioclassica.co.uk). Ladbroke Grove or Notting Hill Gate tube. **Open/food served** noon-midnight Mon-Fri, Sun; 9am-midnight Sat. **Credit** AmEx, MC, V. Wine bar

This is a slice of buttoned-up Italy amid the bric-a-brac and occasional market stalls of Portobello Road – and the efficient staff manage to make it work. Lacquered wood, steel and spotless worktops set the sleek tone, with a few tables to sit by the front, or lean-back seating in the rear of the bar. People who fill these tend to be either wealthy Americans or visitors from the country of *La Dolce Vita*, trying the outstanding

West

coffee from a Faema espresso machine. Or there are plates such as thick slices of sweet, rich parma ham sitting amid rich, melting buffalo mozzarella and tiny figs. But Negozio specialises in the mouth-puckering, rose and tar flavours of Barolo too, with bottles lining the walls to take away, or a few available to sample if you stay. Borgogno's 2001 Riserva, or at less cost the same producer's 2005 Dolcetto d'Alba offer great drinking. Negozio Classica is uncompromisingly Italian, and all the better for it.

Babies and children admitted (until 6pm). Off-licence. Tables outdoors (2, pavement). **Map p279 Z6.**

Trailer Happiness

177 Portobello Road, W11 2DY (7727 2700/ www.trailerhappiness.com). Ladbroke Grove or Notting Hill Gate tube. **Open** 5-11pm Mon-Fri; 6-11pm Sat. **Food served** 5-10.30pm Tue-Fri; 6pm-10.30pm Sat. **Credit** AmEx, MC, V. **Bar**
Tongue in cheek decor matched with a serious attitude to booze sums up the approach here. The basement is a riot of oranges and browns, with '60s furniture, huge smoked-glass mirrors and Tretchiko prints all over the walls. The bar takes pride of place and glows with a huge array of backlit bottles (many of them rum). Clued-up staff mix tikis and other rum cocktails, plus a number of house favourites such as the luscious grapefruit julep (Wyborowa vodka shaken with pink grapefruit, lime and pomegranate juices and a drizzle of honey over crushed ice) and the zingy Stone Pole (Zubrówka bison grass vodka with fresh lime, apple and ginger juices, plus ginger beer). Cocktails start at £6.50, and can be accompanied by snacks ('TV dinners') such as Thai squid salad and jerk chicken sandwich. This is one bar that's definitely worth spending some time in.

Music (DJs 8pm Thur-Sat). Tables outdoors (4, pavement). **Map p279 Z6.**

Shepherd's Bush

Albertine ★

1 Wood Lane, W12 7DP (8743 9593). Shepherd's Bush tube. **Open** 10am-11pm Mon-Thur; 10am-midnight Fri; 6.30pm-midnight Sat. **Food served** noon-10.30pm Mon-Fri; 6.30-10.30pm Sat. **Credit** MC, V.
Wine bar
The vast Westfield shopping site that has popped up next door might have felled some, but Albertine, the 1980s-style wine bar next to Shepherd's Bush Green, has character where so many branded pâtisserie joints don't. Its core group of BBC regulars have helped. And the place has been given a paint job too, with shelving added for bottles to take away. Albertine

has tried to respond to the trend for the Italian enoteca-style all-in-one shop and bar. The result is a clear listing of both drink-in and drink-at-home prices under each bottle that shows how low the mark-ups are at Albertine. Food is regulation wine bar fare, with smoked mackerel pâté and french onion tart featuring prominently. But there's great drinking to be done here, in the shape of a 2004 Les Auzines 'Fleur de Garrigues' Corbières, 2003 Abadia Retuerta Sardon del Duero and 2004 Frederic Mabileau 'Les Rouillères' from the Loire – all lesser-known but outstanding regions. For price and consistency of choice, Albertine has one of the best lists in London.
Babies and children admitted. Function room (up to 40 capacity). Wine shop.

Anglesea Arms ★ HOT 50

35 Wingate Road, W6 0UR (8749 1291). Goldhawk Road or Ravenscourt Park tube. **Open** 11am-11pm Mon-Sat; noon-10.30pm Sun. **Food served** 12.30-2.45pm, 7-10.30pm Mon-Fri; 12.30-3pm, 7-10pm Sat; 12.30-3.30pm, 7-10pm Sun. **Credit** MC, V. **Gastropub**
Situated on pastel-perfect Wingate Road, just off the grimy Goldhawk Road, the Anglesea Arms is a west London gastro institution, with a solid turnover of well-heeled Brackenbury Village folk. The cosy main bar area is a stripped-down clutter of old wooden tables and chairs, plus a supremely comfortable pair of sofas in front of the open fire – the perfect spot to work your way through the impressive wine list. Further back is the rather cramped restaurant area, with the open kitchen to one side. The brief blackboard menu on the back wall is undeniably inventive, but prices are pretty steep and service can be slack – our side order was a no-show, despite repeated requests. There are a few covered tables at the front for summer lounging.
Babies and children welcome: high chairs. Tables outdoors (5, pavement).

Bush Bar & Grill

45A Goldhawk Road, W12 8QP (8746 2111/ www.bushbar.co.uk). Goldhawk Road tube. **Open/food served** noon-11pm Mon-Wed; noon-midnight Thur; noon-1am Fri, Sat; noon-4pm Sun. **Credit** AmEx, MC, V.
Bar/restaurant
Given its proximity to the Shepherd's Bush Empire, this cavernous bar/restaurant can be unnervingly quiet on weekday evenings. Perhaps it's the tucked away location down a bright alley off Goldhawk Road, or the ever-so-slightly dated industrial vibe, but the pre-gig crowd seems notable by its absence. A shame, really – the convivial banquette seating, spacious set up, fairy lights, large (and sheltered) outside area and

Idlewild. *See p109.*

West

super-friendly bar staff combine to make this a fantastic spot for a cocktail (ginger cosmopolitans, singapore slings and margaritas, all £7). Weekend nights see more action, as does the adjoining grill restaurant. *Babies and children welcome: high chairs. Booking advisable. Disabled: toilet. Function room (up to 80 capacity). Tables outdoors (16, patio).*

Crown & Sceptre

57 Melina Road, W12 9HY (8746 0060). Goldhawk Road or Shepherd's Bush tube. **Open** noon-11pm Mon-Thur, Sat; noon-midnight Fri; noon-10.30pm Sun. **Food served** noon-3pm, 6-9.45pm Mon-Fri; noon-9.45pm Sat; noon-8.45pm Sun. **Credit** AmEx, MC, V. Gastropub
Spacious and civilised, the Crown & Sceptre is a great place for lazy Sunday afternoon lunches, as much as for quiet Saturday night drinks. The food is excellent, and decently priced, and there's an inviting array of foreign beers, wines and spirits, and a large selection of whiskies. Regular draught ales are London Pride and Honey Dew, and different seasonal ales are offered throughout the year. Cocktails can also be prepared on demand, although none are advertised. Monthly fancy dress nights, movie nights and themed music nights mean occasional gear-shifts into a more hectic party environment, so it's probably best to ring up in advance if you're hoping for a relaxed evening with a few friends. *Babies and children welcome (until 7pm): high chairs. Disabled: toilet. Games (table football). Quiz (9pm Mon; £2). Tables outdoors (10, garden; 3, pavement). TV.*

Defectors Weld

170 Uxbridge Road, W12 8AA (8749 0008/ www.defectors-weld.com). Shepherd's Bush tube. **Open** noon-midnight Mon-Thur; noon-2am Fri, Sat; noon-11pm Sun. **Food served** noon-3pm, 5-10pm Mon-Thur; noon-3pm, 5pm-midnight Fri; noon-10pm Sat, Sun. **Credit** MC, V. Pub
This clamorous local, decked out in chic Gothic designs – ornately carved furniture, low-hanging crystal chandeliers, intricate art deco wallpaper – is situated right on the corner of bustling Shepherd's Bush Green. Drinks are fairly pricey, but there's a good range, with Amstel, Staropramen, Leffe, Franziskaner, Früli and London Pride on tap, as well as extensive cocktail and wine lists. The crowd isn't quite as trendy as the bar staff, and the average age of the clientele can't be much over 21, but for a

boisterous, boozy, feel-good night out you won't find a pub much better than this west of Soho. *Babies and children admitted (until 5pm). Disabled: toilet. Function room (up to 70 capacity). Games (board games). Music (acoustic 7.30pm Wed; DJs 8pm Thur, 9pm Fri, Sat, 3pm Sun; free).*

Goldhawk NEW

122-124 Goldhawk Road, W12 8HH (8576 6921). Goldhawk Road tube. **Open** noon-11pm Mon-Wed, Sun; noon-midnight Thur; noon-12.30am Fri, Sat. **Food served** noon-4pm, 5-10pm daily. **Credit** AmEx, MC, V. Pub
On a street festooned with Aussie tank-houses, the Goldhawk makes a fine escape from Setanta Sports and travelling talk. With leopard-skin lampshades, low-slung sofas, bead curtains and the odd chandelier, it flirts effectively with retro-kitsch. The beer's jolly good too: Küppers Kölsch and Budvar Dark line up alongside London Pride and Deuchars IPA on draught; chilled bottles include Erdinger Weissbier and Pacifico Clara. And as well as a bountiful back bar and wine list, there are freshly squeezed juices for abstainers. For entertainment there's regular live music, a cracking quiz, Monopoly, Scrabble and a small terrestrial telly. Food stretches to olives and dips, calamares, organic burgers and a Sunday roast. *Disabled: toilet. Games (board games). Music (acoustic 8pm Tue; free). Quiz (8.30pm Sun; £2). Tables outdoors (6, pavement). TVs.*

Havelock Tavern ★

57 Masbro Road, W14 0LS (7603 5374/ www.thehavelocktavern.co.uk). Hammersmith or Shepherd's Bush tube/Kensington (Olympia) tube/rail. **Open** 11am-11pm Mon-Sat; noon-10.30pm Sun. **Food served** 12.30-2.30pm, 7-10pm Mon-Sat; 12.30-3pm, 7-9.30pm Sun. **Credit** MC, V. Gastropub
The Havelock is very much a foodie pub. After a fire gutted the place a couple of years ago, it has since resurfaced pretty much intact, serving up some of the most reliable pub grub in west London, coupled with a decent selection of beers and a newly revamped wine list with a couple of fine Riojas and montepulcianos around the £15-£17 mark. If you want to eat, and you should if you can, it's best to arrive early (or late) to bag a table in the main bar area. The menu has shrunk a little in recent times but the food, chalked up on a blackboard, is as good as ever, and they now accept credit cards as well. Stand-out staples include chargrilled bavette steak and chips and deep-fried monkfish cheeks. There is a patio garden area out the back, which closes at 9.30pm.

West

Babies and children welcome: high chairs. Bookings not accepted. No piped music or jukebox. Tables outdoors (6, garden; 2, pavement).

Mulberry NEW

243 Goldhawk Road, W12 8EU (8748 0229). Ravenscourt Park tube. **Open/food served** 5.30-11pm Mon; noon-11pm Tue-Thur; noon-midnight Fri, Sat; noon-10.30pm Sun. **Credit** MC, V. Bar/restaurant

Formerly the Seven Stars Bar & Dining Room, the Mulberry has high ceilings, large windows and expansive floorspace which – along with a propensity for tall mirrors – can make it seem emptier than it is. But the staff are chatty and extremely friendly, and it's an easy place in which to feel comfortable. Beers on tap include Hoegaarden and Staropramen, and there are decent wine and cocktail lists, as well as a good range of whiskies and rums. Food is served, and although the menu isn't extensive, it's been carefully chosen and the quality is extremely good. An average main costs about £12, but sides and starters are fairly cheap.

Babies and children admitted. Disabled: toilet. Music (pianist evenings Tue-Thur, Sat, Sun; free). Quiz (8pm Mon; free). Tables outdoors (4 long tables, decking). TV (widescreen).

Westbourne Grove

Cow ★ HOT 50

89 Westbourne Park Road, W2 5QH (7221 0021/www.thecowlondon.co.uk). Royal Oak or Westbourne Park tube. **Open** noon-11pm Mon-Thur; noon-midnight Fri, Sat; noon-10.30pm Sun. **Food served** noon-3.30pm, 6-10.30pm Mon-Sat; noon-3.30pm, 6-10pm Sun. **Credit** MC, V. Gastropub

The chairs and tables lining the walls of Tom Conran's small pub are highly coveted, but priority in the larger rear section is given to diners who come for the excellent Irish oysters and other fruits de mer displayed on crushed ice in a glass cabinet on the bar. Still, a confidently stylish crowd of drinkers, happy to stand, gather close by the bar to enjoy pints of ESB, London Pride and the weekly-changing guest ale. Around ten wines are available by the glass and though the list is international, France is the clear favourite. Novelties such as the little-known French aperitif Byrrh, based on red wine and quinine, also make an appearance.

Babies and children admitted (lunch). Restaurant (available for hire, 32 capacity). Tables outdoors (2, pavement).
Map p279 B5.

Crazy Homies

127 Westbourne Park Road, W2 5QL (7727 6771/www.crazyhomieslondon.co.uk). Royal Oak or Westbourne Park tube. **Open** 6.30pm-midnight Mon-Fri; noon-midnight Sat, Sun. **Food served** 6.30-11pm Mon-Fri; noon-11.30pm Sat, Sun. **Credit** MC, V. Gastrobar

Tom Conran's take on the local taquería is hardly downtown Tijuana, but this Mexican themed bar has been packed out with gringos since opening in late 2004. Sleek, fashionable couples from the Westbourne barrio happily chomp down on a 'street food platter' that leaves little change from £40. Variously stuffed tortillas (around £7, main-course versions about £10) do an OK job of soaking up the tequila. There's also a selection of Mexican beers (including a crisp and refreshing wheat beer, Casta Triguera), and micheladas (here, a mix of Sol beer and lime juice in a salt-rimmed glass with a hint of chilli). The basement bar was once a shebeen frequented by Christine Keeler, Aloysius 'Lucky' Gordon and Stephen Ward.

Babies and children admitted. Bar available for hire. Function room (up to 40 capacity). Jukebox. Table outdoors (1, pavement).
Map p279 A5.

Prince Bonaparte

80 Chepstow Road, W2 5BE (7313 9491/ www.the-prince-bonaparte.co.uk). Notting Hill Gate or Royal Oak tube. **Open** noon-11pm Mon-Fri; 10am-11pm Sat; 10am-10.30pm Sun. **Food served** noon-10pm Mon-Fri; 10am-10pm Sat; 10am-9pm Sun. **Credit** AmEx, MC, V. Gastropub

This large, handsome pub went through a bad period when service left a lot to be desired. Those days seem to be over and on a recent Sunday lunchtime visit staff were both plentiful and friendly. There's funky-antique decor and a wood-panelled dining area. The menu is standard gastropub fare but the place is packed with diners all weekend and beyond. At the large horseshoe bar you'll find Timothy Taylor Landlord, London Pride, Leffe, Hoegaarden, Beck's Vier and three different fruit beers on tap. There are also plenty of bottled beers and a 50-strong wine list. For a real treat, splash out on the Torres Mas La Plana.

Art exhibitions. Babies and children admitted (until 6pm). Bar available for hire. Disabled: toilet. Restaurant (available for hire, 50 capacity). **Map p279 A5**.

Tiroler Hut

27 Westbourne Grove, W2 4UA (7727 3981/ www.tirolerhut.co.uk). Bayswater or Queensway

West

tube. **Open** 6.30pm-1am Tue-Sat; 6.30pm-midnight Sun. **Food served** 6.30pm-midnight Tue-Sat; 6.30-11pm Sun. **Credit** AmEx, DC, MC, V. **Bar/restaurant**
Since 1967, Joseph and his lederhosened lads and dirndled lasses have been providing a high-camp version of Austrian hospitality at this basement restaurant. You could easily miss the small street-level doorway, but photographs attest that Hugh Grant, David Walliams, Boris Becker, Elle McPherson and Kate Moss – plus countless stag nights and works parties – have descended those stairs before you. The bar itself is tiny and, disappointingly, has just one beer on tap – Dortmunder Union – although there are a couple of bottled wheat beers. But most people don't come here for the beer or the food; it's the floorshow of yodelling, cowbells and accordion-accompanied singalongs that keep the place packed out.
Babies and children admitted. Booking essential (restaurant). Entertainment (cowbell show 9pm Tue-Sun). Restaurant available for hire (60 capacity). **Map p279 B6**.

Westbourne

101 Westbourne Park Villas, W2 5ED (7221 1332/www.thewestbourne.com). Royal Oak or Westbourne Park tube. **Open** 5-11pm Mon; 11am-11pm Tue-Fri; noon-11pm Sat; noon-10.30pm Sun. **Food served** 7-10pm Mon; 12.30-3pm, 7-10pm Tue-Fri; 12.30-3.30pm, 7.30-10.30pm Sat; 12.30-3.30pm, 6.30-9.30pm Sun. **Credit** MC, V. **Gastropub**
Should you ever find the place empty, a quick gander at the magazine rack of this (usually rammed) bistrobar, gives a fair indication of the regular clientele: *Wallpaper**, *Elle Deco*, *Vogue*… But both staff and punters are friendlier and less pretentious than you might expect. The one big room has a bay of comfy sofas to the left of the zinc bar. Hoegaarden, Leffe, Staropramen and Beck's Vier are on tap, plus Timothy Taylor Landlord and guest ales (Daleside Gravesend Shrimpers on a recent visit). There's also a reasonable wine list to accompany the superior gastro menu. This changes twice a day and is big on seafood and organic British breeds. There's also a large terrace with lots of seating.
Babies and children admitted (until 7pm). Bar available for hire. Tables outdoors (14, terrace). Wi-Fi (free). **Map p279 B5**.

Westbourne Park

Grand Union
45 Woodfield Road, W9 2BA (7286 1886). Westbourne Park tube. **Open** noon-11pm Mon-Thur; noon-midnight Fri, Sat; noon-10.30pm Sun. **Food served** noon-10pm Mon-Sat; noon-9pm Sun. **Credit** AmEx, MC, V. **Pub**
Situated by a desolate stretch of the canal after which it's named, this Fuller's pub comes as something of a welcome surprise. The interior is both light and airy (lots of big windows, fresh flowers galore), but also cosy (fireside sofas and a snug bar down the spiral staircase). Staff are friendly and helpful in a laid-back, unfussy way. London Pride, Leffe and Hoegaarden are on tap. The excellent, if slightly pricey, menu changes daily and includes platters for sharing (we enjoyed the well-chosen charcuterie at £9). The pub's famous for its pies, and it is good to see the staff are still serving camel, despite Stella McCartney's protests. A fantastic canalside terrace has plentiful seating, though the view is chiefly of the bus garage and the occasional despondent duck picking its way around floating Sainsbury's bags. Summer barbecues and weekly film nights offer further attractions.
Babies and children admitted (until 6pm). Function room (60 capacity). Tables outdoors (20, canalside terrace). TVs. **Map p279 A4**.

Metropolitan
60 Great Western Road, W11 1AB (7229 9254/www.realpubs.co.uk). Westbourne Park tube. **Open** noon-11.30pm Mon-Thur; noon-midnight Fri, Sat; noon-10.30pm Sun. **Food served** noon-3.30pm, 6.30-10.30pm Mon-Fri; noon-10.30pm Sat; 1-9pm Sun. **Credit** MC, V. **Gastropub**
Summer or winter weekends see a young and boisterous crowd spilling out onto the pavement in front of the Met; some are smokers, others just taking a breather from the inevitable crush within. Despite its size, this place is so popular that you'll be lucky to get your hands on a table between Thursday and Sunday – unless you arrive early. It's a shame because the food is good – a spinach and asparagus soup was superbly flavoursome, garlicky squid beautifully cooked. Lunchtimes are the best time to sample the fare if you want to avoid the crowds who come for the DJs (5.30pm onwards on Sundays) and themed evenings (Tuesday nights support London buskers). There's a lounge bar upstairs, a small dining room (which can be hired), a roof terrace and a large beer 'garden'. The wine list is good and beers on tap include Adnams, Bombardier and Amstel.
Babies and children welcome (until 7pm): high chairs. Music (acoustic 7pm Tue; DJs 7pm Fri, Sat; 5.30pm Sun; free). Function rooms (up to 80 capacity). Tables outdoors (8, heated garden; 6, roof terrace). TV (big screen). **Map p279 A5**.

West

South West

South West

An afternoon on the King's Road's retail front line requires far greater sustenance than a bag of dry roasted could ever hope to provide. Good job then that Chelsea gives good gastropub – try the **Lots Road Pub & Dining Room** or the much-loved **Pig's Ear**. And it's not just Chelsea either: the **Brown Dog** in Barnes has a loyal local following as does Southfields' **Earl Spencer**. In fact, finding a boozer of the old school variety can prove a challenge; good examples include Barons Court's **Colton Arms**, the **Chelsea Potter**, Wimbledon's **Sultan** and Wandsworth's **Nightingale**. For quirky, oddball appeal head for the **Cat's Back** in Wandsworth; for real ales galore try Putney's **Bricklayer's Arms** or the **White Horse** in Parsons Green; and for swanky champagne swilling, pay **Amuse Bouche** a visit.

Barnes

Brown Dog ★ HOT 50
28 Cross Street, SW13 0AP (8392 2200/ www.thebrowndog.co.uk). Barnes Bridge rail. **Open** noon-11pm Mon-Sat; noon-10pm Sun. **Food served** noon-3pm, 7-10pm Mon-Fri; noon-4pm, 7-10pm Sat, Sun. **Credit** AmEx, MC, V. **Gastropub**
There's much to cherish about this gastropub tucked among the cute backstreet cottages on the border between Barnes and East Sheen. A handsome space by day, with its cream wood panelling and retro metal signs, it positively twinkles by night thanks to the warm wooden furniture, polished red ceiling and copper globe lamps above the central bar. The bar divides the smallish space into drinking and dining areas, and there's a back garden for summer lounging. It's upmarket but not stuffy, and the food can be very good (it was runner-up for Best Gastropub in the 2007 *Time Out* Eating & Drinking Awards). Expect seasonal ingredients and unfussy combinations, whether it's top-notch seafood, a lavish Sunday roast or comforting puds. Dogs (of any colour) are welcome. *Disabled: toilet. Dining room. Games (board games). Tables outdoors (11, garden).*

Bull's Head
373 Lonsdale Road, SW13 9PY (8876 5241/ www.thebullshead.com). Barnes Bridge rail. **Open** noon-midnight daily. **Food served** noon-3.30pm, 6-10.30pm daily. **Credit** AmEx, MC, V. **Pub**
People definitely don't come to the Bull's Head for the riverside garden (there isn't one) or the atmosphere (the big maroon and cream room with its imposing central bar is fairly soulless). They might come for the beer (it's a Young's pub) or the food (Nuay's Thai bistro in the former stables at the back is cheap and popular). But they certainly come for the music: this has been one of London's premier jazz venues since 1959. Coleman Hawkins, Shorty Rogers, Al Cohn, Ronnie Scott, Humphrey Lyttelton, Stan Tracey, Don Weller… anyone who's anyone in the modern jazz world has performed here at one time or another. There are gigs seven nights a week and on Sunday lunchtimes; you can't book and most tickets are a tenner or less. *Babies and children welcome (family area). Function room (10am-7pm Mon-Sat; 100 capacity). Games (board games). Music (jazz 8.30pm Mon-Sat; 1pm, 8.30pm Sun; £5-£15). TVs (big screen).*

Spencer Arms
237 Lower Richmond Road, SW15 1HJ (8788 0640/www.thespencerarms.co.uk). Putney Bridge tube. **Open** 10am-midnight daily. **Food served** noon-2.30pm, 6.30-10pm Mon-Fri; noon-3pm, 6.30-10pm Sat; noon-4pm, 6.30-9.45pm Sun. **Credit** MC, V. **Gastropub**
A drab exterior does this Putney Common boozer a disservice – the interior is far more lively and welcoming. A big, open-plan room curves around three sides of the central bar, and offers a convivial mix of seating at wooden tables and leather sofas. Beer and wine lovers are equally well catered for – draught ales include London Pride and Adnams Broadside, while the diligent wine list has a superb range by the glass. A daily changing menu offers a selection of solidly British recipes and ingredients. A perfect place to end up after a Sunday stroll by the river.

Babies and children welcome (until 9pm): children's menu; high chairs. Disabled: toilet. Games (board games). Music (jazz duo 9pm occasional Tue-Thur). Restaurant (available for hire, 150 capacity). Tables outdoors (8, pavement).

Sun Inn ★

7 Church Road, SW13 9HE (8876 5256). Barnes Bridge rail. **Open** 11am-11pm Mon-Wed, Sun; 11am-midnight Thur-Sat. **Food served** noon-10pm Mon-Thur; noon-11pm Fri, Sat; noon-9.30pm Sun. **Credit** AmEx, MC, V. **Pub**

The Sun's idyllic position across the road from Barnes's duck pond and village green, along with its sun-kissed front terrace, would be enough to bring in the crowds, but there's more. There are three real ales and Weston's organic cider on tap for the traditionalists, bottled beers such as Chimay, Duvel and Paulaner for the sophisticates, a 40-strong wine list for grape fans and even Dom Pérignon at £100 a bottle for the hedonists. The food's not quite up to gastropub standards, but the burgers, fish cakes and suchlike have wide appeal. Soft lighting and a cosy layout of nooks and crannies keep things intimate, and with occasional extras (beer festivals, gigs, sports nights), you've got a deservedly popular local. *Babies and children admitted (until 7pm). Tables outdoors (15, terrace).*

Ye White Hart

The Terrace, Riverside, SW13 0NR (8876 5177). Barnes Bridge rail. **Open** 11am-midnight daily. **Food served** 11am-10.30pm Mon-Sat; noon-10.30pm Sun. **Credit** MC, V. **Pub**

Just up the Thames from the Bull's Head, the White Hart is another big barn of a pub arranged around a central bar, but with a more homely atmosphere thanks to its dark wood decor, capacious chesterfields, fires and friendly local crowd. It's also got a riverside balcony and tables on the towpath, which get packed out in good weather and for the Boat Race – there's a fine view of the finishing stretch to Chiswick Bridge. Hearty pub grub with an international flavour (tempura and chilli squid alongside steak and mushroom pie and a proper Sunday roast) indicates its old-fashioned leanings, as do the well-kept Young's ales. Good sound-proofing keeps the traffic noise to a minimum. A no-nonsense spot, and all the better for it. *Function room (100 capacity). Games (fruit machines; poker 8pm Mon; £5). Music (jazz 8pm Sun, winter only; free). Quiz (8.30pm Thur; £1). Tables outdoors (6, balcony, riverside terrace; 8, garden; 12, towpath). TV (big screen, satellite).*

Barons Court

Colton Arms

187 Greyhound Road, W14 9SD (7385 6956). Barons Court tube. **Open** noon-3pm, 5.30-11.30pm Mon-Thur; noon-3pm, 5.30pm-midnight Fri; noon-4pm, 6.30pm-midnight Sat; noon-4pm, 6.30-11pm Sun. **Credit** MC, V. **Pub**

The Colton Arms is a prime example of an increasingly rare thing this side of the M25 – a proper boozer that time forgot. Which, depending on your outlook, might be just the sort of ale-soaked cubbyhole you've been thirsting for, or the last place you'd hope to find yourself on a Friday night (last time we did, there were only five of us in the place, including the dear old landlord). Fans can't get enough of its tiny, trinket-adorned front bar, dark oak furniture and gentle refusal to refurb. The effect is somewhere between a *Life on Mars* '70s time warp and 'Barons Court does bucolic' (signs above the toilets read 'wenches' and 'sires'). Come to sup on London Pride, Timothy Taylor Landlord and Old Speckled Hen, served up in dimpled beer mugs. There's also a garden out back that's perfect in summer and during June's Stella Artois Wimbledon warm-up at the so-close-you-can-hear-them-serve Queen's Club. *Children admitted (garden). Tables outdoors (4, garden). TV.*

Chelsea

Chelsea Potter

119 King's Road, SW3 4PL (7352 9479). Sloane Square tube, then 11, 22 bus. **Open** 11am-11pm Mon-Fri; 11am-midnight Sat; noon-10.30pm Sun. **Food served** 11am-9pm Mon-Sat; noon-9pm Sun. **Credit** AmEx, DC, MC, V. **Pub**

You could be forgiven for thinking the Potter – an unreconstructed boozer complete with heavy red upholstery and dark wood furniture – had been teleported on to this well heeled stretch of the King's Road from outer space by mischievous aliens. In fact, the one-room pub has been a local institution for decades and, rumour has it, was formerly patronised by the Rolling Stones. The corner location, tall stools and high windows make it a veritable bird hide for watching toffs going about their shopping; turn around and a world of cask ales, fish and chips (£6.99) and sport on the telly awaits. *Babies and children admitted (until 9pm). Games (fruit machines). Tables outdoors (5, pavement). TVs (satellite).* **Map p280 D5.**

Sun Inn. See p121.

Chelsea Ram

*32 Burnaby Street, SW10 0PL (7351 4008).
Earl's Court or Fulham Broadway tube, then
11, 22 bus.* **Open** 11am-11pm Mon-Sat;
noon-10.30pm Sun. **Food served** noon-3pm,
6.30-10pm Mon-Sat; noon-4pm, 6-9pm Sun.
Credit MC, V. **Pub**

Slightly off the beaten track, the Ram is an
attractive, well-run locals' haunt rather than a
destination venue. The familiar Young's
gastropub style – light greens and burgundies,
flickering candles, stripped floors, mix and
match wooden furniture – exploits the pretty
Victorian features such as arched windows,
fireplaces (kept crackling) and cornices, adding
a homely feel. Oldies who've been drinking their
Young's or Bombardier out of personalised
mugs for 20 years still do so with their dogs tied
to handbag hooks at the bar; families with kids
flock in at weekends, and match days bring a
sea of blue shirts. Friendly, dedicated staff serve
high-quality British food (smoked haddock and
cod fish cakes, Cumbrian ribeye steak, apple
crumble) at gastropub prices, alongside a good
selection of international beers on tap.
*Babies and children admitted. Function room
(20 capacity). Quiz (7.30pm 1st Mon of
mth; £1). Restaurant. Tables outdoors
(6, pavement). TV (big screen).*

Cooper's Arms

*87 Flood Street, SW3 5TB (7376 3120/
www.coopersarms.co.uk). Sloane Square tube,
then 11, 22 bus.* **Open** 11am-11pm Mon-Sat;
noon-10.30pm Sun. **Food served** 11am-10pm
Mon-Sat; noon-9pm Sun. **Credit** AmEx,
MC, V. **Gastropub**

Only a short hop from the retail chaos of the
King's Road, the Cooper's Arms is distant
enough in character and clientele from many of
the street's bars and pubs to be worth a short
detour – especially if you like low-key, subdued
surroundings. It's a favourite lunch spot and
evening local for SW3 office workers and old
school Chelsea veterans. The food doesn't justify
much of a journey, but for a pleasant evening
supping Young's ales or continental lagers
(Peroni, Leffe) under the watchful gaze of a
moose's head, the Cooper's really is the business.
*Babies and children welcome (children's
portions). Bar available for hire. Function
room (up to 60 capacity). TV.* **Map p280 D5**.

Cross Keys

*1 Lawrence Street, SW3 5NB (7349 9111/
www.thexkeys.co.uk). Sloane Square tube,
then 11, 22 bus.* **Open** noon-3pm, 7-11pm
Mon-Sat; noon-4pm, 7-10.30pm Sun. **Food**

South West

served noon-3pm, 7-10.30pm Mon-Sat; noon-4pm, 7-9.30pm Sun. **Credit** AmEx, MC, V.

Gastropub

The keys after which this historic Chelsea pub is named are those given to St Peter to gain entry to the Kingdom of Heaven, and with this in mind co-owner and designer Rudy Weller has created his own vision of a magical kingdom. Multicoloured glass mosaics, red velvet sofas, bejewelled candle holders, decorative mirrors and a profusion of fairy lights make an Aladdin's cave of the main bar; upstairs, past a giant gold unicorn's head, a private dining room and first floor gallery are even more outlandish. Despite its other-worldliness, the Keys draws a down-to-earth crowd, including many a bemused tourist, enjoying real ales (Theakston Best and Directors), the usual draught beers and a 28-strong wine list. In addition to the bar menu, a garden-themed conservatory restaurant serves indulgent dishes around a large tree.
Babies and children admitted. Function rooms (up to 100 capacity). Restaurant (available for hire, 70 capacity). TV. **Map p280 C6**.

Fox & Hounds

29 Passmore Street, SW1W 8HR (7730 6367). Sloane Square tube. **Open** 11am-11pm Mon-Sat; noon-10.30pm Sun. **Food served** 12.30-2.30pm Mon-Fri. **Credit** MC, V. **Pub**

This tiny piece of 'Little England' started life as one of the many front room pubs that flourished in the 19th century. Originally beer was served by the landlady through a hatch, but gradually the business overtook her living room and then kitchen – as the still-visible partitions reveal. Stepping into the diminutive bar still feels very much like entering someone's lounge, thanks to its compact cosiness, comfy old chesterfields, bookshelves, hunting-themed oil paintings and weatherworn regulars – many of whom are Chelsea Pensioners. It's now a Young's house; ales on offer include Young's Special and Winter Warmer and Wells Bombardier, complemented by a teensy wine list and reassuringly homely food (bangers and mash, £5.95) served on weekday lunchtimes.
Quiz (8pm last Sun of month; £1). **Map p280 E4**.

Lots Road Pub & Dining Room

114 Lots Road, SW10 0RJ (7352 6645/ www.lotsroadpub.com). Fulham Broadway tube, then 11 bus/Sloane Square tube, then 11, 19, 22 bus. **Open** 11am-11pm Mon-Sat; noon-10.30pm Sun. **Food served** noon-3pm, 6-10pm Mon-Fri; noon-4pm, 6-10pm Sat, Sun. **Credit** AmEx, MC, V. **Gastropub**

Set in a no-man's land near Chelsea Harbour, there's not much to look at from the large windows of this horseshoe-shaped corner pub – but the chefs at work behind the huge L-shaped bar that dominates the interior will monopolise your attention anyway. As the layout implies, food is the main focus here, and has an enviable reputation; on our last visit, poached haddock and spinach fish cake (£7) and roast pumpkin and rosemary risotto with truffle oil (£9.50) were worthy of double the price tag. High ceilings, neutral colours and hard surfaces make for a stylish if cold look; the odd battered church pew can't turn this über-gastropub into somewhere you'd feel particularly at ease just dropping into for a drink.
Babies and children welcome: high chairs. Disabled: toilet. Restaurant (available for hire, 35 capacity). Spirits and wine tastings (6pm Thur; free).

Orange Brewery

37-39 Pimlico Road, SW1W 8NE (7730 5984). Sloane Square tube. **Open** noon-11pm Mon-Fri; 11am-11pm Sat; noon-10.30pm Sun. **Food served** noon-8.30pm daily. **Credit** AmEx, DC, MC, V. **Pub**

Dating back to the 18th century, the Orange Brewery, regrettably, no longer makes its own beer in the basement, but reminders of its industrious past remain with brewing paraphernalia strewn across the maroon walls. Nowadays, the main draw of this slightly shabby boozer is its unpretentious feel and reasonable prices despite its location amid the organic delis and bespoke furniture shops of Pimlico Road. A glass of pinot grigio from the – conspicuously French-averse – wine list is a mere £3.20; a hearty plate of steak and chips can be had for just £6.99 in the more attractive, wood-panelled dining room next door.
Babies and children admitted (until 7.30pm, restaurant). Games (fruit machines, quiz machine). Restaurant (available for hire, 50 capacity). Tables outdoors (7, pavement). TV.

Phoenix

23 Smith Street, SW3 4EE (7730 9182/ www.geronimo-inns.co.uk). Sloane Square tube, then 11, 22 bus. **Open** 11am-11pm Mon-Sat; noon-10.30pm Sun. **Food served** noon-2.45pm, 7-9.45pm Mon-Fri; noon-3.30pm, 7-9.45pm Sat; noon-4pm Sun. **Credit** MC, V. **Gastropub**

Set in a quiet residential street off the King's Road, the Phoenix aspires to be a locals' hangout rather than a trendy Chelsea watering hole. The subsequent 'homely' theme seems to dictate a rather nauseating brown and orange palette stamped with vaguely rustic items including jars of apples, a lone shelf of books and the odd faded rug – all very much belied by the twinkly bar, light wood floor and arty black and white photography. Confused identity aside, the staff are extremely good-humoured, there are more than 20 wines by the glass (starting at just £3) and ales on tap include London Pride and Adnams. The large back dining room offers familiar pub dishes: chargrilled 28-day aged Herefordshire ribeye and chips (£14.50) or slow-roasted pork belly with mustard crackling (£12.50), for example. *Babies and children admitted. Dining room. Tables outdoors (7, patio). TV.* **Map p280 D4**.

Pig's Ear ★ HOT 50

35 Old Church Street, SW3 5BS (7352 2908/ www.thepigsear.co.uk). Sloane Square tube, then 11, 22 bus. **Open** 12.30-11pm Mon-Sat; 12.30-10.30pm Sun. **Food served** 12.30-3pm, 7-10pm Mon-Fri; 12.30-4pm, 7-10pm Sat; 12.30-4pm, 7-9.30pm Sun. **Credit** AmEx, MC, V. **Gastropub**

This much celebrated Chelsea success story proves that it is possible to transform a local boozer into something more refined without making a total pig's ear of it. The appeal lies partly in the characterful yet sympathetic decor – turquoise panelled walls, high red ceilings, beautiful mirrors and eccentric, Victoriana-style collectors' cases full of butterflies and crabs – which lends the place a relaxed, bohemian air. But the real star here is the food, served in an upstairs dining room and, from a more condensed menu, in the bar. Try such delights as hare and foie gras terrine (£8) or caramelised scallops in jerusalem artichoke purée (£18). Bona fide fried swine ears are thankfully no longer available as snacks, but the excellent Pig's Ear ale (from the Uley Brewery in Gloucestershire) is still on tap, along with Deuchars IPA, Kronenbourg and Guinness, in addition to an upmarket wine list. *Babies and children welcome: high chairs. Booking advisable (dining room). Games (board games). Restaurant (available for hire, 40 capacity).* **Map p280 C5**.

Earl's Court

King's Head

17 Hogarth Place, SW5 0QT (7244 5931). Earl's Court tube. **Open** noon-11pm Mon-Sat; noon-10.30pm Sun. **Food served** noon-9.45pm daily. **Credit** AmEx, MC, V. **Pub**

Hidden away down an alley a stone's throw from Earl's Court tube, this is a justly popular local. A sleek black-stone exterior hides an equally sleek interior: a buzzy, low-ceilinged space scattered with chesterfields and overseen by a beautiful old chandelier. A little alcove with vintage wallpaper provides a retro complement to the generally rather modern vibe. On the far side of the horseshoe bar, a smaller area offers views over a pretty little square. Only the Adnams was 'on' when we were last in, but you can usually expect the likes of Timothy Taylor, as well as continental beers such as Paulaner and Früli. Reliable bar grub ranges from wasabi snacks to top-notch sausages. *Disabled: toilet. Games (retro arcade machines). Quiz (8pm Mon; £2). TVs (big screen).*

Warwick Arms

160 Warwick Road, W14 8PS (7603 3560). Earl's Court or High Street Kensington tube. **Open** noon-midnight Mon-Sat; noon-11.30pm Sun. **Food served** noon-3pm, 5.30-11.30pm Mon-Fri; 5.30-11pm Sat; 5.30-10.30pm Sun. **Credit** MC, V. **Pub**

If location, location, location was a landlords' mantra rather than an estate agents', the Warwick would be in deep trouble – stuck on a god-awful stretch of road whose main point of interest is a branch of Homebase. Thankfully, it's considerably better than it needs to be given the lack of competing attractions. The brick interior is lit by nice old lights and decorated with a cornucopia of vintage knick-knacks and nicely burnished old wooden tables. Being a Fuller's pub, the pints themselves are good – London Pride, ESB, plus Adnams – as is the array of whiskies on proud display at the tiny bar. Wednesday nights offer 'Beat The Dice' (throw two sixes for an evening of free booze), but most evenings this is just a welcome spot surrounded by grimness. *Bar available for hire. Tables outdoors (6, pavement). TV.*

Fulham

Cock & Hen NEW

360 North End Road, SW6 1LY (7385 6021/www.cockandhenfulham.com). Fulham Broadway tube. **Open** noon-11.30pm Mon-Thur; noon-12.30am Fri; 11am-12.30am Sat; 11am-11pm Sun. **Food served** noon-10pm Mon-Fri; 11am-10pm Sat; 11am-9.30pm Sun. **Credit** MC, V. **Gastropub**

Perched on a busy road opposite a tiny church-backed green, this is one of the best watering

holes within staggering distance of the Broadway. As you'd expect in a place that makes its own (Bonobo), the beer is one good reason to visit – a changing mix of ales alongside more unusual offerings like extra stout and non-standard wheat beers. The space is eclectic too: stylish modern lights over the bar, a cosy wood-panelled section warmed by a crackling fire in winter, a raised area leading to a patio and a front area lent a modern vibe by pale paint and photos of famous drinkers from Burton to Best. Throw in table football, friendly staff and good vibes, and the appeal is obvious.
Babies and children admitted (until 6pm). Disabled: toilet. Games (table football). Tables outdoors (20, garden). TVs.

Mokssh

222-224 Fulham Road, SW10 9NB (7352 6548/www.mokssh.com). Fulham Broadway tube. **Open** noon-midnight Tue-Thur; noon-1am Fri, Sat; noon-10pm Sun. **Food served** noon-11pm Tue-Thur; noon-midnight Fri, Sat; noon-9.30pm Sun. **Credit** AmEx, DC, MC, V. **Cocktail bar**

Looking like the inside of a red boiled sweet, Mokssh might be a visual challenge for fans of Chelsea's blue-shirted footballers down the way at Stamford Bridge. Lovers of lip-tingling cocktails and tempting Indian tapas, however, will be happier. The bright pinks and reds of the decor light up a depressing stretch of Fulham Road, though some of the decorative touches tip into kitsch. If you're eating, maybe opt for one of the Indian lagers or a robust red, as the fiery Indian tapas (around a fiver each) zap any real appreciation of the flavoursome (lots of ginger and vanilla) cocktails.
Bar available for hire.

Parsons Green

Amuse Bouche ★

51 Parsons Green Lane, SW6 4JA (7371 8517/www.abcb.co.uk). Parsons Green tube. **Open** noon-11pm Mon, Sun; noon-midnight Tue-Thur; noon-1am Fri, Sat. **Food served** 4-10.30pm Mon-Fri; noon-10.30pm Sat, Sun. **Credit** AmEx, DC, MC, V. **Wine bar**

Once you've got used to the fact that this is a champagne bar full of chunky wood seating rather than chandeliers, the appeal of Amuse Bouche becomes clear. We're talking champagne quaffing splendour at non-intimidating prices. Staff will happily talk you through the range of bubbles, although the house champagne Jean-Noel Haton Brut NV over delivers at £5 a glass. For something a little more fancy, Ayala offers

yeasty complexity in its Brut NV, and its 1999 vintage has fantastic depth of flavour. Small, themed plates of food include little soup servings and cones of fish and chips. There's a new Amuse Bouche in Soho, with a younger, more up-for-it crowd, but this is just as good if you have celebration in mind.
Babies and children admitted. Function room (up to 75 capacity). Music (acoustic band, 7pm Sun; free). Tables outdoors (3, courtyard).

Aragon House

247 New King's Road, SW6 4XG (7731 7313/ www.aragonhouse.net). Parsons Green tube. **Open** 11am-11pm Mon-Fri; noon-11pm Sat; noon-10.30pm Sun. **Food served** noon-3pm, 6-10pm Mon-Fri; noon-9pm Sat, Sun. **Credit** AmEx, DC, MC, V. **Pub**

Aragon House is far more discreet than the better-known White Horse (*see p128*) on the opposite side of the Green. Only a small brass plaque indicates anything unusual might lurk behind the plain black front door of what looks like just another dark-brick posh period house. Step inside, though, and you enter a bohemian toff's rustic country retreat. Above a rose-coloured stone floor, pastel yellow walls are adorned with ornate mirrors, large oils and bits of dead deer. Chandeliers cast gentle light over slouchable chesterfields and sturdy chairs clustered around odd-shaped old tables. Interesting beers like Hogsback TEA and Deuchars IPA complement a short but well-chosen wine list and classic cocktails for around the £7 mark. A treasure.
Function rooms (up to 220 capacity). Tables outdoors (7, garden; 3, patio). TV (function room).

Establishment HOT 50

45-47 Parsons Green Lane, SW6 4HH (7384 2418/www.theestablishment.com). Parsons Green tube. **Open** 11am-midnight Mon-Sat; 11am-10.30pm Sun. **Food served** noon-10.30pm daily. **Credit** MC, V. **Pub**

Directly opposite Parsons Green tube, this is a place to stop too, whether for a snifter or a spot of nosh. Inside, clean-lined modernity comes with those all-important clever touches – beautiful giant knobbly glass lampshades, groovy geometric wallpaper, large canvases unexpectedly depicting classic tough guys from 1960s Caine to 1970s *Sweeney*. Though there are good bottled beers like St Peter's and Doom Bar, the drinks list majors on around 100 different wines, with an admirable 40 or so by the glass. There's a good spirits range too and an excellent, inventive bar menu ices the cake.

South West

Babies and children admitted (until 5pm).
Disabled: toilet. Function room (25 capacity).
Restaurant (available for hire, 55 capacity).
Tables outdoors (6, courtyard). TVs.

White Horse ★
1-3 Parsons Green, SW6 4UL (7736 2115/
www.whitehorsesw6.com). Parsons Green
tube. **Open** 9.30-am-11.30pm Mon-Wed, Sun;
9.30am-midnight Thur-Sat. **Food served**
10am-10.30pm daily. **Credit** AmEx, MC, V.
Pub

Ignore the 'Sloaney Pony' clichés and focus in on
what really counts at this stupendously popular
SW6 stalwart – a fantastic (and somewhat mind-
boggling) array of beers. There are 60 (count 'em)
available at any one time, including 30 on
draught, eight of which are cask ales (the likes of
Harveys Sussex Best, Adnams Broadside and a
rotating array of guests). There's always a cask
mild, stout and porter on offer too, so it'll come as
no surprise to hear that the pub hosts regular
beer festivals. Punters are a well-to-do and
decidedly loyal bunch (off-duty chinos and air-
kissing feature heavily) who flock in their droves
to indulge in quality trad pub grub (fish and
chips, sausage and mash), legendary barbecues
on summer evenings and weekends or hearty
Sunday roasts (£13.75) washed down with a pint
(or three – well, it'd be rude not to).
Babies and children admitted. Disabled: toilet.
Function room (up to 90 capacity). No piped
music or jukebox. Restaurant. Tables outdoors
(30, garden).

Putney

Bricklayer's Arms ★ NEW HOT 50
32 Waterman Street, SW15 1DD (8789
0222/www.bricklayers-arms.co.uk). Putney
Bridge tube/Putney rail. **Open** noon-11pm
Mon-Sat; noon-10.30pm Sun. **Food served**
5-10pm Mon-Sat; 1-5pm, 5-10pm Sun. **Credit**
MC, V. Pub

Set back from the Thames close to where the Boat
Race begins, tucked down an unprepossessing
cul-de-sac opposite a red-brick housing estate, is
a plain and staggeringly simple pub, which hails
real ale with gusto and shows little
consideration for anything else. Dating back to
1826, the oldest boozer in Putney has bona-fide
bric-a-brac adorning the walls, wobbly pine
tables on a threadbare floor and a real coal fire
rumbling away beneath a pair of headless
antlers. An incongruous annexe has a disco
mirror, chairs drenched in tapestry and a
raftered roof shaped like an upturned boat.
Design-schizophrenia continues outside with an

L-shaped terrace decked in wrought-iron
furniture. The entertainment options are few
(television, bar skittles or shove ha'penny), which
means you shouldn't be distracted from the real
task at hand: drinking. Named 'Greater London
Pub of the Year 2007' by CAMRA, this is the sole
London pub to serve Taylor's lesser-known gems
on hand-pull: Golden Pride, Dark Mild, Ram Tam
and Best Bitter. The regulars are beer boffins, flat-
capped proprietors of free bus passes and clued-
up locals who can keep a secret. Fulham footy
fans pop in during match days.
Babies and children admitted (until 7pm).
Games (shove ha'penny, bar skittles). Tables
outdoors (7, garden). TVs.

Half Moon
93 Lower Richmond Road, SW15 1EU
(8780 9383/www.halfmoon.co.uk). Putney
Bridge tube/Putney rail. **Open** 4pm-midnight
Mon; noon-midnight Tue-Sat; noon-11pm Sun.
Food served 4-10pm Tue-Thur; noon-9pm
Fri-Sun. **Credit** MC, V. Pub

This great Young's pub has been putting on live
music since the early 1960s – as pictures of the
great, the good and the hirsute of folk, blues and
rock (the Rolling Stones, Dr John, U2) that cover
the walls testify – but a recent refurb has
touched up the sepia-stained ceiling and cream-
and-terracotta walls. Although better known
bands sell out well in advance, the intimate, 200-
capacity music room was only half full on a
recent visit. The gig clientele is swelled by a core
of locals who drop in for just a drink and maybe
a game of pool. Food can be ordered in from a
local Lebanese restaurant.
Bar available for hire. Games (board games,
pool). Music (bands 8.30pm nightly; from
£2.50; jazz 2-5pm Sun; free). Tables outdoors
(8, garden). TV.

Normanby ★ NEW
231 Putney Bridge Road, SW15 2PU (8874
1555/www.thenormanby.co.uk). Putney Bridge
tube/Putney rail. **Open** 11am-11pm Mon-
Thur; 11am-midnight Fri; 10am-midnight Sat;
10am-11pm Sun. **Food served** 11am-10pm
Mon-Fri; 10am-10pm Sat, Sun. **Credit** AmEx,
MC, V. Pub/brasserie

The high-contrast blond, yellow and black
design at the Normanby has the air of a swish
modern brasserie, but the awnings, corner
plasma TV and Adnams Broadside on tap say
'pub'. However, the unusual layout – virtually
S-shaped – means the rear section, done up like
a proper dining room, is more secluded. When
we popped in for Saturday brunch soon after
opening, the place was almost deserted. The fact

Nightingale. *See p131.*

that it still felt welcoming is testament to warm design and an intelligent layout, while the keenly priced mains really impressed (especially a huge hunk of beer-braised lamb with potato gratin). It surely won't stay quiet for long. *Babies and children welcome (until 7pm): high chairs. Disabled: toilet. Games (board games). Restaurant. Tables outdoors (4, garden). TVs.*

Prince of Wales ★ NEW
138 Upper Richmond Road, SW15 2SP (8788 1552/www.princeofwalesputney.co.uk). East Putney tube/Putney rail. **Open** noon-11pm Mon-midnight Thur-Sat; noon-10.30pm Sun. **Food served** noon-3pm, 6-10pm Tue-Fri; noon-4pm, 6-10pm Sat; noon-4pm, 7-10pm Sun. **Credit** MC, V. **Gastropub**
Once a tired old boozer, the Prince has had a generous gastro makeover that has made it a real player. The pub section is smart and cosy, with verdant high-gloss walls and ceiling and pewter tankards hung on little hooks, most of them allocated to specific regular punters. At the bar, chatty staff pull pints of Black Sheep and London Pride or serve superior bar snacks (pork and black pudding sausage roll). The unusual glass-ceilinged restaurant, offering a confidently short menu of mostly delightful modern British food, is separated from the pub by drapes. *Babies and children welcome: high chairs. Quiz (7pm Sun; £1). Restaurant (available for hire, 40 capacity). Tables outdoors (6, pavement). TV.*

Putney Station
94-98 Upper Richmond Road, SW15 2SP (8780 0242/www.brinkleys.com). East Putney tube. **Open** noon-11pm Mon; noon-midnight Tue-Fri; 11am-midnight Sat; 11am-11pm Sun. **Food served** noon-11pm Mon; noon-11.30pm Tue-Fri; 11am-11.30pm Sat; 11am-11pm Sun. **Credit** AmEx, MC, V. **Wine bar**
You would expect this light and spacious bar, ideally located opposite East Putney station, to be packed each evening, but we've never found it to be so. The restaurant always seems quiet, but with everyone seeming to congregate in the rectangular front bar there's a convivial atmosphere. Friendly bar staff dispense cocktails from a list of ten, and the wine list is varied and reasonably priced; draught beer is limited to Peroni. The light wood, chrome and venetian blinds that hang in large, plate-glass windows running the length of the modern frontage give the place a 1990s feel. *Babies and children welcome: high chairs. Disabled: toilet. Function room (70 capacity). Tables outdoors (3, pavement; 13, garden).*

Wandsworth

Alma
499 Old York Road, SW18 1TF (8870 2537/ www.thealma.co.uk). Wandsworth Town rail. **Open** 11am-midnight Mon-Sat; noon-11pm Sun. **Food served** noon-4pm, 6-10.30pm Mon-Sat; noon-9.30pm Sun. **Credit** AmEx, MC, V. **Pub**
Leaving Wandsworth Town station, you can't miss the fine Victorian pub opposite, with its impressive green-tiled frontage and large second-floor turret. Many original features, including lovely hand-painted mirrors depicting wetland scenes, antique carved wood and large mounted mosaics, have also been retained inside this popular local. The large, circular, central bar is often frantic, but bar staff remain affable while tending to the after-work crowd or thirsty rugger fans, serving the usual Young's ales, alongside Hoegaarden and Peroni. Decorated in rustic style and dishing up proper, grown-up food, the light and airy restaurant at the rear looks out on to a colourful courtyard. *Babies and children welcome. Disabled: toilet. Function room (up to 80 capacity). TV.* **Map p283 B2**.

Cat's Back ★
86-88 Point Pleasant, SW18 1NN (8877 0818). East Putney tube/Wandsworth Town rail. **Open** 11am-midnight Mon-Thur, Sun; 11am-2am Fri, Sat. **Food served** 11am-10.30pm Mon-Fri; 11am-10.30pm Sat; 1-4pm Sun. **Credit** AmEx, MC, V. **Pub**
Row upon row of luxury riverside apartments don't prepare you for this oddball gem, named after the owner's cat, which – the story goes – calmly strolled in through the door having been missing for a month. All manner of knick-knacks are scattered around inside, creating a uniquely cosy atmosphere: there's an old Calypso fruit machine, at which one pull costs the princely sum of 1d (old currency), Barbie dolls in glass cases and golliwogs in wooden boxes. The dark red walls are covered in celebrity B&Ws and watercolours, with a pair of resident artists happily painting away the day in a corner. On our most recent visit, the outside seating for smokers was a barber's chair – it could just as easily have been a Victorian dentist's chair with head clamp, since the furniture changes in regular rotation. Built in 1865, this über-friendly local avoided becoming another flatpack new build only because of the owner's determination to preserve it as a pub; the international clientele that packs in here, a good representation of the variety of modern

South West

London life, seem appropriately grateful. If you're feeling in need of some decent entertainment, the live sessions vary from jazz to West African music. The beer, meanwhile, ranges from Sundancer and Queen Bee to Edelweiss.
Babies and children admitted. Disabled: toilet. Function room (30 capacity). Music (alternate Thur & Sat). Tables outdoors (2, pavement).

East Hill
21 Alma Road, SW18 1AA (8874 1833/ www.geronimo-inns.co.uk). Wandsworth Town rail. **Open** noon-11pm Mon-Wed; noon-midnight Thur-Sat; noon-10.30pm Sun. **Food served** noon-3pm, 6-10pm Mon-Fri; noon-10.30pm Sat; noon-4pm, 6-9pm Sun. **Credit** AmEx, MC, V. **Gastropub**
A brisk walk uphill from the station takes you to this backstreet Victorian gastropub conversion. The somewhat clichéd rustic kitchen decor is enlivened by a bar that looks like a set of cupboards. Cheery staff dispense good pints of Scrum Down! from Twickenham Fine Ales, and Hogs Back TEA. A mishmash of wooden tables and chairs, large antique rugs and bookcases keep the atmosphere informal. The smart young post-work crowd enjoy modern British cuisine in the adjoining restaurant room, or quaff quality wines from a well-chosen list.
Babies and children admitted. Games (board games). Quiz (8pm Sun; £1). Tables outdoors (4, paved area). TVs (satellite). **Map p283 B2**.

Nightingale ★
97 Nightingale Lane, SW12 8NX (8673 1637). Clapham South tube/Wandsworth Common rail. **Open** 11am-midnight Mon-Sat; noon-midnight Sun. **Food served** noon-10pm daily. **Credit** AmEx, DC, MC, V. **Pub**
One of the few pubs round these parts to have resisted the ubiquitous gastropub makeover, the Nightingale is a great community local. Witness the prodigious fundraising activities and home-produced newsletter. Built in 1853 by Thomas Wallis, it features green and brown glazed tiles and hanging baskets that front on to an attractive cobblestone street. The decor within is as boisterous and homely as the atmosphere, with the battle between patterned carpets and reupholstered tartan banquettes mollified by the warmth of a modern open fire. Smart and accommodating bar staff serve excellent pints of Young's Special and Bitter or Well's Bombardier to a harmonious mixture of cheery locals, businessmen and doting couples.
Babies and children admitted (until 9pm). Games (board games, darts, fruit machine, quiz machine). Tables outdoors (12, garden). TV.

Ship ★
41 Jew's Row, SW18 1TB (8870 9667). Wandsworth Town rail. **Open** 11am-11pm Mon-Wed; 11am-midnight Thur-Sat; noon-11pm Sun. **Food served** noon-4pm, 6-10.30pm Mon-Sat; noon-5pm, 7-10pm Sun. **Credit** AmEx, DC, MC, V. **Gastropub**
This great Young's local, founded as a waterman's inn around 1786, shines like a riverside beacon. The peaceful and relaxing front bar is ideal for reading or quiet conversation, whereas the much larger conservatory by the Thames attracts a lively mixed crowd, which means seats are always at a premium; an excellent garden overlooks Wandsworth Bridge. The pleasant dining room serves an ambitious seasonal menu that comes – like the list of entertainment (including an informal Irish session on Tuesdays) – printed on a surreal image of a sea captain with a ship for his head and fish for his hands.
Babies and children admitted (until 7pm). Function room (16 capacity). Music (traditional Irish 8.30pm Tue, pop/acoustic duos 8.30pm Sun; free). Quiz (8.30pm Wed, £1). Tables outdoors (30, riverside garden). **Map p283 B1**.

Waterfront NEW
Baltimore House, Juniper Drive, SW18 1TZ (7228 4297/www.waterfrontlondon.co.uk). Wandsworth Town rail/295 bus. **Open** 11am-midnight Mon-Sat; 11am-11pm Sun. **Food served** 11am-10pm daily. **Credit** AmEx, MC, V. **Gastropub**
You have to walk around some rather soulless luxury developments to get to this huge, Young's gastropub. Inside, it feels more like a bar than a pub, decorated as it is in a mishmash of modern styles: floor-to-ceiling windows; chandeliers; centrepiece leather booths; tables of various shapes; numerous outdoor benches overlooking an unlovely stretch of the Thames. The charming staff fill time between punters by diligently polishing the optics behind a central bar that was serving on hand-pump only Young's Bitter of the brewery's many fine beers (there are a few more by the bottle). The wine list is reasonably priced, with a peachy Domaine Condamine L'Evêque viognier coming in at £17. The food (sharing platters, from £12; smoked haddock fish cakes, £10.95; marinated pork loin with puy lentils, £12.95) is of a good standard too.
Babies and children admitted. Bar available for hire. Disabled: toilet. Restaurant (available for hire, 100 capacity). Tables outdoors (20, riverside terrace). TVs (satellite). **Map p283 B1**.

South West

Wimbledon

Alexandra

33 Wimbledon Hill Road, SW19 7NE (8947 7691). Wimbledon tube/rail. **Open** *Pub* 10am-11pm Mon-Wed; 10am-midnight Thur; 10am-1am Fri, Sat; noon-11pm Sun. *Wine bar* noon-11pm Mon-Wed; noon-midnight Thur; noon-1am Fri, Sat; noon-11pm Sun. **Food served** noon-3pm, 6-9.30pm Mon-Thur; noon-9.30pm Sat; noon-7pm Sun. **Credit** AmEx, DC, MC, V. **Pub/wine bar**

Proximity to the station and an earnest attempt to appeal both to young smarty-pants and to bitter-swilling crossword lovers make this one of the better options in an otherwise bland shopping area. Built in 1874, this spacious Young's venue is a pub proper at the front, with a bar to one side and a trendy wine bar area at the rear; the otherwise excellent roof terrace overlooks a busy main road. The pub bit does brisk – occasionally raucous, especially during sporting events – trade during the day, with the wine bar taking most of the strain come nightfall. Young's ales are supplemented on tap by Staropramen and Heineken, while the wine list is well priced (Crystal Brook shiraz, £13.50). *Disabled: toilet (wine bar). Games (fruit machine, quiz machine). Music (rock covers band 9.30pm Fri, last Sat of mth; free). Tables outdoors (15, roof garden; 6, pavement). TVs (big screen).*

Crooked Billet

14-15 Crooked Billet, SW19 4RQ (8946 4942). Wimbledon tube/rail. **Open** 11am-11pm Mon-Sat; noon-10.30pm Sun. **Food served** noon-3pm, 6-10pm Mon-Fri; noon-10pm Sat; noon-9pm Sun. **Credit** MC, V. **Pub**

Located in picturesque Wimbledon village, this appealing local has a friendly, country pub feel, whether you're sitting by the open fire in winter or spending a summer afternoon on the lush patch of green outside (shared with the pub next door). Built in 1776, the Crooked Billet was purchased by Young's in 1888 and the interior has ancient oak beams and walls of bare brick or wood panels, adorned with old paintings and football memorabilia. Well-heeled locals and dog walkers are cheered up with well-kept Young's ales and a great pint of Erdinger Weiss. Keep your wits about you: a ghostly Irishwoman allegedly haunts the cellar. *Babies and children welcome (until 9pm): high chairs. Quiz (8pm Mon; £1). Restaurant (available for hire, 65 capacity). Tables outdoors (5, patio). TV.*

Dog & Fox

24 High Street, SW19 5EA (8946 6565/ www.dogandfoxpub.com). Wimbledon tube/rail/93, 493 bus. **Open** 11am-11pm Mon-Sat; noon-10.30pm Sun. **Food served** noon-10.30pm Mon-Sat; noon-10pm Sun. **Credit** AmEx, DC, MC, V. **Pub**

Sultan ★ HOT 50

In south Wimbledon's backstreets lies this ale drinker's nirvana, named after the famed 1830s racehorse. A much-loved locals' boozer, the Sultan is the only London pub owned by Wiltshire's Hop Back Brewery; on the weekly beer club evenings, chattering middle-aged locals enjoy the delights of GFB, Entire Stout, Summer Lightning and Quad Hop for the princely sum of just £1.90 a pint (carryouts are also available). The saloon bar is named after the beer-loving Ted Higgins, an actor from the original cast of Radio 4's *The Archers*; a smaller public bar shares its decor of cream walls and green panelling. There are also five cosy little open fires dotted about the place. There's a weekly quiz and the dartboard sees enthusiastic use: the patrons' many successes are celebrated with a trophy case full of little silver darts.
For listings, see p134.

This landmark Georgian pub in the heart of Wimbledon village had most remnants of its past eradicated by an extensive makeover at the end of 2006. However, the current interior lends itself nicely to the smart set that drift in from the All England Lawn Tennis Club, just down the road. The main bar is full of elaborate lampshades, leather armchairs and potted plants, but it's the spacious adjoining restaurant that catches the eye with its lofty arches and chandeliers. There's decent entertainment on offer too, in the shape of a very popular Sunday quiz and boisterous Tuesday salsa classes. At the bar, the expected Young's ales are ably backed up by Erdinger, Leffe and Peroni.
Babies and children welcome (until 9pm): high chairs. Dance classes (salsa 7.45pm Tue). Quiz (7.30pm Sun, £2). Restaurant. TV.

Earl Spencer ★

260-262 Merton Road, SW18 5JL (8870 9244/www.theearlspencer.co.uk). Southfields tube. **Open** 11am-11pm Mon-Thur; 11am-midnight Fri, Sat; noon-10.30pm Sun. **Food served** 12.30-2.30pm, 7-10pm Mon-Sat; 12.30-3pm, 7-9.30pm Sun. **Credit** AmEx, MC, V. **Gastropub**

It's obvious that there's a heavy emphasis on food at this inviting Southfields gastropub as soon as you enter and spot the baskets of fresh bread on the bar, shelf packed with cookery books and jars of colourful pickled savouries lined up along the top of the wine rack. Indeed, all the seating is at rustic farmhouse dining tables of various sizes. Yet the proprietors have managed to retain a sense of proper pub in their impressive Edwardian premises, helped by traditional decor, open fireplaces and a great selection of over a dozen beers on tap. On our most recent visit, ales from Hook Norton, Timothy Taylor, Sharp's and Fuller's breweries were on offer beside Hoegaarden and Staropramen. The wine list offers half a dozen of each colour by the glass, including a Navaran cava at £3.40. The food, on a daily changing menu, is not only top notch, but reasonably priced: you might find deep-fried parmesan with cauliflower and mozzarella fritters at £5.50, a bowl of steamed mussels for £7 or an Earl beefburger at £9.50.
Babies and children welcome: high chairs; children's portions. Function room (up to 90 capacity). No piped music or jukebox. Tables outdoors (10, patio). TVs.

Fire Stables

27-29 Church Road, SW19 5DQ (8946 3197). Wimbledon tube/rail then 93, 200, 493 bus. **Open** 11am-11pm Mon-Sat; noon-10.30pm Sun. **Food served** noon-4pm, 6-10.30pm Mon-Sat; noon-4pm, 6-10pm Sun. **Credit** AmEx, MC, V. **Gastropub**

This is one of Wimbledon village's most stylish gastropubs, with quality food served in either

South West

the slouchy minimal front area or the swish, contemporary restaurant section at the rear. The service is friendly, appealing to the mixed-age clientele who come for casual dining. The main bar area has a high ceiling and bare-brick walls decorated with a massive piece of modern art, which can be admired by candlelight from the battered leather sofas. There are a few decent light beers, among them Leffe, Peroni and Kronenbourg Blanc, but the 40-strong wine list is better: an eclectic mix, running from a Montepulciano Abruzzo (£12.70) to a Château Batailley 1999, Grand Cru Classé, Pauillac (£60).

Babies and children admitted. Disabled: toilet. Restaurant (available for hire, 120 capacity).

Fox & Grapes

9 Camp Road, SW19 4UN (8946 5599/ www.massivepub.com). Wimbledon tube/rail. **Open** 11am-11pm Mon-Thur; 11am-midnight Fri, Sat; noon-10.30pm Sun. **Food served** noon-3pm, 6.30-10pm Mon-Thur; noon-10pm Fri-Sun. **Credit** AmEx, MC, V. **Pub**
On the western edge of Wimbledon Common, this popular locals' pub started life as a gin and tea shop in 1787. On one side Caesar's Bar (Julius had a fort down the road) is cosy, with a low ceiling supported by large oak pillars; the other bar is a roomier affair, with a high ceiling of black wooden beams – it used to be a stable, where Dick Turpin apparently once lodged Black Bess. The place can get very busy at times, with legions of dog walkers chattering over the piped jazz, especially in warmer months. The choice of ales provides a good alternative to the dominance of Young's in the area, including Sharp's Doom Bar, Greene King IPA, Courage Directors and Timothy Taylor Landlord.

Babies and children admitted. Function room (50 capacity). TV (big screen, satellite).

Leather Bottle

538 Garratt Lane, SW17 0NY (8946 2309/ www.leatherbottlepub.co.uk). Earlsfield rail. **Open** 11am-11.30pm Mon-Sat; noon-10.30pm Sun. **Food served** noon-10pm Mon-Sat; noon-8pm Sun. **Credit** MC, V. **Gastropub**
Dating back to the early 18th century, this handsome Young's establishment started life as a country pub in the hamlet of Garratt. These days, there's a long, narrow, low-ceilinged, candlelit bar, with wood panelling above a roaring open fire, that feels a bit cottage-like; at its far end, a snug mezzanine with stairs at either end provides a welcome retreat for couples, seated on leather sofas beside a large

brick open fire. On the other side is a small dining area, packed to capacity for Tuesday night poker with local thirtysomethings on our visit. On tap you'll find the familiar Young's Bitter and Special, plus (less usual in these parts) Courage Directors, with Staropramen, Kronenbourg Blanc and Peroni the best of the rest. The kitchen tries to cater for everyone with daily chef's specials and lunchtime snacks, and the food is very popular with families; service is friendly too. Come summer, there's a sprawling two-tier beer garden at the rear, full of bamboo tables and chairs beneath matting roofs that would be more fitting at a Bajan beach bar. Entertainment indoors runs to a flat-screen TV, but seasonal fun includes the likes of Easter Egg hunts and a St Patrick's Day quiz.

Babies and children admitted. Disabled: toilet. Function room (30 capacity). Restaurant (available for hire, 35 capacity). Tables outdoors (50, garden; 11, patio). TVs.

Suburban Bar & Lounge

27 Hartfield Road, SW19 3SG (8543 9788/ www.suburbanbar.com). Wimbledon tube/rail. **Open** 5-11pm Mon-Thur; 5pm-midnight Fri, Sat; 5-10.30pm Sun. **Credit** AmEx, MC, V. **Bar**
This cool little bar, just a couple of minutes' stagger from Wimbledon tube station, remains as popular as ever with a boisterous and undeniably youthful SW19 crowd. Behind the bar, smiley bartenders make a show of twirling glasses and shaking cocktails from an impressive list of over 100 varieties (potent mojitos and caipirinhas were proving popular on our recent visit). The surroundings are unpretentious and friendly, with smart decor of rich brown furniture and chocolate walls, a small terracotta-tiled bar and, at the rear, a snug area where comfy sofas gather around an open fire. A narrow passageway, covered in framed pics of revelry from evenings past, leads to the rear garden. The music has an indie retro feel – a refreshing change from bog-standard dance.

Disabled: toilet. Music (acoustic 8pm Sun; free). Tables outdoors (8, garden). TV (big screen).

Sultan ★ HOT 50

78 Norman Road, SW19 1BT (8542 4532). Colliers Wood or South Wimbledon tube. **Open** noon-11pm Mon-Thur, Sun; noon-midnight Fri, Sat. **Credit** MC, V. **Pub**
For review, *see p132.*

Beer club (6-9pm Wed; free). Games (darts). Quiz (8.30pm Tue, Sept-June). Tables outdoors (8, garden).

South

South

Anyone looking for an upscale night out south of the river needn't look any further than Battersea and Clapham. Both areas are particularly well-blessed with sleek and salubrious bars – **Alchemist**, **Dusk** and the sumptuously turned-out **Iniquity** in Battersea; **Bar Local** and **Clapham North** in its well-heeled neighbour. But there are the more traditional delights of the local boozer to be had here too: we like workers' co-operative **Bread & Roses** and the **Woodman**. There's competition further afield, though, in Balham, which boasts the splendidly idiosyncratic **Balham Bowls Club**, and in Tooting, where its sister establishment the **Tooting Tram & Social** is a welcome addition to the local drinking roster. Gritty Stockwell doesn't miss out either: **Bar Estrela** is a bit of the Algarve transplanted to SW8. And further into town, Waterloo has a dizzying choice of pubs, both gastro and trad. We especially like the **Anchor & Hope** for its superior food, **Fire Station** for its bustle and buzz, and the **White Hart** and **King's Arms** for, well, beer.

Balham

Balham Bowls Club ★ HOT 50

7-9 Ramsden Road, SW12 8QX (8673 4700/ www.antic-ltd.com). Balham tube/rail. **Open** 4-11pm Mon-Thur; 4pm-midnight Fri; noon-midnight Sat; noon-11pm Sun. **Food served** 6-9.30pm Tue-Fri; noon-3.30pm, 6-9.30pm Sat; 1-6pm Sun. **Credit** MC, V. **Bar**
Ignore the 'All visitors must be signed in' request posted up inside the front door – bowls club rules no longer apply at this quirkily cool bar, though the history of the place has been delightfully and sensitively preserved. Witness the framed rosettes, old wooden scoreboard, points plates and worn-out leather sofas and mismatched armchairs. It's not hard to picture the club members of old smoking pipes and mooching about the series of small drawing rooms. Today's punters are happy drinking pints of Grolsch and Peroni, gossiping in secluded corners and plotting how to stop the place getting any more popular than it already is. Real ale drinkers are catered for with Timothy Taylor Landlord, while fruit-beer fans are offered cherry-flavoured Liefmans Kriek. The 'global tapas' menu somehow seems out of keeping with the English vibe, but does its booze-soaking job with aplomb. A recent addition is a snooker room: two full size tables open to anyone who pays the £10 annual membership fee. This place is a real one-off.
Babies and children admitted (until 7pm). Bar available for hire. Function room
(50 capacity). Quiz (8pm Tue; £2). Tables outdoors (10, garden; 4, terrace). TV.

Bedford

77 Bedford Hill, SW12 9HD (8682 8940/ www.thebedford.co.uk). Balham tube/rail. **Open** 11am-midnight Mon-Thur; 11am-2am Fri, Sat; noon-midnight Sun. **Food served** 7-10pm Mon; noon-2.45pm, 7-10pm Tue-Fri; noon-3.30pm, 7-10pm Sat; noon-5pm, 7-9.45pm Sun. **Credit** MC, V. **Pub**
This vast Balham institution attracts a diverse crowd, in part due to Banana Cabaret, comedy nights held in the lofty, lordly Globe Theatre for more than 20 years. The gaping main room of the pub itself is soulless when empty (which it rarely is). There are plenty of other spaces to explore, including an intimate, canopy-covered back yard and three further bars. To drink, there's a good range on tap – four ales and San Miguel among the lagers – plus seven of each colour wine by the glass; to eat, there's upmarket pub grub and light bites.
Babies and children admitted (until 6pm). Comedy (9pm Tue, £3; 7.30pm Fri, £13; 6.30pm Sat, £16). Dance classes (line dancing 7.30pm Mon, £5; swing 8pm Tue, £8-£10; salsa 7.45pm Wed, £5; pole-dancing 7.30pm Thur, £8; tango 7.15pm alt Sun, £8). Disabled: toilet. Function rooms (up to 200 capacity). Games (fruit machines). Music (bands 9pm Mon, Tue, Thur; acoustic 9pm Wed; free). Nightclub (11pm-2am Fri, Sat; £5). Quiz (8.30pm Wed; £1). TV (big screen, satellite).

Grove

*39 Oldridge Road, SW12 8PN (8673 6531).
Clapham South tube/Balham tube/rail.* **Open**
11am-midnight Mon-Sat; noon-11pm Sun.
Food served noon-10.30pm Mon-Sat; noon-
9.30pm Sun. **Credit** MC, V. **Pub**
A clean-cut, well-dressed pub, the Grove is
politely and professionally run, but lacks a bit
of individuality. But this Young's establishment
has just enough going for it to avoid corporate
characterlessness, such as the centrepiece real
log fire; if you can, get yourself one of the comfy
couches that surround it, or dive into the cosy
lounge. There's a helpful drinks menu with tips
and suggestions on the 40 or so wines, along
with the expected Young's ales. Successful just
as it is, the Grove sees no need to depart from a
tried and tested formula.
*Babies and children admitted (restaurant only).
Games (board games). Quiz (8pm Sun; £2).
Restaurant (available for hire, 40 capacity).
Tables outdoors (9, terrace). TVs (big screen).*

Harrison's

*15-19 Bedford Hill, SW12 9EX (8675 6900/
www.harrisonsbalham.com). Balham tube/rail.*
Open 9am-midnight daily. **Food served**
9am-3pm, 6-10.30pm Mon-Fri; 9am-4pm,
6-10pm Sat, Sun. **Credit** AmEx, MC, V.
Bar/restaurant
Formerly the Balham Kitchen & Bar, Harrison's
(owned by Sam Harrison of Sam's Bar &
Brasserie in Chiswick, *see p101*) is predominantly
a restaurant, with three-quarters of its space
occupied by dining tables. Despite this, it
remains relaxed enough for a casual drink. Grab
an armchair stool at one of the high tables
opposite the shiny bar for superior cocktails
(kiwi and cucumber martini) or international
lagers (Staropramen and Beck's Vier on tap;
Asahi, Bohemia and Nova Schin are among the
bottles). The interior is attractively minimalist,
with retro lamp shades providing the obligatory
nod to 1970s lounge chic. The daily changing
menu offers classic brasserie fare such as pasta,
burgers and smoked haddock fish cakes.
*Babies and children admitted. Disabled:
toilet. Function room (up to 40 capacity).
Restaurant. Tables outdoors (6, pavement).*

Battersea

Alchemist

*225 St John's Hill, SW11 1TH (7326 7456/
www.alchemistbar.co.uk). Clapham Junction
rail.* **Open** noon-midnight Mon-Thur, Sun;
noon-2am Fri, Sat. **Food served** noon-10pm
daily. **Credit** MC, V. **Cocktail bar**

This upbeat cocktail bar attracts an up-for-it
crowd of twenty- and thirtysomethings with
drinking, dancing and chat-up lines on their
minds. There's a decadent clubby feel, with
colourful decor – chrome yellow, turquoise and
magenta leather sofas pushed up against loud
patterned wallpaper – and enough space for a
small, well-used (read: rammed at weekends)
dancefloor. As well as the classics there are some
interesting Japanese cocktails based on saké, a
speciality of the bar. For daytime drinking the
verdant back garden comes into its own.
*Babies and children admitted (until 9pm).
Bar available for hire. Music (DJs 9pm Fri,
Sat; £5). Tables outdoors (20, garden). TVs
(big screen, satellite).* **Map p283 C2.**

Le Bouchon Bordelais

*5-9 Battersea Rise, SW11 1HG (7738 0307/
www.lebouchon.co.uk). Clapham Junction
rail/35, 37 bus.* **Open** 10am-midnight Mon-
Thur, Sat; noon-midnight Fri; 10am-11pm
Sun. **Food served** 10am-10pm Mon-Thur,
Sat; noon-10pm Fri; 10am-9pm Sun. **Credit**
AmEx, MC, V. **Bar/restaurant**
Like its counterpart restaurant next door, this
simple, smart yet informal bar is resolutely,
almost fiercely proud of its Gallic DNA. The
French staff will nonchalantly serve you beer
from one of the cluster of Kronenbourg pumps
– the only non-French beer on tap being
Guinness – or you can select from one of the
myriad Burgundy and Loire Valley whites, or
Bordeaux and Rhone Valley reds before settling
down to watch the football or rugby – the other
priorities here – on TF1. Unsurprisingly, given
the quality of the food next door, the bar menu
is worth perusing; onion soup, baguettes, croque
monsieur and snails all feature.
*Babies and children welcome (until 9pm):
children's menu; crèche (Sat, Sun); high
chairs. Bar available for hire. Disabled:
toilet. Restaurant (available for hire,
50 capacity). Tables outdoors (6, terrace).
TVs (big screen, satellite).* **Map p283 E2.**

Dusk ★

*339 Battersea Park Road, SW11 4LF (7622
2112/www.duskbar.co.uk). Battersea Park rail.*
Open 6pm-12.30am Tue, Wed; 6pm-1.30am
Thur; 6pm-2am Fri, Sat. **Food served**
6-10.30pm Tue-Sat. **Credit** AmEx, MC, V.
Cocktail bar
For review, *see p139*.
*Bar available for hire. Dress: smart casual.
Function room (up to 100 capacity). Music
(DJs 9pm Thur-Sat; free). Tables outdoors
(10, terrace).*

Fox & Hounds

66-68 Latchmere Road, SW11 2JU (7924 5483). Clapham Junction rail. **Open** 5-11pm Mon; noon-3pm, 5-11pm Tue-Thur; noon-11pm Fri, Sat; noon-10.30pm Sun. **Food served** 7-10.30pm Mon-Thur; 12.30-3pm, 7-10.30pm Fri, Sat; 12.30-4pm, 7-10pm Sun. **Credit** MC, V. **Gastropub**

Although the regularly changing Mediterranean dishes (pancetta and asparagus risotto, sautéed chorizo and tiger prawn salad), put the Fox & Hounds firmly in the gastro bracket, this corner pub has kept the best aspects of the traditional boozer: welcoming staff, a local crowd, a decent selection of beers on tap (London Pride, Theakston Best, Harveys Sussex Best) and an atmosphere conducive to a good, old-fashioned chat. There's also a lovely back garden, draped in greenery and amply furnished with picnic benches and outdoor heaters.
Babies and children admitted (until 7pm). Disabled: toilet. Tables outdoors (10, garden). TV. **Map p283 E1.**

Freemasons

2 Wandsworth Common Northside, SW18 2SS (7326 8580/www.freemasonspub.com). Clapham Junction rail. **Open** noon-11pm Mon-Thur; noon-midnight Fri, Sat; noon-10.30pm Sun. **Food served** noon-3pm, 6.30-10pm Mon-Fri; 12.30-10pm Sat; 12.30-9pm Sun. **Credit** AmEx, MC, V. **Gastropub**

The focal point for well-heeled, local thirtysomethings, this lively and inviting local has a really sociable feel, enhanced by the warmth of the staff. Chairs and tables are well set up along the curved outer wall of the narrow main room to create a cosy sense of privacy for small groups; almost anywhere you sit, much of the room is lost from view behind the attractive, central, semi-circular bar. Timothy Taylor Landlord makes a nice draught pint, the dozen bottles of each colour slightly favour New World wines over French. Hearty Sunday roasts (£10.95-£16.95) are served in the handsome restaurant, with its exposed brickwork and mood lighting; choose from a short list of gastro classics (sea bass, risotto) during the week.
Babies and children welcome: high chairs. Quiz (8pm Mon; £1). Tables outdoors (11, patio). **Map p283 C2.**

Frieda B

46 Battersea Rise, SW11 1EE (7228 7676/ www.frieda-b.co.uk). Clapham Junction rail/35, 37 bus. **Open** 5pm-midnight Mon-Thur, Sun; 5pm-2am Fri, Sat. **Credit** AmEx, MC, V. **Cocktail bar**

Very much a weekend venue, this compact, keen-to-be-cool cocktail bar is still searching for a market during the week – something a 2008 relaunch under new management aims to address. The monthly wine tasting and mixology nights are a start, the latter consisting of cocktail classes for beginners. The resident musical duo on Tuesday nights has injected life into proceedings too. And though the friendly staff can't be faulted, the slightly awkward ground-floor space still feels like an unsolved puzzle. The cosier, characterful basement full of sofas and mirrors is the perfect antidote. Here an inbuilt DJ booth provides the soundtrack for lively Friday and Saturday nights.
Bar available for hire (Mon-Thur). Music (guitarist and singer 9pm Tue; DJs 10pm Fri, Sat; free). **Map p283 E2.**

Holy Drinker

59 Northcote Road, SW11 1NP (7801 0544/ www.holydrinker.co.uk). Clapham Junction rail/35, 37 bus. **Open** 4.30-11pm Mon-Wed; 4.30pm-midnight Thur, Fri; noon-midnight Sat; 1-11pm Sun. **Credit** MC, V. **Bar**

For Battersea locals keen to avoid the dress-to-impress and who-stole-the-soul establishments that predominate round these parts, Holy Drinker is a place of worship. A laid-back, non-uniform ethos extends throughout, from the casually dressed staff and medley of videos projected onto a crumpled sheet screen, to the hotch-potch furniture and worn and torn cinema seats at the back. Buzzing on Friday and Saturday nights, the Drinker also has plenty of daytime appeal, with punters drifting in to soak up the vibe, sample the impressive array of ales and lagers, and read the papers.
Babies and children admitted (until 6pm). Tables outdoors (4, pavement). TVs. **Map p283 E2.**

Iniquity

8-10 Northcote Road, SW11 1NT (7924 6699/www.iniquitybar.com). Clapham Junction rail/35, 37 bus. **Open** 5-11pm Mon-Wed; 5pm-midnight Thur, Fri; 3pm-midnight Sat; 3-10.30pm Sun. **Food served** 5-10.30pm Mon-Thur; 5-9.30pm Fri; 3-9.30pm Sat; 3-10pm Sun. **Credit** AmEx, MC, V. **Cocktail bar**

Slick, sexy and self-consciously cool, Iniquity is either exactly what you're looking for – or just not your cup of Iniquity. It's all blacks and reds inside, with smart leather seating, low-level lighting from candles and chandeliers, and a well-groomed clientele who pack the place out at weekends. The original and creative cocktail list includes a good number of drinks at the

Dusk ★

Dusk is sleek and modern, and more a proper-night-out venue than a drink-after-work establishment. It fills up on Friday and Saturday nights when DJs take over and the bar effectively becomes a club, though there is no dancefloor as such. Despite the inspection committee staff at the door and dressed-up dolly birds inside, good-time partygoers tend to prevail over the mannequin mafia, as dancers spill from the main room through to the narrower room at the back and, sometimes, down into the half-covered back patio. Two bars offer more than 60 cocktails and, as well as a small number of bottled beers, you can also buy spirits by the bottle; a Havana Club Especial, for example, will set you back £80. *For listings, see p137.*

South

lower end of the price scale (£6.50-£9.50). Music is as central to the experience as the drinks; there's a laid-back soundtrack earlier in the week, taking in jazz, easy listening, soul and rare groove, which gives way to more upbeat funk, dance and electronica for the weekend.
Bar available for hire. Disabled: toilet. Function room (up to 70 capacity). Tables outdoors (12, terrace). TVs (big screen). **Map p283 D2**.

Lost Society ★ [HOT 50]

697 Wandsworth Road, SW8 3JF (7652 6526/www.lostsociety.co.uk). Clapham Common tube/Wandsworth Road rail/77, 77A bus. **Open** 5pm-1am Tue-Thur; 4pm-2am Fri; 11am-2am Sat; 11am-1am Sun. **Food served** 5-10pm Tue-Sun. **Admission** £5 after 9pm Fri, Sat. **Credit** AmEx, MC, V.
Bar/restaurant
Lost Society is one hell of a bar. You probably won't manage to witness all its charms on a single visit – not if you give the cocktail list the level of attention it deserves anyway – but whichever of the six rooms you end up in, you'll find the same sense of stylish decadence. And repeat visits are a given. Like the fantasy country-house party of your dreams, Lost has something of a roaring twenties feel, with aristocratic opulence at every turn, art deco touches, high ceilings, chaises longues and a crystal-bead light shade above the main bar. Drink offerings have suitably glam appeal: a mind-boggling array of bottled beers (from Brahma to Badger), cocktail recipes of yesteryear (juleps, mai tais, pina coladas, £6.50), whole bottles of spirits with free mixers (Mount Gay Extra Old, £95), carefully selected wines galore. The garden out back has a hidden, secret garden feel, DJs spin a crowd-pleasingly eclectic mix and Tuesday night cocktail classes (8pm, £22.50 per person) offer an educational excuse for getting wasted on a 'school' night. No wonder this place is rammed every weekend – there's nowhere else like it for miles.
Bar available for hire. Music (DJs 7pm Thur; 9pm Fri, Sat). Tables outdoors (20, garden). **Map p284 A1**.

Microbar

14 Lavender Hill, SW11 5RW (7228 5300/ www.microbar.org). Clapham Common tube/ Clapham Junction rail/77, 77A, 137, 156 bus. **Open** 6pm-midnight Mon-Fri; 1pm-midnight Sat, Sun. **Credit** AmEx, MC, V. **Bar**
With its low-key feel, quality beers, loungey seating and sociable clientele, this place makes the bar business look like child's play. They've certainly gone the extra mile on the beer front:

you won't find a more varied or original selection anywhere in Clapham. Get your laughing gear around the likes of Sierra Nevada IPA and Blanche de Namur on tap; fridges, meanwhile, are bursting with bottles from Belgium, Holland, Australia, Germany, the US and the Czech Republic. Background noise is kept to a minimum making this place geared more towards civilised chat than pumping basslines. All this attracts a committed crowd of regulars, but newcomers are swiftly welcomed into the fold.
Bar available for hire. Games (board games). Tables outdoors (7, garden). TV (big screen).

Westbridge

74-76 Battersea Bridge Road, SW11 3AG (7228 6482/www.thewestbridge.co.uk). Bus 19, 49, 239, 319, 345. **Open** 11am-11pm daily. **Food served** noon-10pm daily. **Credit** AmEx, DC, MC, V. **Gastropub**
The Westbridge has an upmarket local boozer feel with plenty of personal touches, staff who aren't above whacking Dolly Parton on the sound system and some decent draught (Adnams, Amstel, Guinness and Edelweiss are among the choices) and bottled (Duvel, Anchor Steam) beers. Food is a strong selling point (proper fish and chips, seared tuna niçoise, sausages and mash) but decor manages to steer clear of gastro clichés. Instead of sanded wood and neutral tones, there's a blood-red ceiling, dark green semicircular bar and a hotchpotch of framed pictures clustered into one corner, among them a Billy Bragg poster and a signed print from a Gilbert and George exhibition.
Babies and children welcome: children's menu, high chairs. Function rooms (up to 150 capacity). Tables outdoors (10, pavement; 10, garden). Restaurant (available for hire, 40 capacity). TVs (satellite).

Woodman

60 Battersea High Street, SW11 3HX (7228 2968/www.thewoodmanbattersea.co.uk). Clapham Junction rail then 319 bus. **Open** 11am-11pm Mon-Thur; 11am-midnight Fri, Sat; noon-10.30pm Sun. **Food served** noon-3pm, 6.30-10.30pm Mon-Fri; noon-10.30pm Sat, Sun. **Credit** MC, V. **Pub**
From the outside, the Woodman looks like the archetypal neighbourhood local, nestling discreetly in a terraced row on a Battersea estate. On entering you half expect to be greeted by a stunned silence as everyone within looks up at you from their pints. The reality is nothing of the sort – this friendly, down-to-earth boozer is as welcoming to strangers as it is to its

regulars. Its generous size is equally unexpected, expanding some considerable way back to the cosy yard at the rear. On offer are ales such as Tanglefoot and Fursty Ferret and lagers from the Hofbräu brewery.

Babies and children admitted. Bar available for hire. Quiz (8.30pm, Mon; £1). Restaurant (available for hire, 80 capacity). Tables outdoors (10, garden). TVs (big screen, satellite).

Brixton

Dogstar
389 Coldharbour Lane, SW9 8LQ (7733 7515/www.antic-ltd.com). Brixton tube/rail. **Open** 4pm-2am Mon-Thur; 4pm-4am Fri; noon-4am Sat; noon-2am Sun. **Food served** 5-10pm Tue-Fri; 1-10pm Sat, Sun. **Admission** £5 after 10pm Fri, Sat. **Credit** MC, V.
DJ bar
This gold-corniced DJ bar has always had its finger on the pulse, so it was inevitable that at some point it would attempt to capitalise on the trend for of all things gastro. As ever, expect to find a music-savvy crowd soaking up the range of draught lagers (Grolsch, Beck's Vier, Staropramen). Their diet of hip hop and funk is now spiced up by the addition of El Panzon at the Dogstar, serving up top-notch Mexican food. A taco platter for two is £18 – a fine addition to a cocktail (around the £5 mark) from the brief but appealing list.

Babies and children admitted (until 10pm). Bar available for hire. Disabled: toilet. Function rooms (up to 150 capacity). Music (DJs 9pm daily). Tables outdoors (5, patio). TVs (big screen, satellite). **Map p284 E2.**

Effra ★
38A Kellet Road, SW2 1EB (7274 4180). Brixton tube/rail. **Open** 3-11pm daily. **Food served** 3-10pm daily. **No credit cards. Pub**
Set back from the main drag, this old-school boozer has more of an Afro-Caribbean community feel than many Brixton watering holes. The daily changing menu offers the likes of seaweed callaloo and jerk pork, and palm fronds tower over drinkers in the cosy patio garden (one of SW2's livelier outdoor drinking experiences). The yellowing patterned wallpaper and curtains seem to get progressively more torn each year, but one look at the fading Victorian splendour of the gold-corniced ceiling and pretty domed glass lamps, and it's no wonder die-hard locals pack the place out each night. Join them for excellent Guinness and rowdy sport screenings.

Games (dominoes). Jukebox. Music (musicians 8.30pm Tue-Thur, Sat, Sun; free). Tables outdoors (3, garden). TV. **Map p284 E2.**

Escape Bar & Art NEW
214-216 Railton Road, SE24 0JT (7737 0333/www.escapebarandart.co.uk). Herne Hill rail. **Open** 11am-midnight Mon-Wed; 11am-1am Thur; 11am-4am Fri, Sat; 10am-midnight Sun. **Food served** 11am-7.30pm Thur, Sun; 11am-9pm Fri, Sat. **Credit** MC, V. **Bar**
A textbook case of a bar attempting to be all things to all people, Escape plies yummy mummies with pizzas by day and local media types with beers early evening, before the decks come out, the windows steam up, and dance music throbs until 4am Thursday to Saturday (wretched soulful house on our last visit). Somehow, it manages to pull it off. Bashed leather sofas and a vintage iMac running fractal patterns lend the place an East Village vibe.

Art exhibitions. Babies and children welcome: high chairs, toys. Bar available for hire. Games (chess). Music (DJs 10pm Fri, Sat; free). Tables outdoors (2, pavement).

Far Side
144 Stockwell Road, SW9 9TQ (7095 1401). Stockwell tube/Brixton tube/rail. **Open** noon-11pm Mon-Thur; noon-3am Fri, Sat; noon-10.30pm Sun. **Food served** noon-3pm Mon, Fri; noon-3pm, 6-9pm Tue-Thur; noon-4pm Sat; noon-8pm Sun. **Credit** MC, V. **Pub**
The Far Side's garish exterior may hint at debauchery within, but its crowd is rather more sedate. Expect largely middle aged regulars of a weekday evening and parents bouncing toddlers on their knees on Saturday afternoons. The wine list is fairly short and the draught selection is nothing to write home about. Bottled beers, however, encompass cherry and strawberry varieties of Belle-Vue Kriek, Brahma and two Franziskaners. Head for the dimly lit back room snug where leather sofas and a cosy fireplace make a pleasant spot for tucking into a Sunday roast.

Babies and children admitted (until 7pm). Bar available for hire. Tables outdoors (16, garden). TV (big screen, satellite). **Map p284 D1.**

Hive
11-13 Brixton Station Road, SW9 8PA (7274 8383/www.hivebar.net). Brixton tube/rail. **Open** 5pm-midnight Mon-Wed; 5pm-2am Thur; 5pm-3am Fri; noon-3am Sat; noon-11pm Sun. **Food served** 5-11pm Mon-Fri; noon-11pm Sat, Sun. **Credit** MC, V. **Bar/restaurant**

South

'Hive is a 50ml measure bar' announces the plastic laminate to the side of the bar (and the white writing on the mirror behind the servers, just in case you were in any doubt). As you might expect, there's a heavy spirits focus here, with some 15 whiskies, 19 rums and seven vodkas contributing to an enticingly long cocktail list (most priced around £6.50). Located above a restaurant, Hive has taken a while to catch on with the locals, but a decorative facelift (khaki butterfly-patterned wallpaper, black and white gangster drawings, green leather benches) has popularised it with the area's discerning and more mature drinkers.
Babies and children admitted (restaurant). Bar available for hire. Music (DJ 8pm Fri, Sat; free). Restaurant (available for hire, 34 capacity). Tables outdoors (7, pavement). **Map p284 E2.**

Lounge

56 Atlantic Road, SW9 8PX (7733 5229). Brixton tube/rail. **Open** 11am-11pm Mon-Wed; 11am-midnight Thur-Sat; 11am-6pm Sun. **Food served** 11am-10pm Mon-Sat; 11am-5pm Sun. **Credit** AmEx, MC, V. **Café/bar**
Unique among SW9's array of buzzy DJ bars and yellowing boozers, this café-cum-bar offers a more refined drinking experience. Chatty waitresses operate a friendly table service to customers sampling the Turkish-flavoured meze menu (though there's the odd Caribbean dish in the mix) to a backdrop of candlelight and quiet conversation. There are a few draught lagers and a decent range of cocktails (all around the £5.50 mark), but it's the New World-heavy wine list that's the main alcoholic draw. A word of warning, though: take your toilet trip before getting too drunk – on our last visit a lack of lights left us groping our way blindly around the back room.
Babies and children welcome: high chairs. Bar available for hire. Disabled: toilet. Music (jazz 8pm Wed monthly; free). **Map p284 E2.**

Mango Landin'

40 St Matthew's Road, SW2 1NL (7737 3044/www.mangolandin.com). Brixton tube/rail then 2, 3, 133, 159 bus. **Open** 5pm-midnight Mon-Thur; noon-3am Fri, Sat; noon-11.30pm Sun. **Credit** AmEx, MC, V. **Cocktail bar**
This tropical-inspired bar successfully spans the gap between family-friendly local and party destination. A yellow plastic teddy nestles next to the bowl of cocktail fruit on the bar, the beer garden is littered with kids' toys and there's a framed certificate for community involvement on the wall. But come 11pm, killer cocktails (the signature Mango Landin' – Wray & Nephew rum with mango and strawberry juice – is a must), a late licence and live acts see the place fill up fast. The rest of the time it's dotted with groups of regulars sharing bottles of wine over

Skylon. *See p152.*

South

Caribbean-flavoured tapas (three bowls for £9.95) and mates acting out grudge matches on the proliferation of chessboards. Don't be put off by the location, this is a Brixton must.
Babies and children welcome (until 8pm): high chairs. BBQ (noon Sat, Sun). Food market (Sat). Games (board games, chess, table football). Music (bands/DJs 9pm Thur-Sat, 6pm Sun; free). Tables outdoors (20, garden). **Map p284 E3.**

Prince

467-469 Brixton Road, SW9 8HH (7326 4455/www.dexclub.co.uk). Brixton tube/rail. **Open** noon-midnight Mon-Thur; 11am-4am Fri, Sat; 11am-midnight Sun. **Food served** noon-10pm Mon-Fri; 11am-10pm Sat, Sun. **Credit** AmEx, MC, V. **Gastropub**
Long a popular destination for the post-midnight Brixton drinker, the Prince is currently making a power play for dominance of the SW9 after-hours scene. A nightclub – Dex – recently opened upstairs and there are plans for a two-tier members' club replete with hot tub and outdoor smoking tent, as well as a hotel (although confusion abounded when we attempted to find out an exact opening date). The bar itself has a curious opera-house-meets-après-ski feel (pine slatting and heavy red velvet curtains), which along with a gastropub menu (slow-braised lamb shank, £8.95) and wi-fi provides a relaxed daytime atmosphere. Come nightfall, a hip hop-centric soundtrack pulls in a buzzy, young crowd.
Bar available for hire. Babies and children admitted (until 9pm). Disabled: toilet. Music (DJs 10pm Fri-Sun; £3 after 10pm Fri, Sat). Tables outdoors (12, garden). TV (big screen). Wi-fi. **Map p284 E2.**

Trinity Arms

45 Trinity Gardens, SW9 8DR (7274 4544). Brixton tube/rail. **Open** 11am-11pm Mon-Thur; noon-midnight Fri, Sat; noon-11pm Sun. **Food served** noon-3pm, 6-9pm Mon-Fri; 1-5pm Sun. **Credit** MC, V. **Pub**
The Trinity Arms' discerning selection of beverages – Young's Bitter, Young's Special and a guest ale, plus an impeccable range of single malt whiskies – pulls in a mix of middle-aged after-workers and dressed-down students. It's a demographic reflected in the decor, with antiquated yellowing wallpaper and photos of the Queen rubbing shoulders with the questionable modern addition of harlequin-patterned curtains. The framed 'pub of the year' certificates on the walls prove that this place is a winner, even if the smoking ban has left it with a slight footy smell on occasion.

Babies and children admitted (until 7.30pm, garden only). Games (fruit machine). No piped music or jukebox. Tables outdoors (13, garden; 6, pavement). TV. **Map p284 D2.**

White Horse

94 Brixton Hill, SW2 1QN (8678 6666/www.whitehorsebrixton.com). Brixton tube/rail then 59, 118, 133, 159, 250 bus. **Open** 5pm-midnight Mon-Thur; 4pm-3am Fri; noon-3am Sat; noon-midnight Sun. **Food served** 5-10pm Mon-Fri; noon-10pm Sat, Sun. **Credit** MC, V. **Pub**
Why anyone would choose a boozer based on the presence of a dog is beyond us, but the departure of the landlord's black labrador George has obviously hit the White Horse's drinkers hard. 'Missing George?' queries a blackboard, 'He'll be hanging out in the White Horse's sister pub, the Earl Ferrer in Streatham.' Still, there are more than enough quirky touches to continue to draw a crowd here, with boiled sweets available in tumblers and rotating art exhibitions. The saggy leather sofas, low lighting and candles make this a relaxed lunch destination. In the evening, funk and soul DJs provide a high-octane atmosphere for the ladies loitering on the dancefloor and high-spirited regulars playing pool.
Babies and children admitted (until 9pm). Bar available for hire. Disabled: toilet. Games (board games, pool). Music (DJs 9pm Thur-Sat; jazz/DJ 4pm Sun; free). Tables outdoors (6, courtyard). **Map p284 D3.**

Windmill

22 Blenheim Gardens, SW2 5BZ (8671 0700/www.windmillbrixton.co.uk). Brixton tube/rail then 49, 59, 118, 133, 159, 250 bus. **Open** 5pm-midnight Mon-Thur; 5pm-1am Fri, Sat; 5-11pm Sun. **No credit cards.** **Pub**
The leopard-print tops, thickly applied eyeliner (boys and girls) and sweeping fringes clustered outside this venue on a Saturday night might put you in mind of a Manic Street Preachers gig circa 1993. Inside, though, the landscape couldn't be more contemporary, with a selection of the finest indie bands taking to the stage. Eternally chipped paintwork and sticker-plastered walls ensure the venue retains its squat/student bedsit feel year-in, year-out. Red Stripe and San Miguel are the draught highlights of an unremarkable drinks list, but with a past performers' list containing most successful London guitar bands, it's not the beverages that people come here for.
Bar available for hire. Disabled: toilet. Games (fruit machine). Music (8pm nightly; £3-£5). Tables outdoors (4, garden; 4, pavement). TV (big screen).

South

Clapham

Bar Local

4 Clapham Common Southside, SW4 7AA (7622 9406/www.barlocal.co.uk). Clapham Common tube. **Open** 5pm-midnight Mon-Wed; 5pm-1am Thur, Fri; noon-1am Sat; noon-midnight Sun. **Food served** 5-10pm Mon-Fri; noon-10pm Sat, Sun. **Credit** MC, V. **Bar**

For many visitors to Clapham Common, Bar Local is a first port of call. It's a mere five-yard stumble from the tube, so when the Common hosts festivals like Get Loaded in the Park revellers spill out onto the street. It doesn't help that it's tiny either. Inside, the walls are plastered with local art, DJs spin tunes at the end of the bar and the friendly staff do a fine job of keeping things moving. The floor and booths are starting to show their age, but if you like dance music and pretension-free vibes, this is a worthwhile find.
Music (DJs 8pm Thur-Sun; free).
Map p284 A2.

Bread & Roses ★ [HOT 50]

68 Clapham Manor Street, SW4 6DZ (7498 1779/www.breadandrosespub.com). Clapham Common or Clapham North tube. **Open** 5-11pm Mon-Thur; noon-midnight Fri, Sat; noon-10.30pm Sun. **Food served** noon-3pm, 6-9.30pm Mon-Fri; noon-4pm, 6-9.30pm Sat; noon-6pm Sun. **Credit** MC, V. **Pub**

The Workers Beer Company is a funding organisation for trade unions and other campaigns which has been running festival beer tents for over 20 years. This WBC-run pub, which takes its name from a James Oppenheim poem associated with a textile strike ('Hearts starve as well as bodies, give us bread but give us roses'), is proud to sport its socialist credentials. There's a massive union banner in the conservatory, said to represent a model for staff working conditions. Popular with local families for its world street food, it can lack atmosphere in the evenings, though that's being rectified by an unlikely move into burlesque with monthly Clapham or Bust nights. There are also regular reggae and world music DJs at weekends.
Babies and children admitted (until 9.30pm). Disabled: toilet. Entertainment (burlesque monthly; check website). Function room (up to 100 capacity). Games (board games). Music (band monthly; check website). Tables outdoors (15, garden; 8, conservatory; 8, patio). TVs (big screen, satellite).
Map p284 B1.

Clapham North

409 Clapham Road, SW9 9BT (7274 2472/ www.theclaphamnorth.co.uk). Clapham North tube. **Open** 11am-midnight Mon-Wed; 11am-2am Thur, Fri; 10am-2am Sat; 10am-midnight Sun. **Food served** 11am-10pm Mon-Thur; 11am-9pm Fri; 10am-8pm Sat; 10am-10pm Sun. **Admission** £2-£3 after 10pm Fri, Sat. **Credit** AmEx, MC, V. **Bar**

Cleverly rebranded, this bar is seriously in danger of putting Clapham North on the map. Since its brassy Manhattan brew-pub style makeover – high-backed leather booth seating, copper pendant lights, exposed brickwork, *Wonder Woman* on the plasma screens – it's almost been a victim of its own success, filling up fast every night with the kind of punters who linger over two glasses of wine. The beer choice is rudimentary but there are three healthy shelves of premium spirits and extensive wine and cocktail lists. Sunday sessions offer chilled music, lazy brunches and horizontal lounging.
Babies and children admitted. Disabled: toilet. Music (DJs 8pm Thur, 9pm Fri, Sat, 5pm Sun). Tables outdoors (6, terrace). TVs (big screen, satellite). **Map p284 C1**.

Falcon [NEW]

23 Bedford Road, SW4 7SQ (7274 2428). Clapham North tube. **Open** noon-11pm Mon, Sun; noon-1am Tue-Thur; noon-1am Fri, Sat. **Food served** noon-3pm, 5-10pm Mon-Fri; noon-10pm Sat, Sun. **Credit** MC, V. **Pub**

Circa Britpop, the garishly yellow-fronted Falcon was the last word in Clapham cool. It was the first pub in the area to introduce such exotic fare as Staropramen and Thai food. It hasn't changed much but is noticeably quieter since Clapham North and Green & Blue opened on its patch of SW4. Nevertheless, it may well be time to get reacquainted. The Eurostar may no longer rattle past the terraced suntrap beer garden (complete with beach bar and barbecue on weekends), but the bashed leather sofas, new tapas-style bar snacks and superior dance music make this a worthy precursor to a Brixton club crawl.
Babies and children admitted (until 7.30pm, back area and garden only). Tables outdoors (12, front garden; 30, back garden). TVs.
Map 284 C1

Green & Blue

20-26 Bedford Road, SW4 7HJ (7498 9648/ www.greenandbluewines.com). Clapham North tube. **Open** 7am-midnight Mon-Thur; 7am-1am Fri, Sat; 9am-1am Sun. **Food served** 6pm-11pm Mon-Fri; 9am-11pm Sat, Sun. **Credit** MC, V. **Wine bar**

South

Despite its unpromising location sandwiched between a key cutter and a burnt-out chip shop, this branch of East Dulwich's favourite wine bar/wine merchant has been an instant hit in Clapham. A lot of that's down to the staff, who are passionate about their business and will chat engagingly about future plans. The space might be slightly cramped, the fittings functional and the Mediterranean-inspired sharing platters a little too insubstantial to soak up all that plonk, but settling down here to sample decadent wines cheaply by the glass is still a treat. There's also organic lager and cider on offer, while the area's mums swear by the coffee and carrot cake. All-day breakfasts are served at the weekend. *Bar available for hire. Babies and children admitted. Function room (35 capacity). Wine shop. Wine tastings (phone for details).* **Map p284 C1**.

Grey Goose NEW

100 Clapham Park Road, SW4 7BZ (7720 8902/www.thegreygoose.co.uk). Clapham Common tube. **Open** 5pm-midnight Mon-Thur; 5pm-1am Fri; noon- 1am Sat; noon-midnight Sun. **Food served** 5-10.30pm Mon-Fri; noon-10.30pm Sun. **Credit** AmEx, MC, V. **Gastropub**

For years, the bar on this site made a living trading as the moderately funky, student-pleasing 100, until a makeover by the team behind Tooting's Smoke bar tried to capitalise on the nearby White House's (*see p146*) menu of funky house and cocktails. Now, with the Grey Goose, everything's gone grown-up. The chef works hard to locally source a great menu of gastropub classics (massive pork chops with slices of black pudding and apple sauce), and there are hand-pulled ales and wheat beer. A pretty, heated outdoor deck space plus the elegant upstairs Blue Bar (available for private hire) complete the picture. A fireplace, sofas and brioche bread and butter pudding make it a difficult place to leave. *Babies and children welcome: high chairs. Function room (up to 100 capacity). Music (acoustic/jazz 7pm Sun; free). Tables outdoors (14, rear garden; 7, front garden). TV.* **Map p284 B3**.

Landor

70 Landor Road, SW9 9PH (7274 4386/ www.landortheatre.com). Clapham North tube. **Open** noon-11.30pm Mon-Thur; noon-midnight Fri, Sat; noon-10.30pm Sun. **Food served** noon-2.30pm, 6-9.30pm Mon-Fri; 1-8.30pm Sat; 1.15-5pm Sun. **Credit** MC, V. **Theatre pub**

'What theme's that? Old shite?' were Brian Potter's words when they redecorated his beloved Phoenix Club in Irish pub style in TV comedy *Phoenix Nights*. The eccentric look of the Landor (canoe hanging from the ceiling, old transistor radios atop the bar, dusty books that no one can reach) is similarly eccentric, but the locals wouldn't have it any other way. A huge 360-degree bar (with embedded plasma screens) is the key feature, and the energetic staff work hard to satisfy drinkers coming at them from all angles. A tiny upstairs theatre that specialises in mini-musicals ensures there's always an entertaining mix of people and, despite those TVs and pool tables, people-watching over a pint of London Pride is the order of the day for most people here. *Comedy (8pm Sun monthly; £6-£10). Games (fruit machines, pool). Quiz (8pm 1st Sun of mth; £2). Tables outdoors (16, garden). Theatre (7.30pm Tue-Sun; £7-£10). TVs (big screen, satellite).* **Map p284 C1**.

Loft NEW

67 Clapham High Street, SW4 7TG (7627 0792/www.theloft-clapham.co.uk). Clapham North tube. **Open** 6pm-midnight Mon-Thur; 6pm-1.30am Fri; noon-1.30am Sat; noon-midnight Sun. **Food served** 6-10pm Mon-Thur; 6-9pm Fri; noon-9pm Sat, Sun. **Credit** MC, V. **Bar/restaurant**

This glass-fronted space, courtesy of the good folk behind Brixton's Plan B, takes its music, and its food, seriously. And its minimal breeze block walls, low-slung leather chairs and smoky glass windows make it just about possible to forget you're sitting above Tesco. Word of Loft's charms must be filtering through slowly as it was seats all round on our last visit – and plenty of attention from the bar staff. There's a £5 'cocktail club' menu and reasonably priced bar snacks (chorizo and mash, pork belly sandwich) too. But with a huge DJ set-up embedded into the high concrete bar and a Clapham High Street location, it surely won't be long before the hordes descend. *Babies and children admitted. Disabled: toilet. Music (DJs 9.30pm Fri, Sat; 4.30pm Sun; free). Restaurant (available for hire, 50 capacity).* **Map p284 B2**.

Prince of Wales

38 Old Town, SW4 0LB (7622 3530). Clapham Common tube. **Open** 5-11pm Mon-Wed; 5pm-midnight Thur; 5pm-1am Fri; 1pm-1am Sat; 1-11pm Sun. **Food served** 6-10.30pm Tue-Sun. **Credit** AmEx, MC, V. **Pub**

South

And you thought the Landor was eccentrically decorated? Here there's an inflatable Spider Man in a fishing net and a plastic lobster climbing out of a birdcage – and that's just on the ceiling. The toilets, meanwhile, have been likened to a fairground ghost train by many. Such carnival-esque clutter can distract from the fact that this is one of the few pubs in the area to challenge the palate with well-chosen real ales (Harveys on our recent visit). But, really, Virgin Radio as a soundtrack? Surely 6 Music's Freakzone would have been more fitting.
Babies and children admitted (until 6pm). Quiz (8pm Thur; free). Tables outdoors (4, pavement). TV. **Map p284 A2**.

Stonhouse NEW

165 Stonhouse Street, SW4 6BJ (7819 9312/ www.thestonhouse.co.uk). Clapham Common or Clapham North tube/Clapham High Street rail. **Open** 11am-midnight daily. **Food served** noon-3.30pm, 6-10.30pm Mon-Fri; noon-4pm, 6-11pm Sat; noon-9pm Sun. **Credit** AmEx, MC, V. **Bar/restaurant**
Clapham's back roads sometimes seem like its last refuges of character and civility. While the High Street attracts binge-drinking weekenders galore, joys await away from the main drag. This corner redevelopment is a case in point: an old man's pub given a nifty '70s-referencing refit, a meaty menu (the biggest and best burgers in the area, £9) and a new lease of life. A rotating selection of well-kept real ales (always good to see Harveys Sussex bitter), holds its own among some dazzling contemporary cocktails (chilli and lemongrass bloody mary), while the kitchen reflects modern working trends by serving until late in the evening.
Babies and children admitted (until 7pm). Restaurant (available to hire, 85 capacity). Tables outdoors (7, garden). TV (big screen). **Map p284 B2**.

Tim Bobbin

1-3 Lilleshall Road, SW4 0LN (7738 8953). Clapham Common tube. **Open** noon-11pm Mon-Wed; noon-midnight Thur-Sat; noon-10.30pm Sun. **Food served** noon-3pm, 7-10pm Mon-Fri; noon-10pm Sat; noon-9pm Sun. **Credit** MC, V. **Pub**
The dartboard here is the first surprise – and a sure sign that some pubs work best when they're left intact. Offering some of the best real ale in the area (wonderfully refreshing Crane Sundancer on our visit), as well as decent pub grub (own-made chicken kebabs), the Shaker-style pale green and cream decor and discreet plasma screens are the only sign that this local

haunt has been brought into the 21st century. Less is more, and it's significant that on a damp Tuesday night Tim Bobbin was busier than any of the area's more celebrated watering holes. It exudes a casual friendliness that's perfectly in keeping with its Old Town location.
Babies and children welcome: high chairs. Games (darts). Restaurant (available for hire, 40 capacity). Tables outdoors (11, garden). TVs. **Map p284 A1**.

White House ★ NEW

65 Clapham Park Road, SW4 7EH (7498 3388/www.thewhitehouselondon.co.uk). Clapham Common tube. **Open** 5.30pm-2am Wed; 5.30pm-3am Thur; 5.30pm-4am Fri; 6pm-4am Sat; 5pm-2am Sun. **Food served** 5.30-10pm Wed-Fri; 6-10pm Sat; 5-10pm Sun. **Credit** MC, V. **DJ bar/restaurant**
The overhaul in spring 2007 is still looking remarkably fresh, considering the hammering it receives from the hedonistic and mobbed parties that frequent this hugely popular Clapham bar. From top down, it's gorgeous, modern and worth a visit. Best bit? The large roof terrace with sweeping lengths of wood and full sun nearly the whole day, which sees tanned types lounging their way through the cocktail menu in warmer months. The main bar with its long banquette seating and sunken area sees plenty of house nights from local DJs and Antipodean breaks and D&B parties. The members' lounge – all flocked wallpaper, own kitchen and loos – is available to hire. The short food menu is reasonably priced and offers mostly South-east Asian fare.
Bar available for hire. Function rooms (up to 250 capacity). Music (DJs 9pm Wed-Sun; free-£12). Restaurant (available for hire, 22 capacity). Tables outdoors (10, terrace). **Map p284 B4**.

Windmill on the Common

Clapham Common Southside, SW4 9DE (8673 4578/www.windmillclapham.co.uk). Clapham Common or Clapham South tube. **Open** 11am-midnight Mon-Sat; noon-11pm Sun. **Food served** noon-10.30pm Mon-Sat; noon-10pm Sun. **Credit** AmEx, MC, V. **Gastropub**
Since Wandsworth's Young's brewery joined forces with Charles Wells of Bedford in 2006, its pubs have stayed reassuringly the same (as has – it must be said – the beer). Not so the Windmill, which had traded on its rep as *the* place for an outdoor pint on sunny Clapham Common for too long (well, there has been an inn here since 1655). Over the last two years, it's

gradually smartened up to include welcoming leather sofas, open fires, swirly contemporary art 'inspired' by the area, wicker lamps, and a cluster of cylindrical red lampshades. The attached B&B now styles itself as a boutique hotel, which perhaps stretches the point, but this great Sunday lunch venue now exhibits the touch of class its location deserves.
Babies and children admitted. Disabled: toilet. Function room (35 capacity). Games (fruit machine). Quiz (8pm Sun; £1). Restaurant. Tables outdoors (12, garden). TV (big screen, satellite). **Map p284 A3**.

Kennington

Beehive
60-62 Carter Street, SE17 3EW (7703 4992/ www.thebeehivebar.co.uk). Kennington tube/ 12, 68, 68A, 171, 176, P5 bus. **Open** noon-11pm Mon-Sat; noon-10.30pm Sun. **Food served** noon-3pm, 5.30-10pm Mon-Fri; noon-10pm Sat, Sun. **Credit** MC, V. **Pub**
You might not expect to find abstract expressionist art in a south London boozer just off Walworth Road, but then this graceful neighbourhood pub refuses to adhere to stereotypes. Bang in the middle of a large council estate, the Beehive attracts a pleasingly mixed set of punters who come here for a straightforward pint of Pride or Bombardier: no fruit machines, no theme nights… even the TV screen is discreetly placed. A real effort has been made to create an inviting, unpretentious local meeting place with character and charm. Although reluctant to call itself a gastropub, the Beehive is certainly food-driven, with a tantalising menu of well-crafted and carefully sourced pub staples.
Babies and children admitted (until 7pm). Tables outdoors (35, patio). TV.

Dog House
293 Kennington Road, SE11 6BY (7820 9310). Kennington or Oval tube. **Open** noon-midnight Mon-Thur, Sun; noon-1.30am Fri, Sat. **Food served** noon-3pm, 6-10pm Mon-Fri; noon-10pm Sat, Sun. **Credit** MC, V. **Pub**
Depressed by the dominance of identikit chain pubs? Fed up with ubiquitous refurbishments? Want cod and chips not pan-fried sea bass with curly fries? Has it all gone too far? The Dog House is here to help. The faded paintwork, chipped woodwork, fireplace coated in candle wax, carpet-lined bar and badly hung pictures all help make this place a breath of fresh air. Board games in tatty boxes are piled up in one corner, and there's a good range of beer on tap,

such as Bombardier and Black Sheep. It's cluttered, homely and, triumphantly, a bit of an odd shape.
Babies and children admitted (upstairs). Function room (70 capacity). Games (board games). Music (jazz/Latin American 8.30pm alternate Tue; DJs 9pm Sat; musicians 9pm alternate Sun; free). Tables outdoors (20, pavement). TV.

Prince of Wales
48 Cleaver Square, SE11 4EA (7735 9916). Kennington tube. **Open** noon-11pm Mon-Sat; noon-10.30pm Sun. **Food served** noon-2.30pm, 6-9pm Mon-Thur; noon-2.30pm Fri, Sat; noon-3pm Sun. **Credit** AmEx, MC, V. **Pub**
Tucked away in the corner of an archetypal, residential Georgian square is this delightful, traditional, Shepherd Neame pub, which wouldn't be out of place on the edge of a village green and is frequented by the local hobnobbing media gentry. Well kept inside and out, the pub has flower boxes along the front window, while the walls of the snug and cushioned interior are lined with Victorian adverts for things like St Jacob's Oil and framed portraits of 19th-century cricketers, with cricket a subtle but definite theme here. Suitably English, the beers at the dinky bar are Spitfire and Kent's Best, with additional seasonal ales on rotation.
Babies and children admitted (until 9pm). Tables outdoors (2, pavement).

White Hart
185 Kennington Lane, SE11 4EZ (7735 1061/www.thewhitehartpub.co.uk). Kennington tube/196 bus. **Open** noon-11pm Mon-Wed; noon-midnight Thur; noon-1am Fri, Sat; noon-10.30pm Sun. **Food served** noon-3.30pm, 6-10.30pm Mon-Fri; noon-4pm, 6-10.30pm Sat; 12.30-9.30pm Sun. **Credit** AmEx, MC, V. **Pub**
In stark contrast to the endearingly dishevelled Dog House across the road (*see left*) is the smarter, trendier but less characterful White Hart, with its office crowd, sharply dressed staff, sleek interior and minimalist decor. This is as much a bar as a pub, with an excellent selection of wines, a cocktail list and a choice of champagnes – including a Bollinger (£44.50) and a Veuve Clicquot (£69.95) – served to a dance music soundtrack in the evenings. Food is top-notch: flavourful regulars include corn-fed chicken with chorizo bubble and squeak, supplemented by daily specials chalked on a blackboard by the mirror-backed bar.
Babies and children admitted. Function room (100 capacity). TVs (big screen, satellite).

South

Stockwell

Bar Estrela ★ HOT 50

*111-115 South Lambeth Road, SW8 1UZ
(7793 1051). Stockwell tube/Vauxhall tube/rail.*
Open/food served 8am-midnight Mon-Sat;
10am-11pm Sun. **Credit** AmEx, MC, V.
Bar/restaurant
If it wasn't for the trouble that wearing a bikini
and sarong on the mean streets of Stockwell
could cause, a sunny afternoon spent at one of
the pavement tables outside this fabulous bar/
restaurant would feel like a week on the
Algarve. As you sup on a cold Portuguese beer
(Super Bock, £1.80 a bottle) gruff waistcoated
waiters amble past, laden with perfectly
presented shellfish for tables of boisterous
Portuguese locals. Inside, the deli counter is
heavy with cream cakes and the infamous
custard tarts. A real must-visit.
*Babies and children admitted. Bar available
for hire. Tables outdoors (10, pavement).*

Canton Arms

*177 South Lambeth Road, SW8 1XP (7587
3819). Stockwell tube.* **Open** noon-11pm Mon-
Wed; noon-midnight Thur-Sat; noon-10.30pm
Sun. **Food served** noon-3pm, 6-10pm Mon-
Fri; noon-9pm Sat, Sun. **Credit** MC, V. **Pub**
A whopper of a pub with plenty of seating,
including a large sofa beneath a rather bizarre
stained glass ceiling, the Canton's sweeping bar
holds all the standard lagers – including Red
Stripe – and an excellent selection of beers in
the form of Harveys, Deuchars IPA, Timothy
Taylor Landlord, Wadworth and Hobgoblin.
The clientele is younger and trendier than most
places in the area, with lots of big loud groups
taking advantage of the ample space – there's
also wi-fi for those who just *have* to know who's
recently thrown a virtual sheep at them on
Facebook. The wine list is short and sweet; a
large glass of chardonnay comes in at £4.70.
*Babies and children admitted (until 9pm).
Bar available for hire. Games (table football).
Tables outdoors (7, patio). TV (big screen,
satellite). Wi-fi.*

Priory Arms

*83 Lansdowne Way, SW8 2PB (7622 1884).
Stockwell tube.* **Open** 11am-11pm Mon-Sat;
noon-10.30pm Sun. **Food served** noon-
2.30pm, 6.30-9.30pm Mon-Fri; noon-9.30pm
Sat; 1-6pm Mon. **Credit** MC, V. **Pub**
A true community pub with a cricket team,
weekly quiz night and a dizzying respect for real
ale, it makes sense then that the Priory Arms
should feel less like a pub and more like a club

house. The bar itself is lined with the hundreds
of labels provided by the guest ales it's hosted
over the years, and remains heaving with
Harveys, Adnams and two guests on the pumps,
a vast selection of Belgian fruit beers and 16
country fruit wines, ranging from parsnip to
dandelion. The gastro and Thai dishes are
wolfed down by a packed house on any day of
the week. A select drinker's heaven.
*Children admitted (Sun lunch only). Function
room (up to 60 capacity). Quiz (8.30pm Sun;
£1). Tables outdoors (4, patio). TVs (satellite).*

Royal Albert

*43 St Stephen's Terrace, SW8 1DL (7840
0777). Stockwell tube.* **Open** 4-11pm Mon-Fri;
noon-midnight Sat; noon-10.30pm Sun. **Food
served** 6-10pm Mon-Fri; noon-10pm Sat, Sun.
Credit MC, V. **Pub**
Set well off the main drag, this is definitely a
those-in-the-know local. Loads of gentlemen's
club style leather sofas with hairy cushions and
stacks of board games make this a fine place for
weekend lounging, but the slightly over-lit
atmosphere during the week means lingering is
less likely. The bar staff, however, do a fine job
of manning pumps of Harveys Best, Batemans
Hooker, Old Rosie Scrumpy, Amstel, Guinness
and San Miguel. There's always a £2 pint of ale
deal before 7pm during the week, which implies
that those who frequented the place prior to the
revamp remain well catered for. Quite right too.
*Babies and children welcome (until 7pm
Mon-Fri): high chairs. Disabled: toilet. Games
(board games, golf machine, table football,
quiz machine). Music (jazz 8pm Thur monthly;
free). Tables outdoors (4, pavement). TV
(big screen, satellite).*

Surprise

*16 Southville, SW8 2PP (7622 4623). Stockwell
tube/Vauxhall tube/rail.* **Open** 11am-11pm Mon-
Sat; noon-10.30pm Sun. **Food served** noon-
3pm Mon-Fri. **Credit** MC, V. **Pub**
Cheesy as its name sounds, this Young's pub
really is just that. Hidden down a side street, it
has everything a traditional pub lover needs:
Young's Bitter and Special, cheery staff, higgledy-
piggledy seating, a heated outside area and a
soppy golden retriever who wants to be more
than friends. The back room is full of caricatures
of the regulars and a pull-down screen shows the
football. On our visit, they were still talking about
when the American came in four months ago –
we were amazed he ever left.
*Babies and children admitted. Games (board
games, boules pitch, darts, fruit machine).
Tables outdoors (12, patio). TV (satellite).*

South

Tooting

Tooting Tram & Social ★ NEW

46-48 Mitcham Road, SW17 9NA (8767 0278/www.antic-ltd.com). Tooting Broadway tube. **Open** 5pm-midnight Tue-Thur; noon-2am Fri, Sat; noon-midnight Sun. **Credit** MC, V. **Bar**

The people behind the much-loved Balham Bowls Club (*see p136*) have transformed this vast former warehouse and – you guessed it – tram shed into a bar that's intimate and incredibly eclectic. A birdcage filled with fairy lights and six gloriously grandiose chandeliers dangle from up on high, while funky fabrics soften the tile-clad walls. To drink there's a selection of not-too-inspiring wines and a simple list of cocktails. Timothy Taylor Landlord is the sole hand-pulled beer, but Grolsch Weizen makes a tasty accomplice. Peckish? There are only fancy snacks for the moment, but plans are afoot for a restaurant on the mezzanine. And when you tire of gawping at the decor, there are occasional DJs, bands, art exhibitions and the odd burlesque show.

Babies and children admitted (daytime). Bands/DJs Fri, Sat (times vary; free-£5). TVs.

Vauxhall

Fentiman Arms

64 Fentiman Road, SW8 1LA (7793 9796/ www.geronimo-inns.co.uk). Oval tube/Vauxhall tube/rail. **Open** noon-11pm Mon-Thur; noon-midnight Fri, Sat; noon-10.30pm Sun. **Food served** noon-3pm, 7-10pm Mon-Thur; noon-3pm, 7-10.30pm Fri; noon-4pm, 7-10.30pm Sat; noon-5pm, 6-9pm Sun. **Credit** AmEx, MC, V. **Gastropub**

This gastropub has got it covered whatever the season, with lots of snug corners for winter boozing sessions and a compact back garden, brimming with potted and wall-growing plants, for alfresco drinking and dining in the sun. Upmarket, clean cut and tasteful (though the arty black and white photographs adorning the walls verge on corny), the Fentiman attracts well-spoken City boys and shiny haired career blondes who'd rather hide out with a decent bottle of wine and a plate of good food than face the mean streets of SW8 of an evening. The Sunday menu is particularly mouth-watering, featuring grilled sea bass and courgette risotto alongside the usual roasts.

Babies and children admitted. Function room (up to 80 capacity). Quiz (8pm Tue; £1). Tables outdoors (25, garden). TV (satellite).

Insider Knowledge
Bread & Roses

You are?
David Lime, manager of Bread & Roses in Clapham. I've been working here for five years, and managing the pub for the last year.

Where does the name Bread & Roses come from?
It's from a socialist song that was sung by female textile workers at the beginning of the 20th century: 'Hearts starve as well as bodies; give us bread but give us roses'. The lyrics are painted above the bar.

So this is a pub with a socialist heart?
It was opened by the Workers Beer Company, which is the trading arm of the Battersea & Wandsworth Trades Union Council. They're a non-profit organisation that works at grassroots level, lobbying for workers' rights.

How does that translate into the way the pub is run?
The company looks after its staff really well in terms of wages, sick pay and support. Everyone's a member of the union. We also let out our function room for free to local community groups like South London Gays, Lambeth Cyclists and the Cuba Solidarity Campaign. And our policy is to make this a real community pub, so we have a very eclectic schedule of events each month.

What kind of events happen here?
We have a chess club, a war-games society, a monthly film club showing politically charged films. There's lots of live music, DJs every weekend and even burlesque nights. In the summer we host a real ale and cider festival.

South

Royal Vauxhall Tavern

372 Kennington Lane, SE11 5HY (7820 1222/www.theroyalvauxhalltavern.co.uk). Vauxhall tube/rail. **Open** 7pm-midnight Mon-Fri; 9pm-2am Sat; 2pm-midnight Sun. **No credit cards.** Pub

The grand dame of this so-called 'gay village', the RVT is a true icon. Gloriously faded, a bit louche and with a colourful past (the gay Kray used to drink here, and Lily Savage got her start behind the bar), it just keeps surviving. Built in 1863, and serving confirmed bachelors since long before Kylie was born, it has withstood wrecking balls and outlasted many a trendier bar. The main attraction is Duckie, the eccentric Saturday club night, hosted by New Jersey's most famous lesbian expat, Amy Lamé. There, DJs the London Readers Wifes (sic) keep the sweaty, studenty crowd entertained with an irreverent mix of trash, thrash, punk and pop – expect to hear the Smiths, Human League, Bowie and Bolan as you fight your way to bathroom and bar. At midnight, there is postmodern cabaret (edgy performance art, yes; lip-synching Chers, no). The RVT also hosts a hodgepodge of cultural happenings during the week: drag queen bingo nights (Monday), comedy (Wednesdays), cabaret (Thursdays). The biggest laughs come on Sunday afternoon at SLAGS Chill-Out, with the Dame Edna Experience being rude and singing like Karen Carpenter from 5pm. In the evening, Muscle Marys whip off their tops and gear up for an evening of debauchery at the nearby clubs. *Bar available for hire. Entertainment (bingo Mon; show Tue; comedy Wed; free–£5). Music (cabaret Thur; DJs 9pm Sat; 2pm Sun; £5-£7).*

Waterloo

Anchor & Hope ★ | HOT 50 |

36 The Cut, SE1 8LP (7928 9898). Southwark or Waterloo tube/rail. **Open** 5-11pm Mon; 11am-11pm Tue-Sat; 12.30-5pm Sun. **Food served** 6-10.30pm Mon; noon-2.30pm, 6-10.30pm Tue-Sat; 2pm sitting Sun. **Credit** MC, V. Gastropub

Waterloo's most famous gastropub remains a good place for a drink, though dining is certainly the main event, and it can become impossibly busy. Nibbles such as polish sausage (delicious, £3) arrive with gherkins and pickled cabbage, to complement a fine variety of Old World wines, including on our visit an Austrian blaufränkisch (£22 a bottle) and a Rioja Alta (£44). Five whites and six reds come by the glass. In the maroon-painted drinking area, a profusion of little stools are scattered around small tables on bare wooden boards, while tall chairs line the bar. Young's and Bombardier are the real ales, along with a fortnightly guest such as Bread of Heaven. A set Sunday lunch is now bookable, perhaps the best way to get the full flavour of this very popular pub. *Babies and children admitted. Booking essential (Sun). Tables outdoors (4, pavement).* **Map p282 N8.**

Baltic

74 Blackfriars Road, SE1 8HA (7928 1111/ www.balticrestaurant.co.uk). Southwark tube/ rail. **Open/food served** noon-11pm Mon-Sat; noon-10.30pm Sun. **Credit** AmEx, MC, V. Bar/restaurant

An unlikely find on Blackfriars Road, the Baltic is sleek, chic and discreet. The exceptional north-east European restaurant is a bright and airy Grade II-listed warehouse, but it's reached via a long, low-lit, moody bar stocked with some 47 different vodkas. Most are Polish (hence strictly 'wodka'), although Russian and Finnish distillations also get a look in. The Baltic's famous on-site infusions – lemon, peppercorn, dill or caramel for example (£2.75 a shot, £33.50 a bottle) – are based on Latvian Hlebnaja. The teetering bar stools and wall-recessed banquettes get bagged quickly by local after-workers during the week, while at weekends the Baltic attracts a more sophisticated crowd. *Babies and children admitted. Disabled: toilet. Function rooms (up to 30 capacity). Music (jazz 7pm Sun; free). Tables outdoors (4, terrace).* **Map p282 N8.**

Concrete | NEW |

The Hayward, Southbank Centre, Belvedere Road, SE1 8XX (7928 4123/www.concrete-daynight.co.uk). Waterloo tube/rail. **Open/ food served** 10am-6pm Mon, Sun; 10am-11pm Tue-Thur; 10am-1am Fri, Sat. **Credit** MC, V. Bar/café

Thank the Lord. Starbucks has gone and in its place is a classy little bar/café with the tongue-in-cheek name of Concrete (set, as it is, in the vast Brutalist environs of the Southbank Centre). And yet, despite its exposed piping, original factory lights and industrial-style seating, the place is cosy and fun. There are fresh flowers, candlelit tables, and, at the entrance, a pink neon-covered cement mixer. There's also a decent drinks list, though prices are high: £3.70 for a pint of Russian Baltika lager. Bar snacks (75p) are pickles (egg, beetroot, cucumber), and lunches (hotpot with bread, £5.50) are also available. The coffee comes from

Union Hand-Roasted. Events and drinks offers frequently coincide with exhibitions held at the Hayward art gallery next door.
Art exhibitions. Babies and children admitted (until 6pm Mon-Thur, Sat, Sun; 10pm Fri). Bar available for hire (Mon, Sun). Disabled: toilet. Music (DJs/jazz 8pm Fri; free). Tables outdoors (16, terrace). **Map p282 M8**.

Crown

108 Blackfriars Road, SE1 8HW (7261 9524/ www.thecrownbarandkitchen.co.uk). Southwark tube/rail. **Open** 11am-11pm Mon-Fri. **Food served** noon-3pm, 5-10pm Mon-Fri. **Credit** MC, V. **Pub**
A thoroughly successful pub renovation, the Crown is worth the walk down bleak Blackfriars Road. Often less crowded than nearby locals, it's a comfortable, vaguely scruffy place, lit by candles, chandeliers and shaded standard lamps. It stocks at least 35 different malt whiskies (some much more expensive than others: check before you choose, because prices are not necessarily as advertised on the blackboard). Champagnes are another forte. Flowers IPA or another guest beer and the usual lagers are on draught. Decent enough pub food (steaks, sausages, risotto) is reasonably priced at two courses for £10 and the roomy back yard has been ably converted into an airy, lamp-heated smoking tent.
Babies and children admitted. Bar available for hire. Function room (up to 50 capacity). Music (karaoke 6.30pm 1st Wed of month). Tables outdoors (12, garden; 4, pavement). **Map p282 N9**.

Fire Station

150 Waterloo Road, SE1 8SB (7620 2226). Waterloo tube/rail. **Open** 11am-11.30pm Mon-Sat; noon-10.30pm Sun. **Food served** *Bar* 11am-10.30pm Mon-Sat; noon-9.30pm Sun. *Restaurant* noon-3pm, 5.30-11pm Mon-Fri; noon-11pm Sat; noon-9.30pm Sun. **Credit** AmEx, MC, V. **Pub**
The London County Council's grand Edwardian fire station on Waterloo Road was converted into one of the city's early gastrobars in the 1990s. The restaurant's in the back, while the large, high-ceilinged appliance bays out front ring with the shrill sound of office parties, sometimes not a far cry from wailing sirens. Thankfully, the only emergency now is likely to be choosing from a wide-ranging selection of faintly mediocre wines from around the world. Or perhaps plumping for a real ale (Pedigree, Pride and, on our visit, the interesting Jenning's Cross-Buttock) or draught lager (Paulaner, Foster's,

Staropramen, Kronenbourg). Loud and busy, but convenient for the station.
Babies and children admitted. Disabled: toilet. Restaurant (available for hire, 100 capacity). Tables outdoors (6, pavement). **Map p282 N9**.

Hole in the Wall

5 Mepham Street, SE1 8SQ (7928 6196). Waterloo tube/rail. **Open** 11am-11pm Mon-Thur; 11am-11.30pm Fri, Sat; noon-10.30pm Sun. **Food served** noon-9pm Mon-Sat; noon-4pm Sun. **No credit cards.** **Pub**
Better than an ATM, the HITW is an unreconstructed drinking hole in 'the wall' of the old South Eastern Railway's line into Charing Cross. In a calculated snub to the London & South Western Railway, the viaduct was constructed directly in front of the main entrance to Waterloo station in the 1860s. The windowless brick cavern of the main bar now makes a surprisingly cheery place to enjoy sport on the big screen and a variety of well-kept real ales at sensible prices: Young's Ordinary, Greene King IPA and Abbot, Adnams Best and Broadside as standard, along with a couple of guests such as Hog's Back TEA or Sharp's Doom Bar. Lagers on tap are Leffe, Staropramen and Hoegaarden.
Babies and children admitted (until 8pm). Games (fruit machines, quiz machine, pinball). Tables outdoors (4, garden). TV (big screen, satellite). **Map p282 M8**.

King's Arms

25 Roupell Street, SE1 8TB (7207 0784). Waterloo tube/rail. **Open** 11am-11pm Mon-Fri; noon-11pm Sat; noon-10.30pm Sun. **Food served** 11am-3pm, 6-10.30pm Mon-Fri; 6-10.30pm Sat; noon-4pm Sun. **Credit** MC, V. **Pub**
For review, see p152.
Babies and children admitted (until 5pm). Function room (up to 80 capacity). TV. **Map p282 N8**.

Rose & Crown

47 Columbo Street, SE1 8DP (7928 4285). Southwark tube/rail. **Open** 11.30am-11pm Mon-Fri. **Food served** noon-2.30pm Mon-Fri. **Credit** AmEx, MC, V. **Pub**
Probably the oldest pub in the area, oddly marooned by World War II bomb damage to the surrounding houses and their subsequent redevelopment into offices, the Rose & Crown is one of Shepherd Neame's finest public houses. Landlord Matt Quick has won CAMRA awards and swears that he never uses blanket pressure

(added carbon dioxide or nitrogen) to pump his barrels dry. In summer, the large grassy garden is a wonderful boon, on the edge of shady Christchurch churchyard and lined with hop-strewn trellises. A proper local.

Function room (up to 50 capacity). Games (fruit machine). Tables outdoors (50, garden). **Map p282 N8**.

Skylon ★ NEW

Royal Festival Hall, Belvedere Road, SE1 8XX (7654 7800/www.skylonrestaurant.co.uk). Waterloo tube/rail. **Open** 11am-midnight daily. **Food served** *Grill* noon-10.30pm Mon-Wed, Sun; noon-11.30pm Thur-Sat. *Restaurant* noon-2.30pm, 5.30-10.30pm daily. **Credit** AmEx MC, V. **Bar/restaurant**

There can't be many better transport views than this in all of London. Sit at the cocktail bar (in between the two restaurant areas), and gaze out of what seems like a mile of plate glass, three storeys high, offering views (to the left) of trains trundling out of Charing Cross station, (to the right) of cars and red buses whizzing across Waterloo bridge, and in between boats and cruisers pootling along the Thames. In spite of its aircraft-hangar proportions, the space feels surprisingly intimate: plenty of bronze, walnut and slate, along with 'chandeliers' resembling elegant, elongated car filters, softened with spectacular flower arrangements, candles, and solicitous service. The drinks menu includes ten bellinis, nine martinis and a list of 1950s classics (manhattans, sidecars, and so on), as well as wines, champagnes and beers. Naturally, all are made with the finest ingredients – none of which comes cheap, but then at what price that view? Bar snacks include welsh rarebit (£6.50) and a selection of cheeses (£8).

Babies and children admitted. Bar available for hire. Restaurant (available for hire, 100 capacity). **Map p282 M8**.

Three Stags

67-69 Kennington Road, SE1 7PZ (7928 5974). Lambeth North tube/159 bus. **Open** 11am-midnight daily. **Food served** noon-10pm daily. **Credit** MC, V. **Pub**

The Three Stags has been through a turbulent period of late. Following an ill-advised flirtation with admitting diners only, new ownership has seen it recapture its clientele. During the day its location next to the Imperial War Museum attracts a touristy bunch, while evenings see a younger crowd attracted by an impressive range of draught beers including Leffe, Amstel, Hoegaarden, Peroni and Heineken, alongside Greene King IPA, Abbot Ale and Ruddles.

King's Arms

On one of central London's last remaining terraces of Victorian workers' cottages, this corner pub is now firmly on the tourist map, but also remains a firm favourite with locals and loud office workers. In the same hands as the Windmill and the Ring nearby, it's more traditional than either, with separate public and saloon bars (both very cosy and convivial in winter) and an unusual conservatory at the back where Thai meals are served. A recent refurb hasn't detracted from the charm of the place, though much of the decor is generic pub knick-knackery. Beers include Pride, Bombardier and Adnams' gimmicky Spindrift; the wine list is predominantly New World. *For listings, see p151.*

'Chaplin's corner' is a wooden booth homage to Charlie's father, who allegedly drank himself into oblivion here.

Babies and children admitted (until 8pm). Bar available for hire. Disabled: toilet. Music (open mic 9pm Mon; free). Tables outdoors (10, pavement).

Waterloo Brasserie NEW

119 Waterloo Road, SE1 8UL (7960 0202/www.waterloobrasserie.co.uk). Waterloo tube/rail. **Open** 8am-3am Mon-Fri; 10am-3am Sat, Sun. **Food served** 8am-11pm Mon-Fri; 10am-11pm Sat, Sun. **Credit** AmEx, MC, V. **Bar/brasserie**

Like a true brasserie, this one is open all day, covering breakfast, supper and everything in between. Segregated bar and restaurant areas have a self-consciously contemporary look.

South

The wine list is impressively extensive, with a wide selection, from both the Old World and New, by the glass; there are fair-priced cocktails, draught lagers served by the half-pint and a few bottled beers (including Kasteel Cru and Estrella) to choose from too. Groups of post-work parties dominated on our visit; the place occupies a prominent corner site near the Cut, and is obviously handy for both Waterloo station (just three minutes' walk away) and the Young and Old Vic theatres. May 2008 saw the welcome opening (not least for smokers) of an outside terrace.

Babies and children admitted. Bar available for hire. Restaurant (available for hire, 150 capacity). Function room (up to 100 capacity). Music (jazz 9pm Thur, Fri; free).
Map p282 N8.

White Hart
29-30 Cornwall Road, SE1 8TJ (7401 7151). Waterloo tube/rail. **Open** noon-11pm Mon, Sun; noon-midnight Tue-Sat. **Food served** noon-10pm daily. **Credit** MC, V. **Pub**
Popular with employees from South Bank media offices, this bustling corner pub has big windows looking onto the short cut to Waterloo station. As well as several wheat beers on tap (including Weissbrau and Maredsous), there are three real ales, three draught ciders (one of which is Weston's hefty Organic Vintage) and several draught wines to keep a lively crowd refreshed day and night. A few tables outside provide welcome relief from the jolly crush within.
Babies and children admitted (until 6pm). Disabled: toilet. Tables outdoors (4, pavement).
Map p282 N8.

South East

South East

Barflies south of the river enjoy a smörgåsbord of fine drinking opportunities. Boho Bermondsey has the bistro-cool **Garrison**, fine wines and cocktails at **Village East** and Thames views at the historic **Mayflower**. Blackheath's villagers head for the beer garden at the **Princess of Wales** or the old-school **Hare & Billet** for bucolic vibes. In Camberwell, the freshly scrubbed up **Bear** is a hit. Deptford's much-loved **Dog & Bell** continues to do no wrong. The **Rosendale** flies the flag for gastro in Dulwich, while the **Palmerston** does the same in East Dulwich. Retro bar **Inside 72** offers intimate, divey appeal. Greenwich has the fabulous **Greenwich Union** and kitsch cocktail den **Inc Bar**. London Bridge and Borough reveal further delights, not least the utterly one-off **Boot & Flogger**. Peckham's **Gowlett** has a fuss-free feel and award-winning ales. The revamped **Old Nun's Head** is relaxed, low-key and lovely, while the **Rye Hotel** offers quality wines and British classics, and **Perry Hill** has makes its mark with good ales and food.

Bermondsey

Garrison ★

99-101 Bermondsey Street, SE1 3XB (7089 9355/www.thegarrison.co.uk). London Bridge tube/rail. **Open** 8am-11pm Mon-Fri; 9am-11pm Sat; 9am-10.30pm Sun. **Food served** 8-11.30am, noon-3.30pm, 6.30-10pm Mon-Fri; 9-11.30am, 12.30-4pm, 6.30-10pm Sat; 9-11.30am, 12.30-4pm, 6-9.30pm Sun. **Credit** AmEx, MC, V. **Gastropub**

It's hard to ascertain where exactly the pub is in the self-declared Garrison Public House, but it's a Bermondsey Street highlight all the same. The venue is more bistro than boozer (it's low on standing space), but if you're after top-quality food, a laid-back vibe and character by the bucketload you've found the right place. The interior is an eccentric cross between an old mountain lodge and a 19th-century aristocratic dining room, full of eye-catching touches like the William Morris-style wallpaper on the back wall, curvy tables and chairs, and free-standing floor lamps. The intimate and prettily lit ground-floor space has 'romantic dinner' written all over it. A cosy basement room – complete with jukebox – handles overspill and private parties. *Disabled: toilet. Function room (35 capacity). Jukebox.*

Hide Bar

39-45 Bermondsey Street, SE1 3XF (7403 6655/www.thehidebar.com). London Bridge tube/rail. **Open** 10am-11pm Mon; 10am-midnight Tue; 10am-1am Wed, Thur; 10am-2am Fri; 5pm-2am Sat; noon-8pm Sun. **Food served** noon-4pm, 5.30-10pm Mon-Fri, Sun; 5.30-10pm Sat. **Credit** AmEx, MC, V. **Cocktail bar**

Stylishly informal, Hide has a laid-back sense of bonhomie that makes it difficult to leave – the fact that it's stuffed with soft furnishings and slump-back sofas doesn't help much either. Things are equally relaxed at the bar, but staff know their stuff. The drinks list is outstanding: meticulously prepared cocktails, beers from the Meantime Brewery in Greenwich, international bottled beers and a seemingly endless list of wines and spirits. Try to bag (better still, book) the carpeted chamber at the back of the bar where the black wallpaper and sunken ceiling lights tranquillise the mood even further. *Babies and children admitted. Bar available for hire. Drink tasting (7pm Tue; free). Function room (50 capacity).*

Mayflower

117 Rotherhithe Street, SE16 4NF (7237 4088/ http://themayflowerpub.co.uk). Rotherhithe tube. **Open** *Winter* 11am-3pm, 5.15-11pm Mon-Thur; 11am-11pm Fri-Sun. *Summer* 11am-11pm daily. **Food served** *Winter* noon-2.30pm, 6-9.30pm Mon-Sat; noon-9pm Sun. *Summer* 11am-11pm daily. **Credit** MC, V. **Pub**
For review, *see p158.*
Babies and children admitted (restaurant). Restaurant. Tables outdoors (12, riverside jetty).

Village East ★

*171-173 Bermondsey Street, SE1 3UW
(7357 6082/www.villageeast.co.uk). London
Bridge tube/rail.* **Open** *noon-11.30pm Mon-
Thur; noon-1.30am Fri, Sat; 11am-10.30pm
Sun.* **Food served** *noon-3.30pm, 6-10pm
Mon-Fri; noon-4pm, 6-10pm Sat; 11am-9.30pm
Sun.* **Credit** AmEx, MC, V. **Bar/restaurant**

Sleek and determinedly stylish, Village East takes itself seriously in the best possible way. The 'Scandinavia meets New York' interior – all exposed piping, crisp wood and curvaceous lines – is impeccably laid out, with a canteen, restaurant, two lively bar areas and a private dining room to choose from. Music is on the right side of cutting edge and a weekend late licence ensures the crowd at the bar is as much SE1 hipster as it is after-work media clone. There are 18 house cocktails, draught beers include Staropramen and Guinness, and the wine list offers plenty of choice by the glass. The food (lunchtime sandwiches and salads, swanky meat and fish mains) is a cut above too.

*Babies and children admitted (until 6pm). Bar
available for hire. Disabled: toilet. Function
rooms (up to 50 capacity). Restaurant.*

Blackheath

Crown

*47-49 Tranquil Vale, SE3 0BS (8852 0326).
Blackheath rail.* **Open** *11am-11pm Mon-Sat;
noon-10.30pm Sun.* **Food served** *noon-9pm
daily.* **Credit** AmEx, DC, MC, V. **Pub**

The Crown has been serving regulars and travellers alike since the 1740s; previous incarnations would have seen stagecoaches roll up for business where now there are 4x4s. Rugby fans take their seats inside for ale and big screen sport, while media types herd shrill children around the patio garden out front. The rugby theme continues with Swing Low heading the pumps. Theakston Best, Greene King IPA and London Pride hold up the rear along with Foster's and Hoegaarden. Pleasingly, the busy wine list is very reasonable, to the point that even champagne is guilt free – Lanson at £27.50? Magic.

*Babies and children admitted (until 8pm).
Games (fruit machines, video games). Tables
outdoors (8, pavement). TVs.*

Hare & Billet

*1A Elliot Cottages, Hare & Billet Road, SE3
0QJ (8852 2352). Blackheath rail.* **Open**
*11am-11pm Mon-Thur; 11am-midnight Fri,
Sat; noon-11pm Sun.* **Food served** *noon-*
3.30pm, 5.30-9pm Mon-Fri; noon-7.30pm Sat,
Sun. **Credit** MC, V. **Pub**

This perfectly located watering hole on the edge of the heath has been providing well-earned sustenance for the best part of 400 years. The crowd lean towards ruddy-cheek-and-tweed types who see their Sunday constitutional as a means to an end – the end being a foaming pint with the broadsheets. Food offerings are fairly standard but the pumps are well stacked; Greene King IPA, Flowers, Abbot, Hoegaarden, Strongbow, Heineken and Guinness are all here as well as some bottled Leffe and a reasonably priced wine list.

*Babies and children admitted (lunch only).
Games (darts, quiz machine). TV (big screen).*
Map p285 E3.

Princess of Wales

*1A Montpelier Row, SE3 0RL (8297 5911).
Blackheath rail.* **Open** *noon-11pm Mon-Sat;
noon-10.30pm Sun.* **Food served** *noon-10pm
Mon-Sat; noon-9pm Sun.* **Credit** MC, V.
Pub/bar

A revamped pub that's kept its integrity, not only is the Princess of Wales pleasingly heath-side, it's got its own heated beer garden too. The premises look out across the heath via three, high-ceiling rooms, with a bright conservatory out back. You'll be fighting the well-heeled locals for a seat at the weekend. There's only the merest of nods to the pub's part in rugby's history – England gathered here before their first international game (1871) – the rest is all about relaxing with a cheeky glass of something or other. As with its sister pub, the Railway (see below), the bar is laden with delights: Kirin, Paulaner, Spitfire, Old Speckled Hen, Bombardier and London Pride, and the short wine list holds a decent malbec for £10.

*Babies and children admitted (until 7.30pm).
Conservatory available for hire (50 capacity).
Disabled: toilet. Games (darts, fruit machine,
golf machine). Quiz (9pm Tue; £1). Tables
outdoors (30, garden).*

Railway

*16 Blackheath Village, SE3 9LE (8852 2390).
Blackheath rail.* **Open** *noon-11pm Mon-Wed;
noon-midnight Thur-Sat; noon-10.30pm Sun.*
Food served *noon-10pm daily.* **Credit**
AmEx, MC, V. **Pub/bar**

A pub for all seasons offering up a smörgåsbord of drinking experiences: from lazy Sunday afternoon lounging to dimly lit evening soirées; fresh air in the garden to fags on the roof terrace. And just take a look at those pumps! A festival of beers, ales and ciders awaits:

South East

Liefmans Frambozen, Franziskaner, Maredsous, Früli, Erdinger, Belle-Vue Kriek, Budvar… the list is endless. And there's more coming too – Red Stripe, Bulmers and Applebocq are imminent. Fridges gleam with delights in the form of Singha and Cusqueña while the select wine list hovers around the £4 a large glass mark with a Domaine La Roche Chablis at £4.20. *Babies and children admitted (until 7pm). Disabled: toilet. Music (guitarist 6pm Wed; pianist 6pm Sun; free). Tables outdoors (5, garden; 10, terrace).*

Zerodegrees

29-31 Montpelier Vale, SE3 0TJ (8852 5619/ www.zerodegrees.co.uk). Blackheath rail. **Open** noon-midnight Mon-Sat; noon-11.30pm Sun. **Food served** noon-11pm Mon-Sat; noon-10.30pm Sun. **Credit** AmEx, MC, V. **Bar**
Think the *Crystal Maze*'s 'Industrial Zone' and you've nailed the look of Zerodegrees. This brilliant microbrewery, bar and restaurant (now also in Reading, Cardiff and Bristol) serves its young, buzzy clientele with beers from the very same vats housed in the entrance. Beers can be accompanied by the excellent pizzas or taken away in anything from a four-pinter to a 50-litre keg. At £2.60 a pint full price, £1.90 during happy hour (4-7pm weekdays) is a steal. *Babies and children welcome: high chairs. Restaurant (available for hire, 180 capacity). Tables outdoors (10, terrace). TV (big screen, satellite).*

Camberwell

Bear NEW

296A Camberwell New Road, SE5 0RP (7274 7037/www.thebear-freehouse.co.uk). Oval tube. **Open** 4-11pm Mon-Thur; 4pm-midnight Fri; noon-11pm Sat, Sun. **Food served** 6-10pm Mon-Fri; noon-3pm, 6-10pm Sat; noon-5pm Sun. **Credit** MC, V. **Pub**
A pub as amiable as the Bear comes as something of a surprise on this least appealing arm of Camberwell's beleaguered crossroads. A former Victorian gin palace dominated by a horseshoe bar, the place has scrubbed up nicely and oozes warmth, especially when it is illuminated by candlelight. Despite this, it's still very much a locals' boozer with Ram's Revenge and Old Trip complementing the usual suspects lager-wise. The rear room, decorated with stopped clocks and china dogs, makes for a great place to sample the affordable and hearty British food. *Babies and children admitted. Quiz (8pm Tue; £2).*

Mayflower

If you're looking for a relatively authentic olde worlde environment in which to sup your pint, the Mayflower, hidden in the riverside backstreets, is just the ticket. Around the corner from the little-known Brunel Museum, this 18th-century pub is reassuringly withered and cramped yet totally charming. Seating is snuggled tight around the bar, from which Old Speckled Hen, Greene King IPA and Stella are among the options dispensed on draught. There's a coal fire in one corner, a waterfront terrace and an upstairs dining room (steak and cheese pie, £12.25). *For listings see p156.*

Dark Horse

16 Grove Lane, SE5 8SY (7703 9990/ www.barbarblacksheep.com). Denmark Hill rail. **Open** 11am-11pm Mon, Tue, Sun; 11am-midnight Wed, Thur; 11am-1am Fri, Sat. **Food served** noon-10pm daily. **Credit** AmEx, DC, MC, V. **Pub**
The Dark Horse fights to blend progressive aesthetics with the common touch and comes up not entirely wanting – the bar fronts a dramatic equestrian painting and seating mixes wooden chairs, deep leather thrones and corner couches. Most unusually, the scent of vanilla wafted about us on our last visit – something of a coup in the miasma of sweat and stale beer that is the post-smoking era. Sweet smells aside, it's a down-to-earth place popular with nearby residents, and while there are no surprises on tap, the menu of pub standards is a cut above the average, cheap and eminently cheerful. *Babies and children admitted (until 7pm). Disabled: toilet. Function room (50 capacity). Outdoor tables (10, pavement). Restaurant (available for hire, 40 capacity).*

South East

Hermit's Cave

*28 Camberwell Church Street, SE5 8QU
(7703 3188). Denmark Hill rail.* **Open**
10am-midnight Mon-Wed; 10am-2am Thur-
Sat; noon-midnight Sun. **Food served** noon-
4pm daily. **No credit cards. Pub**
Few places live up to their name as completely
as the Hermit's Cave, a matchbox boozer
cluttered with more cheerful tat than most
museums – framed ornithological prints,
decrepit accordions and cocktail shakers that
look like they've not been used since the '80s.
And rightly so because this is a pub for beer
lovers – not to mention the odd local chancer
and wastrel. The range of ales on our last visit
included Pure Gold, Cheval Mort and
Gravesend Shrimper, plus draft cider from
Weston's. Bright and breezy it ain't – the
garishly upholstered bar stools constitute the
only splash of colour and the windows let in
less light than the walls – but that's all part of
the Hermit's charm.
*Tables outdoors (3, pavement). TV
(big screen, satellite).*

Deptford

Bar Sonic

*1 Deptford Broadway, SE8 4PA (8691 5289).
Deptford Bridge DLR.* **Open** 11am-1am Mon-
Thur; 11am-2am Fri, Sat; noon-midnight Sun.
Food served noon-9pm Tue-Sun. **No credit
cards. Bar**
A cross between a West Indian diner and DJ bar,
this friendly venture at the anchor end of
Deptford High Street serves up pan-fried
snapper and jerk chicken, along with a range of
rums, and bottles of Red Stripe. TV sports and
a pool table also play a leading role, as do live
music nights. Beck's Vier and Carlsberg Export
are draught options, while a row of tables
outside catches the mid-morning sun and
encourages the enjoyment of proper coffee or a
selection of fruit teas.
*Babies and children admitted (restaurant only).
Bar available for hire. Games (fruit machines,
pool). Music (DJ 9pm Thur; bands 9pm Fri,
Sat; free). Restaurant. Tables outdoors (10,
pavement).* **Map p285 C2.**

Rosendale

Dog & Bell ★
116 Prince Street, SE8 3JD (8692 5664/ www.thedogandbell.com). New Cross tube/ rail/Deptford rail. **Open** noon-11pm Mon-Sat; noon-10.30pm Sun. **Food served** noon-2pm, 6-10pm Mon-Fri; noon-10pm Sat; noon-7pm Sun. **Credit** AmEx, MC, V. **Pub**

The much-loved Dog & Bell is Deptford's best bar. That it's dark, foreboding and located in no man's land matters not a jot. Regulars beat a path to its door for a cherry-picked selection of real ales (currently two from the Dark Star stable and Sparrow's Nest) and Beck's at less than £3 a pint. More than that, they come for the communal atmosphere. The bar billiards table stands neglected as everyday folk and Deptford's age-old boho crowd mingle, usually in the side room now dominated by Fred Aylward's striking punk art. Proper meals (liver and bacon, chicken masala) are served too. *Babies and children admitted. Bar available for hire. Disabled: toilet. Games (bar billiards table, board games). Quiz (9pm Sun, £1). Tables outdoors (4, garden).* **Map p285 C1.**

Royal Albert
460 New Cross Road, SE14 6TJ (8692 3737/ www.antic-ltd.com). New Cross tube/rail. **Open** 4pm-midnight Mon-Thur; 4pm-1am Fri; noon-1am Sat; noon-midnight Sun. **Food served** 5-10pm Tue-Thur; 5-9pm Fri; 1-9pm Sat; 1-5pm Sun. **Credit** MC, V. **Pub**

This successful makeover of a notorious late-night dive has positive indications for the area and where it's going. Goldsmiths' students, young professionals and long-term local empty-nesters gather around carefully chosen second-hand furniture to commune over a pint of Grolsch or Heineken, Young's or Timothy Taylor Landlord. Bottled beers include Chimay, Duvel and Budvar. Wine is equally popular and affordably drinkable. A grill in the convivial back room produces burgers and the best Sunday roast around. *Babies and children admitted (until 5pm). Film screenings (8pm alternate Mon; free). Quiz (8pm alternate Mon; £2). Tables outdoors (9, garden). TV.* **Map p285 B2.**

Dulwich

Crown & Greyhound
73 Dulwich Village, SE21 7BJ (8299 4976). North Dulwich rail. **Open** 11am-11pm Mon-Wed; 11am-midnight Thur-Sat; 11am-10.30pm Sun. **Food served** noon-10pm Mon-Sat; noon-9.30pm Sun. **Credit** AmEx, MC, V. **Pub**

This Victorian behemoth was once two pubs – the Crown for the gentry, the Greyhound for the great unhosed – that have long since been united by a democratic unbricking. The cavernous interior comprises a central bar and three rooms with wooden benches overlooked by an ornately moulded ceiling, while the enormous two-tiered beer garden gets packed in summer. As the only pub in the village it's also a community centre of sorts; film screenings, wine and chess club meetings, and even weddings are hosted. The pub is planning a series of real ale festivals, while Young's Bitter, Harveys Sussex Best and London Pride are served up daily.
Babies and children admitted (restaurant and conservatory only). Disabled: toilet. Entertainment (chess club Mon; bridge club Tue, Wed; wine club Wed). Function room (100 capacity). Games (chess). Restaurant. Tables outdoors (50, garden).

Rosendale ★ NEW
65 Rosendale Road, SE21 8EZ (8670 0812/ www.therosendale.co.uk). West Norwood/West Dulwich rail. **Open/food served** noon-11pm Mon-Sat; noon-10pm Sun. **Credit** MC, V. **Gastropub**
Winner of *Time Out*'s Best Gastropub award in 2007, the Rosendale is housed in a fine old coaching inn, three floors of generously proportioned Victorian rooms, with the ground-level façade covered in original tiles. The cavernous, echoey space (much shiny wood and leather banquettes) on the ground floor is divided in two: a superb restaurant run by South African chef Mark Foxon at the back, and a bar with its own shorter menu (including superb burgers for under a tenner) at the front. The vast wine list – the work of sommelier and co-owner Mark Van der Goot – takes precedence over the beers, with the only real ale on our visit being Spitfire.
Babies and children admitted (until 7.30pm). Disabled: toilet. Function rooms (up to 130 capacity). Restaurant available for hire (70 capacity). Tables outdoors (48, garden).

East Dulwich

Franklins
157 Lordship Lane, SE22 8HX (8299 9598/ www.franklinsrestaurant.com). East Dulwich rail. **Open** noon-11pm Mon-Wed; noon-midnight Thur, Fri; 10am-midnight Sat; noon-10.30pm Sun. **Food served** noon-10.30pm daily. **Credit** AmEx, MC, V. **Bar/restaurant**
Franklins has always managed to appear superior above other gastronomic endeavours

on Lordship Lane. Perhaps it's the imperial blue façade, or the elevated position from which it literally looks down on the competition. Maybe it's the assured separation of the drinking den from the British restaurant out back, the former a cosy bolthole of bare wooden floors and benches, the latter a well-aired space for indulging the owners' near-medieval obsession with meats. Young's is the best of a limited selection of ale on tap, although there are also a few European bottles (Leffe, Budvar, Estrella Damm) and a well-edited and affordable wine list featuring six bottles of both red and white for under £20.
Babies and children welcome: high chairs. Disabled: toilet. Function room (35 capacity). Restaurant. Tables outdoors (3, pavement).

Herne Tavern
2 Forest Hill Road, SE22 0RR (8299 9521/ www.theherne.net). East Dulwich or Peckham Rye rail/63, 363 bus. **Open** noon-11pm Mon-Thur; noon-1am Fri, Sat; noon-10.30pm Sun. **Food served** noon-2.30pm, 6.30-9.45pm Mon-Fri; noon-3pm, 6.30-9.45pm Sat; noon-4.30pm Sun. **Credit** MC, V. **Gastropub**
'A proper family pub!' exclaims the chalked billboard outside this dark pub on a busy main road, which looks anything but. However, the Herne's sensitive gastro refurbishment by the same management as East Duwich's celebrated Palmerston– stained glass, dark wood floots, old theatre posters – proves you can have the best of both worlds. On our visit, a sweaty five-a-side team supping pints of Petermans happily mingled with two Czech students reclining on the Chesterfields with big glasses of wine, and a sqaud of real ale bores lamenting that the Deuchars was off (but pleased to see Moorhouse's, one of 25 rotating guest bitters). Meanwhile, in the side dining room, the intrepid (and, frankly, more wealthy) can tuck into fried brawn with sauce gribiche or organic salmon fillets with cockles and samphire. Definitely worth a visit for May's real ale festival or a special Sunday lunch.
Babies and children admitted. Function room (60 capacity). Restaurant. Tables outdoors (25, garden).

Inside 72 ★
72 Lordship Lane, SE22 8HF (8693 7131). East Dulwich rail. **Open** 5pm-midnight Mon-Fri; noon-midnight Sat, Sun. **Food served** noon-4pm Sat, Sun. **Credit** MC, V. **Bar**
Lordship Lane's very own Brooklyn dive bar, much loved by trendier locals. 'Cool' doesn't even come close: the '70s rock the stereo, the

walls are plastered with everything from vintage skate mag covers to Soviet propaganda posters, and the shelves behind the bar groan beneath a retro army of loveable Tomy robots. Seating is split between sofas, bar stools and rickety chairs, and the fact that there isn't room to swing a cat only adds to the unpredictable intimacy of the evening. The draught selection disappoints, but bottles include Chimay, Duvel and Anchor Steam Beer.
Games (board games, cards).

Palmerston ★

91 Lordship Lane, SE22 8EP (8693 1629/ www.thepalmerston.net). East Dulwich rail. **Open** noon-11pm Mon-Thur; noon-midnight Fri, Sat; noon-10.30pm Sun. **Food served** noon-2.30pm, 7-10pm Mon-Fri; noon-3pm, 7-10pm Sat; noon-3.30pm, 7-9pm Sun. **Credit** MC, V. **Gastropub**
Few refits are as thorough as the one that in 2004 turned the grimy old Lord Palmerston into a streamlined gastropub with all the trimmings. The original wood panelling remains along with a gorgeous mosaic floor in the rear room, but these days it's eating rather than drinking that draws both crowds and critical acclaim. As a result, the beer selection suffers in favour of the extensive wine list (although Kronenbourg Blanc and Timothy Taylor appease local media types and their dads respectively), and tables tend to be universally reserved for diners tucking into rumps of lamb, line-caught sea bass and superb Sunday lunches.
Art exhibitions. Babies and children welcome: children's portions; high chairs. Booking advisable. Restaurant available for hire (75 capacity). Tables outdoors (6, pavement).

Forest Hill

Dartmouth Arms ★

7 Dartmouth Road, SE23 2NH (8488 3117/ www.thedartmoutharms.com). Forest Hill rail/122, 176, 185 bus. **Open** noon-midnight Mon-Thur; noon-1am Fri, Sat; noon-11pm Sun. **Food served** noon-3.30pm, 6.30-10.30pm Mon-Fri; noon-4pm, 6.30-10.30pm Sat; noon-9pm Sun. **Credit** MC, V. **Gastropub**
An erstwhile community boozer, the Dartmouth Arms' recent refurbishment stripped away years of aesthetic apathy and created a gastropub on a street formerly famous for its takeaways. The front bar is now a well-aired, sepia-tinted space perfect for chilling out over papers or free Wi-Fi, plus there's an adjoining 'snug bar' (the red walls of which boast exhibitions by local artists) and a rear dining

room for lingering over affordable gastro fodder. Cocktails are just £5.50 (champagne cocktails £6.25) and there's an extensive wine list, but beers are limited: Brakspear and Bombardier for ale heads; Staropramen and Kronenbourg for lager lovers.
Babies and children welcome: high chairs. Disabled: toilet. Restaurant available for hire (45 capacity). Tables outdoors (10, garden). Wi-Fi (free).

Gipsy Hill

Mansion

255 Gipsy Road, SE27 9QY (8761 9016). Gipsy Hill rail. **Open** noon-11pm Mon-Thur, Sun; noon-midnight Fri, Sat. **Food served** noon-4pm, 6-9pm Mon; noon-4pm, 6-10pm Tue-Thur; noon-4pm, 6-10pm Fri; noon-5pm, 6-10.30pm Sat; noon-9.30pm Sun. **Credit** MC, V. **Gastropub**
There's more than a hint of Hammer Horror in the Mansion's looming tower and black turret windows and interior with its endearing mix of camp and vamp thanks to the grand piano, enormous gilt mirrors and elaborate candelabras. Boris Karloff, erstwhile resident of nearby Peckham Rye, would have felt right at home. For all that, the place feels anything but sinister; it's hugely popular and often packed with punters lounging on sofas and tucking into top-end pub food (there's a barbecue in the back garden during summer months). One guest ale accompanies Young's Special, plus there's Staropramen, Leffe and Weston's cider, a range of cocktails and a decent wine list.
Babies and children admitted (until 7pm). Disabled: toilet. Music (jazz 7pm Sun; free). Over 21s only after 7pm. Quiz (8pm Tue; £2). Tables outdoors (15, garden).

Numidie

48 Westow Hill, SE19 1RX (8766 6166/ www.numidie.co.uk). Gipsy Hill rail. **Open** 6pm-midnight Tue-Sun. **Food served** 6-10pm Tue-Sun. **Credit** MC, V. **Gastrobar**
Numidie's ground floor bistro is one of south London's most cherished cultural retreats, and this subterranean cocktail cave is the jewel in its crown. As upstairs, the marriage of French and Algerian influences couldn't be more harmonious – from the Jacques Brel poster on the peeling red walls to barman Hamed's globe-trotting musical mixes, which deliver plenty of African and Middle Eastern promise when jazz bands aren't treading the boards. Hamed is also a dab hand at inventing cocktails – his Berbere Fruit Cup (£5.50) mixes eight-year-old Wild

Turkey with fresh lemon and orange juice and maraschino – plus there's a reasonably priced wine list alongside Kronenbourg on tap and Leffe, Casablanca and London Pride in bottles. *Babies and children welcome: booster seats (restaurant only). Bar available for hire (Tue-Thur). Restaurant.*

Greenwich

Ashburnham Arms
25 Ashburnham Grove, SE10 8UH (8692 2007). Greenwich rail/DLR. **Open** noon-11pm Mon-Wed, Sun; noon-midnight Thur-Sat. **Food served** noon-2pm, 6-9pm Tue-Sat; noon-6pm Sun. **Credit** MC, V. **Pub**
Cricket, well-chosen ales and a children's selection on the dining menu – this could easily be a pub on the village green. Instead, it's tucked down a quiet Greenwich backwater street. That is not to say it's undiscovered, though; a stream of SE10 locals pass by for a pint of Shepherd Neame Spitfire, Master Brew, Bishops Finger or Kent's Best (Oranjeboom and Holsten are also on offer) and a pizza (£7.50-£8) and a natter in the neat backroom. Wine has also been carefully chosen. The pub first XI get a decorative look-in, along with a rather splendid mural of Greenwich cartography and less impressive album covers from the 1970s.
Babies and children admitted (conservatory). Games (board games). Quiz (9pm Tue; free). Tables outdoors (15, garden; 10, patio). **Map p285 D2**.

Bar du Musée ★
17 Nelson Road, SE10 9JB (8858 4710/ www.bardumusee.com). Cutty Sark DLR. **Open** noon-1am Mon-Thur; noon-2am Fri, Sat; 11am-midnight Sun. **Food served** noon-3pm, 6-10pm Mon-Fri; 11am-4pm, 6-10pm Sat; 11am-8pm Sun. **Credit** MC, V. **Wine bar**
Once an intimate late-night and often louche drinking hole, the BDM is now a serious operation with a huge dining area at the back and a more limited selection of the thing that makes it tick – wine. This is not to say that the front bar, with its French soldier's uniform, red walls, wrought-iron and candlelight, is no longer a fine place to move seamlessly from chat to romance – it most certainly is. Help things along with a merlot - malbec (£3.45/£13) or Guerrieri Rizzardi pinot grigio (£3.60/£15.50) – perhaps even a Pannier Brut Champagne (£6.50/£29). Accompaniments include platters of cured meats or French cheeses. The basement offers more intimacy but comes with kitchen smells.

Babies and children welcome: high chairs. Bar available for hire. Function room (40 capacity). Restaurant. Tables outdoors (20, garden). **Map p285 E1**.

Coach & Horses
13 Greenwich Market, SE10 9HZ (8293 0880/ www.greenwich-inc.com). Cutty Sark DLR. **Open** noon-11pm Mon-Thur; 11am-midnight Fri, Sat; 11am-10.30pm Sun. **Food served** noon-9pm daily. **Credit** MC, V. **Pub/Bar**
This super-professional gastrobar is located in a corner of the covered area of Greenwich Market. Little of the old pub feel remains but the Coach offers as good a range of beers and ales as you'll find anywhere in SE10 – Paulaner Hefe-Weizen, Amstel, Oranjeboom, Leffe, Brakspear, Old Speckled Hen, Greene King IPA, Timothy Taylor Landlord – complemented by a dozen wines, most by the glass. Add decent food, the day's papers, a fireplace and a little art, and you're sorted.
Babies and children admitted (until 8pm). Tables outdoors (16, patio). **Map p285 E1**.

Cutty Sark Tavern
4-6 Ballast Quay, SE10 9PD (8858 3146). Greenwich rail/DLR/Cutty Sark DLR. **Open** 11am-11pm Mon-Sat; noon-10.30pm Sun. **Food served** noon-9pm Mon-Fri, Sun; noon-10pm Sat. **Credit** MC, V. **Pub**
A decorative discrepancy over dates – the façade says 1795, the glazed front-door windows insist on 1695 – can't hide the historic nature of this riverside hostelry. Ales are another attraction (St Austell Tribute, Abbot, Fuller's London Pride) as well as bloody great dinners such as ribeye steak (£12.95) with all the trimmings. There are fine whiskies too – Dalwhinnie, Talisker and Lagavulin – somehow fitting with the ground floor's nautical decor. Upstairs is less claustrophobic, while the rows of seats outside overlooking the river come into their own in summer.
Babies and children admitted (until 9pm). Games (quiz machine). Tables outdoors (10, terrace).

Gipsy Moth
60 Greenwich Church Street, SE10 9BL (8858 0786). Cutty Sark DLR. **Open** noon-11pm Mon-Thur; noon-midnight Fri; 11am-midnight Sat; 11am-10.30pm Sun. **Food served** noon-10pm Mon-Fri; 11am-10pm Sat; 11am-9.30pm Sun. **Credit** AmEx, DC, MC, V. **Pub**
The Mitchell Brothers' funky makeover of this formerly traditional boozer – just a gangplank away from another famous ship, the *Cutty Sark*

South East

– has proved a great success. An impressive range of beers (Schneider Weisse, Früli, Budvar, Paulaner, Franziskaner and at least six others) and well-priced selection of wines can be enjoyed in either the split-level back beer garden or the relaxed, multi-spaced interior. The food isn't shabby either, from full breakfasts (£5) through bar snacks (pint of prawns, aïoli, rustic bread) to solid mains such as glazed bacon loin with free-range eggs and chips.

Babies and children admitted (until 6pm). Games (board games). Quiz (8.30pm Thur; £1). Tables outdoors (40, garden). **Map p285 E1**.

Greenwich Park Bar & Grill

1 King William Walk, SE10 9JH (8853 7860/ www.thegreenwichpark.com). Greenwich rail/ DLR/Cutty Sark DLR. **Open** noon-1am Mon-Fri; 11am-1am Sat; 11am-midnight Sun. **Food served** noon-6pm Mon-Thur; noon-8.30pm Fri, Sat; 11am-6pm Sun. **Credit** MC, V.
Bar/restaurant

Busy with people seeking refreshment after afternoon lazing in neighbouring Greenwich Park, the GPB&G has yet to find its feet where a regular after-dark clientele is concerned. It's an Inc bar – that is, under the same umbrella as almost every prominent venue in Greenwich – so the drinks selection is decent. Franziskaner, Boddingtons and Leffe are the picks on draught, while many of the three-dozen cocktails (most under £6) have a tropical flavour and there are ice-cream varieties too.

Babies and children welcome (until 7pm): children's menu; high chairs. Disabled: toilet. Function room (70 capacity). Games (2 pool tables). Tables outdoors (6, courtyard; 4, pavement). **Map p285 E1**.

Greenwich Union ★

56 Royal Hill, SE10 8RT (8692 6258/ www.greenwichunion.com). Greenwich rail/ DLR. **Open** noon-11pm Mon-Fri; 11am-11pm Sat; 11.30am-10.30pm Sun. **Food served** noon-10pm Mon-Fri, Sun; 11am-9pm Sat. **Credit** MC, V. **Pub**

Alistair Hook's laudable Meantime Brewery flagship is based on the training and recipes he gleaned at age-old institutions in Germany. In-house Meantime produces London Stout, Pale Ale, Helles, Kölner, Union, Strawberry and Raspberry varieties, available on draught at reasonable prices. Hook has also been at pains to provide a global selection by the bottle: rare Cantillon Gueuze from Anderlecht, Brussels, Aecht Schlenkerla Marzen smoked beer from Bamberg, and so on. Wines, starting at £3.15 a glass, include a Spy Valley sauvignon blanc and

Punto Alto pinot noir. Throw in proper cheeses, steak and stout pies and it's no wonder the Union is reliably busy.

Babies and children admitted (until 9pm). Tables outdoors (12, garden). **Map p285 E2**.

Inc Bar ★

7A College Approach, SE10 9HY (8858 6721/ www.incbar.com). Cutty Sark DLR. **Open** 6pm-1.30am Wed, Thur; 7pm-3am Fri, Sat; 5pm-midnight Sun. **Credit** MC, V. **Cocktail bar**

Inc is more than this rather smart, two-level cocktail and DJ lounge bar in Greenwich's covered market – it's also a dozen-strong empire of drinks outlets (Bar du Musée, *see p163*; Greenwich Park Bar & Grill, *see left*) clustered in the SE10 postcode. More recently, the group has installed an Inc Brasserie in the O2 Arena at the Dome. Inc Bar is, however, the jewel in the crown, as illustrated by the images of rare stones that are part of Laurence Llewelyn-Bowen's borderline kitsch design concept; decorative nods towards timepieces are another nice touch. The longest cocktail list in south-east London offers nearly three dozen classic and imaginatively mixed drinks using top-notch spirits, nearly all in the £6-£6.50 range: an apple and melon martini with Zubrowka vodka and Midori; a jamaican sunset with Appleton VS, sloe gin and fresh redcurrants; and an aphrodisiac with Stoli vanilla, Chartreuse and fresh ginger. Wines begin at £4/£14 and include a £45 Montmains Chablis, but most people in the mildly erotic upstairs rooms are more interested in eye contact than vintage labels.

Bar available for hire. Function rooms (up to 50 capacity). Music (DJs 10pm Thur, Fri; 11pm Sat; free-£5). TVs. **Map p285 E1**.

North Pole

131 Greenwich High Road, SE10 8JA (8853 3020/www.northpolegreenwich.com). Greenwich rail/DLR. **Open** noon-midnight Mon-Wed; noon-1am Thur; noon-2am Fri, Sat; noon-11.30pm Sun. **Food served** noon-10.30pm daily. **Credit** AmEx, MC, V. **DJ bar**

In place for nearly a decade, this bar-club-restaurant still does a roaring trade. There's a downstairs club (South Pole) and upstairs restaurant but the street-level lounge bar, its modest VIP area with cowhide seating off to one side, provides some 30 cocktails (£6-£7), Greene King IPA, Hoegaarden and Staropramen on draught (plus Peroni and San Miguel by the bottle), and quality bar food (North Pole burger, £7). High-end spirits – Grey Goose vodka, Bombay Sapphire gin, Sauza tequila – are used in the martinis and tequinis, while the house

Florence. *See p166.*

South East

bloody mary is a potent combination of Finlandia, a touch of red wine and all the sauces. Six wines by the glass complete the classily upbeat picture.

Function room (30 capacity). Music (DJs 9pm Thur-Sat, £5 after 10pm; band 8.30pm Sun, free). Restaurant available for hire (80 capacity). Tables outdoors (8, pavement). TVs (satellite). **Map p285 D2.**

Plume of Feathers

19 Park Vista, SE10 9LZ (8858 1661/ www.plume-of-feathers.co.uk). Cutty Sark DLR/ Maze Hill rail. **Open** 11am-11pm Mon-Thur; 11am-midnight Fri, Sat; 11am-11.30pm Sun. **Food served** noon-3pm Mon; noon-3pm, 6-9pm Tue-Fri; noon-4pm, 6-9.30pm Sat; noon-5pm Sun. **Credit** MC, V. **Pub**

Sue and her popular staff run a lovely locals' favourite here, the longest established pub in Greenwich, some three centuries old. Tucked behind Greenwich Park, the Plume doesn't get many tourists but the throng is so thick around the little square bar it's just as well. Pints of Ruddles County, Old Speckled Hen, Fuller's London Pride, Adnams and standard lagers are quaffed in a cosy interior decked out with military, nautical and Victorian memorabilia. The food is something else: tagines, house beefburgers and outstanding roasts. There's a summer terrace on which to dine en famille. *Babies and children admitted. Restaurant available for hire (75 capacity). Tables outdoors (30, garden).* **Map p285 E1.**

Richard I ★ HOT 50

52-54 Royal Hill, SE10 8RT (8692 2996). Greenwich rail/DLR. **Open** 11am-11pm Mon-Sat; noon-10.30pm Sun. **Food served** noon-3pm, 6-9.30pm Mon-Sat; noon-9.30pm Sun. **Credit** MC, V. **Pub**

One might assume that this traditional Young's pub would suffer from standing next door to one of the most successful outlets in south London, the Greenwich Union (*see p164*), but that's far from the case. Regulars gather in droves at the lovely, two-bar boozer, much as they did for the hop-picking organised here 50 years ago, the

photographic evidence of which complements the venue's nautical prints. Seats in the beautiful bay window are the best in the house, along with those in the beer garden out back. As well as Young's usual range and Bombardier, there is Peroni and Bitburger by the bottle, a standard merlot, pinot grigio and shiraz, fairly priced pub grub and board games.
Babies and children admitted (until 5.30pm, saloon bar). Chess club (6pm Tue; free). Games (board games). No piped music (public bar). Quiz (8.30pm Sun; £1). Tables outdoors (15, garden). **Map p285 E2.**

Trafalgar Tavern

Park Row, SE10 9NW (8858 2909/www. trafalgartavern.co.uk). Cutty Sark DLR/Maze Hill rail. **Open** noon-11pm Mon-Thur, Sun; noon-1am Fri, Sat. **Food served** noon-10pm Mon-Sat; noon-5pm Sun. **Credit** MC, V. **Pub**
This landmark boozer lapped by the Thames is not as historic as it seems – its impressive Georgian appearance is actually down to a 1968 makeover – but the TT still pulls in the tourists thanks to its riverside location and nautical get-up. The beers bring in the locals (Flowers, Boddingtons, Franziskaner and Leffe) as does the food, hearty if pricey mains such as beer-battered cod and chips (£9.95). Famous guests of yesteryear include Dickens who set a breakfast here in *Our Mutual Friend*. There is a proper restaurant at the back, a dining area at the front but most are here for the simple, addictive pleasure of watching vessels glide along the Thames.
Babies and children admitted (until 7pm). Function rooms (up to 200 capacity). Music (jazz, 8pm alternate Sun; free). Restaurant. Tables outdoors (20, riverside). **Map p285 E1.**

Herne Hill

Commercial

210-212 Railton Road, SE24 0JT (7501 9051). Herne Hill rail. **Open** noon-midnight daily. **Food served** noon-10pm Mon-Thur; noon-11pm Fri, Sat; noon-9.30pm Sun. **Credit** MC, V. **Pub**
Blimey! This former railway pub has had quite a refit. From our vantage point on a sofa at the back, we spotted four different types of chandelier, blue fairy lights, Shaker-style panelling and exposed brickwork. And, if the pub looks like it's trying too hard, you should see the dressy, too-cool-for-school regulars. Still, there's a lot to like amid the noise (aural and visual), not least the most interesting selection of beers and spirits in the area including Budvar

Dark, Paulaner and guest ales such as Pedigree served in dimply retro pint mugs.
Babies and children admitted. Disabled: toilet. Games (board games). Tables outdoors (5, garden).

Florence ★ NEW

133 Dulwich Road, SE24 0NG (7326 4987/ www.florencehernehill.com). Herne Hill rail. **Open** noon-12.30am Mon-Thur; noon-1.30am Fri; 11am-1.30am Sat; 11am-12.30am Sun. **Food served** noon-10pm Mon-Fri; 11am-10pm Sat; 11am-9.30pm Sun. **Credit** MC, V. **Pub**
The proprietors of this light, airy pub stirred some local antagonism when they took over the space vacated by dank old sports bar Ganleys. Though you may no longer be able to catch Sky Sports here, you can pore over the match reports in the Sunday papers while enjoying burgers from the open kitchen and interesting beers (it's a genuine free house, with tasting notes on every pump; we recommend Meantime's Kölner lager). Proximity to Brockwell Park and Brixton Beach – the Lido – means that the Florence has been colonised by families. But there's enough space amid its cowhide banquettes, conservatory and seemingly endless beer terrace for everyone to enjoy a visit. And those copper vats aren't for show: they pump out an above-average bitter called Weasel, brewed on the premises.
Babies and children welcome: high chairs. Function room (conservatory, 30 capacity). Games (table football). Tables outdoors (5, pavement; 15, garden).

Half Moon NEW

10 Half Moon Lane, SE24 9HU (7274 2733/www.halfmoonpub.co.uk). Herne Hill rail. **Open** noon-midnight Mon-Thur; noon-1am Fri, Sat; noon-10.30pm Sun. **Food served** 6-10.15pm Mon-Fri; 1-10pm Sat; 1-9pm Sun. **Credit** MC, V. **Pub**
A cavernous corner pub, built as a hotel in 1896, the Half Moon is the hostelry that most benefits from proximity to Brockwell Park. But, while it's easy to be put off by the crowds on the tarmac outside, there's always space inside, something that's easy to miss through elegant stained-glass windows offering 'Luncheon' and 'Billiards'. The back room has hosted bands since the late 1970s and – while its owners dine out on the fact the Police and U2 played here – these days the fare is an eccentric mix of pub rockers (Chicken Shack, Albert Lee) and avant-garde noiseniks (arts station Resonance FM hosts a night).

Babies and children admitted (until 8pm).
Function room (up to 220 capacity). Music
(open mic 8pm Tue, free; bands 8pm Fri,
Sat, £3-£12). Quiz (8pm Thur; £1). Tables
outdoors (2, pavement). TV (satellite).

Prince Regent ★
69 Dulwich Road, SE24 0NJ (7274 1567).
Herne Hill rail. **Open** noon-11pm Mon-Wed;
noon-midnight Thur-Sat; noon-10.30pm
Sun. **Food served** noon-3pm, 7-10pm
Mon-Sat; noon-5pm, 6-9pm Sun. **Credit**
MC, V. **Gastropub**
A firm favourite among Herne Hill's young
professionals, the Prince Regent is an elegant
Victorian boozer – etched glass panelling, dark
wood stripped floors – which went gastro in
2005. A relaxed dining room offers comfort food
classics (including perhaps the best vegetarian
sausage and mash in London), while the main
bar is an excellent place to pull up a stool and
savour interesting independent real ales – on
our visit, Wooden Hand Brewery's Pirates Gold.
Some locals have complained about the number
of precocious toddlers scampering around the
place at weekends (an adults-only upstairs room
offers sanctuary) but, whether for a romantic
dinner, a bargain brunch or a sneaky Monday-
night session under the guise of the pub quiz,
this still feels like a proper pub. And, if you're
eating, leave room for dessert…
Babies and children welcome (until 7pm):
high chairs. Disabled: toilet. Function rooms
(60 capacity). Games (board games). Tables
outdoors (12, pavement). **Map p284 E3.**

London Bridge & Borough

Boot & Flogger ★ NEW HOT 50
10-20 Redcross Way, SE1 1TA (7407 1184).
Borough tube. **Open** 11am-8pm Mon-Fri.
Food served 11am-7pm Mon-Fri. **Credit**
MC, V. **Wine bar**
A marvellous anachronism, the Boot & Flogger
was until recently the only hostelry in the UK
that had the right to sell wine without having a
licence, thanks to a charter granted by Queen
Elizabeth I in 1567. And there's something
wonderfully old-school about the place itself,
from its dark wood panelling, little nooks and
deep leather button-back wing chairs, to the pinstripe suited gent behind the bar. It's part of the
venerable wine bar chain set up by the Davy
family, which has been trading in wine since
1870. The Boot first opened in 1964 and has the
feel of a gentlemen's club, but without the
stuffiness. This is a place for settling back,
relaxing and enjoying unsurprisingly top-notch

wine, ports and champagnes. Service is
charming and solicitous, and food also deserves
a mention: reasonably priced and served until
7pm. Options run from olives (with cloves of
garlic, £1.50) to solid English fare such as potted
shrimps, ham sandwiches or steak and chips.
But what of the name? The boot and flogger
was a corking device comprised of a leather
'boot' that the bottle was placed in, with a
wooden 'flogger' – a piece of flat wood – which
was used to 'flog' the cork into the bottle.
Function rooms (up to 50 capacity). No
piped music or jukebox. Tables outdoors
(10, courtyard). **Map p282 P8.**

Charles Dickens
160 Union Street, SE1 0LH (7401 3744/
www.thecharlesdickens.co.uk). Southwark tube.
Open noon-11pm Mon-Fri; noon-6pm Sat, Sun.
Food served noon-2.30pm, 6-8.30pm Mon-Fri;
noon-5pm Sat, Sun. **Credit** MC, V. **Pub**
You would have to know it's here, this
unprepossessing freehouse by the mainline rails
heading out from London Bridge station, but
regulars can always be found as you step into its
scuffed-wood and few-frills interior. Further
inspection reveals a wonderful collection of
caricatures (if not characters) from Dickens'
novels; by then you would have noticed the
pumps of Sharp's Eden Ale, Harveys Best,
Slater's Queen Bee, Wethergate Essex Bomber
and Dirty Dick and Golden Arrow, and taps of
Bitburger and San Miguel. There's a choice of a
dozen wines, too, that make ideal
accompaniments to the hearty mains (lamb
shank, £8.25).
Babies and children admitted (until 7pm).
Bar available for hire. Quiz (8.30pm Wed;
free). Tables outdoors (3, pavement).
Map p282 O8.

George Inn
77 Borough High Street, SE1 1NH (7407
2056). London Bridge tube/rail. **Open** 11am-
11pm Mon-Sat; noon-10.30pm Sun. **Food**
served noon-5pm, 6-9.30pm Mon-Sat; noon-
5pm Sun. **Credit** AmEx, MC, V. **Pub**
Part pub, part museum piece, the galleried
George Inn consists of a number of
interconnecting bars, upstairs function rooms
and a wide courtyard where you expect horses
to be tethered. Instead tourists fill much of the
space, although local workers take their lunch
breaks here, laying into the likes of steak and
ale pie. As well as the house variety, ales include
Greene King IPA, Abbot and Old Speckled Hen,
Peroni is the surprising lager choice, and there
are 14 wines by the bottle.

South East

Insider Knowledge
Boot & Flogger

You are?
Peter Common, manager of the Boot & Flogger (*see p167*), Borough. I've been here since 1987.

The pub's owner, John Davy, is a Free Vintner – what does that mean?
Since 1567, members of the Vintners Company have had the right to sell wine in the City of London and within three miles of the walls without an excise licence. Under the so-called 'Vintners' Privilege', you could only sell wine, however, not beer or spirits.

What happened to the Vintners' Privilege under recent changes to the licensing laws?
We lost our privilege and had to get a licence. But we still don't serve beer or spirits. We're a respectable wine bar. Beers and spirits cause problems.

What's the average age of your customers?
The average age is 55 upwards. One man who comes here was born in 1918.

Is it quite an old boys' club atmosphere?
Definitely. My clientele are the old boys. They have a sherry when they come in, then a glass of claret or port and, in the old days, a cigar. We serve cold meats, steak and chips. I know most people's names, and we'll greet them when they walk in the door and get them their usual table.

Who are your regulars?
A lot of people from the wine trade. Lords, ladies, gentlemen, ministers.

How would you describe the decor – it's quite dark isn't it?
I'd describe it as old, grotty and Dickensian. It's a traditional wine bar.

Babies and children admitted. Function rooms (up to 100 capacity). Games (darts, fruit machine). Restaurant. Tables outdoors (35, courtyard). **Map p282 P8.**

Gladstone Arms ★ NEW HOT 50
64 Lant Street, SE1 1QN (7407 3962). Borough tube. **Open** *noon-11pm Mon-Fri; noon-midnight Sat; noon-10.30pm Sun.* **Food served** *noon-3pm daily.* **Credit** MC, V. **Pub**
This may just be the coolest little pub in south-east London. The landlord has form, having run the equally bijou (and largely undiscovered) Smersh in Shoreditch and the famously debauched Islington 'whiskey café' Filthy McNasty's (*see p217*). The living-room sized Glad – visible from Borough High Street thanks to its garish mural – has become a second home for indie-folk types the Moon Music Orchestra, and has hosted many other hip shindigs. But it works equally well as a local pub. You can simply sit at the bar with a pint of Black Sheep bitter and watch the circus unfold, although it's worth checking in advance to see whether there's anything on – otherwise you might be left wondering what the fuss is about.
Babies and children admitted (until 7pm). Games (board games). Music (bands 8pm Sat, Sun; free). **Map p282 P9.**

Lord Clyde
27 Clennam Street, SE1 1ER (7407 3397/ www.lordclyde.com). Borough tube. **Open** *11am-11pm Mon-Fri; noon-11pm Sat; noon-6pm Sun.* **Food served** *11am-2.30pm, 5.30-11pm Mon-Fri; noon-5.30pm Sat, Sun.* **Credit** AmEx, DC, MC, V. **Pub**
A marvellous neighbourhood boozer. Through a red-curtained entrance, cherry banquettes surround a neat bar counter, a fireplace, timeless pub paraphernalia and no little frosted glass. A set of bar prices is listed from, of all months, July 1966, while a back room contains a dartboard behind wooden shutters. Greene King IPA, Shepherd Neame Spitfire, Fuller's London Pride, Young's and Adnams are the beers of choice now – it would have been 1/6d pale ale when England last won the World Cup – with San Miguel as the draught lager choice. A chiming clock breaks occasional conversation.
Babies and children admitted (until 9pm). Function room (30 capacity). Games (darts). TVs (satellite, widescreen). **Map p282 P8.**

Lord Nelson ★ NEW
243 Union Street, SE1 0LR (7207 2701/ www.lordnelsonsouthwark.co.uk). Southwark tube. **Open** *noon-11pm Mon-Sat; noon-*

10.30pm Sun. **Food served** noon-10.30pm Mon-Sat; 1-4.30pm Sun. **Credit** MC, V. Pub
A drab 1950s council estate façade hides one of the funkiest little pubs in south London. Kitsch and cosy thanks to a wall-length beach theme, the Nelson's decor also includes figures from *The Simpsons* hanging upside down over the bar, original works by stencil artists Shephard Fairey and Faile, and a container-load of fairy lights. Popular with media and muso types, the heated alfresco area boasts a barbecue which gets fired up most days (winter months included) – customers are welcome to bring their own grub and use it for free. The simple, gastropub menu changes every few days, while the guest real ale changes every four days. *Babies and children admitted (lunchtime). Disabled: toilet. Games (poker 7pm Mon). Restaurant (available for hire, 40 capacity). Tables outdoors (6, garden).* **Map p282 O8**.

Market Porter

9 Stoney Street, SE1 9AA (7407 2495/www. markettaverns.co.uk). London Bridge tube/rail. **Open** 6-8.30am, 11am-11pm Mon-Fri; noon-11pm Sat; noon-10.30pm Sun. **Food served** noon-3pm Mon-Fri; noon-5pm Sun. **Credit** AmEx, MC, V. Pub
Few market bars have this range of beers or ambitious quality of cuisine. In an invariably cramped main bar area – there'll be more room in the back – market traders and regulars gather around taps of Okell's Maclir, Vale Brewery Best, Acorn Brewery Kashmir, Harveys Best, Lund's Bitter, although most will be glugging the standard lager. There are choices from Greenwich's Meantime Brewery too. A dextrous hand in the kitchen is revealed by Swedish crayfish with apple salad, and pancetta welsh rarebit; ingredients are sourced as much as possible from next-door Borough market. *Babies and children admitted (Mon-Fri restaurant only). Disabled: toilet. Function room (60 capacity). Games (fruit machines). Restaurant.* **Map p282 P8**.

Rake ★

14 Winchester Walk, SE1 9AG (7407 0557). London Bridge tube/rail. **Open** noon-11pm Mon-Fri; 10am-11pm Sat. **Credit** (over £10) AmEx, MC, V. Pub
Utobeer runs this incongruously modest bar, a small antiseptic room and adjoining heated patio containing a range of beers that would put a Belgian bar to shame. In truth, this is simply a more convivial outlet than the Utobeer's stall in Borough Market round the corner – but welcome nonetheless. The half-dozen taps are changed every week – you can usually count on Veltins and Sierra Nevada – while in the fridge are beers made from seaweed, mango and heather. Friendly staff will dispense their knowledge, and perhaps even entice you to try an 11% proof Belgian type. *Babies and children admitted. Disabled: toilet. Tables outdoors (7, patio).* **Map p282 P8**.

Royal Oak ★ HOT 50

44 Tabard Street, SE1 4JU (7357 7173). Borough tube. **Open** 11am-11pm Mon-Fri; 6-11pm Sat; noon-6pm Sun. **Food served** noon-3pm, 5-9.45pm Mon-Fri; 6-9.45pm Sat; noon-4.45pm Sun. **Credit** MC, V. Pub
A pub for luvvies and lovers of Lewes brewery Harveys, the Royal Oak seems wonderfully trapped in time. Its ales from the Sussex stable – Mild, Pale, Old, Best and Armada – are all under £3, keg cider includes Thatcher's Heritage and Weston's Stowford Press, while a felt-tipped menu boasts classics such as game pie, rabbit casserole, Lancashire hotpot and braised lamb shank. Music hall stars Harry Ray and Flanagan & Allen, here celebrated in framed, hand-bill form, would have tucked into the same decades ago. These days there's wine too. Nevertheless, an unused hatch for off sales remains, as do the shell-effect washbasins in the lavatory. *Disabled: toilet. No piped music or jukebox. Function room (40 capacity).* **Map p282 P9**.

Wine Wharf ★

Stoney Street, Borough Market, SE1 9AD (7940 8335/www.winewharf.com). London Bridge tube/rail. **Open** noon-11pm Mon-Sat. **Food served** noon-10pm Mon-Sat. **Credit** AmEx, DC, MC, V. Wine bar
There are many places to grab a drink while at Borough Market, but none has a better wine list than this temple to the grape. Leather sofas are stuffed in among wood beams, and wood tables provide surfaces on which to rest dishes such as welsh rarebit and potted salt beef while drinking. The sheer number of wines by the glass is to be commended and, unlike many places, Wine Wharf gives the list a big going-over every six months. One that's survived the recent cut is Firesteed's Oregon pinot gris, demonstrating that this grape doesn't have to be boring, thin and tasteless as is so often the case. And if you can't choose, consult the staff – they know their stuff. *Babies and children welcome (before 8pm): high chairs. Booking advisable. Disabled: toilet. Music (jazz 7.30pm Mon). Wine shop.* **Map p282 P8**.

South East

Dolphin. *See p172.*

New Cross

Hobgoblin

272 New Cross Road, SE14 6AA (8692 3193). New Cross Gate tube/rail. **Open** noon-1am daily. **Food served** noon-10pm Mon-Fri, Sun. **Credit** MC, V. **Pub**
Opposite New Cross Gate station and close to Goldsmiths College, this hangout for students and locals who haven't grown up yet is an obvious spot for a rendezvous. A wide main bar showing TV football or playing jukebox favourites gives way to a beer garden at the back. On the island bar stand taps of Timothy Taylor Landlord, Young's, Wychwood Hobgoblin, John Smith's and Stella; behind, a kitchen produces pretty decent Thai grub (green curries, stir fries). A limited 20% student discount encourages weekday drinking but in truth the Hobgob would pack them in whatever the deal.
Babies and children admitted (until 7pm). Disabled: toilet. Games (fruit machines, quiz machines). Music (DJs 8pm Thur-Sat; free). Tables outdoors (8, conservatory; 12, garden). TVs. **Map p285 A2.**

New Cross Inn

323 New Cross Road, SE14 6AS (8692 1866). New Cross Gate tube/rail. **Open** 1pm-2am Mon-Sat; 1pm-midnight Sun. **Credit** MC, V. **Pub**
'For the dreaming, the drowning and the drunk' says the mural on the back wall behind a shin-level stage whose activities have pushed this former workaday Irish pub into the vortex of what outsiders term the New Cross Scene. And, certainly, spiky, pierced student types from nearby Goldsmiths College and beyond flock around the horseshoe bar or make out on the squishy black sofas while Cop On The Edge or Lime Headed Dog thrash indiely. And it's contagious. The team behind this ('Rocklands' – yeuch!) has taken over the former miserable market pub the Deptford Arms and turned it indie. Here, it's still nitrokeg lagers till 2am, with free admission and youth hostel beds next door should it come to it.
Bar available for hire. Games (pool table). Music (DJs/bands daily; free-£5). **Map p285 A2.**

Peckham

Bar Story

213 Blenheim Grove, SE15 4QL (7635 6643/ www.barstory.co.uk). Peckham Rye rail. **Open** 3.30pm-midnight Mon-Fri; noon-11.30pm Sat, Sun. **Food served** 4-9.30pm daily. **Credit** AmEx, DC, MC, V. **Bar**

Under the arches of Peckham Rye station, there's more than a hint of the east European squat bar about this establishment. With its white walls, lap-tops with internet access, open kitchen and blackboard menu (affordable pies and burgers feature largely) there's a communal atmosphere to the place made all the more convivial by the outdoor bar where smokers puff away on railway sleepers converted into benches. As well as the bottled beers (including Duvel, Erdinger, Guinness, Lech and Zywiec), there are at least 34 cocktails and 16 wines (four of which are organic). DJs play remixed hip hop, funk and indie rock and the Sassoon Gallery (which is available to hire as a licensed venue) next door showcases local artists' work.
Function room (200 capacity). Music (DJs 8pm Tue, Fri, Sat; 3pm, 7pm Sun; free). Tables outdoors (8, patio).

Gowlett ★

62 Gowlett Road, SE15 4HY (7635 7048). East Dulwich or Peckham Rye rail. **Open** noon-midnight Mon-Thur; noon-1am Fri, Sat; noon-11.30pm Sun. **Food served** 12.30-2.30pm, 6.30-10.30pm Mon-Fri; 12.30-10.30pm Sat; 12.30-9pm Sun. **Credit** AmEx, MC, V. **Pub**
This CAMRA award-winning boozer has long been a favourite and has maintained the high standards that won its award in 2005. The decor may be simple – even a little bland – with wooden tables and worn leather banquettes beneath three-quarter wood panelling, but the place is familiar, comfortable and relaxed. The choice of drinks is also eminently democratic with excellently kept ales (Adnams and three guest beers – including Harveys and Brakspear on our last visit) and two choices of Fairtrade wine (the house white and red) as well as a totally organic, vegetarian wine list. 'Lucky 7s' night (Thursday) invites punters to bring in and play seven of their favourite seven-inch records.
Babies and children welcome (until 9pm). Disabled: toilet. Games (pool, tournament 8pm Tue; £3). Music (DJs 6pm Sun; free). Quiz (8.30pm Mon; £1). Tables outdoors (3, heated terrace; 4, pavement).

Old Nun's Head **NEW**

15 Nunhead Green, SE15 3QQ (7639 4007). Nunhead rail/78, P12 bus. **Open** noon-midnight Mon-Thur, Sun; noon-1am Fri, Sat. **Food served** noon-2.15pm, 6.30-10.15pm Mon-Fri; noon-10.15pm Sat; noon-9pm Sun. **Credit** AmEx, MC, V. **Pub**
Standing on the site of a nun's decapitation, this place is now home to rather more civilised goings on. A good selection of beers matches

South East

the well thought out wine list (including organic and vegetarian options) with Brakspear, Coach House and Wells on the pumps. An unobtrusive telly shows football, while old tabletop arcade machines double up as, well, tables – both nice touches. Upstairs houses a function room for exhibitions and gigs, and the popular acoustic night, Easycome, every Wednesday. The regularly changing art on the walls is for sale. *Art exhibitions. Babies and children admitted (until 9pm). Disabled: toilet. Function room (80 capacity). Music (open mic Wed 8.30pm; £3). Tables outdoors (7, garden). TVs (satellite).*

Rye Hotel ★
31 Peckham Rye, SE15 3NX (7639 5397). Peckham Rye rail. **Open** noon-11pm Mon-Thur, Sun; noon-midnight Fri, Sat. **Food served** noon-4pm, 6-10pm Mon-Fri; noon-10pm Sat; noon-9pm Sun. **Credit** MC, V. **Gastropub**
Elegant yet unpretentious, the Rye is still one of the most popular gastropubs round these parts. The well-executed English fare complements rather than overshadows the booze: there's an interesting and reasonably priced wine list (try Piemonte Cortese; £17.50/£4.70); some classic cocktails, such as strawberry daiquiri (£6), and changing ales (Wadworth 6X, Exmoor and Hound Dog), as well as Hoegaarden, Leffe and Staropramen, on tap. There's a mellow vibe in the evenings, with lounge beats and candlelight, while the weekends draw families for the perennially popular Sunday lunch. *Babies and children welcome (until 7pm): highchairs. Function room (60). Games (board games). Quiz (8pm Wed; £2). Tables outdoors (45, garden).*

Sydenham

Dolphin NEW
121 Sydenham Road, SE26 5HB (8778 8101/ www.thedolphinsydenham.com). Sydenham rail. **Open** noon-11.30pm Mon-Fri; noon-midnight Sat; noon-11pm Sun. **Food served** noon-3.30pm, 6.30-10pm Mon-Fri; noon-10pm Sat; noon-4pm, 5-9pm Sun. **Credit** MC, V. **Pub**
Set on the grim Sydenham Road, the light and spacious Dolphin is a local mecca. Though it is overflowing with children on a Sunday afternoon, weeknights see relaxed boozing and dining amid the candles and dark wood panelling. The pumps are a little light, with just London Pride, Timothy Taylor and Broadside, but the fridges hold both West and Budvar for the more discerning bottle drinker while the wine list starts at £11.95 for a Ponte Pietra

merlot. The Dolphin's delight, however, is out back: the newly renovated garden comes complete with fountains, sculptures and an apple orchard. *Babies and children admitted (until 9pm): high chairs. Tables outdoors (25, garden).*

Dulwich Wood House
39 Sydenham Hill, SE26 6RS (8693 5666). Sydenham Hill rail/63, 202 bus. **Open** noon-11.30pm Mon-Wed; noon-midnight Thur-Sat; noon-11pm Sun. **Food served** noon-10pm Mon-Sat; noon-9pm Sun. **Credit** AmEx, DC, MC, V. **Pub**
Constructed in the mid 19th century as a private residence by Joseph Paxton (the architect of the Crystal Palace), the Dulwich Wood House has a quirkily friendly feel. Bottles include Young's Light Ale and Ramrod and a rotation of Young's specials, and there's Bombardier on the pumps. It's the Pimms and lemonade on tap that says it all, though. This is a prime spot to end up after a summer rummage through Dulwich Woods. Weekends find the wrap-around garden packed with pink-cheeked souls and should you fancy it, there's a good quiz on Tuesdays. *Babies and children admitted (restaurant only). Games (darts, fruit machines, poker 8pm Wed). Quiz (8pm Tue; £2). Restaurant. Tables outdoors (50, garden). TVs.*

Perry Hill NEW
78-80 Perry Hill, SE6 4EY (8699 5076/ www.theperryhill.co.uk). Catford Bridge or Lower Sydenham rail. **Open** noon-midnight daily. **Food served** 6-10pm Mon; noon-3pm, 6-10pm Tue-Sat; noon-10pm Sun. **Credit** AmEx, MC, V. **Gastropub**
The people behind the Perry Hill have avoided the classic gastropub mistake of giving great gastro but piss-poor pub: this pub keeps very good ale (a hoppy Shepherd Neame Spitfire bitter went down a treat). Food is worth having – hot chocolate soufflé with crème fraîche is a must-order. And while the decor shouts 'Harvester' – it's a big roadhouse squatting on a bleakish suburban thoroughfare, with a large decked backyard, a restaurant at the side and a public bar sprinkled with lads drinking lager and older couples having a pension-day pint – this is the Harvester from heaven. The wine list needs some attention but, that aside, this place is excellent. *Babies and children welcome: high chairs. Music (jazz 6pm Fri; free). Restaurant (available for hire, 60 capacity). Tables outdoors (20, garden).*

East

East

Though Shoreditch remains the East End's nightlife mecca, these days it faces stiff competition from its neighbours where drinking is concerned. Which isn't to say you can't get a decent pint in Hoxton and its environs: the **Wenlock Arms** is heaven for real ale lovers, while the **Fox** offers respite from the hectic nocturnal whirl. Further east in Bethnal Green, the **Camel** and the **Approach Tavern** update the traditional boozer, while the **Bistrotheque Napoleon Bar** is an unlikely island of sophistication. The denizens of Brick Lane are as well served as ever by DJ bars like **Exit** and the **Big Chill**, but there are proper pubs here too, notably the **Pride of Spitalfields**. East London hasn't missed out on the gastropub boom either: the **Gun** on the Isle of Dogs is a more or less flawless example of the genre, while Gordon Ramsay's **Narrow Street Pub & Dining Room**, upriver by Limehouse Reach, remembers that pubs, however gastronomically refined, are also for drinking in. There are options further afield too, at the splendid **Palm Tree** in Mile End and the classy **Morgan Arms**.

Bethnal Green

Approach Tavern
47 Approach Road, E2 9LY (8980 2321). Bethnal Green tube. **Open** noon-11pm Mon-Thur, Sun; noon-midnight Fri, Sat. **Food served** noon-2.30pm, 6-9.30pm Mon-Fri; noon-9.30pm Sat; noon-5pm Sun. **Credit** MC, V. Pub

Comfortably negotiating Bethnal Green's changing fortunes, the Approach sticks to a tried and trusted formula: good beer plus good food equals good pub. The pumps have almost the full run, from Fuller's to several Czechs. Two blackboards list a host of unpretentious snacks and mains (jerk chicken, £9.50), enjoyed by a multinational clientele (French, Spanish, even cockney) of arty bohos and local families. Blazing heaters ensure the covered front beer garden is popular all year round. TV sport plays silently so the jukebox is uninterrupted, and cab telephone numbers are helpfully chalked up by the door to the popular upstairs art gallery (www.theapproach.co.uk).
Art gallery (noon-6pm Wed-Sun). Babies and children admitted. Jukebox. Quiz (8.30pm Tue; £1). Tables outdoors (12, heated patio). TV. **Map p278 U3.**

Bistrotheque Napoleon Bar
23-27 Wadeson Street, E2 9DR (8983 7900/ www.bistrotheque.com). Bethnal Green tube/ Cambridge Heath rail/55 bus. **Open** 6pm-midnight Mon-Sat; 4pm-11pm Sun. **Credit** AmEx, MC, V. Cocktail bar

Off an unprepossessing street in Hackney, its entrance marked only by a planter and some smoking tables, this narrow ground-floor bar is sombre and a little austere in decor (warehouse bricks painted gunmetal grey, black and grey striped carpet). It's grown-up in attitude (wood panels and a Courvoisier Napoleon mirror behind the bar, chandeliers in front, a bossa 'Blue Monday' on the stereo). Ignore the familiar beers in favour of the 30-strong wine list and two dozen cocktails – the dark 'n' stormy (Goslings dark rum, ginger ale, lime, bitters, £6) was unimpeachable, a slightly underpowered lemon drop (Ketel Citron, lemon juice, lemon bitters, £7) delivered an impressively nostalgic hit of 1980s sweetshop.
Babies and children admitted. Disabled: toilet. Music (cabaret dates vary, ticket only). Function room (64 capacity). Restaurant. **Map p278 U3.**

Camel ★
277 Globe Road, E2 0JD (8983 9888). Bethnal Green tube. **Open** 4-11pm Mon-Wed; noon-11pm Fri, Sat; noon-10.30pm Sun. **Food served** 5-9.30pm Mon-Wed; 1-9.30pm Fri-Sun. **Credit** MC, V. Gastropub

The Camel is a low-key local favourite. Lovely plain brown exterior tiles, an etched Camel mirror and archive shots offer reminders of its past, while dark wallpaper with red roses and

bronze spherical lampshades create a modish retro interior thanks to a sensitive refit a few years back. The booze (Adnams and some continentals on draught, premium spirits, reasonable wine) and hearty gourmet pies (chicken, tarragon and bacon; asparagus and wild mushroom) do the essentials nicely; piles of books and scruffy games tempt you to surrender your afternoon. Even half-empty, there can be quite a racket here, and service is usually chaotic, but the chilled crowd of families and local arty types happily trade-in efficiency for beguilingly cosy.
Babies and children admitted. Games (board games). Tables outdoors (4, pavement). **Map p278 U3.**

Florist

255 Globe Road, E2 0JD (8981 1100). Bethnal Green tube. **Open** 2.30-11pm Mon-Sat; noon-10.30pm Sun. **Credit** MC, V. Pub/bar
The barmaid rather charmingly refused to make us a martini on our most recent visit to the Florist because she didn't know how – a sign things are now a little less sophisticated than the stained-glass floral motif above the front door of this little corner pub suggests. On a Saturday, the DJ was rocking a young crowd of drinkers with populist beats, and a throat-kickingly good bloody mary (£6) suggested hangovers are regularly created and successfully dealt with on the premises. The taps are fairly unimpressive, but there's Pride, Modelo Especial and Weston's Organic in the fridge and, in case of emergencies, a bottle of absinthe lurks next to the wine. Post-smoking ban, the tiny outdoor shelf seat has been made a little more commodious.
Babies and children admitted. Games (board games). Music (DJs 6pm Thur-Sat; free). Benches outdoors (10, pavement). Quiz (8pm Mon, free). **Map p278 U3.**

Royal Oak

73 Columbia Road, E2 7RG (7729 2220/ www.royaloaklondon.com). Bus 26, 48, 55. **Open** 6-11pm Mon; noon-11pm Tue-Thur; noon-midnight Fri, Sat; noon-10.30pm Sun. **Food served** 6-10pm Mon; noon-4pm, 6-10pm Tue-Sat; noon-4pm, 6-9pm Sun. **Credit** AmEx, MC, V. Gastropub
Rammed to the gunwales with vintage-clad creatives, the Royal Oak wasn't performing as it might on our recent Saturday night visit. There's a handsome, oval, central counter – low-backed like a cocktail bar – surrounded by small tables where you might snag a seat for the estimable Sunday roast (otherwise book at the first floor restaurant). The fine blackboard wine

list (a Picpoul de Pinet caught our eye) is a better bet than the draughts (Adnams Bitter was the sole cask alternative to continental lagers, Bulmers and Guinness that night), which are poured efficiently by staff worked beyond cheeriness well before closing time.
Babies and children welcome. Restaurant (available for hire, 50 capacity). Tables outdoors (4, yard). **Map p278 S3.**

Brick Lane

Big Chill Bar

Old Truman Brewery, off Brick Lane, E1 6QL (7392 9180/www.bigchill.net). Aldgate East tube/Liverpool Street tube/rail. **Open** noon-midnight Mon-Thur; noon-1am Fri, Sat; 11am-midnight Sun. **Food served** noon-11pm Mon-Sat; noon-10.30pm Sun. **Credit** MC, V. DJ bar
The Big Chill dishes up drinks and dance music in a setting relaxed enough to take in all-comers, from straggly kids to grey-haired know-betters. A bull's head with huge horns stares out the DJ across the loungey front area, before the busy bar recedes into the large main room and its overwhelmed chandelier. People squeeze up around shared tables, stand about yacking or fight their way on to the covered front terrace to smoke – even the large open-air courtyard is full to bursting come summer. Refinement isn't the point, but the £6.50 cocktails are respectable and bottles like Duvel make up for weak draught options.
Babies and children admitted (until 6pm). Disabled: toilet. Music (DJs 7pm Tue-Sat; noon-11.30pm Sun). Tables outdoors (4, patio). **Map p278 S5.**

Café 1001 NEW

1 Dray Walk, 91 Brick Lane, E1 6QL (7247 9679/www.cafe1001.co.uk). Liverpool Street tube/rail. **Open/food served** 6am-midnight daily. **Credit** MC, V. Bar/café
Laid-back, bohemian and artfully shambolic, Café 1001 has been dishing up breakfasts, coffees and experimental beats to E1's starving artists and hungover wastrels for aeons. And with Brick Lane and Spitalfields now firmly established on the tourist trail, it's busier than ever. Join the throng of east European cool kids, freaky clubbers and trilby-sporting musos (seriously, sometimes it feels like you've accidentally gatecrashed a modelling agency's fancy-dress party) on the picnic tables outside for bottled beers, barbecued burgers and the finest mango juice in town. After dark, DJs spin everything from jazz to dancehall to a chilled-out party crowd.

East

Narrow ★

Mr Ramsay's first foray into gastropub territory (now joined by west London's Warrington, *see p108,* and Devonshire, *see p96*) remains well received by Limehouse's more moneyed residents. And it's a good 'un. For a start, there's plenty of space for actual drinking – the spacious bar, decked out in stylish stripes and greys, makes a fine place to indulge in quality ales (Deuchars IPA, Meantime wheat beer, London Pride) and wines (a Sancerre la Vigne Blanche at £20 a bottle perhaps?). Bottled beers include St Peter's Organic and Wells' Banana Bread. There are quality bar snacks (pint of prawns, scotch egg with HP, traditional ploughman's) with not a pack of Nobby's Nuts in sight. The excellent restaurant boasts superb Thames views, as does the sunny beer terrace. *For listings, see p181.*

East

Babies and children admitted (until 7pm).
Bar available for hire. Function room (up
to 200 capacity). Music (experimental 8pm
Tue; jazz 8pm Wed; DJs 8pm Thur-Sun;
free). Short film screenings (8pm Mon; free).
Tables outdoors (12, garden). **Map p278 S5.**

Carpenter's Arms ★ NEW

73 Cheshire Street, E2 6EG (7739 6342).
Liverpool Street tube/rail. **Open** noon-11.30pm
Mon-Thur; noon-12.30am Fri, Sat; noon-
11.30pm Sun. **Credit** MC, V. Pub
This was once a right naughty little boozer deep
in East End gangsterland. It was bought by the
Kray twins in 1967 for their dear old mum,
Violet. Used as a safe spot for a swift half, it was
here that Ronnie tanked up on dutch courage
before murdering Jack 'The Hat' McVitie. In
short, it wasn't the sort of pub where you'd want
to spill someone's pint. Today, the coffin-lid bar
top, supposedly installed by the Krays, may
have gone but the chunky tables, swathes of
dark wood and historic windows make for a
cosy place in which to hunker down with a pint
to plan a bank job. There's also an intimate back
room (with an incongruous picture of shrink-
wrapped toilet roll) and a heated back garden.
Tap talent includes four Dorothy Goodbody ales
from Hereford's wonderful Wye Valley Brewery
and a pair of Adnams bitters on draught. They
pour alongside Germany's Licher Weizen and
Früli fruit beer. Fridge-dwelling gems include
Schneider Weiss, Paulaner, Duvel, a trio of
Chimays and stout from the Brooklyn Brewery
in New York. The kitchen will be open by
summer 2008. These days, the regulars are more
Thompson Twins than Kray Twins: Hoxtonites,
fashionistas, the odd ironic moustache and a few
ambitious hats.
Babies and children admitted. Games (board
games). Tables outdoors (6, garden). **Map**
p278 T4.

Exit

174 Brick Lane, E1 6RU (7377 2088).
Whitechapel tube/Liverpool Street tube/
rail/8, 388 bus. **Open** 4pm-1am Tue-Thur;
4pm-2am Fri; noon-2am Sat; 10am-2am Sun.
Food served 4-10pm Tue-Fri; 11am-8pm Sat;
10am-8pm Sun. **Credit** (over £10) MC, V.
DJ bar
'Mark Plays Good House Music' said the
sandwich board outside – and indeed he did.
This tiny venue on Brick Lane follows the DJ bar
template to the letter: front section of squishy
sofas, amid cream and red Aztec wallpaper
stylings; bar in the middle dispensing cocktails
and a scant handful of beers; unfurnished area

in front of the DJ for dance ramblings when the
alcohol versus time equation finds its happy
solution. Cocktails are a mixed bag – the
caipirinha delivered a solid punch, sloe tequila
(sloe gin, tequila, lime) was too astringent – but
staff and clientele were equally charming.
Babies and children admitted (Sundays only,
until 4pm). Bar available for hire (120
capacity). Music (DJs 9pm daily; free). Tables
outdoors (5, pavement). **Map p278 S5.**

Green & Red ★

51 Bethnal Green Road, E1 6LA (7749
9670/www.greenred.co.uk). Liverpool Street
tube/rail/8, 26, 48 bus. **Open** 5.30pm-
midnight Mon-Thur; 5.30pm-1am Fri, Sat;
5.30-10.30pm Sun. **Food served** 6-11pm
Mon-Sat; 6-10.30pm Sun. **Credit** AmEx,
MC, V. Bar
This Mexican bar/cantina – not themed as such
but dressed in neatly appropriate bar shack
distressed wood and generic Latin American
propaganda posters – is an absolute triumph.
You can drop in for a hangover-straightening
Michelada (your choice of beer – from Bohemia,
Dos Equis, Sol or the imperious Negra Modelo
– 'seasoned and spiced', around £4) with a
'brunch' of Jaliscan bar snacks, or wade into the
unparalleled selection of premium tequilas,
perhaps best encountered as a 'tasting flight' of
three shots (£12 to £59.40, accurately reflecting
the range of quality). Grab a stool at the counter
in the small, ground floor Cantina Bar for
quality cocktails: perhaps a tall diablo (tequila,
lime juice, ginger ale, crème de cassis) or
pomegranate margarita (salt and sugar rim)
accompanied by pan-fried chorizo and 'yam
bean' salad with cucumber and peanuts. When
we admired his craftsmanship, the gently
evangelical barman was pleased enough to
provide discreet tasters of one of the superb
visiting tequilas. But don't let such
gourmandism suggest a po-faced attitude:
Green & Red is as comfortable dishing out litre-
jug cocktail options to Friday night tables of
work carousers as talking you through the
niceties of £50 a shot aged tequila.
Babies and children welcome: high chair.
Disabled: toilet. Music (DJs 9pm Fri, Sat; free).
Restaurant. Tables outdoors (6, terrace).
Map p278 S4.

Indo

133 Whitechapel Road, E1 1DT (7247
4926). Aldgate East or Whitechapel tube.
Open noon-1am Mon-Thur, Sun; noon-3am
Fri, Sat. **Food served** noon-3pm, 6-9pm
daily. **Credit** MC, V. Bar

East

This narrow pub is a splendid, if slightly affected, mishmash. There's all manner of clutter behind the bar, changing art on the walls (on our visit, a painting declared 'Will have sex for fish'), smart floor tiles and a wonderful aquatic mosaic out back. The most coveted spot is at the front, on scruffy sofas under a gorgeous arched window, where stained glass sets off a railway clock. Among requisitioned cinema seats and faded chessboard tables, Indo runs an espresso machine alongside an eccentric beer selection (Mort Subite beside Bombardier on draught) and a troupe of high-end spirits. You'll usually encounter grizzled barflies, young bohos and slightly adventurous City types, nodding to alt-folk or soul-jazz.
Babies and children admitted (until 6pm). Music (DJs 9pm Sat, Sun; free). Tables outdoors (2, pavement). TV (big screen). **Map p278 T6.**

Pride of Spitalfields

3 Heneage Street, E1 5LJ (7247 8933). Aldgate East tube. **Open** 11am-11pm Mon-Sat; noon-10.30pm Sun. **Food served** noon-2.30pm Mon-Fri; 1-5pm Sun. **Credit** MC, V. **Pub**
Tucked down a side street, the Pride steadily walks its time-honoured path, treating decks and the £20 pub roast as figments of a fetid imagination. Excellently kept real ale (Fuller's Pride and ESB, Brewers Gold) is the focus, with a bottle of Dubonnet telling the rest of the story. All around are archive photos and maroon upholstered seating that clashes magnificently with the bright red carpet. And as if that wasn't enough suburban 1980s, our visit also saw a punter strike up 'Ebony and Ivory' on the piano. The clientele remains a jolly blend of Japanese hipsters and old codgers. Smokers now avail themselves of the two tables outside – that aside, nothing changes.
Babies and children admitted. Tables outdoors (2, pavement). TV (big screen, digital). **Map p278 S5.**

Redchurch ★

107 Redchurch Street, E2 7DL (7729 8333 www.theredchurch.co.uk). Liverpool Street tube/rail. **Open** 5pm-1am Mon-Thur; 5pm-3am Fri, Sat; 2pm-1am Sun. **Credit** AmEx, MC, V. **DJ bar**
This little DJ bar has two advantages over fellow Underdog-owned venue Green & Red: later opening and surprisingly good beer, including Brooklyn and Anchor Steam in bottles, and tall silver taps of Sierra Nevada and Maisie's Weisse. An insipid pisco sour steered us away from the well-considered

cocktail selection (featuring some rarities like an Applejack Rabbit of calvados, maple syrup, lemon and orange juice) towards the short wine list. During the day, the dark brick front section of the bar makes for good lounging; by night, the teeny DJ booth midway back whisks things into an inoffensively crowded stumble, during which people will stand on your feet – but you won't need steel toecaps.
Babies and children admitted. Disabled: toilet. Music (DJs 9pm Thur-Sun; free). **Map p278 S4.**

Rhythm Factory

16-18 Whitechapel Road, E1 1EW (7247 9386/www.rhythmfactory.co.uk). Aldgate East or Whitechapel tube. **Open** 11am-midnight Mon-Fri; 7pm-2am Sat. **Food served** 11am-8pm Mon-Fri. **Credit** (over £10) MC, V. **Bar**
During the day this east London institution is a quiet place filled with high chairs, good coffee, Thai food and continental vibes. By night, however, myriad club nights in the two buzzing back rooms see everyone, from chin-stroking music industry types to hedonistic Hoxtonites, descend for eclectic programming: Polish hip hop? Dubstep? Join the (hefty) queue. The gigs, including the delightfully named Let Them Eat Gak series, are also winners. Pete Doherty seems to play here about once a week.
Bar available for hire. Function room (700 capacity). Music (bands/DJs; check website for details). **Map p278 S6.**

Vibe Bar

Old Truman Brewery, 91-95 Brick Lane, E1 6QL (7377 2899/www.vibe-bar.co.uk). Aldgate East tube/Liverpool Street tube/rail. **Open** 11am-11.30pm Mon-Thur, Sun; 11am-1am Fri, Sat. **Food served** 11am-3pm Mon-Thur; 11am-7pm Fri, Sat; 11am-5pm Sun. **Admission** £3.50 after 8pm Fri, Sat. **Credit** AmEx, DC, MC, V. **DJ bar**
The vibe here is classic student party, especially when a band bring all their friends ('We're huge in Suffolk!' announced a wispy-haired singer, trying to flog copies of a Kinks-indebted concept album). Graffiti-style wall murals and limited booze options pretty much confirm the feel; there are a lot of taps, but not much on them to get excited about, so spirits prove popular. This is a fine place for some messy fun, though, especially in summer when the large courtyard comes into its own and you can shuttle between bar and outdoor hot pie counter until you're far too late for that gig at 93 Feet East across the road.

Disabled: toilet. Function room (200 capacity). Music (bands 7.30pm Mon-Wed, Sun; DJs 8pm daily). Tables outdoors (70, courtyard and marquee). **Map p278 S5.**

Clapton

Anchor & Hope
15 High Hill Ferry, E5 9HG (8806 1730). Clapton rail/53, 393 bus. **Open** noon-11pm Mon-Sat; noon-10.30pm Sun. **No credit cards. Pub**
The Anchor & Hope is wedged on the bottom of a hill, between a housing estate and the River Lea. The lack of impressive decor is more than made up for by the hearty cheer of the red-faced locals. Its position also attracts walkers who sit quietly sucking bitter through their beards. Sports lovers might be disappointed to find the flat-screen TV is not tuned in to Sky. Aside from the standard draughts there's the option of London Pride, ESB and a guest beer – plus bottles of Honeydew and Magners in the fridge. On warm days unwind on the fixed metal bench and table sets outside.
Babies and children welcome. Games (darts, fruit machine). Quiz (8pm Mon; free). Tables outdoors (10, riverside). TV.

Biddle Bros
88 Lower Clapton Road, E5 0QR (no phone). Clapton or Hackney Central rail. **Open** 6-11pm Mon-Fri; 1-11pm Sat, Sun. **No credit cards. Bar**
One time builders' merchant Biddle Bros now has art on the walls where tools used to be stacked, and students drinking Beck's instead of brickies buying shovels. Don't expect any real ale, this is a bar rather than a pub, with Beck's, Stella, Staropramen and Guinness on tap. The owner has kept the shop front and name, but has transformed the interior into a comfortable lounge where no one bats an eyelid if you take your shoes off, put your feet up on a leather sofa and order in pizza. There's an open mic night every other week and a piano in the corner. Well worth a visit.
Music (DJs and open mic nights, times vary).

Elderfield
57 Elderfield Road, E5 0LF (8986 1591). Hackney Central or Homerton rail. **Open** 4-11pm Mon-Wed; 4pm-midnight Thur, Fri; 1pm-midnight Sat; 1-11pm Sun. **Food served** 4-10pm Mon-Fri; 1-10pm Sat, Sun. **Credit** MC, V. **Pub**
Formerly the Eclipse, the Elderfield lies on the cusp of a council estate and some of Clapton's more gentrified housing. A friendly vibe prevails, with board games galore and plenty of low-key local banter. The sweeping bar offers a nice selection of draught beers: Timothy Taylor Landlord, Sussex Best, Adnams Broadside, Staropramen, Guinness and Hoegaarden. Quality coffee is also served. The regular piano player has shut the lid on his regular night but the management is open to offers from anyone who fancies a tinkle. Pavement seating attracts a small throng for summer drinking.
Games (board games, cards, dominoes). Tables outdoors (10, pavement). Quiz (8pm, first Tuesday of the month; £2).

Princess of Wales
146 Lea Bridge Road, E5 9RB (8533 3463). Clapton rail. **Open** noon-midnight Mon-Sat; noon-10.30pm Sun. **Food served** noon-3pm, 6-8.30pm Mon-Sat; noon-5pm Sun. **Credit** MC, V. **Pub**
This Young's pub isn't exactly brimming with character but it has a wonderful lockside location on the River Lea to compensate. Sit at one of the many picnic tables and survey the vista – a seat in the conservatory does the job in bad weather. As well as standard draughts, the bar offers the likes of Bombardier and various Young's brews – the Wells Banana Bread beer in the chiller is dangerously addictive. For entertainment, there's a retina-popping seven-foot screen showing MTV and sport, a pool table and a dartboard. Food runs to industrial pub grub standards: roasts, lasagne with salad and chips.
Babies and children admitted. Games (darts, pool, quiz machine). Music (bands/karaoke 9pm Sat; free). Quiz (9pm Tue; free). Tables outdoors (10, garden). TVs (big screen satellite).

Docklands

Dion NEW
Port East Building, West India Quay, Hertsmere Road, E14 4AF (7987 0001/ www.dionlondon.co.uk). West India Quay DLR. **Open** noon-11pm Mon-Fri. **Food served** noon-3pm Mon-Fri. **Credit** AmEx, MC, V. **Bar**
Housed in part of a converted warehouse, the latest branch of the Dion mini-chain (named after the Greek god of wine Dionysus) makes the most of its features with lots of exposed brick and nightclub-style scrubbed black tiling. Wine and, particularly, champagne are the drinks of choice for the nine-to-five clientele; try the Jacquart Brut Mosaïque, rich, balanced and

East

New Jazz Late

Presented by

Charlie Wright's International Bar

Charlie Wright's International
45 Pitfield St, Hoxton, N1
Old Street Tube
0207 490 8345

For more info visit
www.myspace.com/charliewrights

One of My favourite Bars in London.
- **www.beer in the evening.com**

A notably diverse crowd – in both age and
style. - **the London Paper**

Unmissable -**www.london-drinking.com**

Charlie Wright's International Bar has
attracted some of London finest Jazz
Musician. - **Jazzwise Magazine**

They have Thai food, big screen TV and they show the
footy which makes for a lot of happy punters.
- **Itchy Guide**

A pub that puts together a combination of Belgian
beers and thai food dosen't sound original, yet this one
manages to stand out, even in a part of town
overloaded with bars. - **Fancy a pint .com**

Charlie Wright's was dishing out late-night pints
round these parts when most of the area's current bar
owners were still doing their A-Levels.
It's ideal for a taste of the Hoxton of old, and kind of
worn-in local vibe that newer bars can't hope to
compete with.
- **Time Out Bars Pubs and Clubs Guide 2007**

Open all day 'til late7 days a week

Mon - Weds 12-1
Thursday 10pm - 4am: Entrance Fee £4 two bands a night
Friday Live Jazz and Dj 10pm - 4am: Entrance Fee £5
**Saturday Disco Night 70's, 80's, 90's,Soul and Funk 9pm till
late**: Entrance Fee £4
Sunday Fusion and Funk 9pm - 1am: Entrance Fee £3

one of the more affordable bubbly options. You'll need a few drinks inside you to deal with some of the punters – on our recent visit a Stephen Mangan lookalike was flashing his credit card and braying loudly by the bar. Sadly, par for the course during the week in these parts, but weekend opening (planned for summer) will change that.

Bar available for hire. Disabled: toilet. Function rooms (up to 120 capacity). Tables outdoors (30, terrace).

Ferry House

26 Ferry Street, E14 3DT (7537 9587). Island Gardens DLR. **Open** 2pm-midnight Mon-Fri; 11am-midnight Sat; noon-11pm Sun. **Credit** MC, V. Pub

'The oldest pub on the island' – a mile from the bright lights of Docklands and across the river from Greenwich – is old school in the extreme. Push open the door and enter a world where old men slam pints on the bar, the paint job looks as old as the pub, and Belinda Carlisle plays on the stereo – but not in an ironic way. There's a dartboard, wood-panelling and the kind of carpet that covers a multitude of sins. Good job too – we can't imagine a Saturday night here goes by without a right royal knees up. Fancy it definitely ain't, but for a reminder of what pubs were like before the foodies invaded, this is a fine place to sink a few.

Games (darts, London Fives dartboard, pool table). Music (karaoke 9pm Fri; free). Tables outdoors (3, pavement).

Gun ★

27 Coldharbour, E14 9NS (7515 5222/ www.thegundocklands.com). Canary Wharf tube/DLR/South Quay DLR. **Open** 11am-midnight Mon-Fri; 11.30am-midnight Sat; 11.30am-11pm Sun. **Food served** noon-3pm, 6-10.30pm Mon-Fri; 11.30am-4pm, 6-10.30pm Sat; 11.30am-4pm, 6.30-9.30pm Sun. **Credit** AmEx, MC, V. Gastropub

If the 'oldest pub on the island' (Ferry House, *see above*) sounds like it won't offer enough marinated olives for your liking, you'd better head straight for the Gun. A fine example of gastro as it should be done, the Gun is thoughtfully decked out in dark wood and grey slate tiles, with sofas, bookshelves and huge barrels as stand-up tables. Punters are a classy but unpretentious bunch happy to pay for quality dishes such as braised shin of beef with parsnip purée (£18) and pan-fried lemon sole with new potatoes (£16.50). There are cocktails (espresso martini, £6.50) and endless wines, as well as Abbot Ale, Adnams Broadside,

Young's, Guinness, Hoegaarden and more on tap. Best of all is the fantastic decked terrace (heated in winter) with views of the O2 and sporadic river traffic.

Babies and children welcome: high chairs. Disabled: toilet. Function rooms (up to 80 capacity). Restaurant. Tables outdoors (11, terrace).

Limehouse

Grapes ★

76 Narrow Street, E14 8BP (7987 4396). Westferry DLR. **Open** noon-3pm, 5.30-11pm Mon-Thur; noon-11pm Fri, Sat; noon-10.30pm Sun. **Food served** noon-2pm, 7-9pm Mon-Fri; noon-2.30pm, 7-9pm Sat; noon-3.30pm Sun. **Credit** AmEx, MC, V. Pub

As old school as they come, the Grapes ticks all the right boxes with a creaky wood-panelled interior, open fire and quirky memorabilia galore. Take a pew at one of the wonky wooden tables after a bracing Thames walk or join the blokey after-work crowd for banter at the bar. There's plenty of good drinking on offer here – Brakspear Oxford Gold, Timothy Taylor Landlord and Adnams are among the many alternatives to standard draughts (the likes of Carlsberg, Stella, Guinness). There's no music to distract you from the pint-supping task at hand, though the upstairs restaurant's superior fish and chips are rather diverting. Oh, and there's no need to leave Fido shivering on the pavement either – there's a rather thoughtful water bowl provided by the door for man's best friend.

Booking advisable (restaurant). No piped music or jukebox. Restaurant.

Narrow ★

44 Narrow Street, E14 8DQ (7592 7950/ www.gordonramsay.com). Limehouse DLR. **Open** noon-11pm Mon-Sat; noon-10.30pm Sun. **Food served** noon-3pm, 6-10pm Mon-Fri; noon-10pm Sat, Sun. **Credit** AmEx, MC, V. Gastropub

For review, *see p176*.

Babies and children admitted. Disabled: toilet. Restaurant. Tables outdoors (36, riverside terrace).

Mile End

Morgan Arms ★

43 Morgan Street, E3 5AA (8980 6389/ www.geronimo-inns.co.uk). Mile End tube. **Open** noon-11pm Mon-Thur, Sun; noon-midnight Fri, Sat. **Food served** noon-4pm, 7-10pm Mon-Sat; noon-4pm Sun. **Credit** AmEx, MC. V. Gastropub

A grand corner location, made welcoming at night by fairy lights and glittery glass-beaded chandelier lamps in the large windows, makes the Morgan an automatic choice for the better off denizens of Bow. The place is handsome, with stained-glass window insets and a pale wood bar (presumably recovered from elsewhere: the legend 'Fine wines' above one alcove is bafflingly joined by 'Playwrights' above another), the somewhat baronial feel offset by bold pieces of modern art. With more space giving priority to diners than drinkers things can get crowded, but the beer is well kept (Adnams, Timothy Taylor Landlord), there's a decent selection of wine, and the bar snacks (perhaps a charcuterie plate) are unfussily classy.

Babies and children admitted (restaurant only). Disabled: toilet. Restaurant. Tables outdoors (4, pavement; 3, garden).

L'Oasis

237 Mile End Road, E1 4AA (7702 7051/ www.loasisstepney.co.uk). Stepney Green tube. **Open** noon-11pm Tue-Sat; noon-10.30pm Sun. **Food served** noon-9.30pm Tue-Thur; noon-10pm Fri, Sat; noon-9pm Sun. **Credit** MC, V. Gastropub

Fronting on the Mile End Road, L'Oasis doesn't quite feel like part of the city. The bar is in a single rectangular room, with benches (now padded) and upholstered chairs at broad, heavy tables under a handsome green and white panelled roof. The food is gastropub proper, rather than posh pub nosh (pork chop with Amaretto jus, salmon tartare with pickled cucumber), with new tasting evenings (courses paired with wines) and an upstairs dining/events room with country kitchen dresser suggesting food is a key focus. Indeed, a lack of nooks and corners means the layout isn't perfect for casual boozing, but there are fine wines and Adnams Bitter and Timothy Taylor Landlord on draught.

Babies and children admitted (upstairs only). Disabled: toilet. Function room (30 capacity). **Map p278 U5.**

Palm Tree ★

127 Grove Road, E3 5BH (8980 2918). Mile End tube/8, 25 bus. **Open** noon-midnight Mon-Thur; noon-2am Fri, Sat; noon-1am Sun (last admission 10.45pm). **No credit cards.** Pub

If you wanted to demonstrate there's still life in the embattled East End boozer, head to this two-room pub isolated by the canal in Mile End park.

Gastro nothing, fancy cocktails nowhere (although there are half a dozen single malts we'd not noticed before), you'll get a fine pint of one of two cask ales (Batemans XB and Piddler on the Roof for our last visit), wine from a Stowells dispenser or generic liquor out of an optic. You'll also receive that pearl beyond price: atmosphere. There's the wonderful bronze glow of the wallpaper (an original, albeit now coveted by a million retro-stylists playing catch-up), a maroon pelmet around the curved central bar that adds a theatrical spin to the old photos of cabaret nonebrities (Paul Wood? Maxine Daniels?), a shelf of porcelain plates and dried hops hung above the drum kit. Any fears this is becoming a hollow heritage experience are soon allayed by the crammed music nights, when a jazz combo is joined by students, new residents and to-the-nines husband-and-wife teams who've seen the generations move through the nearby estates. There are still ashtrays on the bar (empty, of course) and a manual cash till – almost against expectation, it rings up in decimal rather than farthings.

Games (London Fives dartboard). Music (jazz 9.45pm Fri-Sun; free). Tables outdoors (4, park).

Shoreditch

Anda de Bridge

42-44 Kingsland Road, E2 8DA (7739 3863/ www.andadebridge.com). Old Street tube/rail/ 242, 243, 26, 48, 55 bus. **Open** 10am-midnight Mon-Sat; 10am-11.30pm Sun. **Food served** 11am-midnight Mon-Sat; noon-10pm Sun. **Credit** AmEx, DC, MC, V. Bar

The bridge in question may be a particularly shabby piece of town planning, but Anda de Bridge makes a reasonable fist of bringing some Caribbean bonhomie to Shoreditch. The deceptively large concrete interior could be more atmospheric, although the fairy lights add a bright and typically unpretentious glow, but the lilting ska, reggae and R&B soundtrack and cheery service should help you sink into the sofas. Good for a bite to eat in the early evening (dumplings, plantain, ackee and the like) or a rum cocktail later on, when DJs lift the tempo and you can almost imagine yourself a part of the colourful wall murals.

Babies and children admitted. Bar available for hire. Disabled: toilet. Music (DJs, times vary). **Map p276 R3.**

Bar Kick

127 Shoreditch High Street, E1 6JE (7739 8700/www.cafekick.co.uk). Liverpool Street or

East

Old Street tube/rail. **Open** noon-11pm Mon-Wed, Sun; noon-midnight Thur-Sat. **Food served** noon-3.30pm, 6-10.30pm Mon-Wed; noon-3.30pm, 6-11.30pm Thur, Fri; noon-11.30pm Sat; noon-10.30pm Sun. **Credit** AmEx, MC, V. **Bar**

A big square room with a bar on the right, open kitchen straight ahead, flags of all nations tacked to the ceiling and, yes, rarely unemployed foosball tables under TVs that silently screen international football. Cool and excellently boisterous, Kick takes enough of a hint from European cafés (quality food, a curated selection of drinks) to draw in nearly as many women as men. Super Bock stout stood out among the bottles, but there was plenty for non-beerheads on the lists of cocktails and wine. Busy staff remain calm and friendly under the onslaught of twirl-crazed party groups. Good for a big night out, but also no slouch for a swift one with just a couple of friends.

Disabled: toilet. Function room (150 capacity). Games (table football; tournaments 7pm last Thur of mth; from £3). Tables outdoors (4, terrace). TVs (big screen, satellite). **Map p276 R4.**

Beach Blanket Babylon NEW

19-23 Bethnal Green Road, E1 6LA (7749 3540/www.beachblanket.co.uk). Liverpool Street tube/rail/8, 242, 388 bus. **Open** noon-midnight Mon-Thur, Sun; noon-1am Fri, Sat. **Food served** noon-11pm daily. **Credit** AmEx, MC, V. **Bar**

Partner to the Notting Hill establishment of the same name, BBB east is well situated a stone's throw from both the swanky Loungelover bar and Les Trois Garçons restaurant. Sophisticated bling is the look here: it's all gleaming metal and reflective surfaces designed to catch the light. There are giant lamps mounted on the walls, mini chandeliers set atop the white marble bar, silver candelabra on the wooden tables and retro-modernist drop lights in the raised dining area at the rear of the room. Repro classical statues add a humorous note (one is girded with white feathers), but style and opulence are key, as the bar menu emphasises. It's heavy on cocktails (house, champagne and classic), upmarket wines and champagnes and deluxe spirits (a bottle of Richard Hennessey St Louis Decarrier cognac is a snip at £3,605). Beware the cheeky 12.5% 'service charge' – added to your bill even if you sit at the bar.

Babies and children admitted. Bar available for hire. Function room (up to 150 capacity). Music (DJs 9pm Thur-Sat; free). Restaurant (available for hire, 120 capacity). **Map p276 R4.**

Insider Knowledge
Palm Tree

You are?
Val Barrett, manageress of the Palm Tree pub (*see p182*), Mile End. It's a family business. I've been working here for about 30 years.

What's the history of the pub?
There's been a pub here since about 1850 and it's always been called the Palm Tree. I believe it was named after Lord Palmerston. When we took it over, the previous owner had run it for 25 years and it was very old-fashioned. We did it up, but we tried to keep as many of the traditional features as possible, so we've still got the old oak furniture from decades ago.

It's been described as a proper old East End boozer…
I would say that's true. A lot of bars these days can be quite impersonal, but we're very much about getting to know people, being friendly and welcoming. Everyone knows your name and talks to each other. It's a meeting place. We don't have pool tables or games machines – a pub is for talking.

Who drinks here?
All different types and age groups, from 18 to 80. When we came here, 30 years ago, it was a lot of old East Enders, but now the area is evolving and we're getting a lot of new people moving in.

You've got a piano in the corner – do you have some good knees-ups here?
I don't like the term 'knees-up', but yes, we have live music a couple of nights a week. We have a house band who can play anything from jazz to rock 'n' roll. It's good, middle-of-the-road music – no head-banging or garage.

East

Cantaloupe

35-42 Charlotte Road, EC2A 3PD (7613 4411/www.cantaloupe.co.uk). Liverpool Street or Old Street tube/rail. **Open** noon-11pm Mon, Tue; noon-midnight Wed-Sat; noon-10.30pm Sun. **Food served** noon-10.30pm Mon-Sat; noon-9pm Sun. **Credit** AmEx, MC, V. **Bar**

One of the Shoreditch originals, Cantaloupe has long since eased into a comfy chair to let the young guns tire themselves out at the cutting edge. It simply carries on serving up groovy world-inflected music and booze, to be sopped up by unambitious Latin American tapas (a nibble of olives for £2; Argentine beef stew, £6), in two large rooms of exposed pipework and artfully worn furniture. Hungrier folk head for the Spanish-influenced food in the restaurant out back. Tap beers are less enticing than the cocktails – maybe a Caipa de Acai and Maracuja (cachaça, acai, passion fruit) or London caipirinha (Bombay gin instead of cachaça, plus crème de mure and blackberries) – but the bottles span Estrella Galicia and Lancaster Bomber. Few thrills then, but perfectly hospitable.
Babies and children admitted (Sun only). Bar available for hire. Disabled: toilet. Music (DJs 8pm Fri-Sun; free). Restaurant (available for hire, 50 capacity). **Map p276 R4.**

Catch

22 Kingsland Road, E2 8DA (7729 6097/ www.thecatchbar.com). Old Street tube/rail. **Open** 6pm-midnight Tue, Wed; 6pm-2am Thur-Sat; 6pm-1am Sun. **No credit cards.** **DJ bar**

An engagingly mixed up beast, this poky late-night bar/club has the trademarks of a trendsters' hangout and the atmosphere of a student union. This means you get intimate wooden booths, hip but dancefloor-orientated tunes from the DJs, a pool table during the day and a lot of crazed dancing as night rolls on. While the ground floor is essentially a late-night boogie den – there's no entry fee and it fills up pretty promptly with Staropramen and Guinness-toting young punters after 11pm – the small upstairs room can be hired out and hosts live music of a rocking bent later in the week.
Games (pool table). Music (bands/DJs 9pm Tue-Sun; free-£5). **Map p276 R3.**

Charlie Wright's International Bar ★ HOT 50

45 Pitfield Street, N1 6DA (7490 8345). Old Street tube/rail. **Open** noon-1am Mon-Wed; noon-4am Thur, Fri; 5pm-4am Sat; 5pm-2am Sun. **Food served** noon-3pm, 5-10pm

East

Mon-Fri; 5-10pm Sat, Sun. **Admission** £4 after 10pm Fri, Sat; £3 Sun. **Credit** MC, V.
DJ bar
It's just a few metres from Old Street, but this no nonsense bar feels miles away from the Shoreditch scene. Decent Thai food (you can eat well for a fiver) keeps things buzzing through the day, and the spacious side room makes an atmospheric spot for watching footie (there's an Arsenal bias); regular jazz nights and a 4am licence at weekends ensure it's rammed after dark too. The bottled beer and spirit selections are solid enough, but if fancy cocktails and gleaming glassware are your prerequisites for fun, you'll miss the point of this place entirely. CW's is all about late-night debauchery, spilling Guinness down your new T-shirt and engaging in friendly banter with the genial owner – an ex-weightlifter.
Games (darts, fruit machine, pool tables). Music (DJs 8pm Thur-Sun). Restaurant. TV (big screen, satellite). **Map p276 Q3.**

dreambagsjaguarshoes

34-36 Kingsland Road, E2 8DA (7729 5830/ www.dreambagsjaguarshoes.com). Old Street tube/rail. **Open** noon-1am Tue-Fri; 5pm-1am Sat; noon-12.30am Sun. **Credit** MC, V.
DJ bar

Still as painfully trendy as the day it first opened, this bar – the result of two shops being banged together – offers a fast-track education in what made (and continues to make) Shoreditch cool. Grungey but glam scruffs lounge on the battered sofas, surrounded by scrawled-on walls and lots of tatty art; bar staff look like they have modelling contracts on the side; the background music is self-consciously edgy. Drinks – Belgian beers, lots of bottled lager, cocktails – are nothing special but the laid-back vibe and cosy party cellar make up for it in spades.
Art gallery. Bar available for hire. Function room (100 capacity). Music (DJs monthly, 9pm; call for details). **Map p276 R3.**

Drunken Monkey

222 Shoreditch High Street, E1 6PJ (7392 9606/www.thedrunkenmonkey.co.uk). Liverpool Street tube/rail. **Open** noon-midnight Mon-Fri; 6pm-midnight Sat; noon-11pm Sun. **Food served** noon-11pm Mon-Fri; 6-11pm Sat; noon-10.30pm Sun. **Credit** AmEx, MC, V.
Cocktail bar
Some of the Chinese theming at this dim sum destination is a bit hokey and the music can be ear-splittingly loud, but this is a great bar – which means it's seriously packed Thursday to

Palm Tree. *See p182.*

East

e best guides t
oying London

on't just take our word for it)

CHEAP EATS IN LONDON

'No nonsense, hard-hitting reviews'
Sunday Times

'More than 700 places where you can eat out for less than £20 a head... a mass of useful information in a genuinely pocket–sized guide'

Mail on Sunday

2008
SPAS
ELECTRONICS
KIDS' STUFF
FASHION
COLLECTABLE VINYL
BRITISH DESIGN
SHOPS & SERVICES
Over 1,000 addresses, websites and ideas
HAIRDRESSERS
PETS
LINGERIE
BOOKS
GARDENS & FLOWERS
ART
TAILORS
AFFORDABLE ANTIQUES
MasterCard

'I'm always asked how I ke date with shopping and se city as big as London.This the answer'

Red Magazine

LONDON FOR LONDONERS

The ultimate handbook to living in the city

'Get the inside track on the capital's neighbourhoods'and places to visit in the capital'

ndependent on Sunday

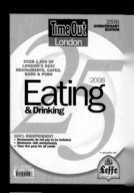

25th ANNIVERSARY EDITION

OVER 1,500 OF LONDON'S BEST RESTAURANTS, CAFES, BARS & PUBS
25
Eating & Drinking 2008

100% INDEPENDENT
• Restaurants do not pay to be included
• Reviews visit anonymously
• Time Out pays for all meals

Leffe

Rated 'Best Restaurant Guide'

Sunday Times

m over 15 London guides at all good
and timeout com /shop from only £6 99

Saturday. On any other day, you can opt for Asian-slanted, generally sweet-toothed cocktails (lemongrass in a gin gimlet, lychee martinis) at your leisure or commandeer one of the big wooden tables for decent wine (the list is arranged by category rather than price) and dim sum. Large red paper lanterns, clustered over the DJ booth, combine with dark wood, mirrors and low lighting to give the place a satisfying San Francisco Chinatown feel.
Babies and children admitted. Function rooms (up to 30 capacity). Music (DJs 8.30pm Tue-Sun; free). Restaurant. **Map p276 R4.**

East Room ★ NEW

2A Tabernacle Street, EC2A 4LU (7374 9570/0700 847 876/www.thstrm.com). Moorgate or Old Street tube/rail. **Open** 11am-1am Mon-Wed; 11am-3am Thur, Fri; 7pm-3am Sat. **Food served** noon-3pm, 6-10pm Mon-Fri; 7-10pm Sat. **Credit** AmEx, MC, V. **Cocktail bar**
Private clubs seem to have had their day, but Jonathan Downey's East Room won't have any difficulty in getting would-be members to cough up £350 per year: it's a very good-looking space that's been very well designed. Most importantly – it's a first-rate bar. Once you've gained entry (non-members must book in advance for admissiont before 11pm, thereafter it's members-only) you walk along a corridor lined with Enomatic wine preservation and dispensing machines, dispensing 36 New World wines by the glass. Pay to charge up a smartcard (a bit like an Oystercard), then help yourself to measures from a taster sip of 50ml up to full glass sizes of 125 or 175ml. The spirits and cocktails list is also exemplary, with the finer armagnacs and malt whiskies shown off in display cases. Walk past some diner-style booth seating and you're in the main lounge bar, with comfy sofas and chairs around tables (the latter used mainly by diners). The food is excellent (the buffet is a particularly good deal too), Matt Skinner is director of wine, and Gilles Peterson is director of music. We like.
Function room (15 capacity). **Map p276 Q4.**

Electricity Showrooms NEW

39A Hoxton Square, N1 6NN (7739 3939/ www.electricityshowrooms.co.uk). Old Street tube/rail. **Open** noon-midnight Mon-Thur; noon-1am Fri-Sun. **Food served** noon-11pm daily. **Credit** MC, V. **Bar**
Irony is almost overwhelming as Shoreditch's once feted minimalist original returns to its (almost) former name after a brief spell as a Nuevo Latino restaurant/bar, but is reinvented

as an old-school boozer. Instead of kitschy cool, however, the owners have oddly opted for unreconstructed, chain-pub decor. On entering through a revolving wooden door, punters are met by a riot of framed butterfly collections, repro Victorian portraits and military prints, model ships and standard lamps, beneath a stucco ceiling painted fuchsia pink. A semi-circular bar dominates, serving draught Red Stripe, Erdinger, Kirin, Guinness, Crest, Munchen, Timothy Taylor and Bombardier, bottled Pacifico, Estrella, Hoegaarden and the like, plus wines and spirits. A blackboard menu boasts sausages and mash with onion gravy, salmon and haddock pie and other neo-traditional fare. Seating is at the vast bar, one of the numerous wooden tables and chairs, or in the small, carpeted lounge area beyond three stained-glass panels, their light bulb imagery an acknowledgement of this now rather unconvincing bar's former identity.
Babies and children admitted. Disabled: toilet. Games (bar billiards; darts). Music (DJs 8pm Thur-Sun; free). Karaoke (8pm Wed; free). **Map p276 R3.**

Favela Chic

91-93 Great Eastern Street, EC2A 3HZ (7613 4228/www.favelachic.com). Old Street tube/rail. **Open** 6pm-1am Tue-Thur, Sun; 6pm-2am Fri, Sat. **Food served** 7-10.30pm Tue-Sat. **Credit** AmEx, MC, V. **DJ bar/restaurant**
With its odious name and a website that gabbles on about 'a big eclectic family that has grown organically throughout time', it's easy to distrust this ultra-hip venture, sister to the original Parisian enterprise. Yet Favela Chic gets away with its pretensions. The spacious interior mixes circus hoops, abundant greenery, bits of timber and flock wallpaper in entertaining fashion, and the events calendar is full to bursting: chilled, with a funky multinational crowd and jazzy DJs early in the week, and lively, with a cover charge (after 9pm), and bands playing anything from garage to world music, at the weekend. Drinks (cocktails or Brahma beer) aren't cheap.
Music (DJs 8pm Fri, Sat; free). Restaurant. **Map p276 Q4.**

Foundry

84-86 Great Eastern Street, EC2A 3JL (7739 6900/www.foundry.tv). Old Street tube/rail. **Open** 4.30-11pm Tue-Fri; 2.30-11pm Sat; 2.30-10.30pm Sun. **No credit cards.** **Bar**
The name suggests industry, but the Foundry, stuck right in Shoreditch's epicentre, goes for an artfully tatty look. Old school chairs and scruffy sofas sit alongside flickering monitors, chaotic

graffiti, weird sculptures and bookshelves full of thrillers. It can seem a little try-hard when empty, but this long-standing bar does the walk to match its boho talk, with regular art, poetry and music events, left-field tunes and right-on beverages (including Pitfield Organic Lager), while the staff are a pretty friendly bunch. On a good evening, it can even feel properly happening – some achievement, given the unforgiving lighting.
Art exhibitions (free). Babies and children admitted (until 9pm). Games (chess). Music (pianist 6pm Tue; free). Poetry readings (9pm Sun; free). Tables outdoors (5, pavement). **Map p276 Q4.**

Fox ★
28 Paul Street, EC2A 4LB (7729 5708/ www.thefoxpublichouse.com). Old Street rail/ tube. **Open** noon-11pm Mon-Fri; 6pm-midnight Sat; noon-5pm Sun. **Food served** noon-3pm, 6-10pm Mon-Fri; 6-10pm Sat; noon-4pm Sun. **Credit** MC, V. **Gastropub**
A real post-work magnet on Thursday and Friday nights, when you can hardly see the bar for bodies, the Fox is a delight the rest of the week. Plus points include an attractive ground floor room (modernised but not ruined) with a big central bar and etched glass windows, moreish bar food (tapas-style plates that come from the kitchen serving the lovely first floor restaurant) and a relaxed vibe. Drinks feature something for everyone: real ales are Bombardier plus a guest beer such as Harveys Sussex Bitter; Red Stripe, San Miguel and Foster's are the lagers; and there's a much better than average choice of wines. What's more, the Fox is just far away enough from Shoreditch's main drag to ensure that the place isn't dominated by bright young things.
Babies and children admitted. Bar available for hire. Disabled: toilet. Function room (12 capacity). Restaurant (available for hire, 40 capacity). Tables outdoors (5, terrace; 3, pavement). **Map p276 Q4.**

George & Dragon ★
2 Hackney Road, E2 7NS (7012 1100). Old Street tube/rail. **Open** 6pm-midnight daily. **Credit** MC, V. **Bar**
Luring trendy kids in skinny jeans and black eyeliner, the George & Dragon is scruffy but stylish. It's a cosy space with crimson walls and a womb-like interior enlivened by kitsch touches: twinkly lights (it always looks like Christmas here) and knick-knacks galore (pink flamingos, a rhinestone-studded cowboy hat, a stuffed weasel). A cardboard cut-out of Kim Wilde surveys a knowing, mostly gay crowd who plant tongues firmly in cheek as they dance to cheesy pop (Kylie and Girls Aloud), vintage gems (Kate Bush, Pulp) and forgotten oddities (Culture Club's 'The Medal Song'). Most punters drink pints from plastic cups (San Miguel, Blanc, Kronenbourg and Foster's). Arrive early at weekends if you want to snag a table, otherwise it's standing room only.
Disabled: toilet. Music (DJs 8pm nightly; free). **Map p276 R3.**

Great Eastern
54-56 Great Eastern Street, EC2A 3QR (7613 4545/www.greateasterndining.co.uk). Old Street tube/rail. **Open/food served** *Ground-floor bar* noon-midnight Mon-Fri; 6pm-midnight Sat. *Below 54 bar* 7.30pm-1am Fri, Sat. **Credit** AmEx, DC, MC, V. **Bar**
This broodingly handsome Will Ricker bar-restaurant serves high-end cocktails and exquisite dim sum bar snacks (four cubes of crispy pork belly with black vinegar, £6.50). There's a funnelled, glassed-in flame heater in one corner, an organic cluster of chandeliers, black roses on the cream wallpaper, black furniture – and a lighting level that purrs along never a tweak higher than intimate. Even the array of premium spirits behind the bar are lent a serious demeanour by their steel shelving. City-sleek funk does little to disguise this bar's emptiness early in the week, but a sazerac of H by Hine cognac, Woodford Reserve, Peychaud's bitters and absinthe rinse (£6.50) may well soften the void.
Babies and children admitted (restaurant only). Bar available for hire. Music (DJs 9pm Fri, Sat; free). Restaurant. **Map p276 R4.**

Hoxton Square Bar & Kitchen
2-4 Hoxton Square, N1 6NU (7613 0709). Old Street tube/rail. **Open** 11am-1am Mon-Thur; 11am-2am Fri, Sat; 11am-midnight Sun. **Food served** noon-11pm daily. **Credit** MC, V. **Bar**
One of the Hoxton originals, Hoxton Square Bar & Kitchen has seen plenty of action in its time. Still hip – check the gig nights and album launches – and packed to bursting at weekends, it attracts a cheerful mix of hip young things and weekend style tourists with its acres of scuffed concrete and on-the-square location. The cavernous space can feel soulless at times but not so's you'd notice once the party is in full flow in the windowless back-room. The main bar is long and buzzy, while the upmarket diner-style food in the restaurant area definitely hits the spot. The pleasant outside area fills up quickly in summer – arrive early.

East

*Babies and children admitted (until 6pm).
Disabled: toilet. Music (live music 9pm Mon-
Thur, Sun; DJs 9pm Fri, Sat; free-£5).
Restaurant. Tables outdoors (10, patio).*
Map p276 R3.

Light Bar & Restaurant

*233 Shoreditch High Street, E1 6PJ (7247
8989/www.thelighte1.com). Liverpool Street
tube/rail.* **Open** noon-midnight Mon-Wed;
noon-2am Thur, Fri; 6.30pm-2am Sat; noon-
10.30pm Sun. **Food served** noon-10.30pm
Mon-Fri, Sun; 6.30-11pm Sat. **Admission**
(upstairs bar) £2 Thur-Sat. **Credit** AmEx,
DC, MC, V. **DJ bar**

Light manages the unusual trick of being a
damn sight groovier when it's quiet and you
can savour the hip grandeur of its cavernous
main room, exposed brickwork complemented
by the old winch on the ceiling. On busy
evenings, by contrast, you can't move for
booze-hungry drones, who celebrate the end of
the day by invading each others' personal
space and shouting loudly. Shame, really,
because there are a number of high points,
from the large beer garden and lengthy wine
list to the loft-style top floor and balcony, which
hosts the odd proper rave-up and lots of funky
house. Developers have their eye on this place,
so get there while you can.
*Disabled: toilet. Dress: no suits in upstairs
bar. Function room (Mon-Thur, Sun only;
up to 200 capacity). Music (DJs 9pm Thur-
Sat). Restaurant. Tables outdoors (15,
courtyard). TV (projector).* **Map p276 R5**.

Loungelover ★

*1 Whitby Street, E1 6JU (7012 1234/
www.loungelover.co.uk). Liverpool Street
tube/rail.* **Open** 6pm-midnight Mon-Thur,
Sun; 5.30pm-1am Fri; 6pm-1am Sat. **Food
served** 6-11.30pm Mon-Fri, Sun; 7-11.30pm
Sat. **Credit** AmEx, DC, MC, V. **Cocktail bar**

Owned by the same concern as the feted Les
Trois Garçons restaurant around the corner, this
famously louche cocktail lounge may have had
some of its thunder stolen by neighbourhood
newcomer, Beach Blanket Babylon. Tasteful,
low-lit decadence is still the decor key, with
distressed wooden armoires, hot-house plants,
vintage palm-frond chandeliers, a stuffed
hippo's head, man-sized Chinese urns, antlers
made of red, mirrored mosaic, a giant disco ball
and tea lights set on elegant, glass-topped tables
establishing a unique, upmarket ambience.
Chinese-print-covered menus list cocktails by
genre (Hot Lover, Old Flame [house specialties],
First Love [classic mixes], Sweeties) and average

Insider Knowledge
Charlie Wright's

You are?
John Nash, owner of Charlie Wright's
International Bar (*see p184*), Shoreditch.
So who's Charlie Wright?
About 50 years ago, the pub was owned
by a guy called Charlie Wright, who was
an old East End boxer. Growing up as
a black kid in Wales, I spent my youth
boxing and, funnily enough, my boxing
nickname was Charlie, so when I took
the place over I named it after him.
**You used to be a body builder – what
made you decide to take over a bar?**
I spent a lot of time in Spain and hung
around in a fair few bars. When I came
back to London, I decided to open my
own. I used to come here in the '80s
when it was the Queen's Head. It had
been going for about 100 years and was
where all the East End gangsters used
to drink. Back then it was full of white,
East Enders and I was the only black
man in the bar, but I really liked it. I said,
'One day I'm going to buy this place.'
Has Shoreditch changed much?
When I came to Shoreditch there
were only three bars that opened late.
Now there are so many new bars around
and it's a lot more expensive. Everyone
wants to come to Shoreditch.
What kind of people come in here?
We get people who've lived here for
years, as well as all the artists and the
new young trendy people from outside.
We haven't changed much over the
years – that's why people love it.
You've been hosting live jazz recently.
In June I'm organising the Hoxton Jazz
Festival. The area is full of clubs that
only have DJs. We need more live music.

East

around £9, while a glass of champagne is £8, but watch out for the 12.5% service charge added to your bill. It may be slightly pretentious, but staff are helpful to the cocktail-confused and if you're out to impress, the place can hardly be bettered.

Booking advisable. Disabled: toilet. Music (DJs 7pm Fri, Sat; live music: cabaret/soul Sun, call for details). **Map p276 R4.**

Mother Bar

333 Old Street, EC1V 9LE (7739 5949/ www.333mother.com). Old Street tube/rail. **Open** 8pm-3am daily. **Credit** MC, V. **DJ bar**

As part of the legendary 333 Club, Mother is something of a Shoreditch institution. Tthough its sleazy, late-night allure has had the edge taken off it with the increasing proliferation of post-pub watering holes, it remains open long after other bars have shut up shop. Via an unmarked door at street level, you climb a shabby staircase and enter the first of two boxy rooms, decorated with red and gold wallpaper, a black padded bar – on which is set a small dressed mannequin – squashy black vinyl seats, gilt-framed mirrors and a chequer-board floor. Adjacent to the lounge area is the dance room, where well-oiled revellers let loose to the DJ's choices beneath a glitter ball or stand back to check out the live bands – a fairly recent re-introduction to this venue. Beers are your basic draught (Red Stripe, Guinness) and bottled choices and the cocktail neon sign seems a hangover from the past, rather than a current advertisement, but then, no one visits Mother for posh drinks. Late and lairy is what it does best.

Bar available for hire. Music (DJs 10pm daily; free; live music 8.30pm Wed, 8pm Fri, Sat; free). **Map p276 R4.**

Prague

6 Kingsland Road, E2 8DA (7739 9110/ www.barprague.com). Old Street tube/rail. **Open/food served** 10am-midnight daily. **Credit** MC, V. **Bar**

With its unassuming front and proximity to a perennially busy intersection, you could be forgiven for giving Prague a miss. But that'd be a mistake, because whether you're in the mood for a liquor-lubricated chat in the evening or a bit of laptop quiet and a decent coffee during the day, this cosy and relaxed eastern European-themed bar/café is well worth a visit. A stripped floor, wooden tables and chairs, exposed brick work, red banquettes, two chesterfield sofas (get there early to bag the one under the window) and

mellow lighting (tiny coach lamps, tea lights on tables) establish the bohemian ambience, which is reinforced by the alcohol selection. Bottled beers are the main draw here – Pilsener Urquell, Budvar (also available on draught), Zatec, Ostrovar, Lobkowicz, among many others – but wines and spirits are also well represented and the cocktail/shooter menu is impressive, offering a Cheeky Monkey (spiced rum, coconut liqueur, crème de banana, milk) and cucumber and mint martini alongside more familiar classics.

Babies and children admitted (until 6pm). Bar available for hire. Disabled: toilet. **Map p276 R4.**

Princess ★

76-78 Paul Street, EC2A 4NE (7729 9270). Old Street tube/rail. **Open** noon-11pm Mon-Fri; 5.30-11pm Sat; 12.30-5.30pm Sun. **Food served** 12.30-3pm, 6.30-10.30pm Mon-Fri; 6.30-10.30pm Sat; 1-4pm Sun. **Credit** AmEx, MC, V. **Gastropub**

Just like the Fox down the road, the Princess has a ground floor bar topped by a very decent restaurant. The differences are all about style. The look here is less pub and more gastrobar, with groovy wallpaper, dark chocolate paintwork and a wrought-iron staircase leading to the first floor dining room; big blackboards list a fine choice of wines and gastropub dishes. As well as the wines (23 bottles, about half of which are available by the glass) there are real ales in the form of Timothy Taylor Landlord and London Pride, plus Kronenbourg, Red Stripe, San Miguel, Staropramen and Guinness. Being that bit closer to the Shoreditch action means the clientele are younger and edgier here, but the welcome is a warm one, whatever you're wearing.

Babies and children admitted. Restaurant (available for hire, 30 capacity). **Map p276 Q4.**

Red Lion

41 Hoxton Street, N1 6NH (7729 7920/ www.redlionhoxton.com). Old Street tube/rail. **Open** noon-11pm daily. **Food served** noon-10.30pm Tue-Sun. **Credit** MC, V. **Pub**

It's years now since this tiny bar on the 'wrong' side of Hoxton Square saw local resident Jarvis Cocker drop in every now and again to do a spot of DJing. But despite numerous makeovers, the place still retains some of its original, low-rent charm. A bar that is barely long enough to accommodate three pairs of elbows dispenses draught Foster's, San Miguel, Kronenberg and Guinness, plus bottled options like Corona and Newcastle Brown Ale to punters who settle in around one of the round, copper-topped tables, on one of two church pews or the sole sofa to warm themselves around the real, open fire. Regency-stripe wallpaper, standard lamps, a large tapestry, potted plants and kitsch reproduction paintings complete the feeling of drinking in an elderly aunt's front parlour. Upstairs, however, the Dining Room serves tasty fare that is far from old-fashioned: pan-fried whole sea bass with ginger, chilli, spring onion and oyster sauce, or sweet potato and peanut massaman curry with jasmine rice.

Babies and children admitted (restaurant only). Disabled: toilet. Music (DJs 8pm Fri-Sun; free). Function room (50 capacity). Restaurant (available for hire, 40 capacity). **Map p276 R3**.

Reliance

336 Old Street, EC1V 9DR (7729 6888). Old Street tube/rail. **Open** noon-11pm Mon-Thur, Sun; noon-2am Fri, Sat. **Food served** noon-9pm daily. **Credit** DC, MC, V. **Pub**

This small, rather awkwardly shaped bar with worn floorboards, rough brickwork and the vague air of a Parisian bistro could do with being double the size, so perennially popular is its mix of decent drinks, late hours and a generally convivial atmosphere. Punters settle in for the duration at one of the scrubbed wooden tables either upstairs or down (only early birds will bag the couch at the very back). Or else they perch at the bar, which focuses heavily on bottled Belgian beers (Duvel, Belle Vue Kriek, Delirium Tremens et al) while also offering draught Litovel (both strengths), Hoegaarden, Adnams Bitter and blonde Fuller's Discovery. There's also a full selection of spirits, the Fentimans range and a good wine list. A blackboard menu advertises both snacks and mains such as sausage and mash, beef burgers and crab cakes, with a superior jukebox pulling it all together in fine style. *Jukebox.* **Map p276 R4**.

Sosho ★

2 Tabernacle Street, EC2A 4LU (7920 0701/ www.sosho3am.com). Moorgate or Old Street tube/rail. **Open** noon-midnight Tue; noon-1am Wed, Thur; noon-3am Fri; 7pm-4am Sat; 9pm-6am Sun. **Food served** noon-10.30pm Tue-Fri; 7-11pm Sat. **Admission** £5-£12 after 9pm Fri-Sun. **Credit** AmEx, DC, MC, V.

Cocktail bar

For review, *see p192.*

Babies and children admitted (until 6pm). Disabled: toilet. Function room (100 capacity). Music (DJs 8pm Wed-Fri; 9pm Sat, Sun). **Map p276 Q4**.

Three Blind Mice

5 Ravey Street, EC2A 4QW (7739 7746/www.3blindmicebar.com). Old Street tube/rail. **Open** 5.30-11pm Tue-Thur; 5.30pm-midnight Fri; 6.30pm-midnight Sat. **Credit** MC, V. **Bar**

Renamed after an album by Art Blakey's Jazz Messengers, this basement bar was previously called Smersh. But if the owners are redecorating, it's clearly a work in progress: the walls are still painted Soviet red and the odd bit of Russian poster art remains on show, in competition with the new black-and-white mural of three hepcats that decorates the red velvet drape-screened stairwell. It's a basic and unpretentious space, but cosy nonetheless, with stools set both at the weather-beaten bar and against one wall, and more relaxed seating in a small, sunken lounge area through the archway. Serious tipplers can pick from one of several Polish vodkas on offer alongside speciality rums and tequilas or opt for a jug of sangria, while the (bottled) beer choice is limited to two: Budvar or Carlsberg. Fentimans soft drinks are also available. Soft lighting on a low ceiling adds to the intimate feel, as does the music policy – DJs play anything from reggae to ambient electronica, while occasional live acts tend toward the unplugged variety.

Bar available for hire. Music (DJs 8pm Thur-Sat; free). **Map p276 Q4**.

Wenlock Arms ★ HOT 50

26 Wenlock Road, N1 7TA (7608 3406/ www.wenlock-arms.co.uk). Old Street tube/rail. **Open** noon-midnight Mon-Wed, Sun; noon-1am Thur-Sat. **Food served** noon-9pm daily. **No credit cards. Pub**

From the outside, the Wenlock doesn't look like much at all. And to be honest, it doesn't look like much from the inside either: it's just a boxy room that hasn't been much modified in years. Still, God forbid this old boozer should ever tear out its carpet or gastro-up its menu of doorstep sarnies: we like it just fine as it is. The key is the unique mix of people it attracts. On any given night, you might find yourself sitting next to a table of beer-bellied ale-hunters going through the excellent and ever-changing range of beers served across eight handpumps, a group of art students slumming it for the night away from their usual Hoxton haunts, and, of course, the ever-talkative regulars. This is, first and foremost, a local pub for local people, though your welcome will be far warmer here than in Royston Vasey and you'll probably end up talking to a table of strangers. It's at its best for Thursday's popular quiz and for the music on

East

Sosho ★

Disconcertingly quiet from the outside, Sosho is a lively DJ bar with fine cocktails and an 'acoustic lock' that keeps sound firmly inside – no doubt a neighbourly necessity with all-night weekend opening. Although certainly lived in, the place remains pretty handsome – tea lights, chandeliers, dark wood. The floor is clear to leave space for shuffle action, but there's a surrounding raised area for lounging, with chocolate-coloured booth seating and clubbing photos. The largely male City crowd was well into the lager wobble on our latest visit, but the cocktails held our attention. Being part of the Match bar empire, you can expect experienced bartenders and quality drinks: perhaps a neat and pretty Japon Cocktail (Gran Centenario Reposado tequila with cassis, saké, pink grapefruit juice and cucumber) or a clean, classic gin martini, both a snip at £6.50.
For listings, see p191.

East

Fridays and Saturdays, when veteran jazzers set up in the corner and start a session that almost invariably dissolves into a singalong. Perfect, more or less.

Babies and children admitted (until 9pm). Function room (25 capacity). Games (cribbage, darts, dominos). Music (blues/jazz 9pm Fri, Sat; 3pm Sun; free). Quiz (9pm Thur; free).

William IV

7 Shepherdess Walk, N1 7QE (3119 3012). Old Street tube/rail. **Open** noon-11pm Mon-Wed; noon-midnight Thur-Sat; noon-10.30pm Sun. **Food served** noon-3pm, 6-10pm Mon-Sat; 1-7pm Sun. **Credit** MC, V. Gastropub
While nearby Old Street and its environs become an increasingly manic party district, the hidden-away William IV keeps its cool as a civilised, homely pub where you can escape for some laid-back drinks or a square meal. The decor is modestly trendy: walls and wooden furniture are painted white and embellished with a potted assortment of portraits, photographs, stuffed animals and other objects. Downstairs, the main bar is a single room which is small, but the clever use of big communal tables maximises available space, and in good weather additional tables are placed outside. Upstairs there's a dedicated dining room, but the same menu is available throughout. Drinks include Black Sheep, London Pride, Hoegaarden, Leffe on tap and a fair selection of inexpensive wines.

Disabled: toilet. Function room (40 capacity). Games (board games). Screening facilities. Tables outdoors (4, yard).

Stratford

King Edward VII

47 Broadway, E15 4BQ (8534 2313/ www.kingeddie.co.uk). Stratford tube/rail/ DLR. **Open** noon-11pm Mon-Wed; noon-midnight Thur-Sat; noon-11.30pm Sun. **Food served** noon-3pm, 5-10pm Mon-Fri; noon-10pm Sat, Sun. **Credit** MC, V. Gastropub
Squatting between taller buildings, this Grade II-listed pub seems quaintly proportioned, but through the comfy main bar there are a sparsely furnished saloon bar, a further upstairs room and a walled back garden. Amid the handsome etched glass and dark wood, gorgeous bright green tiles along a side corridor really stand out, but the pub is no museum piece: a mix of campus renegades and collared locals, with a nearly rowdy guitar-band soundtrack, keeps thing lively. There were four real ales – Nelson Brewery's Trafalgar Bitter and Nethergate's

Suffolk County the rarities – and ten wines, all by glass and bottle, but no menus in evidence at 8.30pm. Has King Eddie scaled back the gastro ambitions? We hope not.

Babies and children admitted (upstairs only). Function room (up to 100 capacity). Music (acoustic/open mic 9pm Thur; free). Quiz (8.30pm Sun; free). Tables outdoors (5, yard).

Wapping

Prospect of Whitby

57 Wapping Wall, E1W 3SH (7481 1095). Shadwell DLR. **Open** noon-11pm Mon-Wed, Sun; noon-midnight Thur-Sat. **Food served** noon-9.30pm daily. **Credit** AmEx, MC, V. Pub
Located on the Thames foreshore and dating from the 1520s, this old boozer has its original flagstone floor and a wonderful pewter bar from where you'll be served (grumpily, on our visit) Greene King IPA, London Pride, Old Speckled Hen and Timothy Taylor Landlord, as well as eight red and white wines by the glass. The noose hanging outside is a reference to one of its most famous customers – 'Hanging' Judge Jeffreys. These days you're more likely to be jostling for a seat with locals and tourists looking for one of the popular roast dinners. Find a spot overlooking the river out on the terrace or upstairs in the Pepys Room where there's an open fire and – located on a shelf – a human ulna bone found in the pub.

Babies and children admitted (before 6pm, dining only). Disabled: toilet. Function rooms (up to 150 capacity). Tables outdoors (7, garden). TV.

Town of Ramsgate

62 Wapping High Street, E1W 2PN (7481 8000). Shadwell DLR. **Open** noon-midnight Mon-Sat; noon-11pm Sun. **Food served** noon-9pm daily. **Credit** AmEx, MC, V. Pub
Though claiming to be the oldest pub on the river, the Ramsgate looks like it had a refurb in the '70s – all patterned carpet and chunky wood tables. But it's full of nautical bric-a-brac and the odd historic manuscript. This much-loved hostelry serves comforting burgers, roasts and beer-battered fish and chips. Equally comforting was the service – warm and welcoming when we visited on a wet Sunday afternoon. On tap you'll find Adnams, Young's Bitter and even Beck's. We'll be back when the sun's out to take advantage of the terrace overlooking the river.

Babies and children admitted (until 7pm). Games (backgammon, board games, cards, chess). Quiz (8.30pm Mon; £1). Tables outdoors (12, riverside garden). TV.

East

North East

North East

Fling a pint pot in the air in Hackney and these days it seems more likely to land in a gastropub than an old man's boozer: Tom and Ed Martin continue their incursions, with the **Prince Arthur** joining the **Empress of India**, and the **Scolt Head** is another fine exponent. Gourmet food isn't the whole story, though: there's late-night debauchery and cheap cocktails at the **Dalston Jazz Bar** and – despite an *NME* plug – the **Prince George** remains resolute in its status as a pub. Stoke Newington too has a fistful of good pubs – gastronauts dive into the **Prince** or the **Alma**, while boozehounds have the **Auld Shillelagh** and the **Shakespeare**. For a taste of that Walthamstow urban village vibe, drop in on the Sunday afternoon jazz session at the **Nag's Head**. Wanstead is no slouch either, with the characterful **Nightingale** and the handsome **George** to choose from.

Hackney

Cat & Mutton
76 Broadway Market, E8 4QJ (7254 5599). London Fields rail. **Open** 6-11pm Mon; noon-11pm Tue-Thur, Sun; noon-midnight Fri, Sat. **Food served** 6-10pm Mon; noon-3pm, 6.30-10pm Tue-Sat; 12.30-5pm Sun. **Credit** AmEx, MC, V. **Gastropub**
The pub that never sleeps – or rather the pub whose regulars never sleep – often struggles to cope with its popularity, and service has been known to slip. Day after night after day, hip kids with pointy shoes, strange haircuts and seemingly endless collections of elasticated belts fill every inch of space in this wooden tabled and chaired gastropub/bar. They sup bloody marys or pints of San Miguel, tuck into weekend breakfast and roasts, and find out what they got up to last night. There's a decent wine list and the food is good, if a little pricey. An upstairs room offers more space to hang out and/or play pool and look cool.
Babies and children welcome (until 8pm): high chairs. Disabled: toilet. Function room (80 capacity). Games (pool table). Music (DJs 7.30pm Sun; free). Tables outdoors (5, pavement).

Dalston Jazz Bar
4 Bradbury Street, N16 8JN (7254 9728). Dalston Kingsland rail. **Open** 5pm-3am Mon-Thur; 5pm-5am Fri, Sat; 5pm-2am Sun. **No credit cards.** **Bar**
This well established late, late night haunt is reminiscent of a 1960s, purpose-built library. Plonked in the middle of what looks like a municipal car park, it's filled with old retro sofas, and books. Not that much reading goes on here. This is a place for a nightcap, in the form of bottled beers and pink drinks (cocktails are an unbelievably cheap £4.50) on the way to bed. The always random crowd get to dance till the wee hours to an equally eclectic mix emanating from the decks on the bar, from Ella to *Jungle Book* favourites to the Cure. What's not to love?
Bar available for hire (Mon-Fri). Music (DJs 10pm daily; free).

Dove Kitchen & Freehouse
24-28 Broadway Market, E8 4QJ (7275 7617/www.belgianbars.com). London Fields rail. **Open** noon-11pm Mon-Thur, Sun; noon-midnight Fri, Sat. **Food served** noon-10pm Mon-Thur, Sun; noon-11pm Fri, Sat. **Credit** MC, V. **Gastropub**
Perhaps it's the draw of the wonderful beer selection (over 100 Belgian beers, 17 beers on tap, including Delirium Tremens 9%, Belle-Vue Kriek and Früli, at least four real ales and guest beers), but the popularity of this place is beginning to divide its customers. Fans love the cosy candlelit nooks, the board games, the vibe and the extensive menu (own-made burgers, sausages with mash, huge Sunday roasts and pub glasses of chips), while detractors have experienced overbearing (even rude) staff and found the food underwhelming. We've experienced both, and hope that what was once Hackney's finest regains its crown.
Babies and children admitted (until 6pm). Games (board games). Music (jazz 8.30pm Wed, Sun; free). Restaurant. Tables outdoors (6, pavement).

Empress of India

130 Lauriston Road, E9 7LH (8533 5123/ www.theempressofindia.com). Mile End tube, then 277 bus. **Open/food served** 8.30am-11pm Mon-Fri; 9am-11pm Sat; 9am-10.30pm Sun. **Credit** AmEx, MC, V. **Gastropub**
With mosaic floor tiling and mussel-shell chandeliers, the airy, conservatory-feel Empress usually hums with diners contentedly tucking into the likes of veal ossobuco with white truffle mash. So far, a typically accomplished Martin brothers gastropub. But – despite Broadside and Landlord on handpumps, Paulaner, Amstel and Bitburger on tap, Meantime Pale Ale in the fridge and a good wine list – the boozing section is just a couple of clumps of low furniture and a dozen red-cushioned bar stools. So think of the place as a grand subcontinental café (smoothies and quality teas are also offered) and enjoy playing the memsahib by the tiger's head and languorous sitar-player mirror.
Babies and children welcome: changing room, children's menu, high chairs. Disabled: toilet. Restaurant. Tables outdoors (8, terrace).

Pembury Tavern

90 Amhurst Road, E8 1JH (8986 8597/ www.individualpubs.co.uk/pembury). Hackney Central or Hackney Downs rail. **Open** noon-11pm daily. **Food served** noon-3pm, 6-9pm Mon-Sat; noon-9pm Sun. **Credit** MC, V. **Pub**
This vast, brightly lit bar room feels disappointingly like a youth hostel canteen, but 16 handpumps – mostly fine real ale from Cambridge's Milton Brewery (Pegasus, Jericho, Cyclops and their stout Nero on our visit), usually plus a guest cider – soften the blow. The fridge has a couple of dozen Low Countries beers, there's Budvar and plenty of wines by the glass, and nosh includes an £8.95 Neal's Yard ploughman's. Bar billiards and a red-baize pool table on one side give way to bookshelves and games (chess, Scrabble, backgammon, role-playing games) on the other. Wireless internet is available, and beer festivals take place in March, July and November.
Babies and children admitted. Disabled: toilet. Games (bar billiards table, board games, pool table). No piped music or jukebox.

Prince Arthur ★ NEW HOT 50

95 Forest Road, E8 3BH (7249 9996/ www.theprincearthurlondonfields.com). Hackney Central or London Fields rail. **Open** 4-11pm Mon-Fri; 10am-11pm Sat, Sun. **Food served** 6-10pm Mon-Fri; 10.30am-4.30pm, 6-10pm Sat, Sun. **Credit** MC, V. **Gastropub**
For review, *see p198.*

Babies and children admitted. Bar available for hire. Disabled: toilet. Tables outdoors (4, pavement).

Prince George ★

40 Parkholme Road, E8 3AG (7254 6060). Dalston Kingsland rail/30, 38, 56, 242, 277 bus. **Open** 5pm-midnight Mon-Thur; noon-1am Fri, Sat; noon-11.30pm Sun. **Credit** MC, V. **Pub**
Thanks to a plug in the *NME*, one of Hackney's finest is now (on a Saturday night at least) wall-to-wall ironic outfits. We saw beauties (and a few beasties) sporting ocelot, sequins, space invader jumpers and – for some reason we couldn't fathom – a lot of unusual scarves as they supped Czech beer and real ale (Pride, Brakspear Bitter, Woodforde's Wherry). There are plenty of good wines by the glass too (from £3.40). Another draw is one of the best, free jukeboxes in London: Martha & the Muffins, Dolly Parton and the Temptations. No wonder there's always a party going on. Monday's popular quiz sees more beards, fewer sequins. Sadly, prices seem to have risen with the pub's profile: a pint of Guinness at £3.40 – in Dalston!
Babies and children admitted (until 8.30pm). Games (board games, pool table). Jukebox. Quiz (9pm Mon; £2). Tables outdoors (8, heated forecourt). TV.

Royal Inn on the Park

111 Lauriston Road, E9 7HJ (8985 3321). Mile End tube, then 277 bus. **Open** noon-11pm Mon-Sat; noon-10.30pm Sun. **Food served** 12.30-3.30pm, 6.30-10pm Tue-Sat; 12.30-4pm Sun. **Credit** MC, V. **Pub**
Wreaths of lights in the windows of this imposing former hotel, whose hugely popular beer garden backs right on to Victoria Park, makes an appropriate welcome to the roomy old boozer. A yellowed ceiling is the principal reminder of a rowdier past, with the beautiful Victorian counter serving a more grown-up crowd these days – the jazz sophistication of *Kind of Blue* is as likely to hit the jukebox as Led Zep. A couple of guests and plenty of Fuller's on the handpumps, plus the same brewer's Honey Dew, Scrumpy Jack and some Czechs on constant pressure, keep beer-drinkers honest, while dissenters get high-end spirits and decent wine. Roasts are a draw here, but there's always something tempting on the menu.
Babies and children admitted (until 8pm). Disabled: toilet. Function room (120 capacity). Quiz (8.30pm Tue; £1). Restaurant (available for hire, 30 capacity). Tables outdoors (30, garden).

North East

Prince Arthur ★ NEW HOT 50

Another Martin brothers enterprise –
and our current favourite. Outside the
imposing three-storey building, large
coaching lamps preside over four trestle
tables; within, the pub is compact and
cosy, beautifully restored in its original
Victorian dark wood and green Anaglypta
wallpaper. Wrapped round the bows
of a sensationally handsome bar,
the single room properly makes no
distinction between diners and boozers
– take a Pride or Deuchars IPA under the
stuffed pheasants or speculate about
the aristo in tights and a stuffed jaguar
over saddle of rabbit cassoulet or deep-
fried triple jam sandwich with Carnation
milk ice-cream. Even lighting is perfectly
pitched: low enough for atmosphere,
easily bright enough to read a book.
The clientele is a healthy mix of old men,
fashionable young Chinese women and
middle-aged architects poring over
drawings. *For listings, see p197.*

Scolt Head ★ NEW

107A Culford Road, N1 4HT (7254 3965/ www.thescolthead.com). Dalston Kingsland rail. **Open** noon-midnight Mon-Sat; noon-11.30pm Sun. **Food served** noon-3pm, 6.30-10pm Mon-Fri; noon-4pm, 6.30-10pm Sat, Sun. **Credit** AmEx, MC, V. **Gastropub**

In a corner of Hackney where pool tables and a giant TV are still a prerequisite for survival, the Scolt Head has been smartened up. New owner Rosie Haines tore out the old carpets, but left the place feeling like a utilitarian locals' pub. Decent beer is served – Hopback Summer Lightning, Deuchars IPA, London Pride (all £2.80) – and the wine list is brief but thoughtful, listing good producers rather than more obvious choices. The brief, daily changing menu features mains mostly under a tenner, with chicken, leek and potato pie next to gnocchi, and chocolate soufflé cake, each dish benefiting from straightforward, unaffected cooking. There's a small urban garden for smokers.

Babies and children admitted. Function room (150 capacity). Games (pool table). Music (acoustic, last Thur of mth 8pm; free). Quiz (8pm Mon; £2). Restaurant. TVs (satellite). Tables outdoors (10, garden).

Spurstowe

68 Greenwood Road, E8 1AB (7249 2500). Hackney Central rail. **Open** 4.30-11pm Mon-Thur; 4.30pm-midnight Fri; noon-midnight Sat; noon-10.30pm Sun. **Food served** 6-10pm Mon-Fri; noon-9pm Sat, Sun. **Credit** MC, V. **Pub**

The Spurstowe's deep main room is an impressive version of gastro-standard decor: burnished bronze suns and rococo mirrors join the bare bricks and distressed wood, and a pretty curve of leaded glass divides it from a boarded-in outdoor terrace. Only Landlord, Pride and, oddly, Ruddles County are on pull, but there are 'classic' cocktails for £5.50 ('We have some lovely vodkas', the barman grumbled, when we failed to specify for a martini), well-priced premium whiskies and a global list of half a dozen of each colour wine. Baggy woolly hat-wearers and shaved-head-barely-bearded blokes lay into gastro-meals or nod to the Stooges and dinner party trip hop. *Babies and children admitted (until 6pm). Bar available for hire. Tables outdoors (18, garden).*

Leyton

Birkbeck Tavern

45 Langthorne Road, E11 4HL (8539 2584). Leyton tube. **Open** 11am-11pm Mon-Thur;

11am-midnight Fri, Sat; noon-11pm Sun. **Credit** MC, V. **Pub**

A former hotel, the 'Birky' offers a large public bar, a smaller room at the front with a pool table and a garden, plus a bustling but never intimidating demeanour. There's a rotating line-up of guest beers from the likes of Mighty Oak, Archers and Weltons, though you won't find much in the way of food to wash it down. You don't need to be a Leyton Orient fan to drink here, but if you are then you're guaranteed to find a fellow sufferer to discuss the team's travails over a pint of 'Rita Special', named after a previous landlady.

Entertainment (karaoke 8.30pm alternate Sat; free). Function room (100 capacity). Games (darts, fruit machine). Quiz (8.15pm alternate Sun; £1). Tables outdoors (14, garden). TVs.

Leytonstone

North Star

24 Browning Road, E11 3AR (8989 5777). Leytonstone tube. **Open** 4-11pm Mon-Fri; noon-11.30pm Sat; noon-11pm Sun. **No credit cards.** **Pub**

This unmodernised back-street boozer is a surprise find barely 50 metres from Leytonstone High Road and within sight of its vile drive-thru McDonalds. Behind the etched-glass saloon door and half-net curtains, some might describe the basic two-bar interior as tatty. Others would use the word 'comfortable', since friendly service, three pumps dispensing reliably well-kept ales and prints of olde E11 create a lived-in feel – no surprise, since the pub was actually created in the 1850s by knocking together two of the neighbourhood's early Victorian cottages. *Babies and children admitted (until 8pm). Games (darts, fruit machine, quiz machine). Jukebox. Tables outdoors (6, garden; 2, pavement). TVs (satellite).*

Stoke Newington

Alma

59 Newington Green Road, N1 4QU (7359 4536/www.the-alma.co.uk). Highbury & Islington tube/rail/Canonbury rail. **Open** 5-11pm Mon-Thur; noon-11pm Fri, Sat; noon-10.30pm Sun. **Food served** 7-10.30pm Mon-Thur; 12.30-3.30pm, 7-10.30pm Fri; 1-4pm, 7-10.30pm Sat; 1-4pm, 7-10pm Sun. **Credit** MC, V. **Pub**

Stunning bay windows dominate the front bar of this relaxed and friendly foodie pub. On hazy afternoons, light pours through them on to the

North East

mismatched leather sofas, chairs and tables that are scattered about the place. Further back are darker, welcoming snugs, a small courtyard garden, and fittingly (it is still a pub after all), an upright piano. Couples flip through the left-leaning Sunday papers before tucking into a seasonal menu of Modern British fare (kedgeree with curried onion, £8.50, for example). Red Stripe, Bombardier, Hoegaarden, Guinness and Amstel are on tap, with four or five red and white wines available by the glass.
Babies and children admitted. Bar available for hire. Games (board games). Restaurant. Tables outdoors (4, pavement; 8, courtyard).

Auld Shillelagh HOT 50

105 Stoke Newington Church Street, N16 0UD (7249 5951). Stoke Newington rail/73, 393, 476 bus. **Open** 11am-11pm Mon-Sat; noon-10.30pm Sun. **Credit** AmEx, MC, V. **Pub**
Long and narrow 'like a canal boat' (according to Shane McGowan), this low-frills local appears tiny on the outside, but the front bar area extends back unexpectedly far to a beer garden. With no ales on offer, the main attraction is the excellent Guinness – a speciality of the pub – perfectly poured and brought to your table without any fuss. The two big screens show key games for the regulars, more likely to come from the nearby bookies than the nearby branch of Fresh & Wild. Things get more cramped at the weekends, when the banter and black stuff flow in equal measure.
Babies and children admitted (until 7pm). Games (fruit machine). Music (musicians 8pm alternate Fri; free). TVs (big screen, satellite). Tables outdoors (7, garden).

Fox Reformed ★

176 Stoke Newington Church Street, N16 0JL (7254 5975/www.fox-reformed.co.uk). Stoke Newington rail/73, 393, 476 bus. **Open** 5pm-midnight Mon-Fri; noon-midnight Sat, Sun. **Food served** 6.30-10.30pm Mon-Fri; noon-3pm, 6.30-10.30pm Sat, Sun. **Credit** AmEx, DC, MC, V. **Wine bar/restaurant**
This cosy bistro has been a fixture on Church Street in one form or another since 1981, along with its proprietors Robbie and Carol Richards. Patrons are ushered in by the elegant fox swinging outside. Within, deep red tones pervade, with corks piled up by the large plate-glass windows. A kitchen dresser and grandfather clock add to the homely feel. The small bar offers one pump (Stella), but the main focus is on a wine list of 30-odd bottles, with a

selection available by the glass. Premium bottled lagers (Hoegaarden, Leffe) are also on offer, as are steaks and Tuscany sausages (£10.75). A backgammon tournament and wine club remain popular with the refined, mature crowd of regulars.

Games (backgammon, board games).
Restaurant. Tables outdoors (5, garden).
Wine-tasting club (7pm alternate Thur; £10 non-members).

Londesborough ★

36 Barbauld Road, N16 0SS (7254 5865).
Stoke Newington rail/73, 476 bus. **Open** 4.30-11pm Mon-Thur; 4.30pm-midnight Fri; noon-midnight Sat; noon-10.30pm Sun. **Food served** 5-10pm Mon-Fri; noon-4.30pm, 5-10pm Sat; noon-8.30pm Sun. **Credit** MC, V. **Pub**
Slightly adrift from the main hubs of Stokey and Newington Green, this corner pub still capably serves the more affluent folk of those zones. A stripped wood panelled bar leads round to a sunken lounge, with battered sofas, and open fires during the cold winter months. Despite the relaxed air, there are some serious drinking options on offer, on tap Harveys, Timothy Taylor Landlord, Guinness as well as the obligatory Staropramen and Hoegaarden. Chalked up on the board is a fine wine list, and the cocktails include a notorious bloody mary (£3.95) held in a jug at the bar. Food is well portioned, and upmarket English breakfasts are a popular choice. DJs entertain a youngish crowd at the weekends when jeans are of the skinny variety.

Babies and children admitted (until 6pm).
Music (DJs 8pm Fri, Sat; 7pm Sun; free).
Tables outdoors (12, garden).

Prince

59 Kynaston Road, N16 0EB (7923 4766/ www.theprincepub.com). Stoke Newington rail/73, 393, 476 bus. **Open** noon-11pm Mon-Thur; noon-midnight Fri, Sat; noon-10.30pm Sun. **Food served** noon-2.30pm, 5-10pm Mon-Fri; noon-4pm, 5.30-10pm Sat; noon-4pm, 6-9pm Sun. **Credit** AmEx, MC, V. **Gastropub**
Under the management of an amiable brother and sister team since August last year, the emphasis at this corner pub is on good eating. On an average weekday night tables are filled with chattering professionals (laptops out) and family groups tucking into a menu of slow-braised lamb shank and sirloin burgers. Dark shades and velvety curtains create a cosy restaurant feel, while the pub's original fireplace and paintwork (artfully left to peel) contrast with

North East

Auld Shillelagh

the sleek metallic central bar. Wine drinkers can peruse an extensive list that groups grapes under 'Distinctive Soils' and 'Purity of Fruit'. Lagers dominate the pumps, with speciality bottled cider including Weston's Organic and Thatcher's. Sunday roasts are a highlight. *Babies and children welcome: high chairs. Disabled: toilet. Entertainment (comedy 8.30pm monthly Thur, check website; £5). Function room (50 capacity). Tables outdoors (8, garden). TV.*

Shakespeare

57 Allen Road, N16 8RY (7254 4190). Dalston Kingsland rail/73, 141, 476 bus. **Open** 5pm-midnight Mon-Thur; 5pm-1am Fri; noon-1am Sat; noon-11pm Sun. **Credit** MC, V. **Pub**
Milton and Chaucer also get name checks in the streets around this unreconstructed old boozer tucked away off Shakspeare (sic) Walk. Decor veers from a Boudicca-like wood carving dominating one side of the central bar, to art deco cigarette adverts, and a jar of pickled eggs (surely for decorative purposes only). Scuffed wooden benches surround it all, topped off with a nicotine-stained ceiling. The rough-round-the-edges approach is mirrored by the regulars, a mixture of old school *Guardian* readers, and art school bohemians. A full range of Fuller's ales, Hoegaarden, Leffe and the Czech lager Litovel, keep whistles wet, and if you're hungry, you can order in from the takeaway pizza place next door. *Babies and children admitted (until 7pm). Games (board games, cribbage, darts). Jukebox. Quiz (9pm Mon; £1). Tables outdoors (12, covered garden). TV (satellite).*

Walthamstow

Nag's Head

9 Orford Road, E17 9LP (8520 9709). Walthamstow Central tube/rail. **Open** 4-11pm Mon-Thur; 2-11pm Fri; noon-11pm Sat, Sun. **Credit** MC, V. **Pub**
Plonked in a surprisingly middle-England village in Walthamstow, the Nag's Head is a pub with an easy-going attitude. Unwind on a leather sofa and enjoy a coconut Mongoza from the range of Belgian beers on offer, or sit and listen to chill-out jazz over a pint of Oscar Wilde from the ample selection of ales. If the velvet tablecloths are not to your liking you can always retreat to the spacious beer garden, unsurprisingly popular on a sunny afternoon. Too many Mongozas? Treat your beer-gut to a (women only) belly-dancing class upstairs on a Tuesday evening. This is a cat-friendly, rather than a child-friendly pub; they have their own

cat, Billy, and a couple of locals' cats follow their owners into the pub. When the last pub cat, Big Blackie, died last August, they held a funeral for him with a gospel choir. *Belly dancing classes (women only, 7pm, 8.30pm Tue; £7). Life drawing classes (7.30pm Mon; phone for details). Music (jazz 4-8pm Sun; free). Pilates classes (7.30pm Wed, Thur; phone for details). Tables outdoors (8, heated patio; 20, heated garden).*

Wanstead

George

159 High Street, E11 2RL (8989 2921). Wanstead tube. **Open** 9am-midnight Mon-Thur, Sun; 9am-12.30am Fri, Sat. **Food served** 9am-11pm daily. **Credit** MC, V. **Pub**
All the usual Wetherspoons features are in place here – decent hand-pulled ale with regular specials, food and drink deals – but this large and handsome building has overcome its corporatisation with aplomb. Set back from a busy junction opposite Wanstead tube station, its Edwardian etched windows and attractive ironwork have remained intact while a 'throne' depicting historical and mythical Georges adds a kitschy touch. The atmosphere is relaxed, and the place is big enough never to feel cramped. Another large bar upstairs is mainly for diners. *Babies and children admitted (until 9.30pm). Function room (80 capacity). Games (fruit machines). No piped music or jukebox. Tables outdoors (12, garden).*

Nightingale

51 Nightingale Lane, E11 2EY (8530 4540). Snaresbrook or Wanstead tube. **Open** 10am-midnight daily. **Food served** 10am-10pm Mon, Wed; 10am-4pm Tue, Thur; 10am-6pm Fri-Sun. **Credit** MC, V. **Pub**
Wanstead has its fair share of chain-bar monstrosities but this place has kept its character as a much-loved local at the heart of the Victorian Nightingale Estate. A smartly painted exterior announces similar attention to detail within: the brass is gleaming and the glasses polished at the central island bar, where ales such as Woodforde's Wherry, Nelson Pieces of Eight and more familiar offerings from Courage and Fuller's are kept in tip-top condition. There's a reasonable wine list too. Banquettes curve around the interior and the large screen TV to the rear is not too overpowering. The traditional pub grub (with fishy leanings) is popular. *Babies and children admitted. Quiz (8pm Mon; £2). TVs.*

North

North

The fire that claimed the Hawley Arms has left the **Dublin Castle** as Camden's sole destination for aspirant skinny-jeaned indie-popsters. Those looking for a quiet pint in a more traditional setting have more choice: the cosy **Crown & Goose**, for example, or **Quinn's**, which boasts one of the best selections of Belgian beers this side of Brussels. Kentish Town offers a similarly relaxed vibe at the revamped **Pineapple** and the **Junction Tavern**, which also does high-class pub grub. Primrose Hill is heaving with top-notch gastropubs, such as the **Engineer**, the **Lansdowne** and **Queens**. There's no shortage in Islington either; our favourite is the **Charles Lamb**. This corner of north London also has some of London's best bars – we like **Keston Lodge** and the sophisticated **Elk in the Woods**. Outstanding local pubs further north include the **Landseer**, the **Dartmouth Arms** and the splendid **Harringay Arms**.

Archway

Landseer ★
37 Landseer Road, N19 4JU (7263 4658).
Archway or Holloway Road tube/17, 43, 217 bus. **Open** noon-11pm Mon, Tue, Sun; noon-midnight Wed-Sat. **Food served** noon-3pm, 5-10pm Mon-Fri; noon-4pm, 5-10.30pm Sat; noon-5pm, 6-9.30pm Sun. **Credit** MC, V.
Gastropub
High red ceilings, pale walls and huge windows give Landseer a fresh, spacious feel. The style is classic gastropub: plain wood tables, leather sofas, and a smarter dining area at the back. The food is fairly ambitious (the same menu is also served in the bar room), with global touches as in cajun tuna steak with tuscan bean salad; there are good tapas and bar snacks for the merely peckish. The selection of cask ales (Adnams, Timothy Taylor) is complemented by posh lagers (Leffe, Hoegaarden); wines are varied but a bit pricey, starting at £12.75.
Babies and children welcome: high chairs, smaller portions. Games (board games). Restaurant. Tables outdoors (15, terrace).

North Nineteen NEW
194-196 Sussex Way, N19 4HZ (7281 2786/www.northnineteen.co.uk). Archway tube/43, 271 bus. **Open** noon-midnight Mon-Thur, Sun; noon-1am Fri, Sat. **Food served** noon-4.30pm Mon; noon-10pm Tue-Fri; 1-10pm Sat; noon-7pm Sun. **Credit** MC, V. **Bar**
Just an empty Special Brew can's throw from the Holloway Road, this spruced-up boozer is all pine, adventurous colour clashes and swirly flock wallpaper. There's St Austell Tribute from Cornwall on tap and, should you prefer your beer made with bottom-fermenting yeast, Budweiser Budvar. Food is quintessentially English, freshly prepared pub grub carried off with a modern twist. There's open mic on Tuesdays, monthly wine tastings, plenty of board games, and, on our visit, talk at the bar was of the forthcoming (in association with CAMRA) beer festival.
Babies and children admitted. Bar available for hire. Function room (capacity 50). Games (board games, darts). Music (open mic 7.30pm Tue; bands 8.30pm Sat; free). Tables outdoors (8, front garden; 4, back garden). TV (big screen, satellite).

St John's
91 Junction Road, N19 5QU (7272 1587). Archway tube. **Open** 5-11pm Mon-Thur; noon-11pm Fri, Sat; noon-10.30pm Sun. **Food served** 6.30-11pm Mon-Thur; noon-3.30pm, 6.30-11pm Fri; noon-4pm, 6.30-11pm Sat; noon-4pm, 6.30-9.30pm Sun. **Credit** AmEx, MC, V. **Gastropub**
Big windows at the front catch the light beautifully, creating a pleasant feel even when Junction Road is at its greyest. St John's has long been a star in the gastropub firmament, with an adventurous modern menu that's mainly served in a grand hall of a dining room at the back, lined with eclectic art. There's relatively less space for drinkers, especially at weekends when dining tables take over more of the bar; but it's still a welcoming spot that encourages conversation. The wine list is superior, with well-chosen French, Italian and Spanish labels; beers on tap include Leffe, Hoegaarden, Timothy Taylor and Black Sheep.

Babies and children welcome: high chairs. Booking advisable. Games (backgammon, chess). Tables outdoors (6, patio).

Swimmer at the Grafton Arms ★

13 Eburne Road, N7 6AR (7281 4632). Holloway Road tube/Finsbury Park tube/ rail. **Open** 5-11pm Mon; noon-3pm, 5-11pm Tue-Thur; noon-11pm Fri, Sat; noon-10.30pm Sun. **Food served** 5-9.30pm Mon; noon-3pm, 5-9.30pm Tue-Thur; noon-9.30pm Fri-Sun. **Credit** MC, V. **Pub**
For review, *see p208*.
Games (board games). Jukebox. Quiz (8.30pm Mon; £2). Tables outdoors (15, garden). TV. Wi-Fi (free).

Camden Town & Chalk Farm

Bartok

78-79 Chalk Farm Road, NW1 8AR (7916 0595/www.bartokbar.com). Chalk Farm tube. **Open** 4pm-3am Mon-Thur; 3pm-3am Fri; 3pm-4am Sat, Sun. **Admission** £5 after 10pm Fri, Sat. **Credit** MC, V. **Cocktail bar**
An understated oasis of Zen-like calm named after the Hungarian composer, Bartok was founded on a fondness for classical music, but more often than not has DJs spinning chill-out tunes of the electronic variety. The red walls are enlivened by arty configurations of modern light bars and a framed LCD fish tank; seating comes in the form of chocolate leather couches and a smattering of cubic pouffe, place to rock out, which mean, mercifully free of goths and gearhead, there are couples ignoring the bog-st beers and sipping cheap cocktails wi, — miracle! – actually hearing each other speak. *Babies and children admitted (until 6pm Sat, Sun). Disabled: toilet. Music (DJs 10pm Mon, Tue, Fri, Sat). Tables outdoors (5, pavement).* **Map p286 G26**.

Bod NEW

30 Hawley Crescent, NW1 8NP (7482 5937/ www.bodegadetapas.co.uk). Camden Town tube. **Open/food served** noon-11pm Tue-Sat; noon-6pm Sun. **Credit** AmEx, MC, V. **Wine bar**
Just off Chalk Farm Road, this Spanish wine bar (full name Bodega de Tapas) has nearly 50 top-notch tipples in stock, chosen from rising wine regions and top producers. The pick of sherries is more limited, though there is one PX dessert sherry available by the glass. Cruzcampo is the sole Spanish beer on tap. Food comes in the form of tapas (chargrilled chorizo in cava, £4.50) of variable quality. The unlikely location, in an area mostly patronised by twentysomething indie kids, may explain why it was so quiet on our visit – all the better if you fancy having a cavernous, two-storey room and two Spanish waitresses all to yourselves. *Babies and children admitted. Disabled: toilet. Restaurant (available for hire, capacity 60).* **Map p286 H26**.

Gilgamesh. *See p207.*

North

Camden Arms

1 Randolph Street, NW1 0SS (7267 9829/
www.thecamdenarms.com). Camden Town
tube. **Open** noon-11pm Mon, Tue, Sun; noon-
11.30pm Wed, Thur; noon-midnight Fri, Sat.
Food served noon-3pm Tue; noon-3pm,
6-9pm Wed-Fri; noon-5pm Sat, Sun. **Credit**
AmEx, DC, MC, V. **Pub**

Bold and rather beautiful, the Camden Arms
successfully melds a number of striking styles
– from the doll's house corner boasting retro
furniture and a spiralling iron staircase to the
two open fires, elaborate flower arrangements,
artful light fixtures and backlit central bar
straight out of a vintage mobster movie. It's also
far enough off the beaten track to feel relaxed
even at weekends, plus there's a charming beer
garden for the summer months. Shame about
the beer selection: Harveys Sussex Best is the
only draught ale, Staropramen pick of the lagers
and Baltika the most exciting bottle.
Disabled: toilet. Function room (capacity 130).
Restaurant. Tables outdoors (14, garden;
6, pavement). **Map p286 J26**.

Crown & Goose

100 Arlington Road, NW1 7HP (7485 8008/
www.crownandgoose.com). Camden Town tube.
Open 11am-1am Mon-Thur; 11am-2am Fri,
Sat; noon-1am Sun. **Food served** noon-3pm,
6-10pm Mon-Fri; noon-10pm Sat; noon-9pm
Sun. **Credit** MC, V. **Gastropub**

Its popularity breeds contempt among some
people, but the C&G remains an almost perfect
local: far enough off the beaten track to elude
the hordes and packed with Victorian charm,
from the scrubbed furniture to the antique
portraits and gilt-framed mirrors on its pea-
green walls. Small and cosy – never more so
than when evening comes and staff draw blinds
and dim lights – the Crown also turns out simple
but superb pub grub. London Pride is the only
ale on tap, Aspall the only draft cider; but there's
a good wine list featuring four reds and four
whites by the glass for less than £3.60.
Babies and children admitted (until 9pm,
dining only). Disabled: toilet. Function room
(capacity 60). Tables outdoors (6, pavement).
Map p286 J1.

Dublin Castle

94 Parkway, NW1 7AN (7485 1773/www.bug
bearbookings.com). Camden Town tube.
Open noon-1am Mon-Thur; noon-2am Fri-
Sun. **No credit cards**. **Music pub**

The Dublin Castle is square one for aspiring
guitar bands. It's dim despite the skylights, and
far from salubrious: upholstered couches of the
'economy train seat' ilk; mirrors dotted with
fingerprints and dog-eared drinks promotions.
Somehow, though, all this only adds to the sense
of a place about to rock. Posters above the bar
hint at the Castle's musical legacy – mostly nods
to Madness, for whom the pub was once a
second home, although Supergrass, Travis and
Blur also trod the boards of its sweaty rear-
room venue. The four-band bills are normally
big on hair-flicking Arctic wannabes, but there's
no saying when the next legend will be born.
Babies and children admitted (until 6pm).
Jukebox. Music (indie/rock bands 8.30pm
nightly; £4.50-£6). **Map p286 H1**.

Fifty-Five

31 Jamestown Road, NW1 7DB (7424 9054/
www.fiftyfivebar.co.uk). Camden Town tube.
Open 5pm-12.30am Mon-Fri; 1pm-12.30am
Sat, Sun. **Happy hour** 6-8pm daily. **Credit**
MC, V. **Cocktail bar**

Cosmopolitan in more ways than one, Fifty-
Five's glossy cocktail menu has endless
variations on the classics, plus a few original
creations like a pear and orange martini, for as
little as a fiver – thereby educating many people
for whom the definition of a mixed drink was a
snakebite and black. For all that, it's a
refreshingly unpretentious place. Black leather
stools and couches cuddle up to candlelit tables;
the walls are covered with vintage gig posters
from the Bravery to the Beastie Boys; and the
resident mix masters all sport smart branded
shirts to match the deep red hue of the walls.
Function room (capacity 100). Tables outdoors
(13, pavement). **Map p286 H1**.

Gilgamesh ★

Stables Market, Chalk Farm Road, NW1 8AH
(7482 5757/www.gilgameshbar.com). Chalk
Farm tube. **Open** noon-3pm, 6pm-2.30am Mon-
Fri; noon-2.30am Sat, Sun. **Food served** noon-
3pm, 6-11pm daily. **Credit** AmEx, MC, V. **Bar**

It's a struggle to describe Gilgamesh, a
Babylonian theme bar and restaurant so
screamingly over the top that it makes Kubla
Khan's palace look like a bouncy castle. Accessed
by escalator from the market, the carved interior
is reputed to have taken 600 sculptors six months
to create – and that's not hard to believe. Every
surface is embellished to a disorientating degree:
bronze walls depict ancient battles, pillars are
inlaid with polished stones, and ceilings shape-
shift in the coloured spotlights. The restaurant's
retractable glass roof and inspired pan-Asian
cuisine is similarly unexpected, although by the
time you've weaved a path to the lapis lazuli bar
you'll probably be prepared for the cocktail r

North

Swimmer at the Grafton Arms ★

Ah, makeovers. Walk into the Swimmer and you can think you've found a genuine historic artefact, with battered wooden floors, panelling and pew seating. A while back, though, calling itself the Grafton Arms, it was another kind of Victorian local, all plush, carpet and brass. No matter, for as the Swimmer it has a real buzz, helped by a funky, full-of-nice-surprises jukebox and events like the esteemed Monday night quizzes. Food, made with panache in an open kitchen, has a feisty edge, as in a hefty venison burger, grilled swordfish, giant piles of calamares and superior chunky chips. Drinkers have Fuller's ales, a well above average range of draught lagers (Leffe, Litovel), and speciality beers (strawberry-tinged Belgian Früli); wines cover all global bases at good prices. There are free papers and Wi-Fi. Another plus is a plant-lined terrace at the front; smokers have this largely to themselves in winter, but compete with other punters whenever the weather picks up.
For listings, see p205.

original recipe drinks are expertly mixed and rich in eastern promise. The Ziggurat (£9.50) is fresh watermelon juice, 42 Below vodka and chilli; the Anu (£9.50) muddles Absolut Apeach, Plymouth gin, peach purée and cucumber. Prophets of doom still wail at the gates, but there's no sign of this Babylon falling in the near future.
Babies and children admitted. Function room (capacity 250). Music (DJs 8pm Fri, Sat; free). **Map p286 H26**.

Lock Tavern
35 Chalk Farm Road, NW1 8AJ (7482 7163/ www.lock-tavern.co.uk). Chalk Farm tube. **Open** noon-midnight Mon-Thur; noon-1am Fri, Sat; noon-11pm Sun. **Food served** noon-3pm, 5-10pm Mon-Fri; noon-5pm, 6-9pm Sat, Sun. **Credit** MC, V. **Pub/DJ bar**
It remains to be seen how the Lock Tavern will cope with being crowned king of cool during the rehabilitation of the fire-damaged Hawley Arms; it's already a hard enough place to get into at weekends, what with queues of artfully distressed rock urchins and one of the most arbitrary entry policies in Camden Town. And though it teems with aesthetic niceties inside – from cosy black couches and warm wood panelling downstairs to open-air terrace on the first floor – it's the unpredictable after-party vibe that packs in the punters, with big name DJs regularly providing the tunes.
Games (board games). Music (bands 7pm Thur-Sun; DJs 7pm Thur-Sat, 3pm Sun; both free). Tables outdoors (4, roof terrace; 12, garden). TV. **Map p286 G26**.

Lockside Lounge
75-89 West Yard, Camden Lock Place, NW1 8AF (7284 0007/www.locksidelounge.com). Camden Town tube. **Open** noon-midnight Mon-Thur, Sun; noon-1am Fri, Sat. **Food served** noon-9pm Mon-Thur, Sat, Sun; noon-6pm Fri. **Credit** AmEx, MC, V. **Bar**
In the self-conscious wackiness of Camden Market, a bar as artfully understated as the Lockside Lounge makes a pleasant change. Granted, there's little to engage the eye in what is essentially one long first-floor room reminiscent of a boathouse – its walls minimally decorated with modern art, a retro clock and a smattering of flock wallpaper – but it's a decent place in which to unwind during the week (DJs turn up the volume at weekends). Draught beers include Amstel and Kronenbourg Blanc and the fridge stocks a handful of Belgian bottles, such as Mort Subite and Chimay Blue. Best in summer when drinkers and diners spill on to the canalside seating and mingle with the marketgoers.

Babies and children admitted (until 7pm). Disabled: toilet. Games (arcade machine, backgammon 7pm 1st Tue of mth; free). Music (DJs 7pm Fri-Sun; free). Tables outdoors (10, terrace). **Map p286 H26**.

Lord Stanley
51 Camden Park Road, NW1 9BH (7428 9488/www.thelordstanley.com). Camden Town tube/Camden Road rail then 29, 253 bus. **Open** noon-11pm Mon-Thur; noon-midnight Fri, Sat; noon-10.30pm Sun. **Food served** noon-3pm, 6.30-10pm Mon-Thur; noon-3pm, 6.30-10.30pm Fri; noon-4pm, 6.30-10.30pm Sat; noon-9.30pm Sun. **Credit** MC, V. **Gastropub**
A pub that counts Gordon Ramsay among its fans might think it can do what it bloody well likes – though that's not the view of the erstwhile regulars petitioning to turn this pre-eminent gastro-palace back into an ordinary pub. Not that much was ever ordinary about the place, its panelled walls among the most welcoming in London; but these days, it seems it has as many braying property developers knocking back oysters as veteran locals nursing pints of Broadside. There's a good list of European and New World wines on the blackboard, and the food can be disarmingly good. If only tempers weren't so severely tested on both sides of the bar.
Babies and children admitted. No piped music or jukebox. Tables outdoors (10, garden; 5, pavement).

Monkey Chews ★ HOT 50
3 Queen's Crescent, NW5 4EP (7267 6406/ www.monkeychews.com). Chalk Farm tube. **Open** 5-11pm Mon-Thur; 5pm-1am Fri, Sat; noon-10.30pm Sun. **Food served** 7-11pm Mon-Sat; noon-10pm Sun. **Credit** MC, V. **Pub**
As charming as its name and twice as cheerful, Monkey Chews is a little-known, much-loved lounge bar in one of Camden Town's more residential areas. The combination of frosted glass and burly doormen gives no clue to the Chews' gloriously gooey centre. On midweek evenings, its ambient red lighting, low couches and live acoustic acts inspire states of relaxation that border on comatose, although DJs take control at weekends, spinning all manner of funky stuff and turning one cramped corner into an impromptu dancefloor. Leffe and Red Stripe are on tap, cocktails are just £4.75 and there's a good restaurant in the back.
Babies and children admitted (until 9pm). Function room (capacity 60). Games (quiz machine). Music (acoustic band 9pm Tue-Thur; DJs 9pm Fri, Sat; free). Tables outdoors (5, pavement). TV (big screen). **Map p286 G25**.

North

Quinn's ★

65 Kentish Town Road, NW1 8NY (7267 8240). Camden Town tube. **Open/food served** 11am-midnight Mon-Wed, Sun; 11am-2am Thur-Sat. **Credit** AmEx, MC, V. **Pub**

Style warriors may be put off by Quinn's garish yellow exterior – and maybe that's the intention. Few square inches are spared the trappings of the traditional pub treatment, from shelves of pretty plates and stopped clocks to walls plastered with vintage prints; but with Miles Davis on the stereo and a stream of banter from two generations of Quinns behind the bar, it manages to feel like a real sanctuary from the outside world. On top of that, there's a rotating selection of guest ales and one of the longest lists of Belgian and German bottled beers you'll find in the capital. *Babies and children admitted (until 7pm). Tables outdoors (7, garden). TV.* **Map p286 J26.**

Crouch End

Banners

21 Park Road, N8 8TE (8348 2930). Finsbury Park tube/rail, then W7 bus. **Open** 9am-11.30pm Mon-Thur; 9am-midnight Fri; 10am-midnight Sat; 10am-11pm Sun. **Food served** 9am-11.30pm Mon-Thur; 9am-midnight Fri; 10am-4pm, 5pm-midnight Sat; 10am-4pm, 5-11pm Sun. **Credit** MC, V. **Bar/café**

It might be the studied boho atmosphere and beach diner decor, or it might be the huge, something-for-everyone menus; either way, this Crouch End fixture is never short of a crowd. By day, the tables are packed with local kids and their trendy parents, some of whom come back later *sans enfants.* Eating is the main activity, and alcohol is only served with a minimum spend of £3.50 on food, but there are plenty of snacks to go with a drink. The tipples are as global as the music: beers such as Cruzcampo and Leffe on tap, or Mexican, Brazilian and Belgian offerings in bottles, Brazilian cachaça firewater, Cuban rum, juices and cocktails – to name just a few. *Babies and children admitted. TV.*

Harringay Arms ★ HOT 50

153 Crouch Hill, N8 9QH (8340 4243). **Open** noon-1am Mon-Sat; noon-midnight Sun. **No credit cards. Pub**

See review, *see p212.*

Games (darts, fruit machine). No piped music or jukebox. Quiz (9pm Tue; £1). Tables outdoors (4, garden). TV (satellite).

Monkey Chews. *See p209.*

Queen's Pub & Dining Rooms

26 Broadway Parade, N8 9DE (8340 2031/ www.thequeenscrouchend.co.uk). Finsbury Park tube/rail then W3, W7 bus. **Open** 11am-midnight Mon-Sat; noon-midnight Sun. **Food served** noon-10pm Mon-Sat; noon-9pm Sun. **Credit** AmEx, MC, V. **Gastropub**

A grand Victorian dame, the Queen's has survived years of neglect (and plans to knock it down) with its stained glass, ornate ceilings and massive wood panelling magnificently intact. It's so big that its straight-pub and gastro sides have equally ample spaces, and there's also a small garden further back. Food is the familiar gastropub mix of classics and the odd culinary adventure, with interesting snacks, kids' dishes and (in the week) £5 lunches. The bar, an imposing wooden island, serves Bombardier, Erdinger and Eagle IPA, classic cocktails, juices and easy-drinking, good-quality wines.
Babies and children admitted (until 8pm). Disabled: toilet. Function room (capacity 35). Tables outdoors (10, garden).

East Finchley

Bald-Faced Stag NEW

69 High Road, N2 8AB (8442 1201/www.real pubs.co.uk). East Finchley tube. **Open** noon-11.30pm Mon-Wed; noon-midnight Thur; noon-12.30am Fri; 11am-12.30am Sat; noon-10.30pm Sun. **Food served** noon-3.30pm, 6-10.30pm Mon-Fri; 11am-4.30pm, 6-10.30pm Sat; noon-9.30pm Sun. **Credit** MC, V. **Gastropub**

For almost 300 years, the Bald-Faced Stag had been a rough sports bar, live music venue, and a private house where travellers were illegally served ale. In the refurb that chucked out 'four pool tables, 12 televisions, a video jukebox, carpets, microwave oven and crime', the new owners didn't forget that this is a pub. The bar area is still sizeable, and serves three real ales – Flowers IPA, Grand Union Bitter and Black Sheep – plus some bottled beers like strawberry Früli; 13 wines can be had by the glass. Modish bar snacks include wasabi peanuts, olives, whitebait and plates of Spanish titbits. The decor is typical modern gastropub: cool lampshades, greeny-brown paint and panels of floral flock wallpaper. The open-plan kitchen turns out decent grub such as bouillabaisse, tender lamb shoulder, and rhubarb and apple crumble.
Babies and children welcome: high chairs. Disabled: toilet. Music (jazz 7.30pm last Tue of mth; free). Quiz (6.30pm 2nd Mon of mth; £5 per team). Restaurant (available for hire, capacity 80). Tables outdoors (18, garden). TV.

Harringay

Oakdale Arms

283 Hermitage Road, N4 1NP (8800 2013/ www.individualpubs.co.uk/oakdale). Manor House tube/Seven Sisters tube/rail. **Open** noon-11pm Mon-Sat; noon-10.30pm Sun. **Credit** MC, V. **Pub**

A refuge for the beer connoisseur deep in the remote (for many) territories of Harringay. The inventive products of Cambridge's Milton Brewery are the main 'residents', all with Greco-Roman names like Pegasus, Nero or Sparta; but you'll also find other small-brewery ales rare in London, like Jarrow or Slater's, and there's always good cider on tap too. There's a vast international range – Budvar on draught, and Polish, Belgian, German and others in bottles – and a great whisky line-up. There are no modern fripperies in the way of decor, or much food beyond a bit of hearty grub, but this is a friendly, cosy spot – a real local as well as a beer showcase.
Babies and children admitted (until 7pm). Games (air hockey, board games, chess, darts, pool, table football, Wii console). Quiz (8.30pm Thur; free). Tables outdoors (8, garden; 2, forecourt). TV.

Salisbury Hotel

1 Grand Parade, Green Lanes, N4 1JX (8800 9617). Manor House tube then 29 bus. **Open** 5pm-midnight Mon-Wed; 5pm-1am Thur; 5pm-2am Fri; noon-2am Sat; noon-11pm Sun. **Food served** 6-10.30pm Mon-Fri; noon-11pm Sat; 1-7pm Sun. **Credit** MC, V. **Pub**

This Victorian beer palace could be Harringay's largest building; it's certainly the most imposing. The changes in the last few years were a spruce-up rather than a makeover, the better to show off the vast, high-ceilinged rooms, glorious wooden bar, stained glass, statues and other fancies, without alienating the geezers who rub shoulders with the grungey-ish newer punters. Beers are mainly Fuller's, with Litovel lagers on draught and many more in bottles; food is quality pub-grub (burgers, 'handmade sausage of the day', couscous). Live acts, in another spacious room, are a staple: bands, comedy and more.
Babies and children admitted. Disabled: toilet. Function room (capacity 120). Music (bands alternate Fri, Sat). Quiz (8.45pm Mon; £1). TV.

Highgate

Boogaloo ★

312 Archway Road, N6 5AT (8340 2928/ www.theboogaloo.org). Highgate tube. **Open**

North

6pm-midnight Mon-Wed; 6pm-1am Thur; 6pm-2am Fri; 2pm-2am Sat; 2pm-midnight Sun. **Credit** MC, V. **Music pub**
The jukebox is excellent, and the regular DJs and live sessions are a draw; but this music-themed boozer has built its reputation on the B-list indie celebs who favour it. Irregular appearances from Shane MacGowan and Pete Doherty (both pals of owner Gerry O'Boyle from his days running Filthy McNasty's) seem to have inspired other Ryman-League indie celebs to pop in, and their presence has in turn attracted the teens who love them. The drinks are nearly as dreary as the staff, but the consumption of alcohol here is more about quantity than quality. On the last Thursday each month, a 1920s-themed dress-up night brings silent films, jazz, swing and motown. *Babies and children admitted (until 7pm). Disabled: toilet. Jukebox. Music (country band 8.30pm Sun; free). Quiz (8.30pm Tue; £1). Tables outdoors (15, garden).*

Flask
77 Highgate West Hill, N6 6BU (8348 7346). Archway or Highgate tube/143, 210, 214, 271 bus. **Open** 11am-11pm Mon-Sat; noon-10.30pm Sun. **Food served** noon-10pm daily. **Credit** MC, V. **Pub**
If your guests want to see a 'real old English pub', bring them here. The Flask's 18th-century wood-panelled interior, with its fireplaces, bottle-glass windows and labyrinth of snug rooms, is bound to enchant; then you can tell them that Dick Turpin is said to have hidden in the cellar. This is no museum piece, though: it's a favourite with all quiet after-work types, families, and gaggles of local youth some weekends. The big front yard is Highgate's top outdoor eating spot, where space is often at a premium. The food is sturdy grub (great steak sandwiches) with a few gastro touches; the fine drinks list runs to good ales (Adnams, London Pride), Czech lagers and wines. *Babies and children admitted (until 7pm). Disabled: toilet. Tables outdoors (20, garden).*

Red Lion & Sun NEW
25 North Road, N6 4BE (8340 1780/www.the redlionandsun.com). Highgate tube. **Open** noon-midnight Mon-Wed; noon-2am Thur-Sat; noon-1am Sun. **Food served** noon-10pm daily. **Credit** AmEx, MC, V. **Pub**
Brighter and less cluttered since its refurb, this place's best feature is the huge patioed front garden (available for hire) with swanky new archway. Inside, lurid red walls, a fag machine and flat-screen TV have been ditched in favour of a quiet beige and wood colour scheme, dotted with flowers and deer antlers. Decent ales are served: Greene King Mild, Morland Original, Abbot and a succession of guest beers. Pigs are spit-roasted for parties and in the summer. *Babies and children admitted. Disabled: toilet. Music (acoustic 7pm Tue-Thur; free). Tables outdoors (25, front garden; 8, back garden).*

Harringay Arms ★ HOT 50
Long may it serve: an unreconstructed local pub, a snug little haven with no music, no 'design', no food beyond a few sarnies or a bag of pork scratchings; just good beer (Adnams, Bombardier, Courage Best), friendly Irish landlords (so you know that the Guinness will be good), a modest telly and nothing to interrupt the flow of chat. Regulars – a fruity mix of Crouch End elders and many of the younger local intelligentsia who have caught on to the Harringay's qualities – come here to sit philosophically over a drink, read the paper and, above all, enjoy a conversation. This is the kind of pub where you thought the smoking ban could never work, but local puffers have accepted banishment to the yard out the back with equanimity, and the decades-old tobacco fug has vanished from the bar with amazing speed.
For listings, see p211.

Victoria NEW

28 North Hill, N6 4QA (8340 6091). Highgate tube. **Open** 4-11pm daily. **Credit** MC, V. **Pub**
The Victoria's boxy exterior might not catch the eye during the day, but at night, warmly lit, it's a beacon of welcome on fashionably gloomy North Hill. Inside, bent awkwardly around an elongated bar, the pub is roughly divided into a family half and a boozers' half. One side has big tables, an upright piano and a play area for the kids (great rocking horse); the other offers a dartboard and smaller tables with more privacy. Ales include Greene King IPA, Bombardier and Spitfire. Crooners step up to the piano for 'Singalong Sundays' (weekly) and 'Sing Your Heart Out Saturdays' (twice monthly).
Babies and children admitted. Games (board games, darts). Tables outdoors (3, garden). Music (singalong Sundays 8.30pm Sun; free).

Hornsey

Three Compasses

62 High Street, N8 7NX (8340 2729). Hornsey rail/Turnpike Lane tube then 144 bus. **Open** 11am-11pm Mon-Thur; 11am-midnight Fri, Sat; noon-11pm Sun. **Food served** 11am-10pm Mon-Sat; noon-9.30pm Sun. **Credit** MC, V. **Pub**
A likeable marriage of modern (the usual soft leather sofas) and unfussy, old-fashioned boozer styles, the Compasses is a laid-back spot that caters well to all and sundry. Football and rugby on the big screen in the pool room at the back are a big draw, or you can borrow a board game or read the paper in the front bar. There's good comfort food like bangers and mash, Saturday brunches and Sunday roasts, plus more gastroish daily specials. There's also a decent, frequently changing wine list, starting at £10.25 for an Italian cabernet, and a quality beer range: London Pride, Timothy Taylor and Deuchars as regulars, with interesting guests.
Children admitted (over 14yrs, until 9pm). Disabled: toilet. Games (board games, darts, pool, quiz machine). Quiz (8pm Mon; £1). TV.

Viva Viva

18 High Street, N8 7PB (8341 0999/www.vivaviva.co.uk). Hornsey rail. **Open** 5pm-2am Mon-Fri; 10am-2am Sat, Sun. **Food served** 5-10.45pm Mon-Fri; 10am-10.45pm Sat, Sun. **Credit** AmEx, MC, V. **Café/bar**
This 'world music bar and restaurant' packs an amazing range of stuff and events into a tiny space. Decor is a bit 'fantasy night in old Beirut', with fairy lights, burgundy banquettes and camp pictures of Elvis and Marilyn; the live music and DJ menu delivers salsa, flamenco, jazz fusion, acoustic open-mic sets and more, with dancing as each session runs on (once tables have been cleared away). A big cocktail list is the big drinking attraction, with a daily happy hour between 5pm and 8pm; there's also a user-

North

The Triangle Restaurant

1 Ferme park road, N4 4DS (8292 0516)
Finsbury park tube. Open 6pm-12am Mon-Fri; 11am-12am Sat-Sun.
www.thetrianglerestaurant.co.uk

Prepare to be transported to another world. Inside this palace of curiosities between Crouch End and Finsbury Park, with its rich fabrics, beaten metalwork, glowing candles and enchanting alcoves is a food-lover's heaven. Moroccan-inspired but with elements of Asian, European and even Australasian cuisine, the menu is as eclectic as the decor. We ate sardine salad with couscous - the fish moist with a perfectly crispy exterior, the couscous tender and spicy - then Thai green chicken curry, once again the ideal heat, texture and taste. My companion's sirloin steak had a garnish of ginger which had her squeaking with pleasure.

Owner Aziz Begdouri devised both the exotic interior (including a surreal bed with furniture stuck to the ceiling) and the funky fusion menu, having been a chef in both his native Morocco and in London. Triangle won Archant's Best Moroccan restaurant in London award in 2006 and chef of the year 2007.

Combined with the chilled music, the gracious and happy service, the small but idyllic garden, the low-level den where you sit cross-legged on cushions, the inventive wine list (try the Moroccan sauvignon blanc - it's knockout) and the plethora of intricate, lovingly worked details everywhere you look, this is a stunning triumph of a restaurant.

By David Nicholson

Don't be   **Go**   **To The**

Photography by Emily Haley

friendly wine and lager range, and even smoothies. Food is a suitably global tapas-meze-grills range, with a separate kid-friendly menu by day. Private parties are a speciality. *Babies and children admitted (until 9pm). Bar available for hire. Disabled: toilet. Games (board games). Music (bands 8.30pm nightly; DJs 11.30pm Fri, Sat; both free). Tables outdoors (10, garden; 3, pavement).*

Islington

Albion
10 Thornhill Road, N1 1HW (7607 7450/ www.the-albion.co.uk). Angel tube. **Open** noon-11pm Mon-Sat; noon-10.30pm Sun. **Food served** noon-3pm, 6-9.30pm Mon-Sat; noon-3pm, 6-8pm Sun. **Credit** AmEx, MC, V. **Gastropub**
The Albion is less busy on weekday evenings since its gastropub-by-numbers makeover (its beer garden is still the main draw on sunny weekends). It's now all colonial wicker furniture and Bugaboos instead of ramshackle chaos, but the food has improved no end. Well-dressed Highbury mums were enthusiastically tucking into pints of prawns (£9) and roast chicken (£14) on our recent visit. If it's cold outside you'll have to stay indoors with the institutional green paint job and self-consciously mismatched leather armchairs – a pleasant enough spot for a pint. Greene King, Black Sheep and Guinness are on tap, and the wine list is pretty good. *Babies and children admitted (weekends). Bar available for hire. Disabled: toilet. Tables outdoors (5, patio; 20, garden).* **Map p287 N1**.

Angelic
57 Liverpool Road, N1 0RJ (7278 8433/ www.theangelic.co.uk). Angel tube. **Open** noon-midnight Mon-Thur, Sun; noon-1am Fri, Sat. **Food served** noon-10pm Mon-Sat; noon-9.30pm Sun. **Credit** MC, V. **Pub**
The key to this attractive, candlelit corner pub is its location, just far enough from Upper Street to be off the pub-crawler radar. That's not to say it's quiet. The upbeat crowd – verging on raucous – sups standard draught beers, bottles (Corona, Beck's, Duvel) and so-so cocktails (£6.50, also available by the jug) to a background of property chat (local estate agents feature heavily). Key sporting fixtures are shown and decent pub grub includes tapas (£4), sausages and mash (£11) and clam chowder (£6.75). If you want a table on weekend evenings, start camping out at noon. *Babies and children admitted (until 5pm). Disabled: toilet. Games (board games). TV.* **Map p287 N2**.

Barrio North NEW
45 Essex Road, N1 2SF (7688 2882/ www.barrionorth.com). Angel tube. **Open** noon-midnight Mon-Thur; noon-2am Fri, Sat; 3pm-midnight Sun. **Credit** AmEX, MC, V. **Pub**
Filling the space left by the Warwick in laid-back Latino style, Barrio North's funky, New Yorican vibe is going down a storm. Despite clean lines and hard surfaces (graffiti art breeze blocks, tiles galore), there's a warm glow about the place, intensified by the attentive staff (rarely have we seen such care lavished on a virgin mary), Latin rhythms, gaudy bunting and flatteringly low lighting. The best seat in the house has to be the fairy-lit caravan up on the mezzanine at the back; it's the perfect vantage point at which to kick back with a bottle of Brahma and a platter of nachos (£6) and watch the night unfold. *Bar available for hire. Dance classes (7pm Mon, Tue; £8-£10). Music (DJs throughout the week, call for details). Tables outdoors (2, pavement).* **Map p287 O1**.

Charles Lamb ★ HOT 50
16 Elia Street, N1 8DE (7837 5040/www.the charleslambpub.com). Angel tube. **Open** 4-11pm Mon, Tue; noon-11pm Wed-Sat; noon-10.30pm-Sun. **Food served** 6-9pm Mon, Tue; noon-4pm, 6-9.30pm Wed-Sat; noon-6pm Sun. **Credit** MC, V. **Gastropub**
This is everything that a neighbourhood boozer should be, and much-loved by the lucky locals – a highbrow, high-spirited bunch that tend to come in small groups to enjoy the excellent, reasonably priced grub (from exemplary bar snacks to mains like fish pie) or play board games with resident mutt Mascha at their feet. The lovely mint-green central bar – with coffee machine and continuously refilled plate of sausage rolls (£2 each) – is manned by a young team who seem to know many of the punters. There's a well-chosen variety of wines and real ales like Timothy Taylor Landlord and Chiswick Bitter. The traditional vibe and the decor (cream walls, wood floors, blackboards, black lacquer tables) evoke a country-in-the-city vibe that's appealingly fresh in summer and cosy in winter. *Babies and children admitted. Tables outdoors (6, pavement).* **Map p287 O2**.

Crown
116 Cloudesley Road, N1 0EB (7837 7107). Angel tube. **Open** noon-11pm Mon-Sat; noon-10.30pm Sun. **Food served** noon-3pm, 6-10pm Mon-Fri; noon-10pm Sat; noon-9pm Sun. **Credit** AmEx, MC, V. **Gastropub**
Dominated by its picturesque mahogany-and-glass bar that splits the compact interior into a

North

Albion. *See p215.*

series of cosy nooks, the Crown is better suited to one-on-one chats than big groups. It's located in a lovely part of Barnsbury so regulars lean to the well-to-do end of the N1 scale. The decor shows respect for tradition and style, with an elegant teal blue exterior and original etched glass and wood panelling throughout. On tap are Honeydew, Chiswick Bitter and London Pride, plus Scrumpy Jack, Staropramen and Hoegaarden; bottled brews include De Konick, Peroni Blue, Früli and Budvar; and the wine list will satisfy most.
Babies and children admitted (until 6pm). Bar available for hire. Games (board games). Tables outdoors (6, patio). **Map p287 N1.**

Drapers Arms ★
44 Barnsbury Street, N1 1ER (7619 0348/ www.thedrapersarms.co.uk). Angel tube/ Highbury & Islington tube/rail. **Open** noon-11pm Mon-Sat; noon-10.30pm Sun. **Food served** noon-3pm, 7-10.30pm Mon-Sat; noon-3pm, 6.30-9.30pm Sun. **Credit** AmEx, MC, V.
Gastropub

A grand horseshoe bar, wood floors, dark pink walls and higgledy bookshelves set the scene at this upmarket gastropub. The crowd is classic posh Highbury: well-to-do gents supping pints of Greene King at the bar, and hassled thirtysomethings trying to enjoy Sunday lunch as much as they did before they had toddlers in tow. The food is good – the likes of double roast pork chop with cabbage, pancetta and apple (£14.50) or aged ribeye with chips (£16.50). The wines are well chosen, many available by the glass or carafe (the bar staff helpfully pointed out that this would work out cheaper for our order), and there's a fine garden in which to drink them.

Babies and children admitted (until 7pm unless dining). Restaurant (available for hire). Tables outdoors (20, garden). **Map p287 N1.**

Duke of Cambridge ★ HOT 50

30 St Peter's Street, N1 8JT (7359 3066/ www.dukeorganic.co.uk). Angel tube. **Open** noon-11pm Mon-Sat; noon-10.30pm Sun. **Food served** 12.30-3pm, 6.30-10.30pm Mon-Fri; 12.30-3.30pm, 6.30-10.30pm Sat; 12.30-3.30pm, 6.30-10pm Sun. **Credit** MC, V. **Gastropub**

The Duke of Cambridge may take itself rather seriously – but it is, after all, Britain's first certified organic gastropub. Everything from the wines, real ales (some from St Peter's Brewery), spirits and soft drinks to the produce used in the food is sourced with sustainability as the guide, and additional features include green electricity and an exemplary recycling system. This is a civilised space in which to enjoy top-quality food and drink – although the experience isn't cheap: £3.40 for a small glass of house white, £13 for a Sunday roast. The glossy blue ceiling, pendant lights, wooden tables, huge windows and retro radiators create an elegant, fresh and relaxed space in which to sip your Freedom organic lager. *Babies and children welcome: children's portions; high chairs. Function room (capacity 100). Games (board games, chess). No piped music or jukebox. Tables outdoors (5, pavement).* **Map p287 P2.**

Elk in the Woods ★ NEW

39 Camden Passage, N1 8EA (7226 3535/ www.the-elk-in-the-woods.co.uk). Angel tube. **Open** 10.30am-11pm daily. **Food served** noon-10pm Mon; 10.30am-10.30pm Tue-Sat; 10.30am-9.30pm Sun. **Credit** MC, V. **Bar**

Leave the Upper Street mayhem behind and stroll down pretty Camden Passage to this decidedly grown-up drinking hole. Forget bar queues (it's waiter service), standing room only (everyone gets seated) and any sense of spontaneity (reservations are essential from Thursday onwards, advisable the rest of the week) while you indulge your inner sophisticate with cocktails (£7) and classy bar snacks. The decor is laid-back boho, with a sturdy concrete bar, roughed-up wooden tables, a wall of ornate mirrors and a large stag's head – the perfect lounging ground for a well-to-do N1 crowd. *Babies and children admitted. Tables outdoors (4, pavement).* **Map p287 O2.**

Filthy McNasty's

68 Amwell Street, EC1R 1UU (7837 6067/ www.filthymacnastys.com). Angel tube. **Open** noon-11pm Mon-Sat; noon-10.30pm Sun. **Food served** noon-3pm, 5.30-9pm Mon-Fri; 5.30-9pm Sat, Sun. **Credit** MC, V. **Music pub**

You can tell a lot about a bar by its toilet graffiti. To judge from the misspelt poetry and smut scrawled on these walls, Filthy McNasty's is still Islington's most rock 'n' roll boozer – frequented by genuinely tortured rock types lured by the Dickensian setting, murky candlelit tables and fabulous whisky list (the rare Bunnahabhain at £3, Highland Park at £4). It also does risqué shooters like Cocksucking Cowboy (Baileys and butterscotch schnapps) and a great range of stout. Music is a Filthy speciality, and the tiny back room hosts acoustic sessions, sweaty bebop and Latin DJ nights. By day the pub is a surprisingly quiet, bookish refuge from the traffic-choked streets. For peckish punters, it does Pieminster pie and mash for a fiver. *Children admitted (over-14s, until 6pm). Disabled: toilet. Function room (capacity 60). Music (bands, call for dates; free). Poetry readings (call for dates; free). Tables outdoors (7, pavement). TV.*

Hemingford Arms

158 Hemingford Road, N1 1DF (7607 3303/ www.capitalpubcompany.com). Caledonian Road tube/rail. **Open** 11am-11pm Mon-Sat; noon-10.30pm Sun. **Food served** noon-3pm, 6-10.30pm Mon-Fri; 6-10.30pm Sat; 12.30-4pm, 6-10pm Sun. **Credit** MC, V. **Pub**

Tucked away down a Barnsbury backstreet, this ivy clad boozer oozes authenticity. The jumble sale decor is the antithesis of the anodyne gastropub, with stuffed mallards, Greek statues, pewter mugs and various antique curiosities hanging from the ceiling. Good-humoured locals rub shoulders with young professionals drawn by the atmosphere, beer on tap (Adnams, Broadside, Brakspear, Deuchars IPA and Kronenbourg Blanc) and Premier League football. There's a quiz on Thursday nights, live music and reasonably priced roasts on Sunday and Thai food in the evenings. *Babies and children admitted (until 6pm) Function room (capacity 60). Music (b 9pm Mon, Fri-Sun; free). Quiz (9.30 £1). Tables outdoors (6, pavement*

North

218 Time

:kens Theatre Bar

*Road, N1 2NA (no phone/
hickens.com). Highbury &
Isu.... e/rail.* **Open/food served**
4.30pm-midnight Mon-Wed; 4.30pm-1am
Thur; noon-1.30am Fri, Sat; noon-midnight
Sun. **Credit** MC, V. **Theatre pub**
Playing on its theatrical links (the comedy venue
is upstairs), the Hen & Chickens makes an effort
to create a lively setting: stage spotlights and
disco balls fixed to the ceiling, pendulous fairy
lights lining the back of the blackboard-style bar,
and music blaring out from the jukebox. The pub
is filled with sociable groups of twenty- to
thirtysomething student types (and the odd
ageing barfly), many of whom are here for pre-
production food and drink. There's a wide range
of decent enough beverages, and fun extras like
posh squash (£1). Food is cheap and cheerful:
quesadillas (£3.95), panini (£4.25), chicken
wings (£3.90) and a range of puds (£3.50).
*Babies and children admitted (until 9pm).
Theatre (shows most nights from 7.30pm,
box office 7704 2001; £5-£12). Tables
outdoors (3, pavement).* **Map p287 O25**.

Island Queen ★

*87 Noel Road, N1 8HD (7704 7631). Angel
tube.* **Open** noon-11pm Mon, Sun; noon-
11.30pm Tue, Wed; noon-midnight Thur-Sat.
Food served noon-3pm, 6-10pm Mon-Thur;
noon-4pm, 6-10pm Fri; noon-10pm Sat, Sun.
Credit MC, V. **Pub**
This popular local is an architectural gem, with
its high, rust-coloured ceilings, Victorian wood
panels, curved front windows, stunning cut-glass
lamps, beautiful etched mirrors and ceiling fans.
Like the nearby Charles Lamb and the Duke of
Edinburgh, the Island Queen has a strong local
following, with the popular Tuesday-night quiz
and pub grub like fish finger sandwiches (and
more elaborate fare). The curved wooden bar is
a real feature; the taps dispense a good pick of
continental beers – Leffe Blonde, Küppers Kölsch,
Paulaner München, Franziskaner Weissbier and
Früli – and British stuff like London Pride,
Addlestones and Weston's cider. Duvel, Chimay
White, Peroni, Pacifico Clara and Bierra Moretti
are available by the bottle; the wine list tends
towards the New World.
*Babies and children admitted (until 7pm).
Function room (capacity 60). Quiz (8pm Tue;
£1). Tables outdoors (4, pavement). TVs.*
Map p287 O2.

Keston Lodge

*131 Upper Street, N1 1QP (7354 9535/
www.kestonlodge.com). Angel tube/Highbury &*
Islington tube/rail. **Open** noon-midnight Mon-
Wed; noon-1am Thur; noon-2am Fri, Sat; noon-
11.30pm Sun. **Food served** noon-3pm, 5-10pm
Mon-Fri; noon-10pm Sat, Sun. **Admission** £3
after 10.30pm Sat. **Credit** MC, V. **DJ bar**
From the same stable as Camden's Lock Tavern
and Shepherds Bush's Defectors Weld, Keston
Lodge adds a touch of cool to the Upper Street
maelstrom. Although boxy, the place has a cosy
glow about it, with convivial booth seating,
orange fairy lights and a 'Small Disco' with a DJ
booth under the stairs. Cocktails include £7
mojitos, but most drinkers here favour pints,
wine, random spirits – anything that means they
can get away from the bar and back to their chat-
up lines. The tiny beer garden is fine for smokers,
but pretty hopeless for summer drinking.
*Babies and children admitted (until 6pm).
Disabled: toilet. Function room (capacity 75).
Music (DJs 9pm Thur-Sat; 4pm Sun). Tables
outdoors (2, garden).* **Map p287 O1**.

Marquess Tavern ★

*32 Canonbury Street, N1 2TB (7354 2975/
www.underdog-group.com). Angel tube/
Highbury & Islington tube/rail.* **Open** 5.30-
11pm Mon-Fri; 12.30-11pm Sat, Sun. **Food
served** 6-10pm Mon-Fri; 12.30-4pm, 6-10pm
Sat; 12.30-5pm, 6.30-9pm Sun. **Credit** AmEx,
MC, V. **Gastropub**
For review, *see p224.*
*Babies and children admitted. Function room
(capacity 12). Restaurant (available for hire).
Tables outdoors (6, patio).* **Map p287 P26**.

Medicine Bar

*181 Upper Street, N1 1RQ (7704 9536/
www.medicinebar.net). Angel tube/Highbury
& Islington tube/rail.* **Open** 4.30pm-midnight
Mon, Tue; 4.30pm-1am Wed, Thur; noon-2am
Fri; noon-3am Sat; noon-midnight Sun.
Admission £3 after 10pm Sat. **Credit** MC, V.
DJ bar
Its late 1990s glory days may be a hazy memory,
but Medicine is looking good for its age. Perspex
lampshades hang over a long bar twinkling with
fairy lights, from which good cocktails (apple
martinis, bloody marys, £6.50) and pints of
Kronenbourg Blanc and San Miguel are served.
At the back, sofas and boho wallpaper combine
to make a prime spot for weekend lounging, and
two cosy chill-out rooms upstairs have 'party'
written all over them. A huge Muhammad Ali
picture takes pride of place behind the elevated
DJ booth, which still rules the roost most nights
of the week.
*Function rooms (capacity 100). Music (DJs
Wed-Sun, times vary).* **Map p287 O26**.

THE OLD
QUEENS
HEAD

Northgate

113 Southgate Road, N1 3JS (7359 7392).
Essex Road rail/21, 76, 141 bus. **Open**
5-11pm Mon; noon-11pm Tue-Thur; noon-
midnight Fri, Sat; noon-10.30pm Sun. **Food
served** 6.30-10.30pm Mon; noon-3pm, 6.30-
10.30pm Tue-Fri; noon-4pm, 6.30-10.30pm Sat;
noon-4pm, 6.30-9.30pm Sun. **Credit** MC, V.
Gastropub

Despite rumours to the contrary, the Northgate
seemed to appeal to a very varied crowd of
Isilngtonites on our visit, with the feel of a
busy local. Blackboard menus, a super-
abundance of wood, gilded mirrors, spherical
pendant lights, pop-type art (for sale) on the
walls and a large, separate dining area with
open kitchen may suggest archetypal modern
gastropub, but this place does it better than
many. On tap you'll find several real ales, and
the decent wine menu has several options by
the glass. The large outside space out front is
an absolute boon in the summer months.
Babies and children admitted (patio,
restaurant). Games (board games). Restaurant
(available for hire, capacity 50). Tables
outdoors (10, patio).

Old Queen's Head

44 Essex Road, N1 8LN (7354 9993/
www.theoldqueenshead.com). Angel tube.
Open noon-midnight Mon-Wed, Sun; noon-
1am Thur; noon-2am Fri, Sat. **Food served**
6-10pm Mon-Thur; 1-9pm Sat, Sun. **Credit**
AmEx, MC, V. **DJ pub**

The Old Queen's Head has been packing them
in since its 2006 relaunch, and there's no sign of
things slowing. We're talking huge queues at the
weekends and wall-to-wall skinny-jeaned
hipsters, lured by the good DJ roster (the likes
of Freestylers, Eno and Mr Thing). With two
floors and outside seating front and back, there's
plenty of room – though if you're hoping to bag
a seat on a weekend night, you've missed the
point entirely. Saturdays are for dancing, minor
league celeb-spotting and chatting up the bar
staff. Come during the week to sample the
cocktails (there are great deals on Mondays) and
lounge on the battered sofas.
Babies and children welcome (until 6pm).
Function room (capacity 150). Music (bands
7pm Mon-Thur; £2-£5; DJs 9pm Fri, Sat;
£3 after 8pm Fri, £4 after 9pm Sat). Tables
outdoors (6, garden; 6, pavement). TV.
Map p287 O1.

Old Red Lion `HOT 50`

418 St John Street, EC1V 4NJ (7837 7816/
www.oldredliontheatre.co.uk). Angel tube. **Open**

noon-midnight Mon-Thur, Sun; noon-1am Fri,
Sat. **Credit** MC, V. **Theatre pub**
Below the fringe theatre of the same name sits
this old-school boozer. There's an etched glass
partition dividing the saloon from the public bar,
and an impressive roster of draught beers: take
your pick from Staropramen, Leffe, San Miguel,
Broadside, Tetley's and Sussex Best (among
others), and settle into a retro, green velour
booth. Early in the week it can be disconcertingly
quiet (regulars looking up from their pints,
freaky fairground music), but post-show, at
weekends and for sporting fixtures (there's a
large screen), this is a buzzy, unpretentious
alternative to the Upper Street chains.
Babies and children admitted (until 7pm).
Function room (capacity 40). Games (board
games, fruit machine). Tables outdoors (4,
patio). Theatre (7.30pm Tue-Sun; £6-£12). TV.

Rosemary Branch ★

2 Shepperton Road, N1 3DT (7704 2730/
www.rosemarybranch.co.uk). Old Street tube/
rail, then 21, 76, 141 bus. **Open** noon-
midnight Mon-Thur; noon-1am Fri, Sat; noon-
10.30pm Sun. **Food served** noon-3pm,
6-9.30pm Mon-Sat; noon-6pm Sun. **Credit**
MC, V. **Theatre pub**
This idiosyncratic, slightly scruffy pub,
furnished with wooden tables, big mirrors, old
posters and quirky bric-a-brac (like the
enormous model aeroplanes hanging from the
ceiling), manages to be most things to most
punters. A well-stocked bar runs from real ales

North

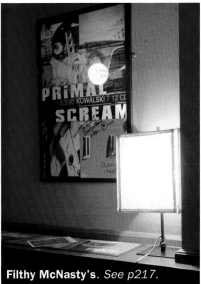

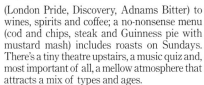

Filthy McNasty's. *See p217.*

(London Pride, Discovery, Adnams Bitter) to wines, spirits and coffee; a no-nonsense menu (cod and chips, steak and Guinness pie with mustard mash) includes roasts on Sundays. There's a tiny theatre upstairs, a music quiz and, most important of all, a mellow atmosphere that attracts a mix of types and ages.
Babies and children admitted. Function room (capacity 80). Games (board games, games night Thur; free). Jukebox. Quiz (9pm Tue, Thur; £1). Theatre (7.30pm Tue-Sat; £8-£10). Tables outdoors (6, patio). TV.
Map p287 P1.

25 Canonbury Lane
25 Canonbury Lane, N1 2AS (7226 0955). Highbury & Islington tube/rail. **Open** 5pm-midnight Mon-Thur; 4pm-1am Fri; noon-1am Sat; 1pm-12.30am Sun. **Food served** 6-10pm Mon-Thur; 1-6pm Sun. **Credit** MC, V. **Bar**
It's out with the Tiffany blue and in with a new (slightly less appealing) brown and gold scheme. And where once there were tapas to go with your tom collins, there's now Thai food (red curry, £5.95). This bar still has merit, though: cosy dimensions, atmospheric lighting, bare boards, and chandeliers; book the small conservatory at the back for a snug soirée, or sink into one of the low-slung sofas by the big window in the front. Cocktails (caipirinhas, whisky sours) are a reasonable £6.50, though the crowd is more of a wine-drinking, in-for-the-long-haul bunch; decent reds and whites start at £14 a bottle.
Babies and children admitted (until 7pm).

Kentish Town

Junction Tavern
101 Fortess Road, NW5 1AG (7485 9400/ www.junctiontavern.co.uk). Tufnell Park tube/ Kentish Town tube/rail. **Open** noon-11pm Mon-Sat; noon-10.30pm Sun. **Food served** noon-3pm, 6.30-10.30pm Mon-Fri; noon-4pm, 6.30-10.30pm Sat; noon-4pm, 6.30-9.30pm Sun. **Credit** MC, V. **Gastropub**
A short hike up the road from Kentish Town tube, this place is worth seeking out for its sterling selection of real ales, picked with a keen eye for smaller regional breweries. On our last visit, a Cornish theme prevailed, with the likes of Doom Bar Bitter, Cornish Knocker and Atlantic IPA tempting regulars away from their usual tipples. The dining area takes up the front of the pub, serving classy comfort food (pork chop with bubble and squeak; pan-fried chicken livers on toast; and broad bean, pea and mascarpone risotto) and Sunday lunches, but there's plenty of space for dedicated drinkers: a cosy (but roomy) panelled main bar and a heated conservatory.
Babies and children admitted (restaurant). Tables outdoors (15, garden). **Map p286 J24**.

Oxford
256 Kentish Town Road, NW5 2AA (7485 3521/www.realpubs.co.uk). Kentish Town tube/ rail. **Open** noon-11.30pm Mon-Thur; noon-midnight Fri, Sat; noon-10.30pm Sun. **Food served** noon-3.30pm, 6-10pm Mon-Fri; noon-

North

4.30pm, 6-10pm Sat; noon-9pm Sun. **Credit** MC, V. Gastropub

The Oxford is a popular meeting place for Kentish Towners, who congregate on its pavement picnic benches or squeeze around ramshackle wooden tables by the bar. Retro orange lampshades, panelled walls and crimson paintwork make this a cosy spot on chilly evenings – particularly if you nab the leather sofa in the front window. There's a good, affordable wine list and a weekly line-up of real ales, and well-executed gastropub grub (braised lamb shank, ribeye steak, wild mushroom risotto) is served in the candlelit dining area. The music policy is nicely unpredictable, though at weekends there's an unfortunate switch to pumpin' dance tracks and long waits at the bar. *Children admitted (until 8pm). Comedy (7pm 2rd Tue of mth; £5). Disabled: toilet. Function room (capacity 70) . Music (jazz 8.30pm Mon). Tables outdoors (6, pavement). TV.* **Map p286 J25**.

Pineapple ★ HOT 50

51 Leverton Street, NW5 2NX (7284 4631). Kentish Town tube/rail. **Open** noon-11pm Mon-Sat; noon-10.30pm Sun. **Food served** 1-3pm, 6-10pm Mon-Fri; 1-10pm Sat, Sun. **Credit** MC, V. Gastropub

The Pineapple's outward appearance hasn't altered in years. Tucked away in a maze of backstreet terraces, it's a dapper, self-respecting little Victorian establishment, adorned with hanging baskets and plaster pineapples. Inside, though, it's all change. Gone are the front bar's cosy, battered red velvet banquettes and moth-eaten curtains; in their place is sleek leather seating, bare windows and metallic fleur-de-lis wallpaper. Happily, the splendid bar remains – a gleaming mahogany affair with etched mirrors and gilt lettering – though the pumps have a pretty lacklustre line-up of ales and ciders. Regulars seem to have taken the transformation in their stride; if it's packed in the front, retreat to the airy conservatory or lovely walled garden. *Babies and children admitted (until 7.30pm). Function rooms (capacity 50). Games (backgammon, cards, chess, darts). Quiz (8.30pm Mon; £1). Tables outdoors (9, garden; 16, pavement). TV.* **Map p286 J24**.

Vine

86 Highgate Road, NW5 1PB (7209 0038/ www.thevinelondon.co.uk). Tufnell Park tube/ Kentish Town tube/rail. **Open** noon-11pm Mon-Wed; noon-midnight Thur-Sat; noon-10.30pm Sun. **Food served** noon-3pm, 6-10pm Mon-Sat; noon-9.30pm Sun. **Credit** AmEx, DC, MC, V. Gastropub

The unabashedly over-the-top decor in the Vine is not to all tastes. Though it looks unremarkable enough from the road, the maroon-painted interior is unexpectedly opulent: lavish hothouse flower arrangements, chandeliers and baroque gilt frames. Yet there's substance behind the style: a respectable range of drinks on tap (Leffe, Hoegaarden, Bombardier, Addlestones cider) and delightfully friendly staff, quick to offer a sample of cider as we dithered by the bar. Out in the front are picnic tables; out in the back, locals convene in the generously-proportioned beer garden. *Babies and children welcome. Function rooms (capacity 30). Music (bands 8pm Thur; free). Tables outdoors (22, garden).* **Map p286 H24**.

Muswell Hill

Victoria Stakes ★

1 Muswell Hill, N10 3TH (8815 1793/ www.victoriastakes.co.uk). Finsbury Park tube/rail, then W3, W7 bus. **Open** 5-11pm Mon-Wed; 5pm-midnight Thur; noon-midnight Fri, Sat; noon-10.30pm Sun. **Food served** 6-10.30pm Mon-Thur; noon-4pm, 6-10.30pm Fri, Sat; noon-9pm Sun. **Credit** MC, V. Gastropub

Poised between Crouch End and Muswell Hill, this superior gastropub is a popular spot with a modish local crowd, especially at weekends. The upstairs dining room is an airy mix of modernity and Victorian plush, but the place to eat at, weather permitting, is the stylish covered patio. Non-diners have plenty of room in the bar, which is equipped with leather sofas and tasty bar snacks. Wines are refined and affordable; the beers include Staropramen and Leffe, but no resident ales; the guest ale tends to be a novelty like Red Squirrel or Rebellion Brewery's Smugglers' Bitter. There's also (at least on our visit) Addlestones cider on tap. *Babies and children admitted (in restaurant; until 7.30pm in bar). Games (board games). Music (acoustic band 8pm 1st Mon of mth; free). Restaurant. Tables outdoors (20, garden).*

Primrose Hill

Engineer ★

65 Gloucester Avenue, NW1 8JH (7722 0950/ www.the-engineer.com). Chalk Farm tube/31, 168 bus. **Open** 9am-11pm Mon-Sat; 9am-10.30pm Sun. **Food served** 9-11.30am, noon-3pm, 7-11pm Mon-Fri; 9am-noon, 12.30-4pm, 7-11pm Sat; 9am-noon, 12.30-4pm, 7-10.30pm Sun. **Credit** MC, V. Gastropub

The Engineer rewards the well organised. Although there's always space at the bar for a

North

swift pint (Bombardier and Hooky Bitter among the draught options), you assume a seat may be available in the dining area at your peril. The gastro offerings (in particular the weekend brunches) at this bright, breezy and very classy boozer are renowned and oversubscribed. Despite the trendy wallpaper and mirror-strewn function rooms, the vibe is well-to-do rather than hip. In the main bar, huge, colourful lampshades reflect a warm glow over a groomed clientele talking bonuses, school fees and the health benefits of pinot grigio. The decked beer garden out back makes a fine escape.

Babies and children admitted (dining only). Disabled: toilet. Function rooms (capacity 30). Tables outdoors (14, garden). **Map p286 G1**.

Lansdowne

90 Gloucester Avenue, NW1 8HX (7483 0409/ www.thelansdownepub.co.uk). Chalk Farm tube/ 31, 168 bus. **Open** noon-11pm daily. **Food served** noon-3pm, 7-10pm Mon-Fri; 12.30-3.30pm Sat, Sun. **Credit** MC, V. **Gastropub**
Pared down to perfection, this easygoing gastropub is a fine place in which to while away an afternoon. The massive windows let plenty of light into the bar, which dispenses run-of-the-mill draught beers (Bombardier, Staropramen, Guinness) and a well-chosen list of wines. If hunger hits, there's a classy, varied bar menu (sardines with lemon, ribeye with chips, Sunday roasts, a whole blackboard of pizzas); if not, just sit back and soak up the banter and bustle of this posh bit of north London.

Babies and children admitted. Disabled: toilet. Restaurant (available for hire, capacity 70). Tables outdoors (5, pavement). **Map p286 G26**.

Queens ★

49 Regent's Park Road, NW1 8XD (7586 0408/www.geronimo-inns.co.uk). Chalk Farm tube/31, 168, 274 bus. **Open** 11am-11pm Mon-Sat; noon-10.30pm Sun. **Food served** noon-3pm, 7-10pm Mon-Fri; noon-5pm, 7-10pm Sat; noon-5pm, 7.30-9.30pm Sun. **Credit** AmEx, MC, V. **Gastropub**
Queens has had its day – as the haunt of the Primrose Hill glitterati, that is. Which makes it all the more appealing to anyone wanting to flee the skinny-jeaned wannabes in the surrounding streets. Whereas the ground-floor bar has a cosy air, the restaurant upstairs has a slightly more decadent feel, with crimson wallpaper and a dining terrace that provides stupendous views. There's a reasonable selection of real ales and beer (Young's Ordinary and Special, Bombardier and unusual guests), knowledgeable staff, and good food like corn-fed chicken with coconut-scented gravy (£12).

Insider Knowledge
Boogaloo

You are?
Gerry O'Boyle. I'm one of the owners of the Boogaloo (*see p212*), in Highgate.
How did you come to open Boogaloo?
I used to own Filthy McNasty's (*see p217*) where the Libertines started out. Our aim was to create a rock 'n' roll bar where bands, artists, writers and music lovers could hang out. Jukebox joints were big in America in the '50s, and we wanted to recreate that.
You've had some quite famous people programming your jukebox…
We get rock stars to do it. At the moment it's Iggy Pop, but prior to that we've had Pete Doherty, Kate Moss, Shane MacGowan and Starsky & Hutch. We only allow them to put in songs that have been around for ten years or more. We don't want to play one-hit wonders.
Who've you had playing live here?
We've had some great Shane MacGowan and Babyshambles gigs. We've also had secret gigs (Dirty Pretty Things, Badly Drawn Boy and the Kooks), and we programme new bands too.
You say you run the bar like a rock 'n' roll band – what does that entail?
It's about attitude. The staff are into their music. We have singer-songwriter nights, MTV movie quizzes, gig nights and club nights on the weekends.
You've said that your mission is to educate people about 'real' music?
We want people who play their own instruments. If you put on bubblegum music, your bar won't be remembered. Do it right and you can make history.

North

Babies and children admitted (restaurant).
Tables outdoors (4, balcony; 2, pavement).
Map p286 G1.

Stroud Green

Faltering Fullback ★
19 Perth Road, N4 3HB (7272 5834).
Finsbury Park tube/rail. **Open** noon-11pm
Mon-Thur; noon-midnight Fri, Sat; noon-
10.30pm Sun. **Food served** 6.30-10.30pm
Mon-Sat; 6.30-10pm Sun. **Credit** MC, V. **Pub**
Tucked away down a side street off busy Stroud
Green Road, this is a dream of a pub.
Consequently, it's always busy, for all its hidden
location. The secret of its success is several
distinct zones: a front room with screens for
match days (provided quirky objets hanging
from the ceiling don't intrude); a smaller, music-
free central area; a barn-like back room with a
raucous, studenty feel, picnic table seating, loud
music and pool; and a pleasant beer garden. A
so-so range of beers includes Leffe and London
Pride on tap, though wine is limited to a couple
of ordinary reds and whites.
Disabled: toilet. Games (fruit machine, pool,
quiz machine). Jukebox. Quiz (9pm Mon; £1).
Tables outdoors (16, garden). TVs.

Marquess Tavern ★
There's a conspiratorial atmosphere
here: groups huddled around tables
by the Victorian fireplace, battered
piano and billiards table. Meanwhile,
the much feted, light-filled dining room
in the back is filled with cheery chatter,
as people tuck into hearty, seasonal
British grub sourced from local organic
suppliers. For each dish, there are
imaginative drink recommendations –
wine and beer (try black pudding with
German lager Köstritzer Schwarzbier,
or chocolate pudding with fruit beer
Kriek). The succulent signature dish –
28-day-hung forerib of Angus beef to
share between four people – is well
worth the 40-minute wait. Cheery,
clued-up staff man the horseshoe bar,
dispensing 40 beers (with a regularly
changing guest beer) and an extensive
wine selection. There are also 50
whiskies, Weston's perry on tap, and
lovely Bramley and Gage gins and
liqueurs. It's rare to find a gastropub
that pleases diehard pub enthusiasts
and fine dining connoisseurs – but this
is it. *For listings, see p218.*

Noble `NEW`
29 Crouch Hill, N4 4AP (7281 7444).
Finsbury Park tube/rail then W7 bus/Crouch
Hill rail. **Open** 5-11pm Mon-Thur; 5pm-
midnight Fri; noon-midnight Sat, Sun. **Food**
served 6-10.30pm Mon-Fri; noon-11pm Sat,
Sun. **Credit** MC, V. **Gastropub**
Noble has a warm welcome, a bedraggled vibe
and a fine drinks selection: Deuchars IPA, Leffe
Blonde and Addlestones cider on tap, plus
strawberry Früli in bottles. A blackboard lists
24 wines by the glass, including champagne and
dessert wines; the brief, well-considered cocktail
list features modish watermelon-basil and
elderflower-ginger martinis, and classics like
caipirinha, bellini and amaretto sour. Service is
perfectly attentive when it comes to ordering
food, too. As well as a full menu, there's a tapas-
style menu of dishes for sharing.
Babies and children admitted (until 8pm).
Tables outdoors (3, front garden).

Tufnell Park

Bar Lorca
156-158 Fortess Road, NW5 2HP (7485
1314). Tufnell Park tube. **Open** 4pm-midnight
Mon-Thur; 4pm-1am Fri, Sat; noon-midnight

Sun. **Food served** 5-11pm Mon-Sat; noon-11pm Sun. **Credit** AmEx, MC, V. **Bar**
You'd be forgiven for not noticing that Bar Lorca is Spanish at all. The slick, softly lit presentation is very salubrious, but its neutral tones could belong to any number of the modern bars you find in central London. However, take a second look and the authenticity shines through. Draught lagers are strictly San Miguel and Estrella Damm; the wine and cocktail lists are predominantly Spanish, and the tapas bar counter serves paella for a fiver at Sunday lunch. DJs every Friday and Saturday and the late licence attract a trendy crowd.
Babies and children admitted (until 7pm). Disabled: toilet. Music (8.30pm Fri, Sat; free).

Dartmouth Arms

35 York Rise, NW5 1SP (7485 3267/ www.dartmoutharms.co.uk). Tufnell Park tube/Gospel Oak rail. **Open** 11am-11pm Mon-Fri; 10am-11pm Sat; 10am-10.30pm Sun. **Food served** 11am-3pm, 6-10pm Mon-Fri; 10am-10pm Sat, Sun. **Credit** MC, V. **Gastropub**
It's a rare thing to find a place that has the trappings of a gastropub *and* the down-to-earth humility of a local boozer – but this place just about pulls it off. The posh crowd happily rubs shoulders with hoi polloi, and tasteful lamps,

decent food menu and fireside bookcase are undiminished by Sky Sports. Drinks reinforce the broad church feel, with Stella and Carlsberg alongside Leffe and quality ciders; there's also a good choice of bitters and wines. The back room serves good and reasonably priced food.
Babies and children admitted (until 8pm). Comedy (8pm every other Thur, call for details; £4). Function room (capacity 60). Quiz (8pm alternate Tue; £1). Restaurant. TV.

Lord Palmerston ★

33 Dartmouth Park Hill, NW5 1HU (7485 1578/www.geronimo-inns.co.uk). Tufnell Park tube. **Open** noon-11pm Mon-Sat; noon-10.30pm Sun. **Food served** noon-3pm, 7-10pm Mon-Sat; noon-9pm Sun. **Credit** AmEx, MC, V. **Gastropub**
The smell of the open fire, crockery-lined shelves and lamplit corners all foster a homely feel, as does the fireside couch area, separate dining room and tasteful decor. The attractive garden is a fantastic place for a pint in the summer; the wide drinks selection includes German lagers, Meantime and Bitburger, and there's an excellent wine list. Frequented mainly by locals, the place strikes a nice balance between friendly local and good dining pub; it's worth making a trip to Tufnell Park just for this.
Babies and children admitted. Function room (capacity 60). Music (live music every mth, call for details; free). Tables outdoors (7, garden; 13, pavement).

Star ★ NEW

47 Chester Road, N19 5DF (7263 9067/ www.thestar-n19.co.uk). Archway or Tufnell Park tube. **Open** 5-11pm Mon-Thur; 4.30pm-12.30am Fri; noon-12.30am Sat; noon-11pm Sun. **Food served** 6-10.30pm Mon-Fri; noon-4.30pm, 6-10.30pm Sat, Sun. **Credit** MC, V. **Pub**
This cavernous corner pub is a cracking space. Lofty ceiling, and full-length windows make it ideal for a bright and breezy weekend lunch, and come the evenings, bare bulbs and fairy lights are turned down low as the broad wooden tables fill up with well-heeled locals. Watched over by three deer (above the open fireplace) and a ram (above the bar), fine gastro servings like grilled chicken with mashed swede are served alongside Timothy Taylor Landlord, London Pride or the current guest ale. Acoustic open-mic sessions liven up Thursday evenings, and there's a jukebox too.
Babies and children admitted. Games (board games). Music (open mic 8pm Wed, free; acoustic musicians 8pm Thur, 7pm Sun, free-£3). Tables outdoors (5, balcony; 10, garden).

North

North West

North West

There are few finer pleasures in life than a bracing stomp across the Heath – trusty hound in tow – followed by a pint of real ale or a hearty Sunday roast at one of Hampstead's cosy boozers. We love the creakily old-school charm of the **Holly Bush**, the locals' banter at the **Flask** and the extravaganza of summer bonhomie that is the beer garden at the **Spaniards Inn** (there's even a doggy wash – like a canine car wash – for that trusty hound). Down the hill in Belsize Park a civilised feel prevails, though we imagine even the area's most genteel punters would be prepared to fight for a seat in the recently refurbished **Freemasons**' huge beer garden. Kensal Green boasts the fantastically quirky **Paradise**, spot on for a leisurely gastro lunch, swift after-work pint or a raucous night of cocktail-swilling. Kilburn's **Black Lion** has characterful appeal (and good food to boot), while St John's Wood's **Clifton** dissolves city stress with its laid-back, bucolic feel.

Belsize Park

Freemasons Arms ★ NEW

32 Downshire Hill, NW3 1NT (7433 6811/ www.freemasonsarms.co.uk). Belsize Park tube. **Open** noon-11pm Mon-Sat; noon-10.30pm Sun. **Food served** noon-10pm Mon-Sat; noon-9pm Sun. **Credit** AmEx, MC, V. **Gastropub**
So shiny is the recent refurb at the Freemasons Arms that you could probably eat straight off the marble-topped tables. The main bar is hotel lobby-like in size, with leather armchairs dotted around a central light-wood bar. There are two dining rooms, but drinkers tend to head for the mirrored and muralled 'Hampstead Room' or, in summer, the pebbled beer garden. There are only two real ales, Timothy Taylor Landlord and London Pride, but interesting draught lagers include Paulaner and Birra Moretti. Diners tuck into fancy cottage pies (£10), pizza (£7) and lamb shank (£14). Staff are friendly, but their logoed tees make them look less like a team of chummy bartenders than members of a militia.
Babies and children welcome: high chairs. Disabled: toilets. Function room (up to 120 capacity). Restaurant. Tables outdoors (50, patio; 15, garden).

Hill

94 Haverstock Hill, NW3 2BD (7267 0033). Belsize Park or Chalk Farm tube. **Open** noon-11pm Mon-Wed, Sun; 11am-midnight Thur-Sat. **Food served** noon-3pm, 6-10pm Mon-Thur; noon-3pm, 6-11pm Fri; noon-11pm Sat; noon-9pm Sun. **Credit** MC, V. **Gastropub**
More gastropub than proper boozer, the Hill is a hit with a smart NW3 crowd who descend in droves for well-executed, if slightly pricey, food: baby octopus, sirloin steak or sea bass, say. During the day, it's a bright, relaxed place for a glass of wine inside or out; the garden's a real suntrap. By night it's warmly lit and the plush sofas are perfect for cosy drinking sessions – though it has to be said that even with all the standard draught beers at the bar, the Hill is more of a wine-drinkers' hangout. It's certainly never rowdy enough to be on anyone's pub crawl list.
Babies and children admitted (until 6pm). Games (board games). Function room (30 capacity). Restaurant. Tables outdoors (15, garden).

Sir Richard Steele ★ HOT 50

97 Haverstock Hill, NW3 4RL (7483 1261/ www.sirrichardsteele.com). Belsize Park or Chalk Farm tube. **Open** 11am-midnight Mon-Sat; noon-11.30pm Sun. **Food served** noon-3pm, 6-10pm Mon; noon-3pm, 6-10.30pm Tue-Fri; noon-10.30pm Sat; noon-10pm Sun. **Credit** MC, V. **Pub**
This old boozer oozes battered character: hand-painted Sistine-esque friezes, dripping candles and weird papier-mâché oddities hanging from the ceiling. Suffice to say it's the antithesis of the Hill (*see above*) across the road. There's real ale – Flowers IPA, Spitfire et al – on tap and a great Sunday roast, as well as the now standard pub Thai food. And since some of the less salubrious locals have been turfed out, the vibe has improved no end. Expect everyone from quietly

loaded Belsize Parkers cosying up in the snugs to pint-downing students in the beer garden preparing for a night out in Camden. *Entertainment (comedy 8.45pm Sat; £10). Function room (120 capacity). Games (fruit machine). Music (trad jazz 9pm Mon; jazz/ soul 9pm Wed; acoustic blues 9pm Fri; jazz 4pm Sun; Irish music 9pm Sun; free). Tables outdoors (16, patio).*

Hampstead

Flask ★

14 Flask Walk, NW3 1HG (7435 4580). Hampstead tube. **Open** 11am-11pm Mon-Thur; 11am-midnight Fri, Sat; noon-midnight Sun. **Food served** noon-3pm, 6-9pm Mon-Fri; noon-10pm Sat, Sun. **Credit** MC, V. **Pub**
The 2007 refit of this fail-safe Young's boozer on a pretty Hampstead alley attracted some local controversy. The result, however, has been kind – not least to the food menu – and the pub's unique charm remains intact. The bar is still partitioned into two separate areas: the (locals') bar and the lounge. In the former, expect to witness Hampstead's old guard propping up the bar and letting rip on a number of topics (the evils of Camden Council being the most popular). The lounge, conservatory and garden are more sedate affairs, with a younger, less intimidating crowd eating anything from beer-battered fish and chips to calf's liver, while sipping pints of Bombardier, Addlestones or the seasonally changing draught. *Babies and children welcome (restaurant only): high chairs. Disabled: toilet. Games (darts). Quiz (8.30pm Tue; £1). Restaurant (available for hire, up to 70 capacity). Tables outdoors (3, pavement). TV.*

Holly Bush ★ HOT 50

22 Holly Mount, NW3 6SG (7435 2892/ www.hollybushpub.com). Hampstead tube/ Hampstead Heath rail. **Open** noon-11pm Mon-Sat; noon-10.30pm Sun. **Food served** noon-10pm daily. **Credit** (over £5) MC, V. **Pub**
For review, *see p230.*
Babies and children admitted. Games (board games). Restaurant available for hire (60 capacity).

Horseshoe

28 Heath Street, NW3 6TE (7431 7206). Hampstead tube. **Open** 10am-11pm Mon-Sat; 10am-10.30pm Sun. **Food served** 12.30-3.30pm, 6.30-10pm Mon-Sat; noon-4.30pm, 6.30-9.30pm Sun. **Credit** MC, V. **Gastropub**
This big corner bar used to be a chain pub of the lowest order. Nowadays, though, it's far from budget. What makes this gastropub stand out is its on-site microbrewery, which produces fine McLaughlin's ale, its long wine list, reflecting the owner's Antipodean roots, and its food. It's proved a real hit in an area surprisingly starved of good-value eateries. And though the bright and frenetic feel doesn't lend itself to cosy romance, the open kitchen's 'farm to fork' sourcing – the cod comes from Cornwall, the beef from Suffolk – makes for an all-round happier meal. *Babies and children welcome: high chairs. Restaurant (30 capacity).*

Roebuck ★

15 Pond Street, NW3 2PN (7433 6871). Belsize Park tube. **Open** noon-11pm Mon-Thur; noon-midnight Fri, Sat; noon-10.30pm Sun. **Food served** noon-3pm, 5-10pm Mon-Fri; noon-10pm Sat; noon-9pm Sun. **Credit** AmEx, MC, V. **Bar**
Run by the same people behind the Eagle in Clerkenwell, by all accounts this is the Royal Free bar that never was. But in stark contrast to the grey monster of a hospital that towers above the place, this pub's a stylish, airy place equally suitable for a quick cuppa or a raucous party in the basement bar. The food is an adventurous take on pub grub – the halloumi burger is still a favourite – and they have a good range of beers on tap, from Früli to Staropramen, as well as guest beers. Venture into the garden in summer and you'll find many a medic nursing a pint. *Babies and children admitted (until 7pm). Disabled: toilet. Function room (100 capacity). Games (board games). Quiz (7pm Tue; £2). Tables outdoors (16, garden).*

Spaniards Inn ★

Spaniards Road, NW3 7JJ (8731 6571). Hampstead tube/210 bus. **Open** 11am-11pm Mon-Fri; 10am-11pm Sat, Sun. **Food served** 11.30am-10pm Mon-Fri; noon-10pm Sat, Sun. **Credit** AmEx, MC, V. **Pub**
The one thing you'll hear about the Spaniards is that Dick Turpin hung out here, and while that may or may not be true (it's been a boozer since 1580 and looks every bit the highwayman's tavern), the fact that there's a 'doggy wash' (a car wash for mucky mutts, £5 for five minutes, £9 for 15) says rather more about the place today. The pub's relative inaccessibility at the side of the heath is also its chief advantage. In winter folk stop off mid-walk and warm up on the splendid pub grub before settling in a booth with one of the 24 draughts – perhaps an

North West

Holly Bush ★ HOT 50

Hampstead may have become part of London in 1888, but no one seems to have told the Holly Bush. As the trend for gutting old pubs claims yet more NW3 boozers, this place's cachet increases. It's as picturesque as they come, tucked away on a quiet crescent and delivering on all fronts: friendly staff, an ancient interior and fine, reasonably priced food, (from spruced-up sarnies to lamb shank in beer). Though the upstairs restaurant does a roaring trade, it's really all about getting the pints in and perching by the fire or in one of the wooden booths. Our one complaint? The backroom's glaring refurb could have been more sympathetic. That, and the place's huge popularity. *For listings, see p229.*

Adnams, Marston's Pedigree or Roosters Special, say – only to stumble out hours later into the dark, dark woods. The traditional British food includes posh mushrooms on toast, two different types of sausage, a 'pie of the day', fish-cakes, citrus-braised Ely Valley lamb shank, and spit-roasted pigs on high days and holidays (and sunny weekends).

Babies and children admitted. Entertainment (poetry 8pm Tue; free). Function room (50 capacity). Tables outdoors (80, garden).

Wells

30 Well Walk, NW3 1BX (7794 3785/www. thewellshampstead.co.uk). Hampstead tube. **Open** noon-11pm Mon-Sat; noon-10.30pm Sun. **Food served** noon-3pm, 6-10pm Mon-Fri; noon-4pm, 7-10pm Sat, Sun. **Credit** MC, V. **Gastropub**

Previously the black sheep of Hampstead pubs, this place has been operating as a fairly high-end gastropub for some years now, kitted out in dark woods and leather. Nobody is here for the decor though, it's the location and the food – posh bangers and mash or scallops downstairs, chateaubriand steaks and the like in the first floor restaurant. In summer, the outside tables are the main draw: a block from the heath, on the way to and from the tube, and looking out onto some of NW3's most picturesque streets. There's nowhere better for a post-stroll meal and a glass of wine.

Babies and children welcome: children's menu; colouring books; high chairs. Disabled: toilet. Function room (12 capacity). Restaurant. Tables outdoors (8, patio).

Ye Olde White Bear [HOT 50]

1 Well Road, NW3 1LJ (7435 3758). Hampstead tube. **Open** 11.30am-11pm Mon-Wed, Sun; 11.30am-11.30pm Thur-Sat. **Food served** noon-9pm daily. **Credit** MC, V. **Pub**

While NW3's house prices are some of the most ridiculous in London, changing the area's demographic immeasurably, this place seems locked in a time warp. And so much the better. Hidden away from the glare of the high street, this is the Hampstead of lore: log fires, muddy dogs, walls of stained press clippings and eccentric punters. There's Bombardier, Ruddles and Adnams on tap and sport on the telly, though it rarely intrudes – the calm is only shattered when battalions of local 18 year-olds invade to bark gap-year plans at each other. Some things never change.

Babies and children admitted. Games (board games). Quiz (9pm Thur; £1). Tables outdoors (6, courtyard). TV (satellite).

North West

Kensal Green

Greyhound

64-66 Chamberlayne Road, NW10 3JJ (8969 8080). Kensal Green tube/Kensal Rise rail. **Open** 4-11pm Mon-Thur; noon-midnight Fri; 10am-midnight Sat; 11am-11pm Sun. **Food served** 6.30-10pm Mon-Thur; noon-3pm, 6.30-10pm Fri, Sat; noon-7pm Sun **Credit** AmEx, MC, V. Gastropub

Sombre lighting, stags' heads, greyhound portraits and a '40s fruit machine create something of an antique shop feel at this gastro boozer. Other oddities on display include a chef's apron signed by Jamie Oliver and a signed print of Ian Brown. The friendly Irish staff serve up Bitburger, Adnams, John Smith's, San Miguel and Aspall Suffolk Cyder to patrons whose dedication might be rewarded by their own framed portrait photo on the wall. Traditional British food is served in the restaurant adjacent to the bar. Decent wines and a good range of aperitifs complete the picture.

Babies and children admitted. Disabled: toilet. Music (DJs 6.30pm Fri, Sun; free). Restaurant (available for hire, 30 capacity). Tables outdoors (7, pavement; 15, garden).

Paradise by Way of Kensal Green ★

19 Kilburn Lane, W10 4AE (8969 0098/ www.theparadise.co.uk). Kensal Green tube/ Kensal Rise rail. **Open** 12.30pm-midnight Mon-Wed; 12.30pm-1am Thur; 12.30pm-2am Fri, Sat; noon-11.30pm Sun. **Food served** 4-10.30pm Mon-Sat; noon-4pm, 6.30-10.30pm Sat; noon-8pm Sun. **Credit** MC, V. Gastropub

Perched in the corner of the quirkily theatrical Paradise is a seven-foot statue of an angel that looks as if it flew over the wall of the nearby cemetery for a cheeky pint. It couldn't have picked a more atmospheric drinking hole: attractively craquelure paintwork; an assortment of decorative chandeliers lighting rooms connected by a spiral staircase; cherubs eavesdropping on hipster locals as they lounge on faux gilt French furniture to sip cocktails (such as moscow mules, £6.50) and pints of Hoegaarden. The restaurant positioned behind the bar has a similarly relaxing atmosphere, offering quality British cuisine (lemon sole with mash, chargrilled ribeye steak with chips) under the direction of Tim Payne, former executive chef to Marco Pierre White. Outside areas are arranged with palms and decking, and the spacious upstairs area has a stage for live acts (burlesque and cabaret often feature). Best of all, though, are the lazy Sunday sessions – roasts to die for (beef, lamb, corn-fed chicken, yorkshire puddings, proper gravy), piles of newspapers and hangover-defying bloody marys. A private dining room, with access to a roof terrace, makes a fine place for parties. Yes, this is the local pub of your dreams.

Babies and children admitted (except evenings Fri, Sat). Function rooms (up to 150 capacity). Restaurant. Tables outdoors (10, garden). TV (widescreen).

Kilburn

Black Lion

274 Kilburn High Road, NW6 2BY (7624 1424/www.blacklionguesthouse.com). Kilburn tube/Brondesbury rail. **Open** 11.30am-midnight Mon-Thur; 11am-1am Fri, Sat; 11am-11.30pm Sun. **Food served** noon-3pm, 6-10pm Mon-Fri; 11am-10pm Sat; noon-9.30pm Sun. **Credit** MC, V. Gastropub

You might expect Bach to fire up the organ on entrance to this, thankfully, listed building. The lavish gilded ceiling would be more likely found in a German church than a pub in Kilburn. Once your head has tilted back to the normal position, relax into a leather sofa with a mojito (£5.50) or order a pint of John Smith's, Bombardier, Adnams or Hoegaarden from the huge bar. A former billiards room has been turned into a restaurant area, offering hearty gastro grub and great Sunday roasts. One too many? Rooms are available upstairs for £40 per person, per night, including breakfast.

Babies and children admitted (until 6pm). Restaurant. Tables outdoors (6, garden).

Kilburn Pub & Kitchen

307-311 Kilburn High Road, NW6 7JR (7372 8668/www.thekilburn.com). Kilburn tube/ Brondesbury rail. **Open** noon-11pm Mon-Wed; noon-midnight Thur, Sun; noon-2am Fri, Sat. **Food served** noon-3pm, 5.30-10pm Mon-Thur; noon-9.30pm Fri, Sat; noon-midnight Sun. **Credit** AmEx, MC, V. Gastropub

Formerly one old-school Irish pub, the Kilburn is now split into an unequal two. The more generous portion is devoted to an American-style diner-cum-bar, with red leather booth seating and quotes from Hank Williams on the walls. Diner menus decorated with disconcerting skulls offer a range of cocktails for a fiver and decent burgers. This is not the place for real ale drinkers (John Smith's is the sole on-tap offering) but the lively young crowd – who later bound upstairs to the award-

North West

Clifton. *See p234.*

winning Luminaire music venue – really couldn't care less. The smaller side is now called McGoverns and resembles an upholstered Irish betting shop, with horse racing on fuzzy TVs and a very male clientele. Both bars are served food by the same kitchen.

Babies and children admitted. Music (DJs 9pm Fri, Sat; free). TVs (big screen, satellite).

North London Tavern
375 Kilburn High Road, NW6 7QB (7625 6634). Kilburn tube. **Open** noon-11.30pm Mon-Wed; noon-midnight Thur; noon-1am Fri, Sat; noon-11pm Sun. **Food served** 6-10pm Mon; noon-10.30pm Tue-Sat; noon-9.30pm Sun. **Credit** MC, V. **Pub**
Head past the smokers huddled under continental-style canvas awnings on this unsavoury stretch of Kilburn High Road to join the North London Tavern's laid-back, boho-leaning crowd on the slouchy leather sofas within. Set below a blood-red ceiling, an island bar terraced with whiskies and rums serves up pints of Harveys, Timothy Taylor Landlord, Deuchars, Adnams, Hoegaarden and Leffe as the buzz of good conversation fills the air. A regularly changing blackboard menu offers above average, reasonably priced pub food (served in the dining room to the rear) and the vibe is friendly and welcoming.
Babies and children welcome. Disabled: toilet. Function room. Restaurant. Tables outdoors (5, pavement). TV.

Salusbury
50-52 Salusbury Road, NW6 6NN (7328 3286). Queen's Park tube/rail. **Open** 5-11pm Mon; 10am-11pm Tue-Thur; 10am-midnight Fri, Sat; noon-11pm Sun. **Food served** 7-10.15pm Mon; 12.30-3.30pm, 7-10.15pm Tue-Sun. **Credit** MC, V. **Gastropub**
Very much part of the gentrified Salusbury Road scene (organic foodshops by the shedload), this gastropub is a firm favourite with NW6's media types, young families and the odd C-list celeb. With its happy-go-lucky, welcoming feel, it's the sort of place where you wander in off the street looking for directions and leave four hours later having made friends with the bar staff and tucked into a damn fine gastro supper. Food has a northern Italian rustic vibe ideally combined with something from the extensive and well-chosen wine list. Ample choice on tap extends to Franziskaner, Peetermans Artois, Adnams, Guinness and Aspall Suffolk Cyder.
Babies and children welcome (until 7pm): high chairs. Restaurant. Tables outdoors (4, pavement).

St John's Wood

Clifton ★
96 Clifton Hill, NW8 0JT (7372 3427). St John's Wood tube. **Open** noon-11pm Mon-Sat; noon-10.30pm Sun. **Food served** noon-3pm, 6-9.30pm Mon-Sat; noon-4pm, 6.30-9pm Sun. **Credit** AmEx, MC, V. **Pub**
This boozer is a couple of hundred years old, and everyone's secret spot – even, at one time, the trysting Edward VII and Lily Langtry. It's long on atmosphere and blissfully short on hubbub: borrow a board game from the bar or toast yourself at the roaring fire in the snug. Wooden panelling abounds, perfectly in harmony with the unobtrusive murals and funky chandeliers in each room. Outdoor types colonise the leafy terrace at the front, warmed in winter by gas heaters. Inside, the line-up of real ales includes Timothy Taylor Landlord, Black Sheep and Everards, and there's a good selection of wines available by the glass and bottle. A proper dining area, some of which occupies the conservatory, serves classic British nosh like bangers and mash with onion gravy; on our visit, a perfect ribeye steak came with chunky chips and a pile of dressed rocket. Service is charming.
Babies and children admitted (until 7pm). Games (board games). Quiz (Wed 8.30pm; £2). Tables outdoors (12, garden). TV.

Ordnance
29 Ordnance Hill, NW8 6PS (7722 0278). St John's Wood tube. **Open** noon-11pm Mon-Sat; noon-10.30pm Sun. **Food served** noon-2pm, 6-9pm Mon-Sat; noon-3pm Sun. **Credit** MC, V. **Pub**
The Ordnance is just up the road from a barracks (hence the name); we thought we might find a few squaddies here, but the punters were largely middle-aged. This is a Sam Smith pub, majoring in lagers and just two bitters, and the pursuit of independence extends to the retro Scintilla soft drinks and a few unusual spirits behind the bar; wine drinkers have a couple of reasonable reds and whites to choose from. The space is warm, woody (tree branches turned into light fittings) and candlelit in winter. The grub is solid stuff, and firmly traditional – various pies, for example, and a couple of fish dishes – and you can choose to eat it in a small conservatory at the back. A couple of enclosed patios front and rear keep smokers happy; staff are a cheerful bunch.
Babies and children admitted (until 9pm). Function room (30 capacity). No piped music or jukebox. Tables outdoors (9, garden).

Outer London

Outer London

London's semi-rural fringe is where stressed-out city dwellers head to unwind. Its acres of green space and riverside paths are also home to some wonderful pubs, making it a perfect destination for daytrippers who like to finish things off with a pint. The **Cricketers** and the **White Cross** in Richmond achieve a kind of idyllic perfection, especially in summer, when the village green and Thames waterfront come into their own. Kingston isn't quite as verdant, but it does boast the splendidly trad **Wych Elm** and top-notch gastropub the **Canbury Arms**. Due north, in Middlesex, Southall has the **Glassy Junction**, the only pub in Britain to accept payment in Indian rupees.

Kew, Surrey

Botanist on the Green ★

3-5 Kew Green, Kew, Surrey TW9 3AA (8948 4838/www.thebotanistonthegreen.com). Kew Gardens tube/rail/65, 391 bus. **Open** noon-11pm Mon-Wed; noon-midnight Thur-Sat; noon-10.30pm Sun. **Food served** noon-3pm, 6-9pm Mon-Fri; noon-9pm Sat, Sun. **Credit** AmEx, DC, MC, V. **Gastropub**
The name is a nod to its floral neighbour, the Royal Botanic Gardens, and this pub's position on the corner of Kew Green truly makes it a perfect place for a relaxing pint after a mooch around the gardens. The substantial space has cosy nooks – one with a fabulous double-sided fireplace – and raised areas that give the place a more intimate feel. The 'contemporary meets retro' interior is a mix of exposed brick walls hung with china plates, retro-1930s grape light fittings illuminating chocolatey-aubergine Anaglypta walls, and dark wood floors, tables and motley seating, while the outdoor space is as twinkly as a fairy grotto. There's a great selection of wines, with nine whites and reds, and a couple of rosés by the glass. On tap there's Birra Moretti, Aspall Suffolk Cyder, Adnams and Erdinger, while bottles include Anchor Steam, Baltika, Duvel, St Peter's Organic and RHS-inspired Gardener's Tipple. There are Gaggia coffees and leaf teas too. The food menu is impressive, including cumberland sausages, cod fillet or a pea, broad bean and spinach risotto. On Sundays there's a clutch of roasts, and decent jazz. In spite of some rather tremulous service on our visit, the Botanist on the Green is somewhere worth 'Kew'ing for.
Babies and children admitted. Bar available for hire. Music (jazz 7pm Sun; free). Tables outdoors (6, courtyard). TVs.

Isleworth, Surrey

London Apprentice

62 Church Street, Isleworth, Surrey TW7 6BG (8560 1915). Isleworth rail. **Open** 11am-11pm Mon-Thur, Sun; 11am-midnight Fri, Sat. **Food served** noon-9.30pm daily. **Credit** AmEx, DC, MC, V. **Pub**
The London Apprentice, just outside Syon Park, opposite Isleworth Ait, was once a favourite of Charles Dickens. Now it's a perfect place to enjoy a drink by the river in the summer. The pub is divided into four areas: a walled riverside terrace, a convivial lounge bar, a dining area, and, upstairs, an ornately decorated river view room. Decor is a mix of the traditional and modern, with light wood flooring and green leaf-motif wallpaper. It's frequented by couples, families, locals of all ages and a smattering of media types from Sky's west London offices. Its choice of real ales (Bombardier, Landlord, Tried and Tested, London Pride, Greene King IPA and Sussex) also make it a popular stop-off for the Twickenham rugby crowd.
Babies and children admitted. Function room (50 capacity). Games (quiz machine). Music (jazz 8pm last Sat of mth; free if dining). Tables outdoors (10, riverside terrace).

Red Lion

92-94 Linkfield Road, Isleworth, Surrey TW7 6QJ (8560 1457/www.red-lion.info). Isleworth rail. **Open** noon-11pm Mon, Tue, Sun; noon-11.30pm Wed, Thur; noon-midnight Fri, Sat. **Food served** noon-3pm, 6-9pm Tue-Sat; noon-4pm Sun. **No credit cards. Pub**
The Red Lion is a proper local pub with character. It sells up to nine real ales at any one time and also offers live music, quiz nights and beer festivals. A blackboard lists a host of real

ales 'coming soon'; on our visit these included Shefford Mild, Atlas Latitude and Dark Side of the Moon. The grand emerald tiled exterior is somewhat at odds with the slightly shabby, white-walled bar that greets you upon entry. Here you can stay and enjoy a retro jukebox, billiards and darts, or go on through to the cosier, quieter lounge bar. The average punter is over 50 and male, but bands and a popular beer garden also draw a younger crowd.

Babies and children admitted. Beer festivals (live music and family events, call for dates). Games (backgammon, board games, cards, chess, darts, pool table). Music (open mic 9pm Wed; rock, blues 9pm Sat; jazz 3pm Sun; free). Quiz (9pm Thur; £1). Tables outdoors (20, garden). TVs.

Kingston upon Thames, Surrey

Canbury Arms ★ HOT 50

49 Canbury Park Road, Kingston upon Thames, Surrey KT2 6LQ (8255 9129/ www.thecanburyarms.com). Kingston rail.
Open 9am-11pm Mon-Sat; noon-10.30pm Sun. **Food served** 9.30-11.30am, noon-4pm, 6-10pm Mon-Sat; noon-4pm, 6-9pm Sun.
Credit AmEx, MC, V. **Gastropub**
In a light, bright, stripped-oak interior, the Canbury's chef – a former employee of TV tyrant Gordon Ramsay – creates reasonably priced food that oozes quality. Spice it up on a Tuesday evening with a curry, or enjoy a 20%

Eel Pie

Here's a pub that slots nicely into what you think a Twickenham boozer ought to be: a little bit rugby, a little bit river, a little bit rock and roll. Well, not really much rock and roll, more 'the Spinners at Christmas'. The Eel does everything well: beer is supplied by the multi-award-winning Badger Brewery from Dorset, with Best at £2.50 a pint and the much-respected Tanglefoot at £2.75. In the summer this pretty street is closed to traffic from Friday evening to Monday morning, so you can enjoy this pub from the outside as well as the inside. *For listings, see p238.*

Outer London

reduction on a Wednesday night. The drinks are top-notch too, with Timothy Taylor Landlord, HSB and Sussex Best on draught, Leffe and San Miguel the pick of the lagers, and an extensive wine list. On the first Tuesday of the month, there's an Irish banjo player, and on the odd Sunday young locals perform easy-going jazz. Parties and quiz nights are held in the spacious conservatory, which sheds its roof in summer. *Babies and children admitted. Games (board games). Music (Irish night 8pm first Tue of month, jazz/pianist 8pm Sun; free). Tables outdoors (8, forecourt; 6, garden).*

Wych Elm

93 Elm Road, Kingston upon Thames, Surrey KT2 6HT (8546 3271). Kingston rail. **Open** 11am-3pm, 5pm-midnight Mon-Fri; 11am-midnight Sat; noon-11pm Sun. **Food served** noon-2.30pm Mon-Sat. **Credit** MC, V. Pub
Located in a quiet suburb, the brass fittings and chintzy fabrics of this charming Fuller's pub testify to an age before stripped floors and sharing platters – it's so traditional, it still holds to mid-afternoon closing. The same family have run the place for 25 years, but they could well have been beaten to the bar by the cheery locals, sat around bantering as if they never move. One side of the split bar has a darts area. Expect Fuller's ESB, Chiswick and a seasonal guest on the pumps.
Babies and children admitted (restaurant only). Bar available for hire. Games (darts, fruit machine). Restaurant (24 seats). Tables outdoors (8, garden). TV.

Richmond, Surrey

Cricketers

The Green, Richmond, Surrey TW9 1LX (8940 4372). Richmond tube/rail. **Open** noon-11pm Mon-Sat; noon-10.30pm Sun. **Food served** noon-7pm daily. **Credit** AmEx, MC, V. Pub
Having Richmond Green as a beer garden is an obvious pull; the crack of leather on willow is the soundtrack for alfresco drinkers in summer. Despite creaky floorboards, this is a modern pub – there's a fruit machine and Sky Sports. Head upstairs for a wonderful view over the Green. Draught beers include Greene King IPA and Ruddles County, and the 18 types of burger that once graced the menu have been edged out by an arguably more fashionable list of pies.
Babies and children admitted. Function room (60 capacity). Games (fruit machine, quiz machine). Tables outdoors (3, pavement). TV (big screen).

White Cross

Water Lane, Richmond, Surrey TW9 1TH (8940 6844). Richmond tube/rail. **Open** 11am-11pm Mon-Sat; noon-10.30pm Sun. **Food served** *Summer* noon-9.30pm Mon-Sat; noon-8.30pm Sun. *Winter* noon-3pm, 6-9.30pm Mon-Fri; noon-5pm Sat, Sun. **Credit** AmEx, DC, MC, V. Pub
The White Cross stands on the site of a monastery. A big, handsome boozer, it has large bay windows that offer none-closer views of the river. Crowds flock here in summer to bask on the waterfront with a cooling drink, but fires and little niches in the many rooms keep things cosy in winter. Happy staff pull pints of Young's Special and Bombardier at the rectangular bar, or pour Pimm's and lemonade. At weekends, book a table if you fancy trying some of the traditional pub nosh.
Babies and children admitted (restaurant and garden only). Restaurant (45 seats). Tables outdoors (15, garden).

Southall, Middlesex

Glassy Junction

97 South Road, Southall, Middx UB1 1SQ (8574 1626). Southall rail. **Open** 11am-11pm Mon-Sat; noon-10.30pm Sun. **Food served** noon-10.30pm daily. **No credit cards**. Pub
The only pub in Britain to accept rupees, the Glassy Junction is peppered with silver and gilt Indian knick-knacks. Highlights of the rather lacklustre drink selection include Cobra and Kingfisher (£4 or 320 rupees a pint), or a sweet or sour lassi – but no India Pale Ale (these days known as IPA) or indeed any ale at all. Regulars include Punjabi elders and Southall 'yoof' (all hair gel, bling and pimp rolls), who hang out in the serious-looking pool room. A giant plasma screen shows Bollywood-style films and pop videos.
Babies and children admitted. Function room. Games (pool tables). TV (satellite).

Twickenham, Middlesex

Eel Pie

9-11 Church Street, Twickenham, Middx TW1 3NJ (8891 1717). Twickenham rail. **Open** 11am-11pm Mon-Wed; 11am-midnight Thur-Sat; noon-10.30pm Sun. **Food served** noon-3.30pm daily. **Credit** MC, V. Pub
For review, *see p237.*
Babies and children admitted (until 7pm). Games (fruit machine). Quiz (9pm Thur; £1). TVs (satellite).

Clubs

Clubs

All change, party people. Urban redevelopment has closed some of the capital's most iconic clubs in the past year: the Cross, Canvas, the Key and Turnmills have all shut their doors for good. But there's no stopping London clubbers; new venues are opening ever further east. And all eyes will be on Fabric's enormous new bespoke gig venue when it opens in autumn 2008 near the O2.

Aquarium

256-260 Old Street, EC1V 9DD (7251 6136/ www.clubaquarium.co.uk). Old Street tube/rail. **Bar Open** 11am-11pm Mon-Wed; 11am-2am Thur, Fri; 6pm-3am Sat. **Food served** noon-8pm Mon-Sat. *Club* **Open** 10pm-4am, 3.30am-11am (after-party) Fri; 7pm-3.30am, 3.30am-11am (after-party) Sat; 10pm-4am Sun. **Admission** £8-£45. **Credit** (bar) MC, V.
Just as Old Street was earning a place on the world's map of cool, this club opened in 1995 to add a healthy dash of knowing cheesiness. Famous as the club with the pool, it also has a bubble-icious jacuzzi (take swimming togs if you like a bit of splish-splash with your disco dancing); its long-running cheese'n'funk fest, Carwash, is another well-known attraction. Hedonistic electro and deep house after-parties like Insomnia and Red Light kick off in the early morning hours, and the large tiered roof terrace is the place at which to have your all-day party come the summer.
Map p276 Q4.

Babalou NEW

The Crypt, St Matthew's Church, Brixton Hill, SW2 1JF (7738 3366/www.babalou.net). Brixton tube/rail. **Open** 7pm-3am Mon-Thur, Sun; 7pm-5am Fri, Sat. **Admission** £5-£8; free before 10pm. **Credit** MC, V.
It's hard to imagine these church crypts as anything but a gorgeous club and bar. The prevailing Moroccan theme – flickering lamps, wooden panels and decadent, red velvet booths – makes the whitewashed, low-ceilinged subterranean space seem positively cosy; the large dancefloor fills up on Fridays and Saturdays with a house crowd; comedy nights, potent cocktails (around the £6.95 mark) and salsa sessions keep the midweek crowd happy. You can reserve an area (a boudoir for ten perhaps, or a kissing booth for two) free of charge for parties.
Map p284 E2.

Bardens Boudoir ★ NEW

38-44 Stoke Newington Road, N16 7XJ (7249 9557/www.bardensbar.co.uk). Dalston Kingsland rail/67, 76, 149, 243 bus. **Open** 8pm-2am Tue-Sat (days vary; check website for details). **Admission** £4-£6. **No credit cards**.
Walk down the steep stairs at Bardens and you'd be forgiven for thinking you'd accidentally crashed a house party. This lovely basement club is tiny – 300 at a friendly squeeze – but it has single-handedly put Stoke Newington High Street on the clubbing map. Mismatched wallpaper, battered leather sofas and scuffed wooden floors give it cosily worn-in vibe, while upcoming indie bands and edgy DJs help make it the last word in cool.

Barfly

49 Chalk Farm Road, NW1 8AN (7424 0800/www.barflyclub.com). Camden Town or Chalk Farm tube. **Open** 7.30pm-midnight Mon-Wed, Sun; 7.30pm-2am Thur; 7.30pm-3am Fri; 1pm-3am Sat. **Admission** £4-£12.50. **No credit cards**.
The Barfly chain does a damned fine job of supporting up-and-coming musical talent, and the Camden outpost is no exception. The battered upstairs-downstairs space is still packed most nights with local 'faces' and wayward kids sporting cool haircuts and their skinniest jeans, all here for next-big-thing bands and club events like Casino Royale, which joyously mixes 1960s garage, northern soul and psychedelia with more recent fare. Indie dance mash-ups like Dirty Sounds (first Friday of the month) and Adventures Close to Home (second Friday) foster boisterously happy dancefloor mayhem.
Map p286 H26.

Bar Rumba

36 Shaftesbury Avenue, W1V 7DD (7287 6933/www.barrumba.co.uk). Piccadilly Circus tube. **Open** 9pm-3am Mon; 6pm-3am Tue;

End ★

End is still mining the rich seams of electronic music after 13 years. Recent additions to the roster include Groove Armada's Lovebox party, grime and dubstep night FWD, and Buzzin' Fly's slice of deep house. The main room boasts an island DJ booth, which some spinners loathe (perhaps because there's nowhere to hide), and others adore (something to do with applause from all sides). Don't be fooled by the laid-back sofas in the lounge; it's a fierce space that can outrun the main room when it fires up. Upstairs, the bricks 'n' steel AKA bar gets its fair share of house jamborees, and gets swept into the maelstrom every Saturday when all three rooms become 'As One'. *For listings, see p244.*

8pm-3am Wed; 8pm-3.30am Thur; 7pm-4am Fri; 9pm-3.30am Sat; 8.30pm-2.30am Sun. **Admission** £3-£12; free before 9pm Tue, Fri, before 8.30pm Thur. **Credit** (bar) MC, V. Bar Rumba says it's a fave with Londoners, and we believe it. Open since 1993 but still packing them in, this West End basement venue puts on some of the most esteemed sessions in town. Still focusing on cool urban sounds, Barrio Latino fires up every Tuesday with a salsa class followed by heavy reggaeton, and Movement is the capital's longest-running junglist jam on Thursdays. Fridays pull in a cool crowd for hip hop slam Front To Back. **Map p273 K7**.

Bethnal Green Working Men's Club ★

42 Pollards Row, E2 6NB (7739 2727/ www.workersplaytime.net). Bethnal Green tube/rail/8, 55 bus. **Open** 8pm-2am Thur-Sat; 10.30am-2am Sun. **Admission** £5-£12 after 8pm Fri, Sat. **Credit** MC, V.
Tucked down a Bethnal Green side street, this East End working men's club has been responsible for the whole burlesque and variety show explosion. It might look like *Phoenix Nights*, with grotty carpets and a cheap as chips bar, but the line-up is inimitable. Lucha Britannia, with its Mexican wrestlers and German nurses, is held one Thursday a month, and Whoopee presents Hip Hip, the essential burlesque try-out night, on the second Friday of the month. Be warned, though: if you're not there by 9pm and dressed in your vintage best, you probably won't get in. **Map p278 T4**.

Bistrotheque ★ NEW

23-27 Wadeson Street, E2 9DR (8983 7900/ www.bistrotheque.com). Bethnal Green tube/ Cambridge Heath rail/55 bus. **Open** *Shows* 9.30pm Fri, Sat (check website for details). **Admission** £8-£12. **Credit** AmEx, MC, V.
Bistrotheque's small cabaret room was launched as an addendum to the fashionable restaurant and bar, but has punched so far above its weight as to be internationally famous among alternative performance types. Jonny Woo's collective of alternative drag stars works from here; the gay burlesque bear troupe Bearlesque met in the back room; and the annual Underconstruction series gives performers a chance to try out works in progress. It's never polished, often wonderfully ad hoc – but is still the capital's most forward-thinking and inspiring cabaret space. **Map p278 U3**.

Black Gardenia ★ NEW

93 Dean Street, W1D 3SZ (7494 4955). Tottenham Court Road tube. **Open** doors open 8pm Fri, Sat; other days vary. **Admission** £5-£7; free before 9pm. **Credit** MC, V.
When this tiny basement club opened in 2007, owner Zimon spent about a tenner on decoration, wrote 'no jeans, no cunts' on his flyers, and opened the doors. Attracting a dressed-up crowd who live and breathe vintage (as opposed to weekend wearers of Topshop replicas), it's as shabby as you'll find, but that only feeds the sleazy, speakeasy vibe. Blues and jazz bands squeeze onto the small dancefloor, feisty burlesque babes work the bar, and a bloke in a straw boater works the piano. **Map p272 K6**.

Cargo

83 Rivington Street, EC2A 3AY (7749 7840/ www.cargo-london.com). Old Street tube/rail/ 55 bus. **Open/food served** noon-1am Mon-Thur; noon-3am Fri, Sat; 1pm-midnight Sun. **Admission** £6-£12. **Credit** (bar) MC, V.
While much of Shoreditch concerns itself with how you look while you're dancing, Cargo's only concern is what you're dancing to. Tinkering for tinkering's sake is out; if it's good, it can call this converted railway arch home for as long as it likes. There's a small restaurant serving tapas, and the first arch has a large, raised seating area for when the dancing gets too much. Summer gets the cool urban garden smoking with barbecues, should you need to refuel before a night's drinking and dancing. **Map p276 R4**.

CellarDoor NEW

Zero Aldwych, WC2R 0HT (7240 8848/ www.cellardoor.biz). Covent Garden or Temple tube. **Open** 4pm-1am Mon-Sat; 6pm-1am Sun. **Admission** free. **Credit** MC, V.
In spite of the futuristic, purple-lit stairs leading down from pavement level, it can be tricky to find this diminutive jazz club in a converted Victorian loo; make the effort, though, and you'll be rewarded. Some staggeringly clever design means that although there's room for just 60, it doesn't ever feel claustrophobic, though the toilets require a bit of courage: the glass doors only cloud over when locked. Cabaret crooners, drag queens singing opera and snuff parties are the order of the evening. **Map p275 M7**.

East Village NEW

89 Great Eastern Street, EC2A 3HX (7739 5173/www.eastvillageclub.com). Old Street

Ministry of Sound
Every Friday & Saturday

The Gallery.
featuring in 2008:

Above & Beyond
Anthony Pappa
Armin Van Buuren
Christopher Lawrence
Dave Seaman
Eddie Halliwell
Ferry Corsten
Gavyn Mytchel
Hernan Cattaneo
Hybrid
Jimmy Van M
John 'Quivver' Graham
John 00 Fleming
John Askew
Judge Jules
Marcel Woods
Marco V
Markus Schulz
Matt Hardwick
Mauro Picotto
Menno De Jong
Nick Warren
Paul Oakenfold
Paul Van Dyk
Peace Division
Randy Katana
Remy & Klinkenberg
Richard Durand
Riley & Durrant
Sander Van Doorn
Satoshi Tomiie
Seb Fontaine
Sister Bliss
Steve Porter
Tall Paul
X Press 2
plus many more...

Saturday Sessions.
featuring in 2008:

Audiofly
Axwell
Bent
Boy 8 - Bit
D. Ramirez
Danny Howells
Darren Emerson
Dave Spoon
David Guetta
David Moralez
Derrick Carter
Derrick May
Dimitri from Paris
DJ Vibe
Dubfire (Deep Dish)
Erick Morillo
Felix Da Housecat
François K
Freeform Five
James Zabiela
Lee Coombs
Mark Knight
Masters at Work
Norman Jay
Pete Tong
Roger Sanchez
S.O.S (Demi, Desyn, Omid 16B)
Sander Kleinenberg
Sebastian Ingrosso
Sharam (Deep Dish)
Spirit Catcher
Stacey Pullen
Steve Angello
Tom Novy
Trentemoller
We're Not Cool!
plus many more...

www.ministryofsound.com/club

Clubs

Volupté ★

One of the pioneers of London's new breed of supper clubs, Volupté caters for people who don't mind blowing £20 on a burlesque show. The ground-floor bar might be part of a 1980s office block, but it still thinks it's a swish NYC cocktail bar. Down the opulent stairwell is a Moulin Rouge-style basement; ivy leaves hang from the ceiling and candlelit tables are gathered around a piano. DJ El Nino runs dressed-up vintage nights here, and there are cabaret shows galore (Wed-Sat). Admission prices are for the shows, and the top price includes a meal. Entrance to the bar is free. *For listings, see p250.*

tube/rail. **Open** 5pm-1am Mon, Tue; 5pm-3am Wed-Sun. **Admission** £8. **Credit** AmEx, MC, V.

Small club, big line-ups, they say – and we wholeheartedly agree. Since the place formerly known as Medicine Bar opened in February 2008, with a classy facelift and killer new sound system, savvy promoters have been queuing up to put on nights here. Though swankier than Medicine – done out in a gorgeous chocolate brown, with plenty of seating on two floors – it's still all about what happens on the basement dancefloor. Stuart Patterson rolls in the Faith house party one Friday a month, and Justin Robertson's Black Rabbit electro party is just as roadblocked. **Map p276 Q4**.

EGG

200 York Way, N7 9AP (7609 8364/www.egg london.net). King's Cross tube/rail then free shuttle bus from York Way. **Open** 10pm-6am Fri; 10pm Sat-2pm Sun. **Admission** £6-£15. **Credit** (bar) MC, V.

A gorgeous, three-floored party palace that's big enough to lose yourself in, yet still manages to have a cosy atmosphere. You get comfy red leather banquettes and waitress service in the loft; a middle floor with pole-dancing columns that seems to belong in a warehouse dance studio; and a ground floor that leads to the spacious, AstroTurf-clad garden. Wrap on some shades, pull up a lounger and do the 'after the after' party in style.

End ★

18 West Central Street, WC1A 1JJ (7419 9199/www.endclub.com). Holborn or Tottenham Court Road tube. **Open** 10pm-3am Mon; 10.30pm-3am Wed; 10pm-4am Thur; 10pm-5am Fri; 10pm-7am Sat; phone for details Sun. **Admission** £5-£16. **Credit** MC, V.

For review, *see p241.* **Map p272 L6**.

Fabric ★

77A Charterhouse Street, EC1M 3HN (7336 8898/www.fabriclondon.com). Farringdon tube/rail. **Open** 9.30pm-5am Fri; 10pm-7am Sat. **Admission** £13-£16. **Credit** (bar) MC, V.

In Fabric's very early days, one promoter suggested that the new venue would become a latter-day Haçienda. Nine years on, the prophecy has come true: you wouldn't be laughed at for saying that Fabric is currently the most important club in the world, and it needs no

1000
things to do in London

No.478
Shop for musical memorabilia at Dress Circle

A luvvies' paradise, Dress Circle is the London authority on musical theatre, with a rich stock of original Broadway and West End cast recordings accompanied by a vast selection of books, souvenir programmes, libretti and sheet music. There's also a collection of British and American musical scores performed in foreign languages, plus musical karaoke backing tracks for those who can't resist a Gilbert & Sullivan sing-along.

Dress Circle
57-59 Monmouth Street, WC2H 9DG,
7240 2227, www.dresscircle.com

For *hundreds* more *great* ideas...

introduction to music fans. Its three rooms still get superstar DJs and regularly introduce spanking new talent to an appreciative audience. **Map p274 O5**.

Herbal
10-14 Kingsland Road, E2 8DA (7613 4462/ www.herbaluk.com). Old Street or Liverpool Street tube/rail/55 bus. **Open** 9pm-2am Wed, Thur, Sun; 9pm-3am Fri, Sat. **Admission** free-£5 Wed, Thur; £5 (women) before 10.30pm, £10 after, Fri; £8 before 10.30pm, £10 after, Sat; £6 Sun (women free before 11.30pm). **Credit** MC, V.
There's a fine line between well worn and falling apart, and the last year or two have seen Herbal wobble somewhat. It really could do with a lick of paint or three. Some people walk into this small two-floor venue (the main area almost fits 300, the top floor barely 200) and walk straight back out, but other punters love it for its catholic mix of hip hop, house and mic-bothering nights. The terrace should – fingers crossed – reopen soon, once the management has sorted out some licensing difficulties. **Map p276 R3**.

Island [NEW]
Hungerford Lane, WC2N 6NG (7389 6622/ www.theisland-london.com). Charing Cross tube/rail. **Open** 10pm-6am Fri, Sat. **Admission** £10-£15. **Credit** AmEx, MC, V.
Fancy splashing your cash? Gorgeous to a fault – all bare brick walls, slick 1970s wallpaper and cream sofas – with a mezzanine to pose on, this new West End grown-ups' playground is just around the corner from iconic rave and gay venue Heaven. It's synchronicity at work, because the star DJs lining up to play Friday nights here include old school house talents Danny Rampling and John Digweed. **Map p273 L7**.

Jamm
261 Brixton Road, SW9 6LH (7274 5537/ www.brixtonjamm.org). Brixton tube/rail. **Open** 5pm-2am Mon-Thur; noon-6am Fri, Sat; noon-2am Sun. **Admission** £3-£8. **Credit** AmEx, DC, MC, V.
Battered but never bruised, Jamm's two rooms make the ideal venue for socially aware, multimedia nights like Rock Against Racism and punchy e-zine Urban 75's free Offline do. The smaller room is equipped with squishy sofas, plants and a friendly bar crew; the main space has a distinctly warehouse vibe (battered floors and steel ceiling girders) and a cracking sound system. This is one place well set up for live gigs.

KOKO
1A Camden High Street, NW1 7JE (7388 3222/www.koko.uk.com). Mornington Crescent tube. **Open** 9.30pm-4am Fri; 10pm-4am Sat; phone to check other times. **Admission** free-£15. **Credit** (bar) MC, V.
Famous for formerly being the Camden Palace, where music legends did legendary things, KOKO is opulent in an unashamedly old-fashioned way: high ceilings, claret and gold gloss paintwork, and plenty of Greek gods holding up columns. The place is all about highs and lows (it started life in 1900 as the Camden Theatre), and it's nearly impossible to avoid getting lost in the many stairwells as you try to drunkenly navigate from one tiered balcony to another. Punters here are a decidedly unpretentious bunch happy to indulge in Club NME's indie-focused Friday nights and the occasional Saturday night Guilty Pleasures cheese-fest courtesy of Sean Rowley. **Map p286 J1**.

Madame Jo Jo's
8-10 Brewer Street, W1S 0SP (7734 3040/ www.madamejojos.com). Leicester Square or Piccadilly Circus tube. **Open** 8pm-3am Tue, Thur; 10pm-3am Wed, Fri; 7pm-3am Sat; 9.30pm-2am Sun. **Admission** £5-£15. **Credit** (bar) AmEx, MC, V.
Virtually all those who sample this Soho stalwart love it. The sumptuous, slightly shabby red decor makes it stand out from the local crowd, and it spins several entertainment plates (cabaret, comedy and club). Saturday evening brings a riot of feathers and hen parties for Kitsch Cabaret, before the doors are thrown open for rockabilly and ska night Lost & Found. Other highlights include Keb Darge's Deep Funk, the last word in rare funk singles and a worthy survivor of the capital's 1980s rare groove scene. **Map p273 K6**.

Mass
St Matthew's Church, Brixton Hill, SW2 1JF (7738 7875/www.mass-club.com). Brixton tube/rail. **Open** 10pm-6am Fri, Sat; phone to check other times. **Admission** £6-£15. **Credit** MC, V.
Former prime minister John Major may have married Norma here, but in more recent times this space has become a bastion for genre-defying hedonism. DMZ is a fave for dubstep acolytes; the fourth Saturday of the month delivers grinding reggaeton, hip hop and salsa at Latin Mass. **Map p284 E2**.

Ministry of Sound

103 Gaunt Street, SE1 6DP (7740 8600/
www.ministryofsound.com). Elephant & Castle
tube/rail. **Open** 10.30pm-5am Fri; 11pm-7am
Sat. **Admission** £8-£15 Fri; £10-£15 Sat.
Credit (bar) MC, V.

With venues in Singapore and, er, on the Red
Sea, not to mention compilations released every
month of the year, the Ministry of Sound makes
no bones about being a mega-successful
clubbing brand. The four rooms of its London
base let promoters spend a pretty penny
booking up talent; the Gallery shifted its hard
house and trance nights here when Turnmills
closed; and other nights bring mainstream
urban and house sounds, and superstar DJs
earning silly money to play to an international
crowd. If you can spare £75 per person (you get
£60 in drinks), buy a VIP table for a night and
walk straight past the queues.
Map p282 O10.

93 Feet East

150 Brick Lane, E1 6QN (7247 3293/
www.93feeteast.com). Aldgate East tube/
Liverpool Street tube/rail. **Open** 5-11pm Mon-
Thur; 5pm-1am Fri, Sat; noon-10.30pm Sun.
Admission free-£8 after 8pm. **Credit** (bar)
MC, V.

There's plenty to be grateful for here, with a
great courtyard that wraps right around the
back, a large balcony terrace, a 'Pink' bar
crammed full of welcoming sofas, a loft, and a
main space that works well as a cinema, gig
venue or club. Ninety Free Fridays showcase up-
and-coming and established bands for free, and
the occasional indie music cum cabaret night
Jealous of the Daylight throws comedians,
bands and alt cabaret stars together on the last
Thursday of the month.
Map p278 S5.

Notting Hill Arts Club ★

21 Notting Hill Gate, W11 3JQ (7460 4459/
www.nottinghillartsclub.com). Notting Hill
Gate tube. **Open** 6pm-1am Mon; 6pm-2am
Tue-Fri; 4pm-2am Sat; 4pm-1am Sun.
Admission free-£8. **Credit** (bar) MC, V.

This is the kind of space that really shouldn't
work in posh Notting Hill, but, thankfully, does.
It's not fancy; in fact, it's quite battered around
the edges, and only accommodates a few
hundred people – if everyone gets up close and
personal, that is. But despite its diminutive
proportions, the club has some of the best far-
flung sounds in town. Seb Chew and Leo
Greenslade's YoYo, the crate-diggin' soul and
funk night at which Lily Allen caused mayhem

before she was famous, is held every Thursday;
Alan McGee Death Disco kicks Wednesdays
into submission with bands and indie DJs.
Map p279 B7.

Pacha

Terminus Place, SW1E 5NE (0845 371 4489/
www.pachalondon.com). Victoria tube/rail.
Open 10pm-5am Fri, Sat. **Admission** £15-
£20. **Credit** (bar) MC, V.

There's been talk of refurbishing this club by
the Victoria bus depot, but nothing looks likely
to happen until the new Pacha Terrace (a five-
floored members' club with roof terrace and live
music rooms) opens in King's Cross, perhaps at
the end of 2008. Until then, this two-roomed
place still pulls in the glitzy, the sleek and the
minted for glammed-up house nights.
Map p281 H10.

Pigalle Club

215-217 Piccadilly, W1J 9HN (reservations
0845 345 6053/enquiries 7644 1420/after
6pm 7734 8142/www.thepigalleclub.com).
Piccadilly Circus tube. **Open** 7pm-2am Mon-
Wed; 7pm-3am Thur-Sat; music from 8.30pm.
Food served 7-11.30pm Mon-Sat. **Admission**
£10 after 10pm Mon-Thur; £15 after 10.30pm
Fri, Sat. **Credit** AmEx, DC, MC, V.

This sleek, chic, basement supper club (part of
the Vince Power stable) is all about 1940s-style
glamour: low lighting, olive-green carpets,
antique fittings and diamond-shaped mirrors.
Tables for diners are clustered around the stage,
where jazz, jive and cabaret crooners serenade
an appreciative audience. The Modern European
food is pricey (£45 for three courses), but non-
diners are welcome; head for the bar and make
like you're Sinatra instead.
Map p273 J7.

Plan B ★

418 Brixton Road, SW9 7AY (7733 0926/
www.plan-brixton.co.uk). Brixton tube/rail.
Open 7pm-3am Thur; 9pm-5am Fri, Sat;
9pm-3am Sun. **Admission** £5 after 10pm
Thur; £6 after 11pm, £8 after midnight Fri;
£8 after 10pm, £10 after midnight Sat.
Credit (bar) AmEx, MC, V.

The ceiling is low, the venue is high spec and
there's even more space in which to breakdance
battle, thanks to B.Low, the self-contained
extension in the neighbouring basement. Nights
push the urban, hip hop and funky house
buttons: Friday's Fidgit has plenty of turntable
trickery; Thursday's Throwdown is all about
graffiti and dance battles.
Map p284 E1.

Madame Jo Jo's. See p247.

Plastic People

147-149 Curtain Road, EC2A 3QE (7739 6471/www.plasticpeople.co.uk). Liverpool Street or Old Street tube/rail/8, 55 bus. **Open** 10pm-2am Thur; 10pm-4am Fri, Sat; 8-11.30pm Sun. **Admission** £5-£10. **Credit** MC, V.
Dark basement? Check. A swung cat would brush its ears on all four walls? Check. A sound system that has had songs written about it? Check – and how! Forward has long called this tiny space home, and is now in residence every Saturday with its heavyweight dubstep and grime beats; CDR (second Thursday of the month) lets bedroom producers play their music-in-progress. **Map p276 R4.**

Punk ★

14 Soho Street, W1D 3DN (7734 4004/ www.fabbars.com). Tottenham Court Road tube. **Open** 5pm-2am Mon-Wed; 5pm-3am Thur, Fri; 9pm-3am Sat. **Admission** £3-£10. **Credit** (bar) MC, V.
When regulars include Kate Moss, Lily Allen and – when he's in town – Mark Ronson, it seems

there's little this basement space can do wrong. It accommodates 270 at a squeeze, and the bespoke Mapplethorpe-style flower prints and Rock Galpin furniture suit the mix of high-heeled girls and indie mash-ups from the Queens of Noize at their fab Smash 'n' Grab parties on Thursdays. **Map p272 K6.**

Scala

275 Pentonville Road, N1 9NL (7833 2022/ www.scala-london.co.uk). King's Cross tube/ rail. **Open** 10pm-6am Fri, Sat. **Admission** £6-£15. **Credit** (bar) MC, V.
This dual-purpose establishment manages to tick the right music boxes as a club and as a live venue, and the variety of nights and gigs means it's bound to appeal to everyone at some point. The layout and design are good, with a balcony and mezzanine-type levels providing great views of the stage and plenty of stairs to get lost in. Nights range from hedonistic dance like Smartie Partie and Kinky Malinki to salsa on a grand scale – this is where the Latin Collective throw their all-nighters.

seOne

41-43 St Thomas Street, SE1 3QX (7407 1617/www.seonelondon.com). London Bridge tube/rail. **Open** 10pm-6am Fri, Sat; 8pm-2am every other Wed. **Admission** £8-£30. **Credit** (advance bookings only) MC, V.

They're absolutely huge, often damp and may leave a strange mark on your jeans after a night out – but these arches host some great nights, along with some of the best loos in London (which goes a long way in our book). The promoters usually open up two arches and a chill out space, but those three rooms need a few thousand to fill them. When they're crammed, it's all 'back in the day' rave, with a cracking atmosphere and plenty of room for lasers. Clubs range from old-school happy hardcore to the Lucha Britannia's occasional Mexican wrestling extravaganzas. **Map p282 Q9.**

Soho Revue Bar

11 Walkers Court, W1F 0ED (7734 0377/ www.sohorevuebar.com). Piccadilly Circus tube. **Open** 8pm-3am Tue-Sun. **Food served** 8pm-1am Tue-Sun. **Admission** £3-£12. **Credit** AmEx, MC, V.

The Raymond Revue Bar was a 1960s cabaret club, notorious for its striptease shows; it was, if we were to believe a towering sign at the front, 'The World Centre of Erotic Entertainment'. Fast forward to today, and girls are still taking their clothes off, but in the much more middle-class guise of burlesque, at variety nights like Sunday's All That Jazz, or the Hurly Girly Show on the first Saturday of the month. The main room has tiered seating for cabaret-watching, and upstairs is a smaller piano bar. London's drag queen du jour Jodie Harsh hosts the Friday night Circus, and Trannyshack encourages a mostly gay crowd to 'release the woman within' every Wednesday. Go with it – even if you don't, the drag queens most certainly will. **Map p273 K6.**

333

333 Old Street, EC1V 9LE (7739 5949/ www.333mother.com). Old Street tube/rail. **Open** *Bar* 8pm-2.30am daily. *Club* 10pm-2.30am Fri; 10pm-5am Sat. **Admission** £5-£10. **Credit** (bar) MC, V.

A haven for the area's cutting-edge crowd for more than ten years, this three-floored, no-frills party space has found its feet again thanks to quality house nights like Reverb, strange gay mash-ups at the midweek Dirty Fairy, and the filthy minimal Zombies Ate My Brain. **Map p276 R4.**

12 Acklam Road

12 Acklam Road, W10 5QZ (8960 9331/ www.12acklamroadclub.net). Ladbroke Grove or Westbourne Park tube. **Open** 9pm-late Thur-Sat; phone to check times Sun. **Admission** free-£10. **Credit** (bar) MC, V.

They've ditched the 'Neighbourhood' tag – this W10 club is now known merely by the first line of its address – and we're waiting to see what the other changes will be. Thankfully, the brushed concrete walls and wraparound steel mezzanine balcony from which to wave at the dancefloor below haven't been pulled out, and long-running nights such as Rodigan's Reggae Lounge and Book Slam still have a home here.

Unit 7 NEW

Cable Studios, 566 Cable Street, E1W 3HB (www.unitseven.co.uk). Limehouse rail/DLR. **Open** times vary. **Admission** varies. **No credit cards.**

Part of the Cable Street Studios (an enormous warehouse full of small artists' and music studios and creative start-ups, a moment away from the Rotherhithe Tunnel), Unit 7 ran on temporary licences for over a year before the local council saw fit to let it open properly. The promoters are still in the middle of making the transition from occasional warehouse parties to regular club nights, so you're as likely to see a masked ball as a thumping great electro rave in the large warehouse unit.

Victory NEW

55 New Oxford Street, WC1A 1BS (7240 0700/www.clubvictory.com). Tottenham Court Road tube. **Open** 8pm-4am Fri; 9pm-4am Sat. **Admission** £15-£20. **Credit** MC, V.

The people who brought you the now defunct Hedges & Butler have magicked this former underground New Oxford Street car park into a Victorian high street film set. Friday nights see the ultra-decadent Chopin Scores; there's a dress-up room for post-work transformations, a library sitting room, street performers, burlesque girls and lashings of fun. We're looking forward to the fashion market for new designers during the day. **Map p272 L5.**

Volupté ★

7-9 Norwich Street, EC4A 1EJ (7831 1622/ www.volupte-lounge.com). Chancery Lane tube. **Open** 11.30am-1am Tue, Wed; 11.30am-3am Thur, Fri; 2.30pm-3am Sat. **Food served** 11.30am-4pm, 6-10pm Tue-Fri; 7-10.30pm Sat. **Admission** *shows* £10-£55. **Credit** MC, V. For review, *see p244.* **Map p275 N5.**

Clubs

Last Orders

Below is a list of bars and pubs that are open a little (or even a lot) later than usual. We haven't reviewed all of them but, where we have, we've included a page number for easy reference. For more late-night options, you'll find a list of clubs on p239.

Central

Belgravia
Blue Bar
p17. 1am Mon-Sat.
Horse & Groom
*7 Groom Place, SW1X
7BA, 7235 6980.* 12.30am
Mon-Fri.
Library
p17. 1am Mon-Sat.
Bloomsbury
AKA
p17. 5am 1st Tue; check
website for opening Wed; 3am
Thur; 4am Fri; 5am Sat, Sun.
All Star Lanes
p18. Midnight Thur; 2am Fri,
Sat.
Bloomsbury Bowling Lanes
p18. 2am Mon-Wed; 3am
Thur-Sat; midnight Sun.
Lamb
p18. Midnight Mon-Sat.
Museum Tavern
p18. Midnight Fri, Sat.
mybar
p21. Midnight Mon-Thur,
Sun; 1am Fri, Sat.
101 Bar
*101 New Oxford Street 7379
3112.* 3am Mon-Thur; 4am
Fri-Sun.
Perseverance
p21. Midnight Fri.
Clerkenwell & Farringdon
Al's Café Bar
p23. Midnight Mon; 2am
Tue-Sat.
Betsey Trotwood
p23. 1am Fri, Sat.
Café Kick
p24. Midnight Fri, Sat.
Cellar Gascon
p24. Midnight Mon-Sat two
Sats a month; call to check.
Charterhouse
p24. Midnight Wed, Sun on
request; 2am Thur; 4am Fri,
Sat.
Dollar
p25. 1am daily.
Easton
p26. 1am Fri, Sat.
Fluid
p26. Midnight Mon-Wed;
2am Thur; 4am Fri, Sat.
Green
p27. Midnight Thur-Sat.
Hat & Feathers
p28. 1am Mon-Sat.
Match
p28. Midnight Mon-Wed;
1am Thur, Fri; 1am Sat.
Medcalf
p28. 12.30am Fri.
Old China Hand
p30. 2am Mon-Sat.
Queen Boadicea
*292-294 St John Street, EC1
7278 9990.* Midnight Mon-

Thur; 2am Fri, Sat.
Slaughtered Lamb
p30. 1am Fri, Sat.
Covent Garden
Café des Amis
p34. 1am Mon-Sat.
Detroit
p35. Midnight Mon-Sat.
Freud
p35. 1am Thur, Sat; 2am Fri.
Langley
p35. 1am Mon-Sat.
Maple Leaf
p36. Midnight Fri, Sat.
Euston
Positively 4th Street
p37. 1am Fri, Sat.
Fitzrovia
Annex 3
p37. Midnight Mon-Sat.
Bourne & Hollingsworth
p39. Midnight Mon-Thur;
12.30am Fri, Sat.
Carpenter's Arms
p39. Midnight Fri.
Eagle Bar Diner
p41. 1am Thur, Fri; 1am Sat.
Hakkasan
p42. 12.30am Mon-Wed;
1.30am Thur-Sat; midnight
Sun.
Long Bar
p42. 2am Mon-Wed; 3am
Fri, Sat.
Market Place
p44. Midnight Mon-Wed;
1am Thur-Sat.
Newman Arms
p44. Midnight Mon-Fri.
Nordic
p44. Midnight Fri, Sat.
Nueva Costa Dorada
p44. 3am Tue-Sat.
Shochu Lounge
p45. Midnight daily.
Social
p45. Midnight Mon-Wed;
1am Thur-Sat; midnight Sun
occasionally.
King's Cross
Big Chill House
p47. Midnight Mon-Thur,
Sun; 3am Fri, Sat.
King Charles I
p48. 1am Fri
06 St Chad's Place
p48. 1am Thur, Fri.
Ruby Lounge
p48. Midnight Thur; 2am Fri,
Sat.
Knightsbridge
Mandarin Bar
p49. 1.30am Mon-Sat.
Townhouse
p49. Midnight Mon-Sat.
Leicester Square
De Hems
p51. Midnight Mon-Sat.
International
p51. 2am Mon-Sat.

Salisbury
p52. Midnight Fri, Sat.
Marylebone
Artesian
p53. 1.30am daily.
Moose
*31 Duke Street, W1U 1LG,
7224 3452.* 4pm-2am Mon-
Thur; 3am Fri, Sat.
Occo Bar & Kitchen
p53. Midnight daily.
Salt Whisky Bar
& Dining Room
p54. 1am Mon-Sat;
12.30am Sun.
Windsor Castle
p55. Midnight Fri, Sat.
Mayfair
Absolut IceBar/Below Zero
p57. Midnight Mon-Wed;
12.30am Thur; 1am Fri, Sat.
Admission £12-£15.
Claridge's Bar
p57. 1am Mon-Sat; midnight
Sun.
Donovan Bar
p57. 1am Mon-Sat; midnight
Sun.
Galvin at Windows
p57. 1am Mon-Wed; 3am
Thur-Sat.
Mahiki
p58. 3.30am Mon-3.30am
Sat. Admission £10 after
9.30pm Mon, Tue; £15 after
9.30pm Wed-Sat.
Mô Tea Room
p58. Midnight daily.
Only Running Footman
p58. Midnight daily.
Polo Bar
p58. Midnight daily.
Trader Vic's
p60. 1am Mon-Thur; 3am
Fri; 3am Sat.
Piccadilly
Brumus Bar
p60. Midnight daily.
Electric Bird Cage
p61. 4am Mon-Sat.
Glass
p61. 1am Fri, Sat.
Rivoli at the Ritz
p61. 1am Mon-Sat.
St James
Aura
*48-49 St James's Sreet,
SW1A 1JT, 7499 6655.*
3.30am Tue-Sat; 1.30am
Sun.
Soho
Ain't Nothin' But...
The Blues Bar
p65. 1am Mon-Wed; 2am
Thur; 3am Fri, Sat; midnight
Sun.
Akbar
p65. 1am Mon-Sat.
Blue Posts
p66. Midnight Fri, Sat.

Café Bohème
*13 Old Compton Street,
W1D 5JQ, 7734 0623.* 3am
Mon-Sat; midnight Sun.
Candy Bar
p66. 2am Fri, Sat.
Edge
p68. 1am Mon-Sat.
Floridita
p69. 2am Mon-Wed; 3am
Thur-Sat.
Freedom
p69. 3am Mon-Sat.
Green Carnation
p70. 2.30am Mon-Sat;
midnight Sun.
Kettners
p70. Midnight Mon-Wed;
1am Thur-Sat.
LAB
p70. Midnight Mon-Sat.
Lucky Voice
p70. 1am Mon-Sat.
Milk & Honey
p71. 3am Mon-Sat
members.
Phoenix Artist Club
p71. 3am Mon-Sat
members.
Player
p71. Midnight Mon-Wed;
1am Thur-Sat.
Polka
p72. Midnight daily.
Two Floors
p74. Midnight Fri, Sat.
South Kensington
Admiral Codrington
p74. Midnight Mon-Thur;
1am Fri, Sat.
Collection
p75. Midnight daily.
Drayton Arms
p75. Midnight daily.
190 Queensgate
p77. 1am Mon-Wed, Sun;
2am Thur-Sat.
Strand
Coal Hole
*91 Strand, WC2R 0DW,
7379 9883.* Midnight Thur-
Sat.
Trafalgar Square
Albannach
p78. 1am Mon-Sat.
ICA Bar
p78. 1am Tue-Sat.
Victoria
Boisdale
p80. 1am Mon-Sat.
Zander Bar
p82. 1am Thur-Sat.

City

Fleet Street & Blackfriars
Mustard Bar & Lounge
p87. Midnight Thur, Fri.
Liverpool Street
George
p88. Midnight Thur, Fri

Golden Heart
p88. Midnight Mon-Sat.
Gramaphone
p89. Midnight Mon-Thur;
3.30am Fri, Sat.
Hawksmoor
p89. 1am Mon-Sat.
Ten Bells
p91. Midnight Mon-Thur,
Sun; 1am Fri, Sat.
1 Lombard Street
p92. Midnight Mon-Fri.

East

Bethnal Green
Approach Tavern
p174. Midnight Fri, Sat.
Bistrotheque Napoleon Bar
p174. Midnight Mon-Sat.
Royal Oak
p175. Midnight Fri, Sat.
Brick Lane
Big Chill Bar
p175. Midnight Mon-Thur,
Sun; 1am Fri, Sat.
Café 1001
p175. Midnight daily.
Carpenter's Arms
p177. 12.30am Fri, Sat.
Exit
p177. 1am Tue-Thur; 2am
Fri-Sun.
Green & Red
p177. Midnight Mon-Thur;
1am Fri, Sat.
Indo
p177. 1am Mon-Thur, Sun;
3am Fri, Sat.
Redchurch
p178. 1am Mon-Thur, Sun;
Sat.
Rhythm Factory
p178. Midnight Mon-Fri; 2am
Sat.
Vibe Bar
p178. 11.30pm Mon-Thur,
Sun; 1am Fri, Sat.
Clapton
Elderfield
p179. Midnight Thur-Sat;
11pm Sun.
Princess of Wales
p179. Midnight Mon-Sat.
Docklands
Ferry House
p181. Midnight Mon-Sat.
Gun
p181. Midnight Mon-Sat.
Via
Port East Building, West
India Quay, E14 4QT, 7515
8549. Midnight Thur-Sat.
Mile End
Morgan Arms
p182. Midnight Fri, Sat.
Palm Tree
p182. Midnight Mon-Thur;
2am Fri, Sat; 1am Sun last
admission 10.45pm.
Shoreditch
Anda de Bridge
p182. Midnight Mon-Sat;
10-11.30pm Sun.
Bar Kick
p182. Midnight Thur-Sat.
Beach Blanket Babylon
p183. Midnight Mon-Thur,
Sun; 1am Fri, Sat.
Cantaloupe
p184. Midnight Wed-Sat.
Catch
p184. Midnight Tue, Wed;
2am Thur-Sat; 1am Sun.

**Charlie Wright's
International Bar**
p184. 1am Mon-Wed; 4am
Thur-Sat; 2am Sun.
dreambagsjaguarshoes
p185. 1am Tue-Sat;
12.30am Sun.
Drunken Monkey
p185. Midnight Mon-Sat.
East Room
p186. 1am Mon-Wed; 3am
Thur-Sat.
Electricity Showrooms
p187. Midnight Mon-Thur;
1am Fri-Sun.
Favela Chic
p187. 1am Tue-Thur, Sun;
2am Fri, Sat.
Fox
p188. Midnight Sat.
George & Dragon
p188. Midnight daily.
Great Eastern
p188. Ground-floor bar
midnight Mon-Sat. Below 54
bar 1am Fri, Sat.
Hoxton Square Bar & Kitchen
p188. 1am Mon-Thur,
midnight Sun; 2am Fri, Sat.
Light Bar & Restaurant
p189. Midnight Mon-Wed;
2am Thur-Sat.
Loungelover
p189. Midnight Mon-Thur,
Sun; 1am Fri, Sat.
Mother Bar
p190. 3am daily.
Prague
p190. Midnight daily.
Reliance
p191. 2am Fri, Sat.
Sosho
p191. Midnight Tue; 1am
Wed, Thur; 3am Fri; 4am
Sat; 6am Sun.
Three Blind Mice
p191. Midnight Fri, Sat.
T Bar
56 Shoreditch High Street,
E1 6JJ, 7729 2973/
www.tbarlondon.com.
Midnight Mon-Wed, Sun;
1am Thur; 2am Fri, Sat.
Wenlock Arms
p191. Midnight Mon-Wed,
Sun; 1am Thur-Sat.
William IV
p194. Midnight Thur-Sat.
Stratford
King Edward VII
p194. Midnight Thur-Sat.
11.30pm Sun.
Wapping
Prospect of Whitby
p194. Midnight Thur-Sat.
Town of Ramsgate
p194. Midnight Mon-Sat.

North East

Hackney
Cat & Mutton
p196. Midnight Fri, Sat.
Dalston Jazz Bar
p196. 3am Mon-Thur; 5am
Fri, Sat; 2am Sun.
Dolphin
165 Mare Street, E8 3RH,
8985 3727. 2am Mon-Thur,
Sun; 4am Fri, Sat.
Dove Kitchen & Freehouse
p196. Midnight Fri, Sat.
Prince George
p197. Midnight Mon-Thur;
1am Fri, Sat.

Scolt Head
p199. Midnight Mon-Sat.
Spurstowe
p199. Midnight Fri, Sat.
Leyton
Birkbeck Tavern
p199. Midnight Fri, Sat.
Leytonstone
Sheepwalk
692 High Road Leytonstone,
E11 3AA, 8556 1131.
Midnight Mon-Thur, Sun;
2am Fri, Sat.
Stoke Newington
Fox Reformed
p200. Midnight daily.
Londesborough
p201. Midnight Fri, Sat.
Prince
p201. Midnight Fri, Sat.
Rose & Crown
199 Stoke Newington
Church Street, N16 9ES,
7254 7497. Midnight daily.
Shakespeare
p202. Midnight Mon-Thur;
1am Fri, Sat.
Three Crowns
175 Stoke Newington High
Street, N16 0LH, 7241
5511. 1am Fri, Sat.
Walthamstow
Flower Pot
128 Wood Street, E17 3HX,
8520 3600. 12.30am Thur-
Sat.
Wanstead
George
p202. Midnight Mon-Thur,
Sun; 12.30am Fri, Sat.
Nightingale
p202. Midnight daily.

North

Archway
Landseer
p204. Midnight Wed-Sat.
North Nineteen
p204. Midnight Mon-Thur,
Sun; 1am Fri, Sat.
Camden Town & Chalk Farm
Bar Vinyl
6 Inverness Street, NW1
7HJ, 7482 5545/www.bar
vinyl.com. Midnight Mon-
Thur, Sun; 1am Sat.
Bartok
p205. 3am Mon-Fri; 4am
Sat, Sun.
Bullet
147 Kentish Town Road,
NW1 8PB, 7485 6040/
www.bulletbar.co.uk.
Midnight Mon-Wed, Sun;
1am Thur; 2am Fri, Sat.
Camden Arms
p207. Midnight Fri, Sat.
Crown & Goose
p207. 1am Mon-Thur, Sun;
2am Fri, Sat.
Cuban
Unit 23, Stables Market,
Chalk Farm Road, NW1
8AH, 7424 0692/www.the
cuban.co.uk. 1am Mon-Thur;
2am Fri, Sat; midnight Sun.
Dublin Castle
p207. 1am Mon-Thur; 2am
Fri-Sun.
Enterprise
2 Haverstock Hill, NW3 2BL,
7485 2659. 1am Fri, Sat.
Fifty-Five
p207. 12.30am daily.

Gilgamesh
p207. 2.30am daily.
Grand Union
102-104 Camden Road,
NW1 9EA, 7485 4530.
1.30am Fri, Sat.
Lock Tavern
p209. Midnight Mon-Thur;
1am Fri, Sat.
Lockside Lounge
p207. Midnight Mon-Thur,
Sun; 1am Fri, Sat.
Lord Stanley
p207. Midnight Fri, Sat.
Monkey Chews
p207. 1am Fri, Sat.
Quinn's
p210. Midnight Mon-Wed,
Sun; 2am Thur-Sat.
Crouch End
Banners
p210. Midnight Fri, Sat.
Harringay Arms
p210. 1am Mon-Sat;
midnight Sun.
Queen's
p211. Midnight Mon-Sat;
midnight Sun.
East Finchley
Bald-Faced Stag
p211. Midnight Thur;
12.30am Fri, Sat.
Harringay
Salisbury Hotel
p211. Midnight Mon-Wed;
1am Thur; 2am Fri; 2am Sat.
Highgate
Boogaloo
p211. Midnight Mon-Wed,
Sun; 1am Thur; 2am Fri;
2am Sat.
Red Lion & Sun
p212. Midnight Mon-Wed;
2am Thur-Sat; 1am Sun.
Hornsey
Three Compasses
p213. Midnight Fri, Sat.
Viva Viva
p213. 2am Mon-Fri; 2am
Sat, Sun.
Islington
Angelic
p215. Midnight Mon-Thur,
Sun; 1am Fri, Sat.
Barrio North
p215. Midnight Mon-Thur,
Sun; 2am Fri, Sat.
Camden Head
2 Camden Walk, N1 8DY,
7359 0851. Midnight Wed,
Thur; 1am Fri, Sat.
Duchess of Kent
441 Liverpool Road, N7
8PR, 7609 7104. Midnight
Fri, Sat.
Hen & Chickens Theatre Bar
p218. Midnight Mon-Wed,
Sun; 1am Thur; 1.30am Fri,
Sat.
House
63-69 Canonbury Road, N1
2DG, 7704 7410/www.the
meredithgroup.co.uk.
1.30am Thur-Sat.
Island Queen
p218. Midnight Thur-Sat.
Keston Lodge
p218. Midnight Mon-Wed;
1am Thur; 2am Fri, Sat.
King's Head
115 Upper Street, N1 1QN,
7226 0364. 1am Mon-Thur,
Sun; 2am Fri, Sat.

Medicine Bar
p218. Midnight Mon, Tue,
Sun; 1am Wed, Thur; 2am
Fri; 3am Sat.
Narrow Boat
*119 St Peters Street, N1
8PZ, 7288 0572*. Midnight
Mon-Sun.
Northgate
p220. Midnight Fri, Sat.
Old Queen's Head
p220. Midnight Mon-Wed,
Sun; 1am Thur; 2am Fri, Sat.
Old Red Lion
p220. Midnight Mon-Thur,
Sun; 1am Fri, Sat.
Rosemary Branch
p220. Midnight Mon-Thur;
1am Fri, Sat.
Salmon & Compass
*58 Penton Street, N1 9PZ,
7837 3891/www.salmon
andcompass.com*. 2am Mon-
Thur; 4am Fri, Sat; midnight
Sun.
25 Canonbury Lane
p221. Midnight Mon-Thur;
1am Fri; 1am Sat; 12.30am
Sun.
Kentish Town
Abbey Tavern
*124 Kentish Town Road,
NW1 9QB, 7267 9449/
www.abbey-tavern.com*.
Midnight Mon-Wed, Sun;
1am Thur-Sat.
Oxford
p221. Midnight Fri, Sat.
Vine
p222. Midnight Thur-Sat.
Muswell Hill
Victoria Stakes
p222. Midnight Thur-Sat.
Stroud Green
Faltering Fullback
p224. Midnight Fri, Sat.
Noble
p224. Midnight Fri-Sun.
Tufnell Park
Bar Lorca
p224. Midnight Mon-Thur,
Sun; 1am Fri, Sat.
Bull & Last
*168 Highgate Road, NW5
1QS, 7267 3641*. Midnight
Fri, Sat.
Star
p225. 12.30am Fri, Sat.

North West

Belsize Park
Hill
p228. Midnight Thur-Sat.
Sir Richard Steele
p228. Midnight Mon-Sat.
Washington
*50 England's Lane, NW3
4UE, 7722 8842*. Midnight
Fri, Sat.
Hampstead
Flask
p229. Midnight Fri-Sun.
King William IV
*77 Hampstead High Street,
NW3 1RE, 7435 5747*.
Midnight Fri-Sun.
Roebuck
p229. Midnight Fri, Sat.
Kensal Green
Greyhound
p232. Midnight Fri, Sat.
**Paradise by Way
of Kensal Green**
p232. Midnight Mon-Wed;
1am Thur; 2am Fri, Sat.

Kilburn
Black Lion
p232. Midnight Mon-Thur;
1am Fri, Sat.
Kilburn Pub & Kitchen
p232. Midnight Thur, Sun;
2am Fri, Sat.
North London Tavern
p234. Midnight Thur; 1am
Fri, Sat.
Salusbury
p234. Midnight Fri, Sat.

South

Balham
Balham Bowls Club
p136. Midnight Fri, Sat.
Bedford
p136. Midnight Mon-Thur,
Sun; 2am Fri, Sat.
Exhibit
*12 Balham Station Road,
SW12 9SG, 8772 6556/
www.theexhibit.co.uk*.
Midnight Mon-Thur, Sun;
2am Fri, Sat.
Grove
p137. Midnight Mon-Sat.
Harrison's
p136. Midnight daily.
Battersea
Alchemist
p137. Midnight Mon-Thur,
Sun; 2am Fri, Sat.
Le Bouchon Bordelais
p137. Midnight Mon-Sat.
Dusk
p137. 12.30am Tue, Wed;
1.30am Thur; 2am Fri, Sat.
Freemasons
p138. Midnight Fri, Sat.
Frieda B
p138. Midnight Mon-Thur,
Sun; 2am Fri, Sat.
Holy Drinker
p138. Midnight Thur-Sat.
Iniquity
p138. Midnight Thur-Sat.
Latchmere
*503 Battersea Park Road,
SW11 3BW, 7223 3549*.
Midnight Thur-Sat.
Lost Society
p141. 1am Tue-Thur, Sun;
2am Fri, Sat.
Microbar
p141. Midnight daily.
Woodman
p141. Midnight Fri, Sat.
Brixton
Commercial
*210-212 Railton Road, SE24
0JT, 7501 9051*. Midnight
daily.
Dogstar
p142. 2am Mon-Thur, Sun;
4am Fri, Sat.
Escape Bar & Art
p143. Midnight Mon-Wed,
Sun; 1am Thur; 4am Fri, Sat.
Far Side
p143. 3am Fri, Sat.
Hive
p143. Midnight Mon-Wed;
2am Thur; 3am Fri, Sat.
Lounge
p143. Midnight Thur-Sat.
Mango Landin'
p143. Midnight Mon-Thur;
3am Fri, Sat.
Prince
p144. Midnight Mon-Thur,
Sun; 4am Fri, Sat.
Trinity Arms
p144. Midnight Fri-Sat.

White Horse
p144. Midnight Mon-Thur,
Sun; 3am Fri, Sat.
Windmill
p144. Midnight Mon-Thur;
1am Fri, Sat.
Clapham
Bar Local
p145. Midnight Mon-Wed,
Sun; 1am Thur-Sat.
Bread & Roses
p145. Midnight Fri, Sat.
Clapham North
p145. Midnight Mon-Wed,
Sun; 2am Thur-Sat.
Falcon
p145. Midnight Tue-Thur;
1am Fri, Sat.
Green and Blue
p146. Midnight Mon-Thur;
1am Fri-Sun.
Grey Goose
p146. Midnight Mon-Thur,
SUN; 1am Fri, Sat.
Landor
p146. Midnight Fri, Sat.
Loft
p146. Midnight Mon-Thur,
Sun; 1.30am Fri, Sat.
Prince of Wales
p147. Midnight Thur; 1am
Fri, Sat.
Stonhouse
p147. Midnight daily.
Tim Bobbin
p147. Midnight Thur-Sat.
White House
p147. 2am Wed, Sun; 3am
Thur; 4am Fri, Sat.
Windmill on the Common
p148. Midnight Mon-Sat.
Kennington
Dog House
p148. Midnight Mon-Thur,
Sun; 2am Fri, Sat.
White Hart
p148. Midnight Thur; 1am
Fri, Sat.
Stockwell
Bar Estrela
p149. Midnight Mon-Sat.
Canton Arms
p149. Midnight Thur-Sat.
Royal Albert
p150. Midnight Sat
Tooting
Selkirk
*60 Selkirk Road, SW17 0ES,
8672 6235/www.theselkirk.
co.uk*. Midnight Mon-Thur,
Sun; 2am Fri, Sat.
Tooting Tram & Social
p150. Midnight Tue-Thur,
Sun; 2am Fri, Sat.
Trafalgar Arms
*148 Tooting High Street,
SW17 0RT, 8767 6059*.
Midnight Mon-Thur, Sun;
1am Fri, Sat.
Vauxhall
Fentiman Arms
p150. Midnight Fri, Sat.
Riverside
*5 St George's Wharf, SW8
2LE, 7735 8129/www.river
sidelondon.com*. Midnight
daily.
Royal Vauxhall Tavern
p151. 2am Sat; midnight
Sun.
Waterloo
Skylon
p154. Midnight daily.
Three Stags
p154. Midnight daily.
Waterloo Brasserie
p154. 3am daily.

White Hart
p154. Midnight Tue-Sat.

South East

Bermondsey
Hartley
*64 Tower Bridge Road,
SE1 4TR, 7394 7023*.
Midnight Mon-Thur; 2am
Fri, Sat.
Hide Bar
p156. Midnight Tue; 1am
Wed, Thur; 2am Fri, Sat.
Village East
p157. 1.30am Fri, Sat.
Blackheath
Hare & Billet
p157. Midnight Fri, Sat.
Railway
p157. Midnight Thur-Sat.
Zerodegrees
p158. Midnight Mon-Sat;
11.30pm Sun.
Camberwell
Bear
p158. Midnight Fri.
Castle
*65 Camberwell Church
Street, SE5 8TR, 7277
2601/www.the-castle.co.uk*.
Midnight Mon-Thur, Sun;
3.30am Fri, Sat.
Dark Horse
p158. Midnight Wed, Thur;
1am Fri, Sat.
Funky Munky
*25 Camberwell Church
Street, SE5 8TR, 7277
1806*. Midnight Mon-Wed,
Sun; 2am Thur; 3.30am Fri,
Sat.
Hermit's Cave
p159. Midnight Mon-Wed,
Sun; 2am Thur-Sat.
Deptford
Bar Sonic
p159. 1am Mon-Thur; 2am
Fri, Sat; midnight Sun.
Royal Albert
p160. Midnight Mon-Thur,
Sun; 1am Fri, Sat.
Dulwich
Crown & Greyhound
p160. Midnight Thur-Sat.
East Dulwich
Clock House
*196A Peckham Rye, SE22
9QA, 8693 2901*. Midnight
daily.
East Dulwich Tavern
*1 Lordship Lane, SE22
8EW, 8693 1316*. Midnight
Mon-Thur, Sun; 1am Fri, Sat.
Franklins
p161. Midnight Thur-Sat.
Herne Tavern
p161. 1am Fri, Sat.
Inside 72
p161. Midnight daily.
Liquorish
*123 Lordship Lane,
SE22 8HU, 8693 7744/
www.liquorish.com*. Midnight
Mon-Thur; 1am Fri, Sat.
Palmerston
p162. Midnight Fri, Sat.
Forest Hill
Dartmouth Arms
p162. Midnight Mon-Thur;
1am Fri, Sat.
Gipsy Hill
Mansion
p162. Midnight Fri, Sat.
Numidie
p162. Midnight Tue-Sun.

Where to go for

Index

Index

Index

A-Z Index

a

**Absolut IceBar/
Below Zero　p57**
29-33 Heddon Street, W1B
4BN (7287 9192/www.below
zerolondon.com).

Admiral Codrington　p74
17 Mossop Street, SW3 2LY
(7581 0005/www.theadmiral
codrington.co.uk).

Admiral Duncan　p63
54 Old Compton Street, W1V
5PA (7437 5300).

**Ain't Nothin' But…
The Blues Bar　p65**
20 Kingly Street, W1B 5PZ
(7287 0514/www.aintnothin
but.co.uk).

AKA　p17
18 West Central Street, WC1A
1JJ (7836 0110/www.aka
london.com).

Akbar　p65
77 Dean Street, W1D 3SH
(7437 2525/www.red
fort.co.uk/akbar).

Albannach　p78
66 Trafalgar Square,
WC2N 5DS (7930 0066/
www.albannach.co.uk).

Albert　p80
52 Victoria Street, SW1H
0NP (7222 5577).

Albertine　p114
1 Wood Lane, W12 7DP
(8743 9593).

Albion　p215
10 Thornhill Road, N1 1HW
(7607 7450/www.the-
albion.co.uk).

Alchemist　p137
225 St John's Hill, SW11 1TH
(7326 7456/www.alchemist
bar.co.uk).

Alexandra　p132
33 Wimbledon Hill Road,
SW19 7NE (8947 7691).

All Star Lanes　p18
Victoria House, Bloomsbury
Place, WC1B 4DA (7025 2676/
www.allstarlanes.co.uk).

Alma　p199
59 Newington Green Road,
N1 4QU (7359 4536/
www.the-alma.co.uk).

Alma　p130
499 Old York Road, SW18 1TF
(8870 2537/www.thealma.
co.uk).

Alphabet　p65
61-63 Beak Street, W1F 9SS
(7439 2190/www.alphabet
bar.com).

Al's Café Bar　p23
11-13 Exmouth Market, EC1R
4QD (7837 4821).

Amuse Bouche　p127
51 Parsons Green Lane,
SW6 4JA (7371 8517/
www.abcb.co.uk).

Anchor & Hope　p150
36 The Cut, SE1 8LP (7928
9898).

Anchor & Hope　p179
15 High Hill Ferry, E5 9HG
(8806 1730).

Anda de Bridge　p182
42-44 Kingsland Road, E2
8DA (7739 3863/www.anda
debridge.com).

Angelic　p215
57 Liverpool Road, N1 0RJ
(7278 8433/www.the
angelic.co.uk).

Anglesea Arms　p75
15 Selwood Terrace, SW7
3QG (7373 7960/www.capital
pubcompany.com).

Anglesea Arms　p115
35 Wingate Road, W6 0UR
(8749 1291).

Annex 3　p37
6 Little Portland Street, W1W
7JE (7631 0700/www.annex
3.co.uk).

Apple Tree　p23
45 Mount Pleasant, WC1X
0AE (7837 2365).

Approach Tavern　p174
47 Approach Road, E2 9LY
(8980 2321).

Aquarium　p240
256-260 Old Street, EC1V
9DD (7251 6136/www.club
aquarium.co.uk).

Aragon House　p127
247 New King's Road, SW6
4XG (7731 7313/www.aragon
house.net).

Argyll Arms　p65
18 Argyll Street, W1F 7TP
(7734 6117).

Artesian　p53
Langham Hotel, 1C Portland
Place, W1B 1JA (7636 1000/
www.artesian-bar.co.uk).

Ashburnham Arms　p163
25 Ashburnham Grove, SE10
8UH (8692 2007).

Audley　p57
41-43 Mount Street, W1K 2RX
(7499 1843).

Auld Shillelagh　p200
105 Stoke Newington Church
Street, N16 0UD (7249 5951).

b

Babalou　p240
The Crypt, St Matthew's
Church, Brixton Hill, SW2
1JF (7738 3366/
www.babalou.net).

Bald-Faced Stag　p211
69 High Road, N2 8AB (8442
1201/www.realpubs.co.uk).

Balham Bowls Club　p136
7-9 Ramsden Road, SW12
8QX (8673 4700/www.antic-
ltd.com).

Baltic　p150
74 Blackfriars Road, SE1 8HA
(7928 1111/www.baltic
restaurant.co.uk).

Banners　p210
21 Park Road, N8 8TE (8348
2930).

Bar Bourse　p91
67 Queen Street, EC4R
1EE (7248 2200/2211/
www.barbourse.co.uk).

Bardens Boudoir　p240
38-44 Stoke Newington Road,

N16 7XJ (7249 9557/
www.bardensbar.co.uk).

Bar du Musee　p163
17 Nelson Road, SE10 9JB
(8858 4710/www.bardu
musee.com).

Bar Estrela　p148
111-115 South Lambeth
Road, SW8 1UZ (7793 1051).

Barfly　p215
49 Chalk Farm Road, NW1
8AN (7424 0800/www.barfly
club.com).

Bar Kick　p182
127 Shoreditch High Street,
E1 6JE (7739 8700/www.cafe
kick.co.uk).

Bar Local　p144
4 Clapham Common
Southside, SW4 7AA (7622
9406/www.barlocal.co.uk).

Bar Lorca　p224
156-158 Fortess Road, NW5
2HP (7485 1314).

Bar Polski　p45
11 Little Turnstile, WC1V 7DX
(7831 9679).

Bar Rumba　p240
36 Shaftesbury Avenue, W1V
7DD (7287 6933/www.bar
rumba.co.uk).

Barrio North　p215
45 Essex Road, N1 2SF (7688
2882/www.barrionorth.com).

Bar Sonic　p159
1 Deptford Broadway, SE8 4PA
(8691 5289).

Bar Story　p171
213 Blenheim Grove, SE15
4QL (7635 6643/www.bar
story.co.uk).

Bartok　p205
78-79 Chalk Farm Road, NW1
8AR (7916 0595/www.bartok
club.co.uk).

bbar　p80
43 Buckingham Palace Road,
SW1W 0PP (7958 7000/
www.bbarlondon.com).

Beach Blanket Babylon　p183
19-23 Bethnal Green Road, E1
6LA (7749 3540/www.beach
blanket.co.uk).

Bear　p158
296A Camberwell New Road,
SE5 0RP (7274 7037/
www.thebear-freehouse.co.uk).

Bedford　p136
77 Bedford Hill, SW12 9HD
(8682 8940/www.the
bedford.co.uk).

Beehive　p147
60-62 Carter Street, SE17
3EW (7703 4992/www.the
beehivebar.co.uk).

Bell　p91
29 Bush Lane, EC4R 0AN
(7929 7772).

**Bethnal Green Working
Men's Club　p242**
42 Pollards Row, E2 6NB
(7739 2727/www.workers
playtime.net).

Betsey Trotwood　p23
56 Farringdon Road, EC1R
3BL (7253 4285/www.the
betsey.com).

Index

Index

Advertisers' Index

Please refer to relevant sections for addresses/ telephone numbers

Index

Maps

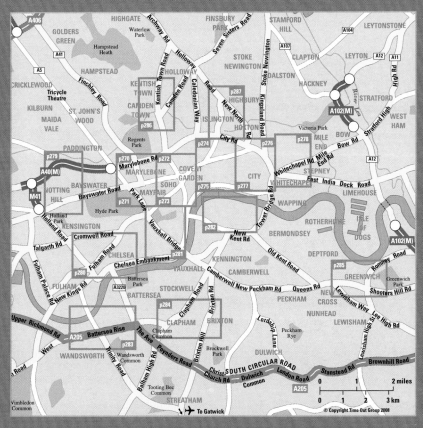

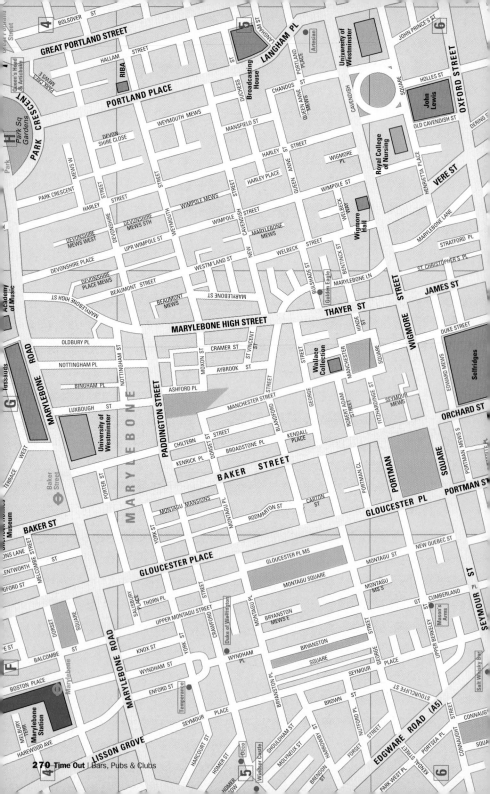

Marylebone & Mayfair

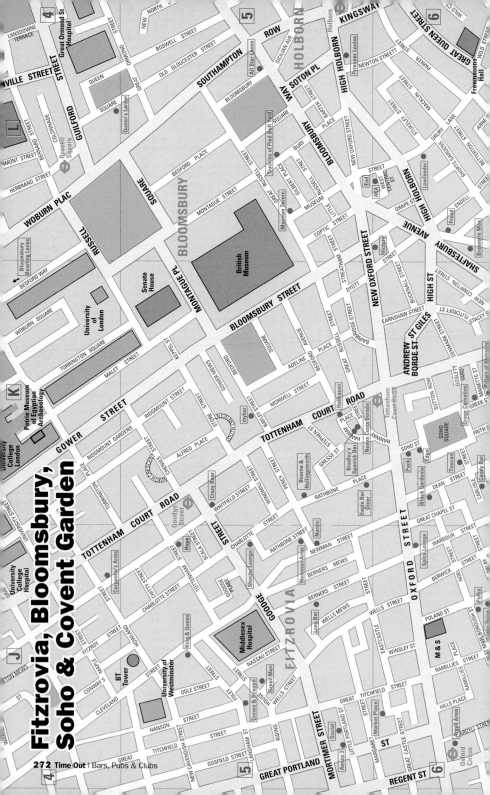

Fitzrovia, Bloomsbury, Soho & Covent Garden

© Copyright Time Out Group 2008

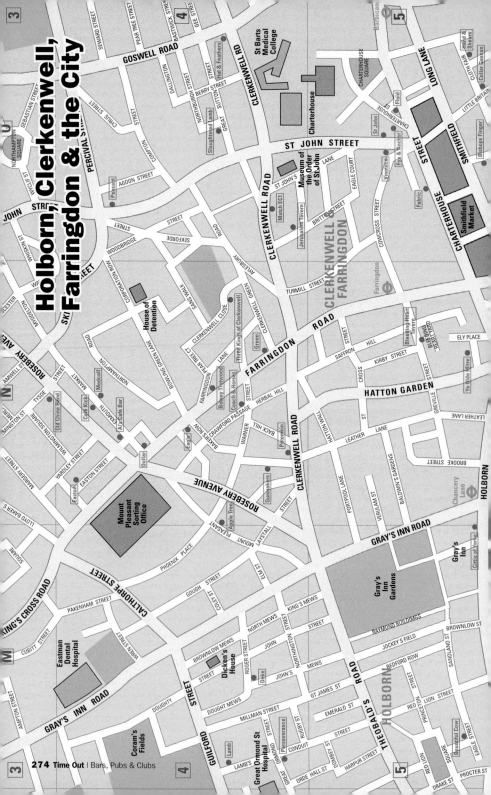

Holborn, Clerkenwell, Farringdon & the City

GOSWELL ROAD

ST JOHN STREET

CLERKENWELL ROAD

CLERKENWELL & FARRINGDON

CHARTERHOUSE STREET

SMITHFIELD

LONG LANE

FARRINGDON ROAD

HATTON GARDEN

ROSEBERY AVENUE

CLERKENWELL ROAD

GRAY'S INN ROAD

HOLBORN

THEOBALD'S ROAD

CALTHORPE STREET

KING'S CROSS ROAD

GRAY'S INN ROAD

GUILFORD STREET

St Barts Medical College

Charterhouse

Museum of the Order of St John

House of Detention

Mount Pleasant Sorting Office

Eastman Dental Hospital

Dicken's House

Gray's Inn Gardens

Gray's Inn

Coram's Fields

Great Ormond St Hospital

Smithfield Market

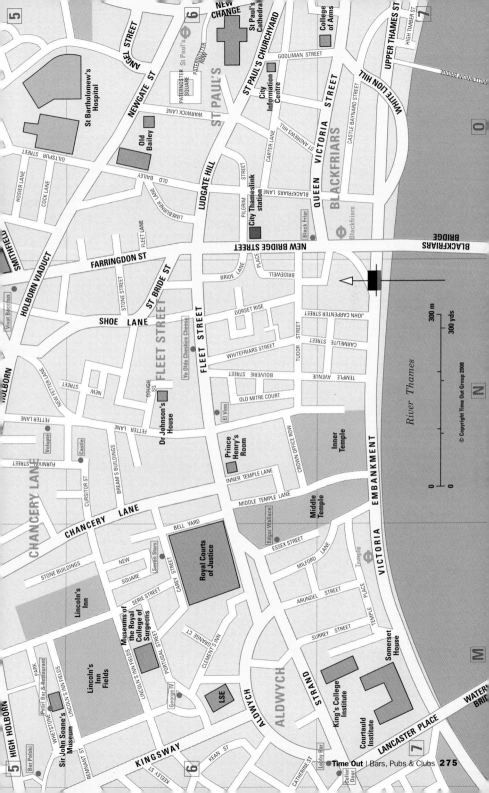

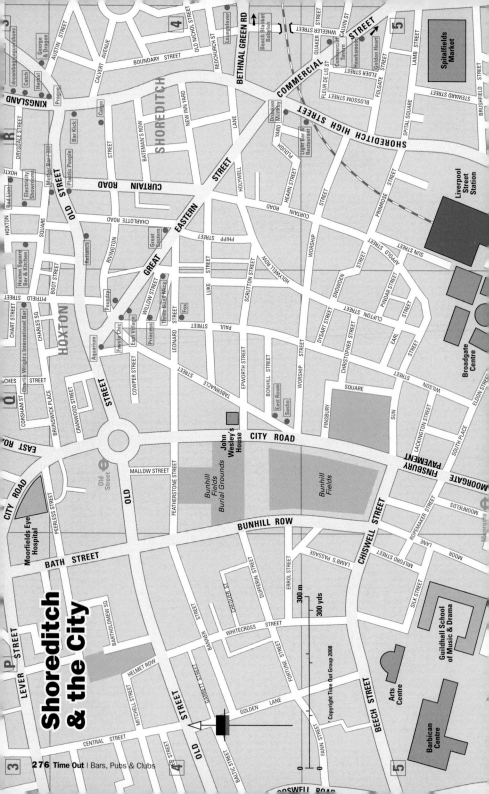

Shoredicth & the City

Spitalfields Market

Liverpool Street Station

Broadgate Centre

Guildhall School of Music & Drama

Arts Centre

Barbican Centre

Moorfields Eye Hospital

John Wesley's House

Bunhill Fields Burial Grounds

Bunhill Fields

Finsbury Square

300 m
300 yds

Copyright Time Out Group 2008

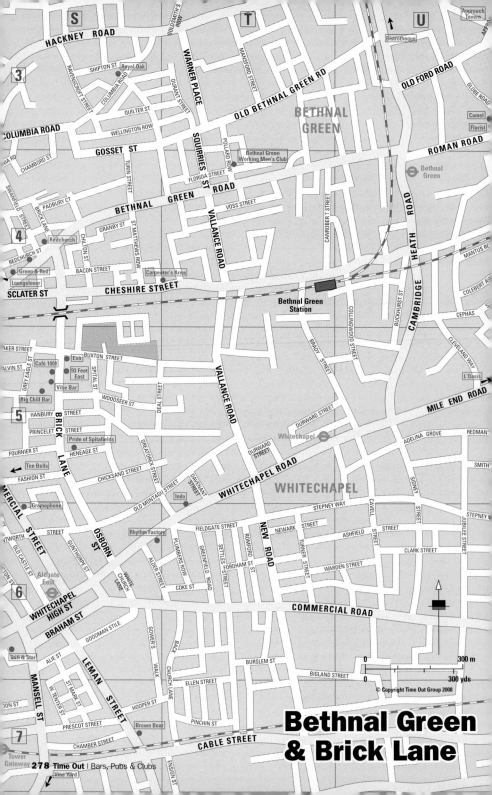

Bethnal Green & Brick Lane

© Copyright Time Out Group 2008

Notting Hill

Chelsea

300 m
300 yds

© Copyright Time Out Group 2008

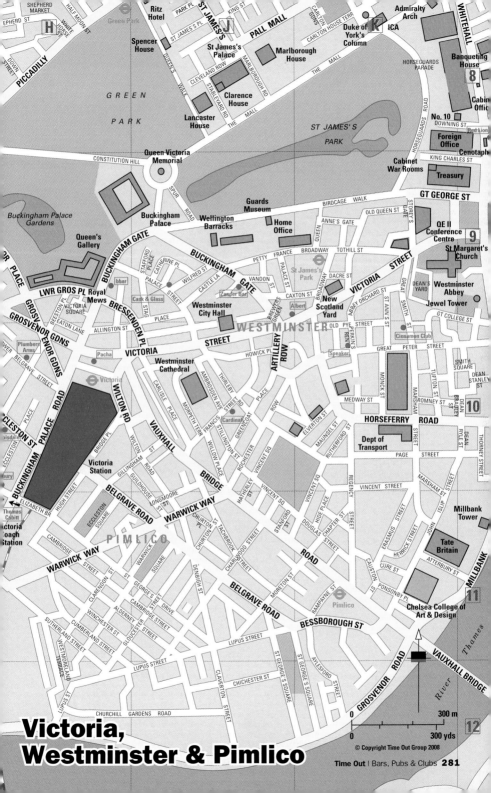

Victoria, Westminster & Pimlico

© Copyright Time Out Group 2008

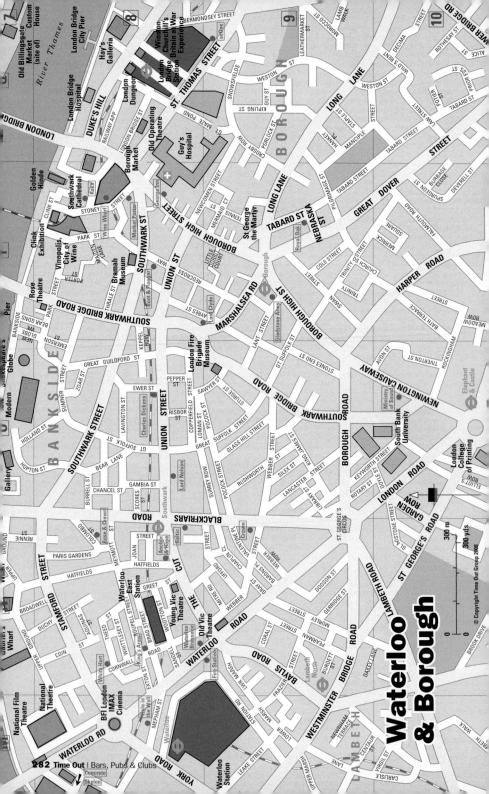

Waterloo & Borough

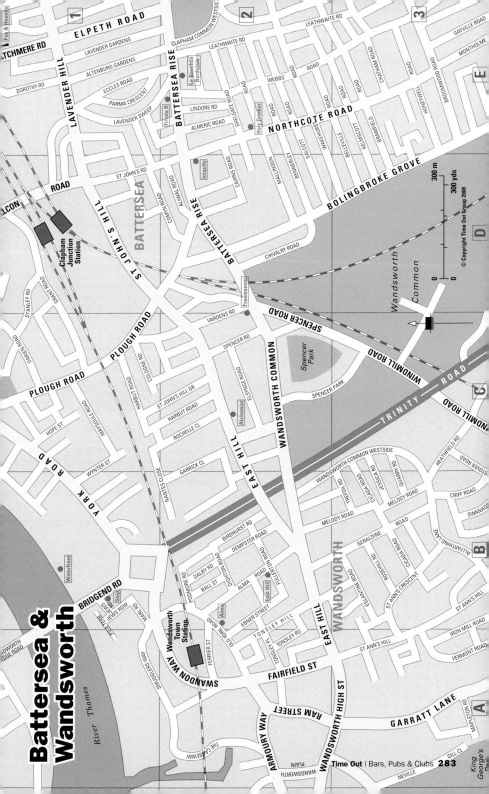

Battersea & Wandsworth

Clapham & Brixton

Map labels

Roads and streets (top / area E–D, columns 1–3):
VILLA ROAD · WILTSHIRE ROAD · GRESHAM RD · WATERWORTH RD · ST JOHN'S CRES · BRIXTON STATION ROAD · COLDHARBOUR LANE · RAILTON ROAD · TALMA ROAD · BARNWELL RD · Prince Regent

BRIXTON ROAD · STOCKWELL PARK RD · CANTERBURY CRESCENT · ATLANTIC RD · ELECTRIC AVE · ELECTRIC LANE · RATTRAY ROAD · KELLETT ROAD · SALTOUN RD · RUSHCROFT RD · DALBERG ROAD · MERVAN RD · BRIXTON WATER LANE · MORVAL ROAD

Brixton Station · Hive · Dogstar · Lounge · Prince · Effra · Mango Landin'

RUMSEY RD · STOCKWELL ROAD · BEEHIVE PL · Plan B · BELLEFIELDS RD · FERNDALE ROAD · NURSERY ROAD · PORDEN ROAD · EFFRA ROAD · ST MATTHEW'S ROAD · BRIXTON WATER ROAD

Far Side · Plan B · St Matthew's Church · Mass · White Horse

Left margin
Clapham & Brixton

STOCKWELL ROAD · LANDOR ROAD · COMBERMERE ROAD · STANSFIELD RD · CHANTREY ROAD · GATELEY ROAD · DALYELL ROAD · PULROSS ROAD · MORDAUNT STREET · HARGWYNE ST · TRINITY GDNS · Trinity Arms · BRIGHTON TERR · CONCANON RD · BAYTREE ROAD · SUDBOURNE ROAD · HAYTER ROAD · HORSFORD RD · LAMBERT ROAD · GLANVILLE ROAD

BRIXTON

KIMBERLEY ROAD · EDITHNA STREET · ARLESFORD RD · HUBERT GROVE · TASMAN ROAD · WILLINGTON ROAD · FERNDALE ROAD · STANLEY ST · TINTERN ST · BALLATER · CORRANCE ROAD · RAEBURN STREET · SOLON ROAD · PLATO ROAD · BONHAM ROAD · BRANKSOME ROAD · STRATHLEVEN ROAD · KILDORAN RD · MARGATE RD · MANDRELL RD

MAYFLOWER RD · HEMBERTON RD · LANDOR ROAD · FERNDALE ROAD · SANDMERE ROAD · KELPER ROAD · HETHERINGTON ROAD · ACRE LANE · LYHAM ROAD · MAULEVERER ROAD

RHODESVILLE RD · STIRLING ROAD · Clapham North · Falcon · BEDFORD ROAD · ARISTOTLE ROAD · CATO ROAD · TREMADOC RD · KENWYN ROAD · NORTHBOURNE RD · WEST ROAD · PARK HILL · CRESCENT LANE · KING'S AVENUE

CLAPHAM ROAD · CHELSHAM ROAD · GAUDEN ROAD · Clapham High Street Station · CLAPHAM HIGH ST · Green & Blue · Clapham North · Loft · ST LUKE'S AVENUE · NELSON ROAD · HAZELRIGGE ROAD · CLAPHAM PARK ROAD · BRIARWOOD RD · ABBEVILLE ROAD · LEPPOC ROAD · CALDERVALE RD · FRANCONIA RD

BRONMELOE ROAD · SIBELLA ROAD · GAUDEN ROAD · VOLTAIRE ROAD · LITTLEBURY ROAD · PRESCOTT PL · CRESSET ST · STONHOUSE ST · White House · Grey Globe · ST ALPHONSUS RD · TABLEY AVE · CRESCENT LANE · HAMBALT RD · WEST ROAD

LARKHALL RD · LANSDOWNE WAY · ELMHURST STREET · SWAFFIELD STREET · MANOR STREET · EDGELEY ROAD · CLAPHAM MANOR ST · Bread & Roses · BELMONT CLOSE · KENN ST · Bar Local · WORSOPP DRIVE

CLAPHAM · CUBITT TERRACE · LISTON ROAD · GRATTON SQ · Stonhouse · STONHOUSE ST · PRESCOTT PL · BROWELL'S LANE · Clapham Common

LARKHALL RISE · GROVE · ROZEL ROAD · TURRET GROVE · NORTH STREET · RECTORY GROVE · FITZWILLIAM RD · GRATTON RD · GRATTON SQUARE · Prince of Wales · ORLANDO ROAD · THE PAVEMENT · LONG ROAD · CLAPHAM COMMON SOUTH SIDE

Tim Bobbin · LYNDON ROAD · OLD TOWN · MACAULAY ROAD · CLAPHAM COMMON NORTHSIDE

Windmill on the Common · Clapham Common

300 m · 300 yds

© Copyright Time Out Group 2008.

NARBONNE AVENUE · CAUTLEY AVE · ELMS ROAD · HAMBALT RD · ABBEVILLE ROAD

Lost Society

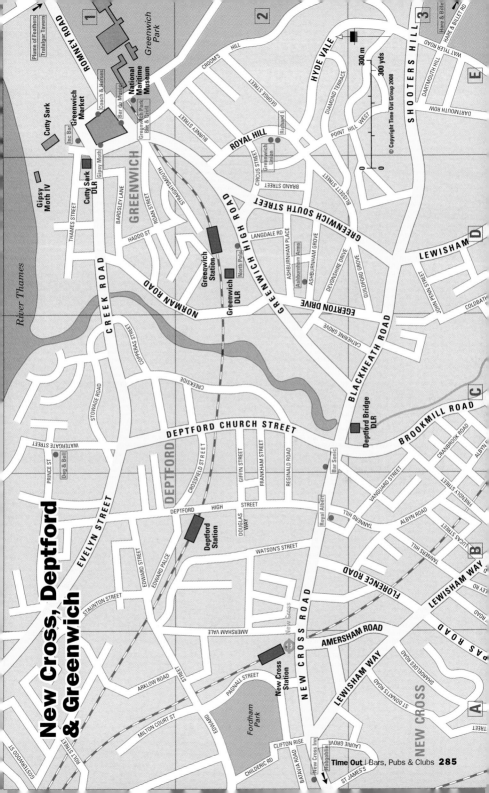

New Cross, Deptford & Greenwich

River Thames

Plume of Feathers
Trafalgar Tavern

Cutty Sark

Greenwich Market
Coach & Horses

National Maritime Museum

Greenwich Park

ROMNEY ROAD

Gipsy Moth IV

Inc. Bar
Bar du Musée

Greenwich Pier Bike & Grill

GREENWICH

Richard I

Cutty Sark DLR

Gipsy Moth

CROOM'S HILL

GEORGE STREET

HYDE VALE

Diamond Terrace

POINT HILL WEST

POINT HILL

SHOOTERS HILL

HARE & BILLET RD
WAT TYLER ROAD

DARTMOUTH HILL
DARTMOUTH ROW

THAMES STREET

BARDSLEY LANE

ROAN STREET

HADDO ST

CREEK ROAD

STRAIGHTSMOUTH

BURNEY STREET

ROYAL HILL

CIRCUS STREET

Greenwich Union

BRAND STREET

BLISSETT STREET

LEWISHAM

JOHN PENN STREET

COLDBATH

NORMAN ROAD

Greenwich Station

Greenwich DLR

North Pole

GREENWICH HIGH ROAD

Langdale Rd

GREENWICH SOUTH STREET

Ashburnham Arms

ASHBURNHAM PLACE

ASHBURNHAM GROVE

DEVONSHIRE DRIVE

GUILDFORD GROVE

EGERTON DRIVE

CATHERINE GROVE

BLACKHEATH ROAD

BROOKMILL ROAD

CRANBROOK ROAD

ALBYN

CUPPERAS STREET

CREEKSIDE

STOWAGE ROAD

WATERGATE STREET

DEPTFORD CHURCH STREET

DEPTFORD

Deg & Bell
PRINCE ST

CROSSFIELD STREET

GIFFIN STREET

FRANKHAM STREET

REGINALD ROAD

Bar Sonic

Deptford Bridge DLR

VANGUARD STREET

ALBYN ROAD

LUCAS STREET

FRIENDLY STREET

EVELYN STREET

EDWARD STREET

EDWARD PALCE

DEPTFORD HIGH STREET

DOUGLAS WAY

WATSON'S STREET

Royal Albert

TANNERS HILL

TANNERS HILL

FLORENCE ROAD

LEWISHAM WAY

LEWISHAM WAY

ROAD

KEY RD

STAUNTON STREET

Deptford Station

AMERSHAM VALE

New Cross

AMERSHAM ROAD

NEW CROSS ROAD

SHARDELOES ROAD

ST DONATT'S ROAD

LEWISHAM WAY

NEW CROSS

ARKLOW ROAD

MILTON COURT ST

PAGNALL STREET

New Cross Station

Fordham Park

CLIFTON RISE

CHILDERIC RD

BATAVIA ROAD

New Cross Inn
Hobgoblin

LAURIE GROVE

ST JAMES'S

GOSTERWOOD STREET

ROLT STREET

EDWARD

300 m
300 yds

© Copyright Time Out Group 2008

Time Out | Bars, Pubs & Clubs **285**

Camden Town
& Kentish Town

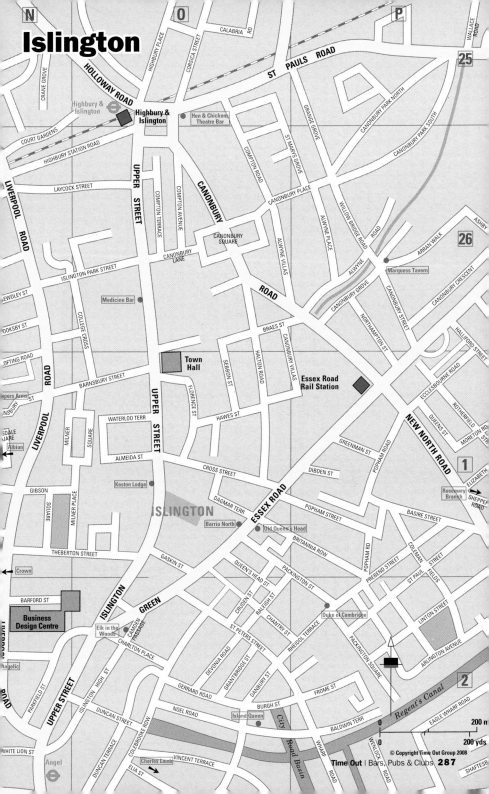

Islington

© Copyright Time Out Group 2008

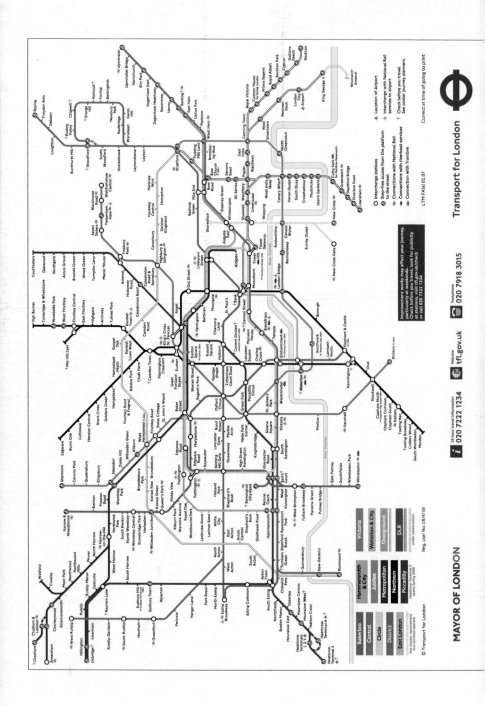